Omnichannel Retailing for the Fashion Business

Omnichannel Retailing for the Fashion Business

Tunmin (Catherine) Jai, PhD
Fulbright Scholar
Associate Professor
Hospitality and Retail Management
College of Human Sciences
Texas Tech University

Jihyun (J.) Kim Vick, PhD
Graduate Studies Coordinator
Professor
Shannon Rogers and Jerry Silverman School of
Fashion Design and Merchandising
Kent State University

FAIRCHILD BOOKS
NEW YORK • LONDON • OXFORD • NEW DELHI • SYDNEY

FAIRCHILD BOOKS
Bloomsbury Publishing Inc
1385 Broadway, New York, NY 10018, USA
50 Bedford Square, London, WC1B 3DP, UK
29 Earlsfort Terrace, Dublin 2, Ireland

BLOOMSBURY, FAIRCHILD BOOKS and the Fairchild Books logo are trademarks
of Bloomsbury Publishing Plc

First edition published 2025

Cover image: We Are/Getty Images
Back cover images: left: Dowell/Moment/Getty Images;
right: seksan Mongkhonkhamsao/Getty Images

A catalog record for this book is available from the Library of Congress.

ISBN: PB 978-1-5013-7709-9
ePDF: 978-1-5013-7708-2
eBook: 978-1-5013-7707-5

Typeset by Integra Software Services Pvt. Ltd.
Printed and bound in the United States of America

To find out more about our authors and books visit www.bloomsbury.com/fairchildbooks
and sign up for our newsletter.

Contents

Extended Table of Contents

About the Authors

Dr. Tunmin (Catherine) Jai, PhD, is an associate professor and a Fulbright Scholar at Texas Tech University in the Hospitality and Retail Management program within the College of Human Sciences. She received a BS in Textile Design and an MA in Culture Study from Fu Jen Catholic University in Taiwan, and PhD in Consumer Behavior from Oregon State University. Dr. Jai had industry experience as a textile designer and market analyst in the global supply chain industry. Since 2010, she has been teaching web-based retailing (e-commerce, and mobile commerce), consumer behavior, and advanced marketing courses at both undergraduate and graduate levels. She has published numerous research papers in peer-reviewed journals on topics such as digital marketing, neuromarketing, consumer privacy concerns in the big data era, and brand-customer relationships on social media. Readers of this book will find her research findings in this book. Drawing from her industry experience in the global fashion supply chain, Dr. Jai believes that our world should not be separated by physical locations and that the Internet and modern technology enable the possibility of providing an omnichannel experience to consumers. Therefore, she has served as chair and board member of the International Relations Committee in the International Textile and Apparel Association and as a member of the IEEE Standard Association's P3141 Standard for 3D Body Processing, Communication, Security, and Privacy Working Group. Because of her academic achievements in consumer behavior and international business, she was selected as a Fulbright US Scholar to represent the United States in cultural exchange and research collaboration. Her Fulbright project includes developing a curriculum incorporating 3D product merchandising and artificial intelligence (AI) for virtual try-ons in the metaverse.

Dr. Jihyun (J.) Kim Vick is a professor and graduate studies coordinator in the School of Fashion Design and Merchandising at Kent State University in Ohio. Dr. Vick earned a BS in Home Economics Education from Korea University, Seoul, an MA in Apparel and Textiles from Michigan State University, East Lansing, and a PhD in Textiles and Clothing from Iowa State University in Ames. In 2004, she began her assistant professorship at Virginia Tech in Blacksburg, where she later held positions, including Associate Professor, Wallace Gallery Coordinator, and Apparel Program Coordinator. In 2013, she joined the current institution as an Associate Professor with Tenure at Hire and taught a variety of undergraduate and graduate courses. She provided leadership as a faculty director of the Fashion School STORE, a live retail laboratory from 2014 to 2019 in downtown Kent. During that time, she also led the curricular and assessment effort of the Fashion Merchandising program. For the past two decades, Dr. Vick has developed theoretical frameworks to deepen our understanding of relationships between the digital transformation of fashion retail and consumer behavior in omnichannel retailing. Her dedication to research and teaching has earned her numerous international and university awards, such as the 2024–25 KSU President's Faculty Excellence Award, the 2021–22 KSU Outstanding Research and Scholarship Award, the Paul L. Pfeiffer Faculty Mentor Award in 2020, and the ITAA Mid-Career Excellence Award in 2018, among others. Her recent industry engagement employed generative artificial intelligence and machine learning to create a collaborative and practical platform for industry professionals and businesses. She is currently serving as a secretary for the ITAA, the global professional organizations in the field of fashion, textiles, and clothing.

Preface

Traditional retailers with brick-and-mortar locations are bolstering their e-commerce efforts and creating new digital experiences. Meanwhile, direct-to-consumer retailers that got their start in e-commerce are looking for smarter ways to engage customers and drive growth. *Omnichannel Retailing for the Fashion Business*, 1st edition, provides an in-depth introduction to the distinct dimensions of the "new standard" in the contemporary retail landscape. With the advancement of artificial intelligence (AI), virtual reality, mobile technology, easily accessible internet, and changes in consumers' consumption patterns, the retail industry has experienced many revolutions over the past two decades. The contents of this book focus on bringing you the principles and practices relevant to the omnichannel retail business. In addition to principles and implementation processes, we also include real-world business cases from well-known fashion/lifestyle brands and the brands you are likely to encounter in daily life.

Content Overview

How to deliver an integrated, cohesive customer experience as an omnichannel retail owner is at the heart of the book content. The book's content focuses on the pragmatic knowledge needed to implement omnichannel customer services. In addition to the consumer experiences perspective, this text introduces students or business owners to operations of omnichannel retailing including omnichannel strategies, supply chain, promotions, and customer relationship management. Each of these topics represents a pivotal pillar of today's omnichannel retail businesses. Moreover, the cross-sectional cases throughout the chapters provide real-world examples for the readers to comprehend the integration of different sectors involved in the omnichannel retail businesses.

What Courses and Students Can Use the Text?

This text is appropriate for courses, such as Omnichannel Retailing, Digital Retailing, Multichannel Retailing, Web-Based Retailing, Fashion Marketing, and Advances Fashion Marketing and more. This book covers examples from countries from North America, Europe, and Asia, with an emphasis on the practical utilization of US-based e-commerce platforms. Given the variations in the regulatory establishments in the United States and European Union, we tried to showcase as many retail formats and e-business models as possible to broaden our readers' perspectives. With technological advancements, digital retailing presents an enormous opportunity for fashion brands to test the water in international markets beyond where they are reading this text. For students who read this book beyond the North American continent, this textbook will be an excellent entry point for them to learn the practices of digital retailing and marketing practices in North America. For United States or Canadian students, this textbook not only serves as a pragmatic guide to what omnichannel retailing is and how those retailers operate, but also provides thought-provoking examples of the fashion/lifestyle brands from which to learn.

Description of the Textbook

The book consists of 10 chapters, organized into three parts, each covering different aspects of omnichannel retailing. Part 1, The Road to Omnichannel Retailing, is divided into three chapters. Chapter 1, Evolution and Impact of Omnichannel Retailing, introduces omnichannel retailing, covering its definition, reasons behind its emergence, retail organization structures, and strategies for creating omnichannel experiences.

Chapter 1 also explores the top omnichannel retailers, methods for evaluating their capacity, and the impact, challenges, and opportunities of omnichannel retailing, including technology changes and consumer trends driving this shift.

Chapter 2, Retail Formats in the Omnichannel Business Environment, focuses on reviewing traditional retail formats, such as brick-and-mortar and direct marketing, along with major retailers in each category. It discusses how these retailers incorporate the e-commerce revenue model into their operations. Electronic retail options for online product sales, including websites, online marketplaces, mobile apps, and social media accounts, are also examined. Examples of each format are evaluated, and students are taught how to assess these options for fashion/lifestyle brands, considering the key stakeholders in the omnichannel retailing arena.

In Chapter 3, Omnichannel Customer Experience, the five-stage shopping journey in consumers' decision-making process is introduced. The chapter delves into the essential factors that promote or hinder omnichannel customer experiences. It provides insights into identifying issues in delivering such experiences through the application of customer journey mapping techniques.

Part 2, Omnichannel Operations, provides comprehensive insights into implementing omnichannel strategies, cross-channel integration, supply chain management, promotional techniques, and customer service approaches tailored for the omnichannel retail environment. Part 2 comprises five chapters.

Chapter 4, titled Implementing Omnichannel Strategies, focuses on the expansion of retailers' retail presence across online and various offline channels. It examines two perspectives: how brick-and-mortar stores can establish an online presence and how direct-to-consumer (D2C) retailers can start online and expand to physical stores. The chapter begins by discussing the different approaches for brick-and-mortar stores to expand their reach online. It covers the establishment of online presences through websites, mobile apps, and social media accounts. By leveraging these online channels, traditional retailers can enhance their visibility and accessibility to a wider customer base. Next, the chapter explores the journey of emerging D2C retailers. It highlights how these businesses often start their operations online and later consider expanding into physical stores as part of their growth strategy. This approach allows D2C retailers to build their brand and customer base online before venturing into the brick-and-mortar realm.

In Chapter 5, Cross-Channel Integration, the focus shifts to one of the fundamental goals of omnichannel retailers: creating a seamless customer experience through the integration of various channels. The chapter emphasizes the importance of gathering invaluable customer information through integrated customer database systems. By understanding customers' preferences, interests, lifestyle, and shopping behaviors, retailers can tailor their offerings and interactions to meet individual needs and wants. The chapter stresses the need for careful planning and development of cross-channel integration. This involves ensuring the availability of data across different systems such as ordering, inventory, fulfillment, and returns. By establishing effective communication and coordination among these systems, retailers can deliver a cohesive and frictionless experience for customers regardless of the channel they choose to engage with.

In Chapter 6, Omnichannel Supply Chain and Logistic Management, the book delves into the differences between supply chain management strategies in multi-channel retailers and omnichannel retailers. The key focus is on the importance of having an integrated database/platform to support an omnichannel consumer experience. This integration allows for the seamless flow of data across various touchpoints, enabling efficient ordering, inventory management, fulfillment, and return processes. By analyzing product return data and sharing insights with relevant departments, retailers can drive continuous improvements in their operations and customer satisfaction.

Chapter 7, Promotion in the Omnichannel Environments, explores how omnichannel retailers can effectively promote their products using multiple touchpoints. The chapter covers both offline and online promotion strategies. Offline touchpoints include brick-and-mortar stores, print media, and pop-up events, while online touchpoints encompass search engine promotions, social media campaigns, and email marketing. By leveraging a combination of these channels, retailers can reach a wider audience and create a consistent brand presence across various platforms.

Chapter 8, Omnichannel Customer Service, emphasizes the significance of carefully planning and executing customer service strategies in the context of omnichannel retailing. The chapter discusses the foundational elements necessary for effective omnichannel customer service and highlights the importance of meeting customer expectations regardless of the shopping channel. It also addresses specific services tied to individual channels and the role of customer service in building long-term relationships with customers.

Part 3, Business Considerations for Omnichannel Retailers, comprises two chapters. Chapter 9, Ethical and Legal Issues in Omnichannel Retailing, delves into the complex ethical and legal concerns that arise in the context of omnichannel retailing. It specifically addresses issues related to consumer privacy and information rights, intellectual property rights, evolving sales tax regulations in the United States, and the regulation of social media marketing. The chapter examines these topics to shed light on the challenges retailers face and the importance of navigating these legal boundaries responsibly.

In Chapter 10, Emerging Trends in Omnichannel Retailing, the chapter explores the technological advancements shaping the retail industry. It discusses consumer-facing trends such as the integration of augmented reality (AR) and virtual reality (VR) into mobile technology, collaborative consumption through digital redistributive channels, the Internet of Things (IoT) applications, and visual search. The chapter also covers retail technological trends like AR and digital garment merchandising, personalized micro-production, location-based technology, digital transformation in supply chain and logistics, and customer relationship management (CRM) and email marketing. Additionally, it highlights emerging trends in other industries that impact fashion, including AI applications, the metaverse, non-fungible tokens (NFTs), and gamification. The chapter concludes by presenting a vision of the future of retail that offers unique and authentic shopping experiences to customers. The top omnichannel retailers listed in this chapter were accurate at the time of publication.

Pedagogical Features

This textbook can be used to introduce students and enhance student learning, each chapter contains following features:

- Chapter Introduction: Provides students with an overview of the content covered in each chapter and how the concepts introduced in this chapter relate to omnichannel retailing practices.
- Learning Objectives: A list of learning objectives to guide students learning the major concepts in each chapter.
- Appropriate tables and figures to provide data and visuals at a glance. These will be important references that students can apply to projects.
- End-of-Chapter Case Studies: Provide real-world business cases related to the chapter content for students to practice critical thinking and synthesizing skills. Case studies may originate from various trade publications, interviews, and personal observations.
- Career Opportunities: A list of entry job titles and their responsibilities related to the chapter content. This feature exposes students to some insights of the rapidly developing job market related to omnichannel retailing and digital marketing.
- Summary: Helps students review the chapter's content.
- Key Terms: A list of key terms/concepts in each chapter helps students review the chapter content and prepare for quizzes and exams.
- Reflection and Discussion Questions: A list of guided discussion questions prompts students to actively learn through applying the concepts covered in each chapter. Instructors can use these questions as chapter assignments, in-class discussions, online discussion boards, or roundtable brainstorming, etc.
- Exercises at the end of each chapter engage students in investigations, research, observations, evaluations, and analysis, as well as to personalize the material. Additional exercises are found in the Instructor's Guide.
- Endnotes gathered at the end of the book. These comprise a list of references offering further information for both students and instructors to deepen their understanding through accessing the sources.

Exercises are designed to move students through a learning experience. Personal experience exercises engage the student and integrate the experience with personal meaning. Here, students experience something new as they draw from past experiences. Next, instructors provide informational/different perspective through presentations, videos, or other methods of material presentation; class discussion is encouraged to aid a greater understanding of the topic. Practice and personalization exercises allow learners to use ideas or concepts from their reflections to draw their own conclusions (e.g., develop theories or generalizations). Lastly, with self-discovery exercises, learners apply theories or generalizations to real-life situations or to practical problems.

Summary

Omnichannel Retailing for the Fashion Business provides an in-depth introduction of the distinct dimensions in modern omnichannel retailing. This text includes the most current and accurate omnichannel content or information at the time of publication. We hope you will find the text provides useful insights into the foundations, operations, ethical, legal, and technological aspects of omnichannel retailing. By exploring the challenges and opportunities associated with these considerations, fashion business can navigate the complexities of the modern retail industry, embrace emerging technologies, and provide innovative and valuable experiences to their customers.

INSTRUCTOR AND STUDENT RESOURCES

Omnichannel Retailing for the Fashion Business STUDIO™

We are pleased to offer an online resource to accompany the textbook—*Omnichannel Retailing for the Fashion Business* STUDIO. The online STUDIO is specially developed to complement this book with rich media ancillaries that students can adapt to their visual learning styles to better master concepts and improve grades. Within the STUDIO, students will be able to:

- Study smarter with self-quizzes featuring scored results and personalized study tips
- Review concepts with flashcards of essential vocabulary

The *Omnichannel Retailing for the Fashion Business* STUDIO here can be accessed as follows:

SIGN IN

1. Go to https://www.bloomsburyonlineresources.com/fairchildbookstudios
2. Follow the instructions to enter your unique access code which is printed on the inside back cover of this book. The code is valid for one registration only.
3. Credentials to access the STUDIOs will be emailed once the code has been redeemed.

Having trouble registering or logging in? Be sure you have entered your access code, not your password when prompted.

STUDIO™ will be live within six to eight weeks of the book's publication date.

Instructor Resources

- The Instructor's Guide provides suggestions for planning the course and using the text in the classroom, including sample syllabi, video suggestions, and teaching ideas such as projects and in-class activities.
- Test bank includes sample test questions for each chapter.
- PowerPoint® presentations include images from the textbook and provide a framework for lectures and discussions

Instructor's Resources may be accessed through https://www.bloomsburyonlineresources.com/fairchildbookstudios

Acknowledgments

This book would not be possible without the unwavering support of many people. We would like to express our heartfelt gratitude to the following individuals who played pivotal roles in bringing this book to life. Emily Samulski, our dedicated Publisher, whose unwavering support and belief in this project made it possible. Edie Weinberg, the brilliant Art Development Editor, whose creative insights and meticulous attention to detail elevated the visual aspects of this work. Julie M. Vitale, our exceptional Development Editor, whose guidance, feedback, and expertise shaped the content and structure of this book. Their contributions were invaluable, and we are deeply thankful for their commitment and collaboration throughout this journey.

Tunmin (Catherine) Jai: I am profoundly grateful to my family, especially my husband, Stephen, and our son, Leo, for their unwavering support, encouragement, and patience throughout this book project. Their love and understanding sustained me during the late nights and countless revisions. Additionally, I extend my heartfelt appreciation to my co-author, Jihyun (J.), whose collaboration and insights enriched every chapter. Together, we embarked on this creative journey. To my colleagues and students, thank you for being my pillars of strength and inspiration. My life has become much richer because of you.

J. Kim Vick: Words cannot express how thankful I am for my husband, Scott, and my family for their continuous encouragement, love, and support on this book writing journey. I am much indebted to my co-author, Catherine, who has been absolutely amazing to work with to make this journey memorable and productive. I would like to end this acknowledgment by paying tribute to my late mother, Dr. Sun-Hee Park, and my father, Dr. Bong-Koo Kim, for their life-long inspiration to dedicate my life to higher education.

Bloomsbury Publishing wishes to gratefully acknowledge and thank the editorial team involved in the publication of this book:

Publisher: Emily Samulski
Senior Development Editor: Julie M. Vitale
Art Development Editor: Edie Weinberg
Assistant Editor: María Francisca Núñez
In-House Designer: Elena Durey
Production Manager: Ken Bruce
Project Manager: Mandy Collison
Fairchild Books/Graphics Rendered by Daniel Kison

PART 1
The Road to Omnichannel Retailing

Welcome to the start of your journey to learn about omnichannel retailing! In the first part of this book, we introduce omnichannel retailing, covering its definition, reasons behind its emergence, retail organization structures, and strategies for creating omnichannel experiences. Part 1 contains three chapters. In Chapter 1, we introduce you to the evolution and impact of omnichannel retailing. In Chapter 2, you will learn the various retail formats in the omnichannel business environment. Chapter 3 explains the omnichannel customer experiences and elaborates the five-stage shopping journeys in consumers' decision-making process.

CHAPTER 1

Evolution and Impact of Omnichannel Retailing

Learning Objectives

Upon finishing this chapter, you will be able to:

- Understand the history and evolution of omnichannel retailing
- Recognize the difference between omnichannel retailing and multichannel retailing
- Evaluate the reasons why retailers are adopting the omnichannel approach
- Differentiate the key strategies to create an omnichannel customer experience
- Identify the top omnichannel retailers
- Analyze the consumer trends and their impact on omnichannel retailing

In Chapter 1, we discuss the history and background of omnichannel retailing, defining omnichannel retailing and its methods. We will also discuss retail organization structures and the strategies to create omnichannel experiences. To give you a perspective on US omnichannel retailers, we provide a list of the top omnichannel retailers in 2023, and discuss how to appraise retailers' omnichannel capacity. (The top omnichannel retailers listed in this chapter were accurate at the time of publication.) We also discuss the different impacts of omnichannel retail business, the challenges and opportunities omnichannel retailing brings, as well as the technology changes and the important consumer trends that drive omnichannel retailing.

Omnichannel Retailing Background and Definition

Retail business encompasses the sale of goods and services to consumers across all cultures and times from ancient history to the present. The modern retail business began during the Industrial Revolution in the mid-eighteenth century in Britain when steam-powered machines gradually filled out factories and attracted a new generation of workers into the cities to work.[1] Before the Industrial Revolution, almost all the products were handmade. The Industrial Revolution changed not only the way people made goods but also their shopping behaviors. With more products made, there were more products to be displayed in the stores. Soon after the Industrial Revolution, a wave of "department stores" emerged in the nineteenth century. For example, Harrods of London (1834), Le Bon Marché (Paris, 1838), Macy's of New York (1858, Figure 1.1), Bloomingdale's (New York, 1861), Saks Fifth Avenue (New York, 1867), etc. Early department stores functioned as cultural centers where consumers congregate and seek entertainment.

Entering the twentieth century, the ready-to-wear industry in America expanded and became a mature industry by 1920. Between 1900 and 1920, women's fashion in Europe and America changed rapidly, moving from Edwardian styles to more narrow silhouettes due to the limited amount of material available during the Great War (1914–1918, known as the First World War). After the First World War, the 1920s witnessed a surge in consumerism in the United States. More women graduated from high schools and colleges and entered the workforce. Many factories had to pivot quickly from producing war supplies to civilian goods.[2] In 1924, Macy's Herald Square location became the largest store in the world.[3] In the following two decades, with the gradual availability of automobiles, more people in the United States began to leave cities and commute from the suburbs. As of 1941, about 88 percent of US households had a family car, although many civilian families struggled to keep their car running during the Great Depression (1929–1939) and the Second World War (1939–1945).[4] After the Second World War, the returning soldiers sought stability and normalcy. The baby boom led to increased demand for consumer goods, fueling exceptionally strong economic growth. In reacting to the increasing consumer demands, retail stores and mall space increased significantly. Supermarkets, warehouse stores, discount stores, and convenience stores occupied vast areas and sold a large variety of goods such as clothing, packaged foods, produce, house cleaning supplies, drugs, etc. Northlake Mall (Southfield, Michigan) became the first open-air shopping mall in the United States in 1954. Founded in 1958, Carrefour opened their first hypermarket in 1963 in Sainte-Geneviève-des-Bois, near Paris, France.[5] The largest shopping and entertainment complex in the United States, the Mall of America (MoA), opened its doors in 1992 in Bloomington, Minnesota. MoA is one of the most visited tourist attractions on the globe and receives roughly 40 million visitors a year.[6] It was not until the late 1990s that online shopping started to become popular with the increasing ownership of personal computers.

Figure 1.1 Macy's department store in New York

Understanding Modern Retailing and Its Evolution

The modern retail industry has evolved significantly over the past few decades. In the early twenty-first century, retailers adopted several technologies and strategies, such as credit card systems, POS systems, and loyalty programs, to improve the in-store shopping experience and compete with other retailers. However, with the rise of online shopping, direct marketing has evolved from sending consumers physical mail to tracking consumers' online behavior in order to provide personalized ads and promotions. Today's consumers have an abundance of choice when it comes to purchasing a product or service, including where, when, what, and how to shop. With the rapid evolution of internet technology, such as broadband access and mobile devices, along with the growth of social media platforms, consumers' technology usage patterns have changed significantly. Figure 1.2 shows Steve Jobs, the late Chief Executive Officer of Apple, who introduced the first iPhone in 2007. In response to these changes, many retail organizational structures have shifted from a single-channel format to multi-channel (meaning operating more than one retail channel), even omnichannel retailing. In the following sections, we will discuss the various retail organizational structures and why modern retailers are updating their omnichannel practices to serve consumer trends and maintain competitiveness.

Figure 1.2 A magical device in your pocket—Steve Jobs, the Chief Executive Officer of Apple, introduced the first iPhone in 2007 and unleashed a revolution in mobile software

Single-Channel Retailers

Single-channel retailer refers to a retailer reaching customers through only one distribution option, regardless of whether it is online, catalog, mail-order, face-to-face selling, or traditional brick-and-mortar retail. This approach reduces marketing investments and organizational complexity. Before the internet era, consumers used to go to brick-and-mortar stores or rely on one channel (such as catalogs or phonebooks) to gather product information and look for relevant products. The downside to taking the single-channel approach, particularly for fashion businesses, is it is no longer effective enough to scale the business. **Pure-play retailers** is a term usually attributed to online retailers that have never operated brick-and-mortar stores nor engaged in other types of nonstore distribution. Customers today are consuming media across several different channels, and marketing in just one runs the risk of missing your ideal targets altogether. Some examples of pure-play retailers are ASOS, Zappos, Etsy, etc. Many new direct-to-consumer (D2C) retailers start their business online as pure-play retailers, too.

Dual-Channel Retailers

Dual-channel retailers operate both in brick-and-mortar stores and online through e-commerce platforms or catalogs, along with a website or mobile apps. The concept of dual-channel retailing emerged in the early days of e-commerce when online shopping became popular in the late 1990s and early 2000s. Traditional brick-and-mortar retailers established an online presence, creating a dual-channel retail model that combined the advantages of both physical and online shopping. Typically, small- to medium-sized retailers or those in the early stages of retail business growth operate dual channels. Brick-and-click retailers refer to those that operate both brick-and-mortar stores and an online channel. In recent years, the trend towards dual-channel retailing has continued to evolve, with many retailers offering a multichannel shopping experience that includes in-store, online, and mobile options. This trend has led to the emergence of multichannel retailers, which we will discuss in the next section.

Multichannel Retailers

Multichannel retailers are companies that operate in brick-and-mortar stores, direct marketing, direct selling, online, and other electronic methods to transact business with customers. Nowadays, consumers tend to use online channels with brick-and-mortar stores to both search for and buy products, leading to the emergence of cross-channel shopping behavior. Shoppers who shop with more than one channel are called multichannel shoppers. A Harvard Business Review study found that customers who use multiple channels rather than a single channel spent an average of 4 percent more when shopping in-store and 10 percent more when shopping online.[7]

Most department stores and mass merchandise retailers became multichannel retailers as they grew their retail business through e-commerce. From the early 2000s until now, these retailers have become multichannel retailers by selling products/services on more than three channels (e.g., brick-and-mortar stores, websites, and catalogs). However, they do not integrate the operations such as pricing, inventory, shipping, and payment systems as one. In other words, each channel may have a separate team for planning, buying, pricing, and distribution. Consumers who purchase products from multichannel retailers may find they can only use mailing services to return the products they purchased online, or a product may be priced differently in a retailer's physical store and on their website. These incongruent shopping experiences may bring down a consumer's trust towards the retailer.

Omnichannel Retailers

Omnichannel retailers are companies that provide customers with an integrated shopping experience across various channels, including brick-and-mortar stores, online stores, mobile apps, social media platforms, and other channels. **Omnichannel retailing** allows consumers to interact with a brand seamlessly, regardless of the channel they use and provides them with a consistent experience and access to the same product information, pricing, and promotions. As consumers are increasingly asking for a smooth experience no matter which channel they are shopping with, an omnichannel retailer integrates data from multiple channels into one platform. If done right, customers can order online and pickup in-store, order at the in-store kiosk and have the product delivered to their home, or even order online with home delivery and return or exchange in-store. Around 80 percent of Top 500 retailers offered buy online, pickup in store in 2021.[8]

The omnichannel shopping experience can be one of the following combinations:

- Buy online, pickup in-store (**BOPIS**)
- Buy online, ship from store
- Buy online, ship from a fulfillment center
- Buy in-store, ship from the store or another store
- Buy in-store, ship from a fulfillment center
- Use loyalty credits online and in-store
- Having a store locator and in-store stock status features on the website and mobile apps
- Making an in-store appointment online
- Buy online, in-store returns

Research has suggested marketing campaigns spread across three or more channels earned a 90 percent higher customer retention rate and 250 percent higher engagement and purchase rates. In addition, personal traits also influence omnichannel shopping behavior. For example, impulsive shoppers make greater use of mobile devices, whereas individuals with a higher level of need for touch are more predisposed to use other online devices in their omnichannel shopping process.[9] In the next section, we will discuss the difference between multichannel retailing and omnichannel retailing, the reasons for omnichannel retailing, and the opportunities.

Why Adopt Omnichannel Retailing?

The word "omni" means all. Omnichannel Retailing refers to the practice of using all available channels to buy or sell goods or services. This includes in-store, internet, mobile, and catalog sales. In this section, we will illustrate the difference between multichannel retailing and omnichannel retailing, the reasons for omnichannel retailing, and the business opportunities presented in omnichannel retailing.

Discerning Multichannel Retailing and Omnichannel Retailing

To discern the difference between multichannel retailing and omnichannel retailing, we need to first have a clear understanding of the terminologies. Retail scholars defined **multichannel retailing** as the set of activities involved in selling merchandise and services through more than one channel or all popular channels. However, the customer cannot trigger the channel interaction, such as specifying a store-pickup order on the website, or the retailer does not control channel integration, like declining a return for an online order in-store because the inventory system was separated among different channels. On the other hand, omnichannel retailing evolved from multichannel retailing. Customers can trigger cross-channel interaction with an omnichannel retailer, and the retailer will be able to provide services to navigate consumers through their shopping journey.[10] Furthermore, an omnichannel experience accounts for each platform and device a customer can use to interact with the company.

A true omnichannel approach must also deliver a consistent brand experience to meet customers where they are while building relationships beyond channels. Learned knowledge about the customer is then used to deliver them an integrated experience. Omnichannel retailers use this technique to align their messaging, goals, objectives, and designs across each channel and device. This comprehensive integration of data and systems is illustrated in Figure 1.3. From the figure, you can see that the multichannel retailers interact with their customers using channels, and there is no integration from one touchpoint to another. However, in the context of omnichannel retailing, consumers will be able to start interacting with the retailer at any touchpoint, and their data is integrated among different channels to provide a seamless shopping experience.

Reasons for Omnichannel Retailing

Because consumers' shopping journey is not linear, oftentimes consumers can shift back and forth among channels like email, website, YouTube, and physical stores before they make a final decision. While the rise of e-commerce has seemingly taken over the retail industry, the roles of brick-and-mortar stores have also changed in the last decade. Nowadays, the most successful retailers are learning how to combine the benefits of their physical and digital channels. For example, Target found that their omnichannel customers (i.e., customers that purchase from stores, mobile, and online) spend four times more than store-only buyers and ten times more than digital-only customers. During the Covid-19 pandemic, many omnichannel retailers rapidly integrated their brick-and-mortar stores as part of their distribution network to fulfill online orders, in-store and curbside pickups, and returns.

Opportunities of Omnichannel Retailing

From the consumer perspective, omnichannel experience levers a consistent shopping experience and provides a complementary rather than conflicting experience. According to eMarketer, almost 50 percent

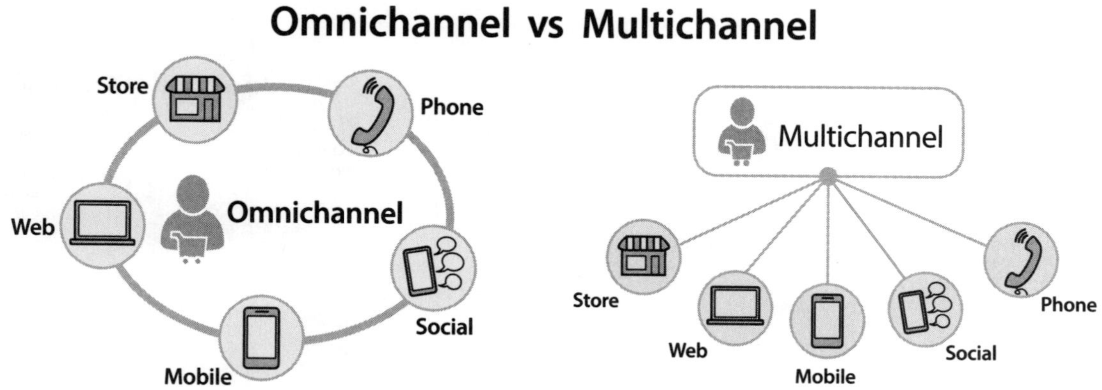

Figure 1.3 Multichannel retailing versus omnichannel retailing

of retail CFOs in the United States were pursuing a digital transformation in 2021 to improve omnichannel experiences. When it comes to where they're investing, 64 percent were planning to increase their e-commerce spend within the next six months, with mobile, social, and physical commerce followed on the priority list.[11] To make the customer experiences between all of these channels seamless, retail leaders are making sure a holistic omnichannel strategy is a part of their digital transformation. Figure 1.4 depicts the multiple touchpoints with an omnichannel retailer in a consumer journey. Perry Belcastro, senior vice president of fulfillment at Saddle Creek Logistics Services, said, "[t]o provide an optimal omnichannel experience, retailers need to ensure consumer-friendly functionality for point of purchase, inventory access, and returns. 'It's also essential to offer optimal economy and priority shipping options.'"

The pandemic also has significantly altered consumer behaviors, with some changes expected to be permanent. In the United States, the availability of e-commerce and health concerns have led to an increase in store-switching behavior. Approximately 17 percent of consumers have shifted away from their primary store. Many customers also tried new omnichannel models, for example buy online, pickup in-store (**BOPIS**) during the Covid-19 pandemic. According to reports, 56 percent of consumers intend to keep using BOPIS, while 45 percent plan to continue using grocery delivery services.[12]

Top Omnichannel Retailers

The 2023 Top 100 Omnichannel Retailers Report ranked 100 leading retailers based on their omnichannel practices. They visited each retailer's website as well as one of its brick-and-mortar stores and judged them on the following eight omnichannel criteria:[13]

1. the ability for customers to buy online, pickup in-store (BOPIS);
2. buy online, pickup curbside;
3. search for in-store product availability on a brand's digital properties (desktop site, mobile site, mobile app);
4. have a shared cart across channels for logged-in shoppers (e.g., mobile site to desktop; app to desktop);
5. earn and redeem loyalty points/rewards across channels;
6. return products cross-channel (e.g., return online purchases in-store);
7. pay for purchases in-store via a mobile wallet and/or app;
8. access customer service help across multiple channels; and
9. make purchases and check in-store stock levels via a mobile app.

All of the 100 retailers ranked offer at least some form of BOPIS and/or curbside pickup and also

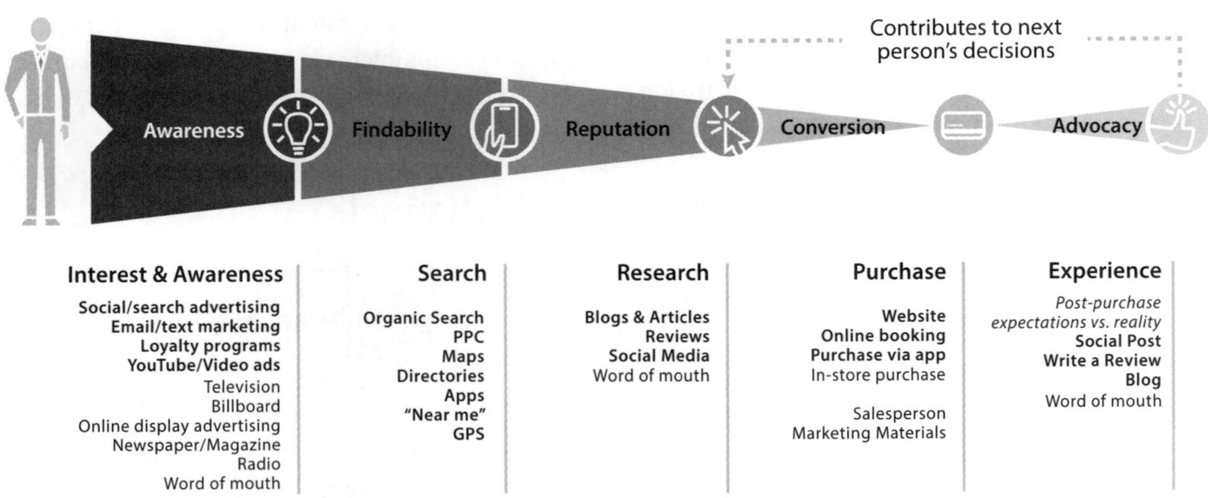

Figure 1.4 Modern consumer journey and the multiple touchpoints with omnichannel retailers
(*Source:* https://www.emailvendorselection.com/crm-vs-marketing-automation-what-are-the-differences/)

Table 1.1 Top 100 Omnichannel Retailers

RANK	RETAILER	BUY ONLINE, PICKUP IN-STORE	BUY ONLINE, PICKUP CURBSIDE	INVENTORY TRANSPARENCY ACROSS CHANNELS	SHARED CART	CROSS-CHANNEL LOYALTY PROGRAM	CROSS-CHANNEL PRODUCT RETURNS	IN-STORE MOBILE PAYMENTS	CUSTOMER CARE	MOBILE APP	TOTAL SCORE
1	Destination XL	14	6	12	10	7	12	7	13	9	90
2	The Home Depot	14	6	6	10	7	12	7	13	13.5	88.5
3	American Eagle Outfitters	14	6	12	10	7	6	7	13	9	84
3	H&M	14	6	12	10	7	6	7	13	9	84
3	Nordstrom	14	6	12	10	7	6	7	13	9	84
3	Staples	14	6	12	10	7	6	7	13	9	84
3	The Vitamin Shoppe	14	6	6	10	7	12	7	13	9	84
4	Amazon.com	14	3	9	10	0	12	7	13	13.5	81.5
5	Carter's	14	3	12	10	7	6	7	13	9	81
5	Hibbett Sports	14	3	12	10	7	6	7	13	9	81
5	Macy's	14	3	12	10	7	6	7	13	9	81
5	Office Depot	14	3	12	10	7	6	7	13	9	81
6	Abercrombie & Fitch	14	6	12	10	7	6	3.5	13	9	80.5
6	Ace Hardware	14	6	12	10	7	6	3.5	13	9	80.5
7	Buckle	14	0	12	10	7	12	7	13	4.5	79.5
7	Michael Kors	14	1.5	12	10	7	6	7	13	9	79.5
8	Dick's Sporting Goods	14	4.5	12	10	7	6	3.5	13	9	79
8	Gap	10.5	4.5	12	10	7	6	7	13	9	79
9	Neiman Marcus	14	6	12	10	1.75	6	7	13	9	78.75
10	Kohl's	14	0	12	10	7	6	7	13	9	78
10	The Container Store	14	0	6	10	7	12	7	13	9	78

Source: Total Retail/Cordial, *2023 Top100 Omnichannel Retailers Report*, p. 6

enable customers to return purchases across channels. However, just 10 percent of the retailers provide frictionless returns across all channels, indicating there is room for improvement to enable cross-channel product returns, particularly the return of online orders in-store. The results provided us with a picture of how omnichannel retailing is a prevalent practice in the United States and who the omnichannel retailing leaders are. Table 1.1 lists some of the Top 100 Omnichannel Retailers. In the following section, we will discuss the leading omnichannel retailers of the department store, sporting goods, footwear, and apparel and accessories categories and their practices.

Department Stores

Nordstrom, Macy's, Neiman Marcus, and Kohl's ranked as the top four department stores in the 2023 Top 100 Omnichannel Retailers Report. Nordstrom, a high-end department store, earned the top spot in 2021 and 2022 reports. The retailer's buy online, pickup in-store (BOPIS) and curbside pickup programs are immensely popular among customers and highly profitable for the company. In fact, BOPIS is the most profitable touchpoint for Nordstrom. CEO Erik Nordstrom stated in a press release announcing the company's 2022 Q1 earnings that the company's "interconnected model with Nordstrom and Nordstrom Rack, a scaled digital platform, and a robust store fleet positioned us to capitalize on demand from customers."[14] To provide customers with a seamless shopping experience, Nordstrom launched small-format "Local" stores in New York City and Los Angeles. These stores serve as hubs for online order pickup and returns, express alterations, free styling help, and other services (Figure 1.5).

Figure 1.5 Order pickup area at the Nordstrom store in Columbia, Maryland
(*Source:* Shatina Chen)

From 2016 to 2022, Macy's closed 170 underperforming stores in the United States in response to the changing consumer shopping habits.[15] With one of the nation's largest e-commerce platforms, including its website and mobile app, Macy's rolled out a new small-store concept called Market by Macy's as part of its omnichannel platform in 2020.[16] Market by Macy's store is an off-mall, small-format strategy to offer "buy online, pickup in-store" and "buy online, ship to store services." The "Market by Macy's" stores range from 25,000 to 50,000 square feet (compared to roughly 185,000 square feet for anchor stores). Joe Hodge, the senior director of real estate at Macy's said they approach Market by Macy's from an omnichannel lens, especially about how their stores fit into their digitally led ecosystem. In addition to narrowing the gap between in-store and online shopping, one objective for Market by Macy's is to provide a physical engagement point for customers after they close a mall-based department store. This approach allows Macy's to maintain and protect market share and serve a loyal customer base in high-quality and viable submarkets. Macy's opened several Market by Macy's stores in Dallas and Atlanta. They observed that the power center locations (big-box shopping centers) generated more foot traffic and increased the number of visits per customer than the other locations.[17]

Apparel and Accessories

Out of the Top 100 omnichannel retailers, thirty-seven are apparel and accessories specialty stores, with Destination XL (DXL), American Eagle Outfitters, and H&M ranked top three in the apparel and accessories specialty stores category. The majority of the apparel specialty stores allow online items to be returned via mail or in-store. However, in-store purchases must be returned in-store. Inconsistencies in pricing are rare, although they still exist on the list. Destination XL (DXL) is the largest retailer of men's clothing in sizes XL and up in the United States, catering to a niche market of men who are big and tall and may have limited options for shopping. DXL is also the only omnichannel retailer in the 2023 Top 100 omnichannel retailers list that earned all the available points for its omnichannel services. In addition, DXL has developed a proprietary fitting approach by measuring real customers and determining sizes that are as close to custom-tailored as they can get off the rack. They have also developed a digital-first strategy and implemented services such as in-store and curbside pickup prior to the pandemic.

American Eagle Outfitters (AEO), a global specialty retailer, ranked third in the 2023 rankings. AEO places a strong emphasis on product innovation, particularly in its core merchandise: jeans. In 2023, AEO unveiled an exclusive collaboration designed by Maddie and Kenzie Ziegler, which resonated with Gen Z shoppers—a key demographic for the brand. AEO's leadership in the denim space remains unwavering, as it continues to engage Gen Z through styling content, #AEJeans reviews, and partnerships with popular creators. The brand's presence on Gen Z's social feeds reinforces its position as a go-to destination for trendy denim styles. The retailer also operates its logistics platform, the Quiet Platforms Delivery Network, which offers nationwide coverage through trusted carriers. By optimizing supply chain efficiency, AEO aims to compete with fast delivery leaders like Amazon.com. Shekar Natarajan, the executive vice-president and chief supply chain officer of AEO, said in a news release, "We are reimagining the way retailers and brands deliver service to their customers, while taking on the complexity of logistics."[18]

H&M, the Sweden-based apparel, accessories, and homeware brand, prioritizes merchandise assortment and customer experience across both in-store and online channels. The brand invests in its supply chain and leverages technology solutions, including artificial intelligence, to manage inventory efficiently.[19] Notable innovations for enhancing the customer omnichannel experience include digital receipts, visual search, radio frequency identification (RFID) for real-time item availability, and smart mirrors in fitting rooms, etc.

Sporting Goods

Among the sporting goods category, Hibbett Sports, Dick's Sporting Goods, and Bass Pro Shops ranked as the top three outdoor specialty retailers in the 2023 Top 100 Omnichannel Retailers Report. Hibbett Sports, an athletic-inspired fashion retailer, rose from eighth place in 2022 to fifth place in the 2023 Omnichannel Retailers list. Hibbett offers both buy online, pickup in-store (BOPIS), and reserve online, pickup in-store (ROPIS) services to leverage their stores. The company didn't launch an e-commerce site until late 2017, and Hibbett Sports capitalizes on the sneaker craze by selling in-demand Nike and Adidas sneakers. To manage high demand, they use a mobile app raffle system for fair access to coveted releases. "We were 20 years late to the party, so you better be good when you walk in," said Bill Quinn, vice president, digital commerce.[20]

Consumer Trends of Omnichannel Retailing

Broadband is the transmission of wide bandwidth data over a high-speed internet connection.[21] From 2010 to 2020, the percentage of Americans with access to broadband internet increased from an estimated 74.5 percent to 93.5 percent.[22] The broadband technology and hardware development make browsing and interactions on the internet a much more efficient and enjoyable experience. Mobile devices with internet access also bring in another driving force to change technology usage patterns. Since the first iPhone was announced in 2007, smartphones have gradually penetrated consumers' daily lives. In 2011, only 35 percent of all US adults owned a smartphone. By 2021, that number increased to over 85 percent.[23] The mobile device penetration rate also reflects on internet traffic. Worldwide, mobile phones generate 58.57 percent of traffic, while desktop/laptops generate 39.25 percent.[24] About 55 percent of page views in 2021 came from mobile phones, while more than half of all video views came from mobile devices. American adults spent 4 hours and 16 minutes daily on their cell phones in 2021; this number is expected to continue to grow, according to eMarketer's forecasting.[25] The global pandemic has made drastic shifts in consumer behavior (Figure 1.6), which in turn has forced retailers

Figure 1.6 Consumer technology usage patterns have largely changed in the past decade

to re-evaluate (and speed up) their technology road maps. Consumers' increasing reliance on digital and omnichannel solutions to engage and transact with retailers has presented a sea change for the industry—or at least accelerated that pace of change. According to McKinsey & Company, the retail industry saw ten years' worth of forecasted e-commerce growth in just three months in Q1 2020.[26]

The last major consumer technology behavior change is social media platform usage, which also tends to happen on mobile devices. According to Pew Research, in 2005, 5 percent of US adults had at least one social media account. By 2011, around half of US adults used at least one social media platform. In 2021, that number had risen to 72 percent.[27] Most importantly, not only are there more people on social media, but they also spend a lot of time using the platforms. For example, globally, an average user spent 2 hours and 31 minutes per day on social media in 2023, up from 1 hour per day in 2012. If we accumulated the time spent on social media in a lifetime, an average user would spend a total of 6 years and 8 months on social media, closely equivalent to the time spent sleeping and watching TV.[28] Take a look at your mobile phone. Do you know how many social media accounts you have? How much time do you spend on these social media platforms? How do you usually message your best friends? When you arrive in a new town, how do you find out where to eat? Chances are you are doing these things using mobile devices by accessing the internet or social media.

Worldwide Apparel Consumption

The revenue generated from online apparel and accessories retail sales is continuing to grow in the United States. In 2019, retail e-commerce revenues from apparel and accessories sales amounted to $102.5 billion and were projected to increase to $153.6 billion by 2024.[29] Amazon.com is the biggest online retailer in the world, and over 80 percent of US households own Amazon Prime memberships. When Amazon Prime members were asked which product categories they purchased in the past month, clothing, shoes, and accessories were the most purchased (Table 1.2).[30]

Around the world, shoppers are buying more apparel and shoes than ever before. By 2025, the global e-commerce fashion industry was projected to grow to $2.25 trillion.[31] Market reports predicted that the e-commerce segment of fashion and apparel would grow at a compound annual rate of 10.6 percent until 2022. The three largest apparel markets in the world are the United States, China, and Japan, in descending order.[30] There are four main product categories for the apparel and footwear market: womenswear, menswear, sportswear, and childrenswear. Womenswear was the bestselling apparel category in the world.[33] During 2020–2021 amid the beginning of the Covid-19 pandemic, consumers and retailers readily adopted new digital and omnichannel shopping behaviors such as curbside pickup and home delivery. According to the McKinsey & Company report, the Covid-19 pandemic stimulated ten years' worth of the penetration rate just three months into the pandemic. Therefore, retailers are facing higher expectations for a post-pandemic marketplace.

In the meantime, the double-digit growth in US e-commerce is expected to continue. E-commerce sales in the US were set to surpass $1 trillion in 2022. By 2023, eMarketer projected worldwide retail e-commerce sales would total $6.169 trillion and make up a 22.3 percent share of total retail sales, up from $3.351 trillion and 13.8 percent in 2019. The US e-commerce sales grew 17.9 percent in 2021 to reach $933.30 billion. E-commerce was expected to surpass 20 percent of total retail by 2024.[34]

Forrester, a market research company, predicted that digital sales in the clothing category will reach 47.5 percent by 2024 in the United States.[35] One thing to keep in mind, though, is that this forecasting may not apply to other industries. Physical retail stores still maintain a firm position and are expected to account for three-quarters of total retail sales. Amazon.com started in 1994 as a virtual merchant. After years of pure online operation, they are beginning to recognize the importance of physical stores. Today, Amazon operates close to 600 physical stores in the United States, the majority of which are locations of grocer Whole Foods Market, which Amazon acquired in 2017. Amazon also operates Amazon-branded stores, including Amazon Go (cashier-less convenience stores), Amazon Fresh (grocery), Amazon 4-star (featuring products with a four-star rating or higher on Amazon.com), Amazon Books (carrying books and electronics), and Amazon Pop Up (shopping center locations that highlight various brands and trends).

As consumers increasingly adopt online purchasing and interaction with retailers through multiple channels that retailers/brands operate, there is a strong demand for a tailored experience based on knowledge learned from an individual consumer via the multiple touchpoints (e.g., website browsing, email sign-up, etc.). More than eight in

Table 1.2 Fashion Purchases of Amazon Prime Members in One Month

	AUG-23	OCT-23	DEC-23	FEB-24	APR-24	JUN-24
Clothing	63%	63%	73%	56%	56%	61%
Food or beverages (nonalcoholic)	41%	44%	48%	47%	40%	47%
Shoes (shoes, boots, sandals, etc.)	43%	39%	48%	40%	35%	42%
Household supplies (cleaning supplies, kitchen supplies, etc.)	40%	44%	48%	41%	34%	41%
Pet products	38%	38%	42%	42%	35%	40%
Beauty products	39%	43%	48%	40%	35%	38%
Pharmacy or health (over-the-counter products such as vitamins)	32%	35%	41%	33%	28%	35%
Books, music, or videos (physical or digital copies)	37%	34%	41%	31%	30%	34%
Toys or games	27%	27%	42%	28%	25%	28%
Accessories (belts, wallets, handbags, backpacks)	29%	28%	35%	26%	21%	26%
Home improvement or tools	27%	26%	32%	23%	23%	25%
Outdoor (including lawn and garden) products	24%	17%	17%	13%	15%	25%
Home, furniture, or small appliances	23%	24%	28%	20%	17%	23%
Computers, computer accessories, software	20%	17%	27%	20%	17%	19%
Office equipment or supplies	24%	24%	21%	20%	16%	19%
Consumer electronics (TV, phone, etc.)	18%	18%	25%	19%	19%	18%
Sporting products	18%	17%	23%	16%	15%	16%
Baby products	13%	13%	12%	10%	12%	14%
Alcoholic beverages	8%	11%	13%	13%	13%	13%
Large appliances	6%	4%	5%	6%	5%	5%
Other	5%	4%	5%	2%	3%	4%

Note: Respondents aged 18–65 who were Amazon Prime members and made a digital purchase in the past month/30 days; surveys were conducted every two months. (*Source:* The EMARKETER E-commerce Survey (June 2024); subscriber access at https://chart-na1.emarketer.com/266366/which-product-categories-have-us-amazon-prime-members-purchased-digitally-past-month-of-respondents-april-2023-feb-2024)

ten (84 percent) consumers say being treated like a person rather than a number is very important to earning their business. In other words, when you ask a customer for their birthday, and you do something on their birthday (like sending coupons or birthday wishes), they feel valued. With advanced technologies such as automation and machine learning, if their birthday is coming and they did not receive a birthday wish with some discount or gift, they will not feel that you "see" them or want their business. In the following sections, we will discuss the evolution of omnichannel retailing and the activities that omnichannel retailers do to provide an exceptional omnichannel customer experience.

Changes in Consumer Behavior

Globally, there are some major changes in consumer behavior that facilitate omnichannel retailing. These changes include social commerce, live stream shopping, personalized retailing, on-the-go consumption, sustainability, ethical and value-based shoppers, re-commerce and sharing economy, consumer privacy and security, and digital transformation in supply chain management. In the following sections, we will introduce these in more detail.

Social Commerce

Social commerce is defined as selling with social media websites, such as Facebook, Instagram, X (formerly Twitter), TikTok, Pinterest, and YouTube, which support user-generated content and social interaction.[36] For omnichannel retailers, communicating with consumers using multiple touchpoints is important as well. Social media platforms have been essential tools to build relationships with individual customers by providing engaging content. As consumers continue to spend more time on social media, brands collaborate with social influencers (content creators) to sell products and services. Social influencers on Facebook can earn money from ads via the in-stream ads program, from the support of their fans (either via subscriptions or paid online events), through the Stars feature (each Star is worth $0.01, so that, for every 10,000 Stars, streamers will get $100), or with paid partnerships via branded content and brand managers. This way, social influencers can choose the mix of products that best matches the community they have built and the content that they share. Many YouTubers create their own community by providing useful or entertaining content on YouTube or TikTok channels.

Consumers can directly place orders through social media without leaving the platform. For instance, Instagram offers Instagram checkout to allow users to directly make a purchase without leaving Instagram.[37] That is, if someone sees a picture of a product they want in the Stories or short video Reel, they can tap to view more details and then place the order right from their phone. Similarly, TikTok Shopping also provides a way for TikTok users to buy products in the app without opening a web browser to go to a separate e-commerce store. Kylie Jenner's store, Kylie Cosmetics, was one of the first to let their customers shop directly on TikTok. Social checkout can increase the conversion rate since shoppers are not leaving the platform. Brands can better monitor the effects of influencer marketing on conversions. Making shoppable content will be introduced more in Chapter 7, Promotion in the Omnichannel Environment.

Live Stream Shopping

Live stream shopping is like modernized TV shopping programs and enables viewers to buy products directly from creator-hosted streamed events. It has been growing rapidly in the Chinese market over the past ten years. In 2021, livestreaming sales in China were around $300 billion. Live stream retailing is also becoming a new trend because it allows the seller to include pictures, descriptions, and prices for customers all in one place (Figure 1.7). Douyin, TikTok's Chinese counterpart also owned by parent company ByteDance, tripled live shopping sales in 2021 during the pandemic. Live shopping is particularly popular in the fashion, beauty, fitness, and home decor categories; while women may be more interested in fashion and beauty products, the fitness and home improvement retailers target male consumers.

Although buying via live streaming or video has grown in popularity in recent years, adoption in the United States is still limited, regardless of age. According to a 2022 survey, adults between 18 and 34 are the heaviest users of this shopping channel, but just 10 percent reported using it regularly. On the other hand, half of US users aged 55 and older stated they had never shopped via video commerce and had no interest in doing so either. However, this could change quickly with Facebook, YouTube, Amazon, X (formerly Twitter), and other tech companies like Pinterest all investing in incorporating live shopping features in their platforms.[38]

Figure 1.7 Fashion vlogger presenting dress to cellphone and selling clothes online using live streaming

Personalized Retailing

In today's market, consumers expect brands to provide a personalized shopping experience tailored to their individual needs. Herzberg's motivation-hygiene theory distinguishes between satisfaction and dissatisfaction, and personalization is considered a "hygiene factor." Although customers take personalization for granted, if a retailer fails to deliver it customers may turn to competitors. An effective personalization operating model consists of four key components: a data foundation, analytics and planning, re-design, and distribution, including cross-functional teams and company culture. Nike has taken personalization to a new level with its #NikeByYou builder, allowing customers to customize their clothes and shoes using a 3D sneaker customization platform. Amazon Prime Wardrobe has launched a personal shopping service exclusively for Prime members, offering personalized recommendations from a wide selection of brands based on customer style and fit preferences. In omnichannel retailing, customers expect personalization throughout their entire experience, including multiple personalized touchpoints that cater to their individual preferences. The best personalized experiences involve the customer in the dialogue, and use data to create unique, one-to-one personalization with tailored products, services, and communications that are relevant to them.

On-the-Go

On-the-go (OTG) consumption denotes the purchase and immediate consumption of food and beverages while in transit from one place to another. Therefore, on-the-go consumers are also called in-transit consumers. For retailers, revenue goals hinge on their ability to steer in-transit consumers to their doorsteps, elevating physical stores as key touchpoints in the omnichannel customer journey. Amazon Go is a convenience store concept developed by Amazon. These stores use advanced technology, including cameras, sensors, and machine learning algorithms, to allow customers to enter the store, grab the items they need, and leave without having to stop at a checkout counter. This technology is called "Just Walk Out," and it tracks the items customers take from the shelves and charges their Amazon account automatically when they exit the store. Amazon Go stores offer a variety of food and beverages, including ready-to-eat meals, snacks, and grocery items. As of early 2023, there were approximately thirty Amazon Go stores operating across the United States, primarily in urban locations such as New York City, San Francisco, and Seattle.[39]

Sustainability

Sustainability has become a critical issue in response to global climate change. The IBM Institute for Business Value (IBV) found that 93 percent of global respondents said that the pandemic had influenced their views on sustainability. A joint study by McKinsey and NielsenIQ found that products making Environmental, Social, and Governance related claims (ESG) averaged 28 percent cumulative growth from 2017–2022, versus 20 percent for products that made no such claims. A survey conducted in February 2022 of 16,000 global consumers found that over half of respondents (51 percent) said that environmental sustainability was more important to them today than it had been twelve months ago. This trend of increasing importance for sustainability is apparent across demographics and shopper groups, with 78 percent of US consumers stating that a sustainable lifestyle is important to them.

In the retail and consumer goods industry, there is a growing tension between two common refrains regarding sustainability. While sustainability is becoming increasingly important to all stakeholders, including consumers, regulators, and companies, there remains an attitude-behavior gap where people may not be willing to pay more for sustainable products and services. However, the willingness to pay more for sustainable products is rising across geographies, with one in four consumers planning to focus more on environmental issues and social aspects in their shopping behavior. Sustainability advocates tend to tilt towards women, Gen Z, and people with higher incomes, although this trend is evident across sociodemographic backgrounds.

Industry experts are calling for government policy changes, as work done on achieving zero upstream emissions can be possible at low consumer costs. For instance, according to the World Economic Forum, the average cost increase for a €40 (around $43) pair of jeans would be less than 2 percent.[40] Industry leaders are also encouraging education to raise awareness among consumers that buying a green product is often an option they have, and the extra price is comparatively small, but the extra impact they have with this responsible choice is significant. Patagonia, an outdoor retailer, ran an ad in *The New York Times* on Black Friday telling people, "Don't Buy This Jacket," to encourage shoppers to think twice before they buy.[41] Some fashion companies—such as Reformation—are ahead of the curve in this sector. They regularly post their sustainability reports on their website to show how they will be "climate positive" by 2025.

Fast fashion brand H&M is also trying to push their own boundary by adopting sustainable products through their Conscious Exclusive collection, which features organic cotton and the use of Tencel and recycled polyester. Sustainability advocates see this as a critical step in promoting a more sustainable future. The retailer gives pieces in the collection, which are priced higher than the Swedish retailer's traditional labels, interesting details with embellishments and trimmings. "We're pushing the boundaries with fashion and sustainability," said Cecilia Brann, sustainability manager. "We're one of the largest users in the world of Tencel and recycled polyester. We used organic cotton in our collection before we launched Conscious Exclusive."

Ethical and Value-Based Shoppers

Ethical and value-based shoppers are defined as "shoppers who purchase goods/services from brands that align with their values whenever practical."[42] The market size of this growing consumer trend makes it very relevant to omnichannel fashion businesses. According to the Centre for Retail Research, these shoppers spend a total of approximately $300 billion on ethical products each year, about a 10 percent increase from the same period in 2017. These shoppers seek out products produced with no animal cruelty, no animal testing, and made sustainably, without excess packaging, and/or packaging made with a carbon-neutral approach and support fair compensation to the makers.[43] As many as 73 percent of Millennials surveyed by DoneGood Collaborator expressed their willingness to pay higher prices for sustainably produced goods.[44] Interest in ethical products is usually higher in consumers with children. Most ethical brands looking at the global market are targeting young, highly educated, and digitally engaged shoppers, usually with high incomes.

Consumers become interested in ethical and value-based consumption when they are educated about the extent of the environmental or human rights problem. Omnichannel retailers who target ethical and value-based shoppers need to demonstrate their values in all touchpoints instead of doing lip service. For instance, if you're an apparel brand that advocates for gender spectrum inclusion, ensure that your merchandising, product lines, search, and navigation reflect that. Sudden boasting about philanthropic work or improved practices can seem disingenuous. Also, the higher price of ethical products along with the lack of transparency and traceability across the supply chain are the main factors preventing consumers from making more ethical decisions. Understanding where products come from and how the materials were sourced, transported, and manufactured could make a difference in their willingness to pay more for ethical products.[45]

Re-Commerce and Sharing Economy

Consumers are increasingly making the connection between the products they buy and their impact on the environment. The apparel resale site ThredUp was founded a decade ago. At that time, there was a stigma around used or gently worn clothing. "The stigma around resale has all but disappeared, and secondhand has gone mainstream," James Reinhart, the founder and CEO of ThredUp, said. What changed? The CEO points to the auto industry, where a few years ago, used cars were highly stigmatized. "Certified pre-owned vehicles allow consumers to trade their old car for a new or used car at the same dealer. The same shift was happening in the clothing industry, with resale offering value to consumers and opportunities for retailers."[46]

Re-commerce and sharing economy are systems where goods and services are shared, bartered, traded, and transacted between individuals free of charge or for a fee.[47] Individual-to-individual or peer-to-peer (P2P)-based activities of acquiring, providing, or sharing access to goods and services are often facilitated by a community-based online platform or profit-based online/mobile-based platform. By 2021, more than 86 million Americans were participating in the sharing economy. The market size of the sharing economy is expected to reach $335 billion by 2025.[48] The two most common examples of the sharing economy are sharing private vehicles through ride-sharing companies such as Uber and private residences and lodging through accommodation websites such as Airbnb.[49]

The re-commerce business caters to consumers who are intensely interested in the sharing economy. Users of Wardrobe, a new peer-to-peer clothing rental service business, can view the virtual Wardrobe on its website, along with rental rates and minimum rentals for items ranging from four days to four months.[50] In addition, any users can lend their clothes to other users via the Wardrobe lender community.[51] Another prominent example of re-commerce in the fashion industry is Poshmark. Poshmark operates both web-based and mobile apps to connect consumers as buyers and sellers through its platform. Consumers are empowered to clean up their closets on their platforms and offer the items to other Poshmark consumers. Even though most items are in "pre-loved" condition, at times, some sellers are posting "brand new items with tags" for reselling purposes. Customers can buy and sell clothing, shoes, handbags, and other accessories through the app and set up virtual closets.[52] On January 14, 2021, Poshmark launched an initial public offering (IPO) at $42 a share, which equates to an initial valuation of more than $3 billion (see Figure 1.8).[53]

Figure 1.8 Poshmark Inc. launched an initial public offering (IPO) in New York, USA, on Thursday, January 14, 2021

Customer Privacy and Security

Internet technologies have enhanced retailers and brands to sell products across physical boundaries such as geographic areas (e.g., across states, countries, etc.) and offer new services (such as virtual try-on, augmented reality, etc.) or new product types (such as subscription boxes, clothing rental, etc.). In the past decade, a series of high-profile data breach scandals have heightened consumers' concerns, and more consumers think companies should be responsible for protecting consumers' online privacy. General Data Protection Regulation (GDPR) and the California Consumer Privacy Act (CCPA) are the two recent privacy regulations introduced in the EU and California, respectively. The advanced e-commerce format, therefore, evokes issues on governance, business tax, and intellectual property management. We will discuss more on these matters in Chapter 9, Ethical and Legal Aspects in Omnichannel Retailing.

Digital Transformation in Supply Chain Management

Fashion retailer H&M has announced a new partnership to develop an enterprise data backbone for its business. H&M is collaborating with Google Cloud for the project that will include a core data platform and the use of machine learning and artificial intelligence (AI) capabilities. A range of Google Cloud's products and services will be used throughout the full organization to create stronger customer experiences—from in-store to online—and optimize internal supply chains. This partnership will also enable further development of data science and AI capabilities throughout H&M Group's business. "We are now further accelerating digitalization as we believe in sustainable growth powered by advanced analytics and tech. Therefore, I'm happy to announce we've found a provider who matches our needs," said Alan Boehme, Chief Technology Officer of H&M Group.[54] More information about supply chain management is provided in Chapter 6, Omnichannel Supply Chain and Logistic Management.

CASE STUDY 1.1

Just Do It™—What We Can Learn from Nike's Omnichannel Strategy

Nike designed all its channels/platforms to communicate with one another so that the consumer experience is close to perfect—leaving the customer wanting to come back for more. Not only does Nike have an efficient marketing strategy, it is also not afraid to tell a story. The brand is constantly evolving with the world and proposes messages with all their brand deals.

Nike has been able to expand its store into the interfaces of several apps, websites, commercials, and more. Every platform is intentionally designed to communicate with one another so that they have the best data/information for each individual customer. The company has taken personalization to a whole new level by allowing customers to configure their own clothes and shoes. Recently, Nike launched a 3D sneaker-customization platform that generates real-time, shareable snapshots of finished footwear.

But personalization doesn't stop at the product level. Nike has also extended personalization to its physical locations. The Nike flagship store in New York City offers a compelling omnichannel shopping experience driven by membership in NikePlus, the company's personalized loyalty program. Members enjoy personalized, exclusive benefits, such as access to Nike Speed Shop, which offers a data-driven, locally tailored assortment of "NYC favorites." Members can also reserve items and retrieve them from pickup lockers by scanning their NikePlus member pass. Nike Shop the Look allows members to use QR code scanning to determine the availability of their preferred sizes and colors and request delivery to their selected pickup location or dressing room. With instant checkout, members can skip the cash register line and check out directly from their own stored-payment device. Other benefits include access to Nike Expert Studio, where members can book personal, one-on-one appointments with Nike experts, and the opportunity to book appointments with Nike by You, where members can view a selection of silhouettes that are uniquely fitted to their specifications.

Whether Nike is collaborating with famous athletes, rappers, or fashion designers, they always seem to be telling a bold and unique story with their products. They strategize an emotional sentiment with their consumers that evoke a sense of emotion in every purchase. For example, Nike's collaboration with Colin Kaepernick that protested police brutality brought a different kind of publicity to the brand and found that more people were interested in what they were selling. Nike not only uses stories to utilize a marketing technique, but they also customize their platforms to the individual. Customers from anywhere in the world will find that their Nike experience is customized to fit their own culture, interests, and even body type.

Discussion Questions:

1. What specific marketing strategy do you think is most effective in Nike's growth (i.e., influencer collaborations, user-friendly interface of Nike's online store, long-form video content, etc.)? Why?
2. Nike is known to have multiple social media accounts, multiple mobile apps, and even multiple websites. Why does Nike use a variety of platforms to reach out to its consumers?
3. Do you think other big-name brands should replicate this kind of marketing strategy? Why or why not?
4. What are the pros and cons of Nike's controversial campaigns and storytelling?
5. Are there any other companies you can think of that use emotional connection as a marketing strategy? How does it compare to Nike's?

Career Opportunities

Job Titles	Key Responsibility
Browse & Search eCommerce Manager (Luxury Department Store)	• Increase search conversion rate by reducing friction in the search experience and help customers find what they want right away. • Provide relevant results to customers based on the search term. Using third-party tools, execute algorithm tweaks to ensure the most relevant products are prioritized within the results. • Uncover customer intent and reveal data about customer's interests. Share with the appropriate cross-functional teams. • Create synonyms for null search results specific to brands that are not carried by us. Redirect commonly misspelled searches to relevant search terms. • Add filters and facets to search results to allow customers to narrow the results. • Partner with site merchandising and category management to understand the key business drivers based on seasonality, receipts, and brand penetration. Collaborate with product management on search and browse enhancements to improve the customer experience (UX). • Identify new data points that should be considered as results are populated on the search results and browse category pages to increase click-through rate, conversion rate, and demand. • Subject matter expert for the design and implementation of personalized search and browse results. **Qualifications:** • Bachelor's degree. • Minimum of 3+ years of relevant retail ecommerce experience. Proven experience successfully driving Search and Browse strategies is preferred. • Skilled in defining the right metrics to measure how your actions are impacting customers and the business. • Strong analytical skills with hands-on experience using data analytics tools. Adobe Analytics experience preferred. Advanced Excel and Microsoft Office skills required. • Technically savvy. Familiar with Machine Learning concepts, Search fundamentals, approaches to personalization. • Strong experience in large-scale enterprise organizations. Luxury retail preferred. • Excellent communication skills—interpersonal, verbal, and written. • Strong commitment to timelines, accuracy, organization, and professionalism. • Thrives in a fast-paced and cross-functional environment with a customer-first mindset. • Proactive, self-motivated, passionate, and accountable. A self-starter approach with an eagerness to consistently meet and exceed objectives and take on more responsibility.

(*Source*: https://www.linkedin.com/jobs/search/?currentJobId=2746245923&f_C=157312&geoId=92000000&start=0&position=17&pageNum=0)

Summary

Retail business has a rich history dating back to ancient times when goods and services were sold to consumers across different cultures. As the twentieth century dawned, the widespread availability of automobiles saw a migration of people to the suburbs, leading to the growth of retail stores and malls that sold a vast range of goods in formats such as supermarkets, warehouse stores, discount stores, and convenience stores. With the rapid evolution of internet technology, consumers' technology usage patterns have changed significantly, and retailers have had to adapt. This led to the emergence of multichannel retailers, which allowed department stores and mass merchandise retailers to sell products/services on more than three channels. However, these retailers did not integrate operations such as pricing, inventory, shipping, and payment systems as one, and each channel may have had a separate team in planning, buying, pricing, and distribution.

Omnichannel retailers, on the other hand, provide customers with an integrated shopping experience across various channels, including brick-and-mortar stores, online stores, mobile apps, social media platforms, and other channels. This allows consumers to interact with a brand seamlessly, regardless of the channel they use and provides them with a consistent experience and access to the same product information, pricing, and promotions. Over 80 percent of Top 500 retailers offered buy online, pickup in-store in 2021. A true omnichannel approach must also deliver a consistent brand experience to meet customers where they are while building relationships beyond channels. Omnichannel retailing is driven by technological changes such as broadband penetration, mobile devices, and social media platforms. It allows consumers to shop through non-traditional platforms such as **social shopping**, live stream shopping, or checkout without having to stop at a checkout counter.

With the aid of information technology, consumers expect brands to provide a personalized shopping experience tailored to their individual needs while also aligning with their ethical values. They demand to know how their purchase decision impacts the environment, economics, and if a brand's practices align with their ethical values. In response to consumers' concerns about sustainability, the market size of the sharing economy is expected to reach $335 billion by 2025. To accommodate consumers' increasingly particular demands, omnichannel retailing seamlessly integrates all the various paths to purchase and makes all retail channels work together. This requires data integration across different channels. However, with high-profile data breach scandals over the past decade, consumers have become increasingly concerned about online privacy, and they now expect retailers to be responsible for protecting their data. This presents a challenge for retailers as they must not only overcome technical challenges but also earn consumers' trust by proving their ability to handle data securely. Despite these challenges, retailers must deliver a seamless and consistent experience across channels while considering the different channels that consumers use to interact with their business.

Key Terms

BOPIS
Brick-and-click retailers
Broadband
Clothing rental service
Dual-channel retailers
Ethical and value-based shoppers
Instagram checkout
Live stream shopping
Multichannel retailers
Multichannel shoppers
Omnichannel retailers
On-the-go (OTG)
Pure-play retailers
Re-commerce
Sharing economy
Single-channel retailers
Social shopping
TikTok shopping
Touchpoints

Reflection and Discussion Questions

1. Name one of your favorite retailers and find out its retail organization structure.
2. As a consumer, what's your favorite omnichannel service(s) among the eight omnichannel criteria suggested by the Top 100 Omnichannel Retailers Report?
3. Explain the difference between multichannel retailing and omnichannel retailing. In your opinion, what omnichannel services bring most value to shoppers?
4. Reflect on your last online apparel shopping experience and briefly describe what you bought and where you bought it. Did you spend a lot of time searching for the right product? Are you satisfied with the purchase? If not, do you have any difficulty with returning the product?
5. Based on the content of this chapter, please describe the three major changing technology usage patterns among consumers. In your opinion, what other factors also contribute to the trend of omnichannel retailing?
6. What impacts did the 2020–2021 Covid-19 pandemic have on the retail industry? In your observation, what have changed since then?
7. What is BOPIS? Do you think retailers will continue to offer this service?
8. Among the major trends mentioned in the chapter, which one do you think is most important for fashion retailers?

CHAPTER 2

Retail Formats in the Omnichannel Business Environment

Learning Objectives

Upon finishing this chapter, you will be able to:

- Describe the various types of brick-and-mortar retailers and their characteristics
- Distinguish the difference between direct marketing and direct selling
- Evaluate the various types of direct marketing and direct selling methods and their characteristics
- Appraise the options of electronic retailing and provide examples

In Chapter 2, we will review traditional retail formats (e.g., brick-and-mortar, direct marketing, sell, etc.), the major retailers in each category, and how they incorporate the e-commerce revenue model into their revenue stream. Following, we will discuss different electronic retail options for retailers selling products on the internet, including websites, online markets, mobile apps, and social media accounts. Examples of each format will be evaluated, and students will learn how to appraise these options that apply to fashion/lifestyle brands and the major stakeholders involved in the omnichannel retailing arena.

Brick-and-Mortar Retailing

Traditionally, a retail format is defined by assortments. Assortment describes the range of choices within a particular classification of goods, such as style, color, size, and price. Within a specific store, an assortment means all the goods carried in that store (in terms of breadth and depth of stock). In this section, we will introduce different types of brick-and-mortar retail formats based on their assortment.

Department Stores

Department stores offer a broad assortment of products, with multiple departments separating product categories. Their assortments have depth within each category, and they have some variety but usually focus mainly on soft goods such as apparel and bedding; some hard goods, like appliances, are usually included as well. A **full-line department store** is a department store that offers many different lines of products, including both soft lines (e.g., apparel and household textile goods), hard lines (e.g., sporting goods, furniture, electrical goods, etc.), and many different services, including wrapping, delivery, and credit. A **limited-line department store** is a department store that carries a narrower range of merchandise than a full-line department store; typically, a limited-line department store usually has high-quality merchandise at high prices for the upscale market. For instance, Saks Fifth Avenue and Neiman Marcus are examples of upscale specialty department stores. Department stores generally account for less than 10 percent of a country's total retail sales, but they draw large numbers of customers in urban areas.

Target Market and Pricing Strategies

Target markets for full-line department stores are determined by more than just age, as lifestyle factors, brand preferences, income, and diverse ethnic backgrounds are all equally important. For example, J.C. Penney features name brands and fashion similar to their Nordstrom counterparts (see Chapter 1), but they appeal to diverse groups of customers from big cities to smaller cities in the United States.[1,2] In contrast, limited-line stores have more narrowly defined target markets and typically offer higher-priced merchandise than full-line department stores. Limited-line department stores, such as Harrods department store (a high-end British department store) or Neiman Marcus (a high-end US department store), particularly those focused on apparel, offer fashion-forward merchandise and operate on gross margins of around 50 percent.

Department Store Strengths

Department stores have several strengths compared with other types of retail stores:

- Wide range of products: Department stores offer a wide range of products, from clothing and accessories to home goods, appliances, and electronics. This means that customers can find everything they need in one place, which is convenient and timesaving.
- Brand variety: Department stores carry products from multiple brands, giving customers a greater choice and selection. This also allows customers to compare prices and quality across different brands.
- Convenience: Department stores are typically located in shopping malls or busy shopping districts, making them easily accessible for customers. They also often have extended hours, allowing customers to shop at their convenience.
- Customer service: Department stores generally offer excellent customer service, with well-trained staff who are knowledgeable about the products they sell. This can make the shopping experience more enjoyable and help customers find what they are looking for more easily.
- Promotions and sales: Department stores often offer promotions and sales, such as discounts or buy-one-get-one-free deals, which can attract customers and help them save money.

- Return policies: Department stores typically have generous return policies, allowing customers to return or exchange items if they are not satisfied with their purchase. This can give customers greater confidence in their purchases and help build trust between the store and the customer.

Overall, department stores offer a one-stop shopping experience with a wide variety of products, good customer service, and convenient locations.

Department Store Weaknesses

Department stores also have some weaknesses compared with other types of retail stores:

- Higher prices: Department stores often have higher prices than discount retailers or online stores, due to higher overhead costs and other factors such as better layout and ambience, special services, etc.
- Competition from e-commerce: With the rise of e-commerce, department stores face stiff competition from online retailers that offer lower prices, wider product selection, and the convenience of shopping from home.
- Large size: Department stores are typically large, which can make it difficult for customers to navigate and find what they are looking for. This can be especially challenging for older adults or customers with disabilities.
- Declining relevance: Department stores have been facing declining relevance since the beginning of the twenty-first century, with many consumers shifting their shopping habits to online retailers or discount stores. This can make it difficult for department stores to attract and retain customers.[3]

Overall, department stores face challenges with higher prices, competition from e-commerce, large size, limited personalization, inconsistent quality, and declining relevance. These weaknesses can make it difficult for department stores to remain competitive in the retail industry.

Specialty Stores

A retail **specialty store** is a store that focuses on selling a specific type of product or a narrow range of related products within a particular niche or category. These stores often have a more targeted and specialized selection of products than larger, general merchandise retailers. Examples of retail specialty stores include clothing boutiques, toy stores, sports equipment shops, pet stores, and bookstores. They cater to a specific customer base that is interested in their particular niche or product offering. Specialty stores often provide a higher level of customer service and expertise, as they are more knowledgeable about their products and can offer more personalized advice and recommendations to their customers.

Target Market and Pricing Strategies

Specialty stores focus on catering to specific markets, such as age, interest, gender, income level, ethnic origin, lifestyle, and fashion orientation, rather than attempting to appeal broadly. This is demonstrated by the higher-priced, exclusive, and fashion-forward apparel collections offered by designers such as Gucci, as opposed to the mass-produced goods found at Walmart. These definitive collections, like Giorgio Armani and Burberry, are sold at a premium price point. To expand their customer base, some designers offer merchandise at multiple price points, with diffusion lines being sold at lower prices than designer collections. Armani, for example, has both collection (Armani) and diffusion lines (Armani Exchange, Armani Jeans, Emporio Armani). Some other notable examples include Ralph Lauren's diffusion line: Polo Ralph Lauren, and Vera Wang's diffusion line: Simply Vera.

Specialty Store Strengths

Specialty stores offer many advantages, including:

- Product expertise: Specialized retail businesses, such as those selling wedding gowns, sports shoes, cosmetics, or suits, are able to provide their employees with comprehensive training that offers in-depth knowledge of their product category. This allows their staff to become expert resources for customers seeking guidance in selecting the right products. As a result, customers can rely on these knowledgeable employees to provide accurate and helpful information during the purchasing process.
- Pleasant atmosphere: Specialty stores are typically designed and laid out in a manner that contrasts starkly with the sterile and impersonal

environment of general merchandise retailers. Rather than the bright fluorescent lighting and endless aisles of stockpiled inventory found in discount supercenters, specialty stores offer a more intimate, home-like setting. The lighting is often softer and products are arranged in visually appealing displays, creating a welcoming and aesthetically pleasing shopping experience.

- Appealing products: Specialty stores cater to a niche market and carry a limited scope of inventory. As a result, these retailers focus on curating a collection of merchandise that appeals to their target market. Product labels often feature buzzwords such as "locally made," "handcrafted," and "sustainably sourced." Customers may prefer to shop at specialty stores as they are the destination to buy well-made, one-of-a-kind items.
- Curated experiences for customers: Many specialty stores offer workshops, lessons, and classes that showcase the products they sell. A kitchen goods store, for example, may offer a cooking class that utilizes cookware and utensils from its inventory. Fashion boutiques may host pop-up events (short-lived events that allow business owners and creators to connect in person with their target audiences) or private parties for VIP guests to preorder new products in advance.

Specialty Store Weaknesses

In contrast with general merchandise retailers that offer a wider variety of products, specialty stores sell a limited scope of products that meet a specific need or match a specific interest. This automatically narrows the list of potential customers. Additionally, specialty stores are not as widespread as mass merchandisers, which can make them harder to locate and more time-consuming to reach, deterring some potential customers. Other weaknesses of specialty stores include:

- Market dependency: Specialty stores can be a risky venture because they operate at the mercy of a market where trends come and go quickly. If the products sold at a particular store lose their popularity, consumers will look elsewhere to find a store that has what they're looking for.
- Seasonal swings: Depending on the nature of product offerings, specialty stores can be susceptible to significant fluctuations in demand. There is more of a drawback to store owners, rather than to customers, when a product is out-of-season and, therefore, in low demand.
- Pricier products: Specialty stores are often associated with higher quality products, which can give the impression that they are more expensive. While this is sometimes true, it is not always the case. Unlike discount retailers, specialty stores typically do not order items in bulk, which can translate to higher costs.

While specialty stores may excel in a particular product category, their limited selection can drive customers to purchase from other retailers in order to complete their shopping lists, as visiting multiple specialty stores can be inconvenient and time-consuming.

A new type of specialty has also emerged online. Such sites typically specialize in offering a specific product category at different price points. For example, Warby Parker specializes in retailing prescription glasses and sunglasses. Casper, another online startup, specializes in selling different kinds of mattresses, while Harry's and Dollar Shave Club offer shaving products.

Discount Stores and Key Characteristics

Selling merchandise below the manufacturer's list price is known as discounting. The discount store has become an increasingly popular means of retailing. Following the Second World War, a number of retail establishments in the United States began to pursue a high-volume, low-profit strategy designed to attract price-conscious consumers. A key strategy for keeping operating costs (and therefore prices) low was to locate in low-rent shopping districts and to offer minimal service assistance. This no-frills approach was used at first only with hard goods or consumer durables, such as electrical household appliances, but it has since been shown to be successful with soft goods, such as clothing. This practice has been adopted for a wide variety of products so that discount stores have essentially become department stores with reduced prices and fewer services. In the late twentieth century, discount stores began to operate outlet malls. These groups of discount stores are usually located some distance away from major metropolitan areas and have facilities that make them indistinguishable from standard shopping malls. As they gained popularity, many discount stores improved their facilities and appearances, added new lines and services, and opened suburban branches. Coupled with attempts by traditional department stores to reduce prices to compete with discounters, the distinction between many department and discount stores has become blurred. Specialty discount operations have grown significantly in electronics, sporting goods, and books.

General Merchandise Discounters

Retailers that sell various brand products at much lower costs are known as **full-line discount stores** (brick-and-mortar stores). Their primary purpose is to generate as many sales as possible by selling their products at lower prices. Some of the characteristics of these retailers include:

- Discounted prices of commodities. They offer subsidized prices on everything they sell, and consumers may benefit from more significant discounts if they are shopping in bulk.
- No or limited customer service. Consumers are expected to guide themselves and choose their products using the labels and directory for guidance. However, consumers get assistance with the billing and packing of goods.
- A variety of different products in one place. Consumers are assured of having a variety of brand products in which they can choose from their preferred preferences.

Full-line discount stores sell almost everything available on the market, ranging from groceries, clothing, shoes, food items, and home appliances, all under one roof. Some of the common examples of full-line discount stores include Walmart and Target.

Category Killers

A category killer is a large retail chain superstore that dominates its product category and puts less productive and highly specialized merchants out of business. Examples of category killers include Home Depot, Office Depot, Bed, Bath and Beyond, Toys"R"Us, PetSmart, etc. The original category killers proliferated during the 1980s and 1990s and generally excelled until the arrival of e-commerce, which paved the way for a new breed of online competitors that not only focus on price but also on convenience and after-sales support. Category killers mainly attain their massive competitive advantage by having a bigger and deeper selection of merchandise as compared to small and independent stores. While Toys"R"Us was founded in 1948, the heyday of category killers was during the 1980s and 1990s. During that time, large companies invested in modern supply chain technologies, which made it a reality for a US corporate office to communicate with overseas suppliers in Asia and other continents. The expansion of suburbs, which led to bigger stores with larger parking lots than in cities, also contributed to the success of these category killers. However, many category killers have fallen out of the business because of the consumer trend of internet shopping.[4] The Covid-19 pandemic added extra pressure onto the category retailers in their ability to move their business practices toward a more digital-oriented environment and offer omnichannel services.[5]

Off-Price Discounters

Off-price retailers are stores that sell high-quality goods at low prices. They offer significant discounts over the retail price. These stores sell designer clothes, branded apparel, etc. An off-price retailer targets end-of-season stock, closeouts, overruns, returns, and inventory excess. The off-price retail model relies on the purchase of over-produced, or excess, branded goods at a lower price, thus being able to sell to consumers at a discount compared to other stores that purchased an initial run. Among the largest retailers of this type are TJX Companies and Ross Stores. For customers, this could seem like a treasure hunt; they can buy the biggest brands at the lowest price. Low-price retailers do not follow the business model of regular retailers. They operate on a lower profit margin. In the United States, the highest low-price retail market share is owned by TJX Companies, accumulating approximately 70 percent of sales. It is followed by two other rivals, Burlington and Ross stores. In addition, TJX owns T.J. Maxx, HomeGoods, Marshalls, Sierra, Trading Post, and Homesense.

Warehouse Clubs

Warehouse clubs offer a more limited range of products than a traditional supermarket and aim to attract shoppers who wish to save money by buying in bulk. A typical Sam's Club has less than 10,000 stock keeping units (SKUs), much less when it compares to 100,000 or more SKUs inside a discount retailer like Wal-Mart Stores Inc.[6] Shoppers need to have a membership and pay a fee to be able to shop in these types of stores. Club stores are responsible for about $114 billion in sales annually in the United States, and Costco, Sam's Club, and BJ's Wholesale Club are three of the biggest warehouse chains in the United States.[7] Club stores offer significant benefits to both retailers and customers. They provide fewer options than most other supermarkets, and it benefits customers who shop often. Costco is a unique yet profitable retailer. In contrast to conventional wisdom, they make the majority of their money on customer memberships, not product margins. Therefore, the goal of the retailer is not selling a lot of products, but providing their club members with the best values. For example, in a pitch meeting, Costco buyers want to hear about what value a product offers their customers and why it's different from the other products in the store. They are much less concerned with how much they will make off every unit than other retailers are.

Factory Outlet Stores

Factory outlet stores, also known as designer outlet stores, are typically located in outlet malls and have become popular destinations for value-seeking shoppers in the United States and many other countries. Shoppers are drawn to these malls for the opportunity to purchase designer goods at discounted prices. Initially, heavy discounts were offered to clear outdated or damaged stock and make room for new inventory. However, in recent years, factory outlets have shifted towards stocking outlet-specific lines due to a decrease in overstock and damaged goods available for sale. Advances in demand forecasting have enabled retailers to order goods more accurately, resulting in fewer excess items. Additionally, as most manufacturing is done overseas, damaged goods are less likely to make it to the United States for sale in outlet stores.

Deep Discounters

Deep discount stores are stores that offer for sale primarily discounted items that are typically surplus, liquidated, out of season, discontinued, salvaged, part of an odd or partially damaged lot of goods, etc. Dollar Trees, Big Lot, Aldi, and Jacks Dollar Stores are some examples of deep discount stores. Beginning with the recession in 2008, value-focused consumers began turning their attention to the dollar stores in their communities. Deep discount retailers like Dollar General and Family Dollar capitalized by tightening up their operations and increasing their assortment of groceries, household goods, and other consumables. Not only did dollar stores manage to seize the moment, they retained many of these customers for the long run and continued to make gains. As of 2021, there were over 35,000 dollar stores across the United States.[8] Dollar stores have a product mix that appeals to the core demographic of low- and middle-income consumers. What's surprising many in the industry—including dollar stores themselves—is that it appeals to Millennials and high-income shoppers, too. According to checkout data gathered by the NPD Group, 25 percent of customers at the three biggest dollar chains are Millennials from households earning $100,000 or more.[9] A recent trend observed is that many affluent Millennials are choosing to save money on consumable products and splurging on experiences and big-ticket items. Dollar stores' growth across income levels has taken a toll on traditional retailers by pressuring their prices and chipping away at margins. Some supermarkets, in response, have cribbed directly from the dollar store playbook, offering more dollar items and deals like ten items for $10. Many stores like Target now have a special section, Dollar Spot, stocked with seasonal products from $1 to $5.[10,11]

Direct Marketing and Direct Selling

This section examines the differences between direct marketing and direct selling. Direct marketing has a long history dating back to the fifteenth century in Europe. Its first form was using catalogs to sell books.[12] The traditional direct marketing methods included catalogs, mailing, and telemarketing. We will first discuss how to distinguish between direct marketing and direct selling and then discuss the techniques. The strengths and weaknesses of catalog, direct mail, and telemarketing retailers are highlighted in the following.

Direct Marketing versus Direct Selling

According to the Data & Marketing Association (formerly Direct Marketing Association, DMA), **direct**

marketing is a form of communicating an offer (usually presented in ways such as advertising), where organizations communicate directly to a pre-selected customer and supply a method for a direct response through various media such as mail (or email), catalog (or e-catalog), TV, mobile phone, or website. Aaron Montgomery Ward of Chicago first produced a catalog designed for direct order via mail in 1872, aiming to remove the middleman from the buying and selling process.[13] The improvements in transportation and railway systems made the mail-order business successful in serving rural customers. By 1971, catalog sales of major United States firms exceeded more than $250 million in postal revenue.[14] As technologies such as telephones, TVs, the internet, and mobile phones emerged, the definition and practices of direct marketing evolved over time as well. Nowadays, almost all the traditional direct marketing media (e.g., mails, catalog, coupons, telephone calls, faxing, etc.) have an online version.

Direct selling is a business model that offers entrepreneurial opportunities to individuals as independent contractors to market and sell products and services, typically through one-to-one selling, in-home product demonstrations, parties, or online.[15] Direct selling companies primarily use **multi-level marketing** compensation plans, in which individuals may earn compensations based on personal sales and/or the sales of others in their sales organizations. **Pyramid schemes** are different from multi-level marketing and are illegal. Many direct-selling companies sell personal care and cosmetics products. According to *Direct Selling News*, Amway, Natura & Co, and Herbalife are the top three direct-selling companies.[16] Mary Kay is also one of the classic direct selling examples, as they often host social events to sell goods and find recruits when they aren't making one-on-one sales.[17] Products sold via direct selling are not typically found in traditional retail locations. The salespeople may be called distributors, representatives, or consultants, depending on the company.

Direct Marketing Methods

As we mentioned earlier, direct marketing methods have been evolving over the past hundred years. The Data & Marketing Association organization's website acknowledged its past and the evolution of its name over time from the Direct Mail Marketing Association to its current name, the Direct Marketing Association. In the following sections, we will discuss the strengths and weaknesses of catalog marketing, direct mailing, and telemarketing.

Direct Mail/Email

Direct mail marketing is a type of advertising that involves sending promotional materials directly to potential or existing customers via postal services or other delivery services. While the idea of having a mailbox full of actual mail seems outdated, there are more and more tech-savvy, digital-first online retailers such as Glossier, Wayfair, Rover, Away, and Modcloth using direct mail to reach their target customers. Direct mail can be targeted to specific demographics, such as age, gender, income, or location, allowing businesses to reach the most relevant audience for their products or services. Retailers can use direct mail to offer a wide range of creative options, including postcards, letters, coupons, or even free samples. This allows businesses to showcase their products or services in a variety of ways and stand out from competitors, which may lead shoppers to their websites.[18]

In addition to what we have mentioned above, here are some other benefits of direct mail marketing:

- Personalization: Direct mail can be personalized with the recipient's name and address, which can help to grab their attention and make them feel valued as a customer.
- Tangibility: Unlike digital marketing, direct mail is a physical item that recipients can touch, feel, and keep. This can make it more memorable and impactful than digital ads, which can easily be ignored or forgotten.
- Builds brand recognition: Consistent direct mail campaigns can help to build brand recognition and loyalty among customers. By staying top-of-mind with customers, businesses can increase their chances of repeat business and referrals.

While direct mail marketing has many benefits, there are also some weaknesses to consider. Generally speaking, direct mail's weaknesses are similar to those of the print catalog. Here are some of them:

- Cost: While direct mail can be a cost-effective option, it can also be expensive, especially if businesses are targeting a large audience or using high-quality materials. Costs can include printing, postage, and mailing list fees, etc.

- Inaccuracy: Direct mail campaigns can be less accurate than digital marketing campaigns, as mailing lists can contain errors, such as outdated addresses or misspelled names. This can result in wasted marketing efforts and higher costs.
- Environmental impact: Direct mail can have a negative impact on the environment, as it requires paper, ink, and other resources. Additionally, recipients may not be interested in the materials and may simply throw them away, contributing to landfill waste.
- Limited interaction: Direct mail is a one-way form of communication that doesn't allow for interaction or immediate feedback. This can make it difficult for businesses to gauge the effectiveness of their campaigns and make adjustments.
- Perception: Some people may view direct mail as spam or junk mail, which can negatively impact the perception of the business and reduce the effectiveness of the campaign.

Overall, while direct mail can be an effective marketing tool, it is important for businesses to consider the potential weaknesses and weigh the costs and benefits before deciding to use it.

Email marketing utilizes sending out emails to a list of accounts and it has become a popular marketing strategy for businesses due to its many benefits over traditional mail marketing. Here are some of the benefits of email marketing:

- Cost-effective: Email marketing is a much more cost-effective option than traditional mail marketing. There are no printing or postage costs, and businesses can send emails to thousands of customers at once for a relatively low cost.
- Greater reach: Email marketing has a wider reach than traditional mail marketing, as businesses can send emails to customers all over the world, without the need for physical mailing addresses.
- Personalization: Email marketing allows businesses to personalize their messages to individual customers, including their name, purchase history, and interests. This can help to build a stronger relationship with customers and increase engagement.
- Immediate results: With email marketing, businesses can see immediate results, including open rates, click-through rates, and conversion rates. This allows them to quickly adjust their campaigns based on customer behavior and improve their results.
- Tracking and analysis: Email marketing provides businesses with detailed analytics and tracking, including open rates, click-through rates, bounce rates, and more. This data can help businesses to better understand their customers and make informed decisions about their marketing strategies.
- Interactive: Email marketing allows businesses to include interactive elements in their emails, such as videos, images, and links to additional information. This can enhance the customer experience and increase engagement.
- Environmentally friendly: Email marketing is much more environmentally friendly than traditional mail marketing, as it doesn't require paper, ink, or other physical resources.

Overall, email marketing offers businesses a cost-effective, personalized, and highly measurable marketing strategy that allows them to reach a wider audience and engage with customers in a more interactive way than traditional mail marketing. More details about email promotion will be discussed in Chapter 7.

Print Catalogs

Catalog marketing is a selling technique of using catalogs to sell. It not only provides the tangibility and power of direct mail, but they have also become an integral part of an omnichannel campaign by driving customers to digital experiences. Studies showed that the combination of email and catalog marketing could increase sales by 15 percent and a 27 percent lift in product inquiries, compared to just using email marketing alone.[19,20]

- Tangible and visual: Catalogs are tangible and visual, which can help customers better understand and visualize the products being sold. High-quality images and detailed product descriptions can provide customers with a comprehensive view of the product and its features. For e-commerce retailers without physical stores, catalogs can effectively mimic stores' sensory experiences to enhance customer affinity.[21]
- Convenience: Catalogs offer the convenience of shopping from home, allowing customers to

browse and purchase products at their own pace without the pressure of salespeople or crowds.

- Personalization: Catalogs can be personalized to individual customers based on their purchasing history, preferences, and interests. This can help retailers better target their marketing efforts and increase the likelihood of a sale.
- Cross-selling and upselling: Catalogs can be used to promote related or complementary products, encouraging customers to make additional purchases. Many catalog retailers now include QR codes in their catalog, and shoppers can use their smartphones to scan the QR code to order or check up for more information.[22]

Overall, print catalog marketing could offer a convenient, personalized, and cost-effective way to reach a broad audience and promote products through tangible, visual, and detailed product descriptions in this overcrowded digital marketing era.

Below are some weaknesses of print catalog marketing:

- Environmental concerns: Catalog marketing can have a negative impact on the environment. The production and distribution of catalogs require resources such as paper and energy, and the disposal of unwanted catalogs can contribute to waste.
- Cost: Catalog marketing can be expensive. The cost of printing and mailing catalogs, as well as the cost of list rental and postage, can quickly add up. This can be a significant barrier for small businesses or those with limited marketing budgets.
- Limited interaction: Catalogs are typically one-way communication, meaning there is limited opportunity for interaction or engagement with potential customers. This can make it difficult to establish a relationship or build brand loyalty.
- Timing: Catalogs can take several weeks to be designed, printed, and mailed. This can make it difficult to respond quickly to market changes or new product launches.
- Over-saturation: In today's digital age, consumers are bombarded with advertising and marketing messages on a daily basis. As a result, catalogs may be seen as intrusive or overwhelming, and may even be ignored or discarded without being read.

Overall, while catalog marketing can be an effective way to reach potential customers, it is important to weigh the potential weaknesses against the benefits and consider other marketing strategies as well.

E-Catalogs

An e-catalog is an electronic catalog that provides information on products and services sold by a vendor. It can be an online publication, generally an HTML page, or a mobile application that supports vendors with online ordering and payment capabilities. From many perspectives, e-catalogs can overcome the weaknesses of the aforementioned print catalogs. For example,

- Accessibility: An e-catalog can be accessed from anywhere, at any time, as long as there is an internet connection. This means customers can browse and shop for products from the comfort of their homes or while on the go.
- Cost-effective: Producing and distributing print catalogs can be expensive, whereas e-catalogs are much more cost-effective. With an e-catalog, there are no printing or shipping costs, which can save businesses a lot of money.
- Interactive: An e-catalog can be more interactive than a print catalog. It can include videos, animations, and links to additional product information. This can enhance the customer experience and increase engagement.
- Easily updatable: Making updates or changes to an e-catalog is much easier and faster than making changes to a print catalog. This allows businesses to make changes to their products, prices, and inventory in real-time.
- Environmentally friendly: Printing and distributing large numbers of print catalogs can have a negative impact on the environment. E-catalogs are a more sustainable option, as they do not require paper or ink and can be easily shared digitally.
- Analytics: E-catalogs can provide businesses with valuable analytics about customer behavior, such as which products are viewed the most or which pages are visited the most frequently. This data can help businesses make informed decisions about their marketing strategies and product offerings.

One study that was conducted on iPad users and their intentions of adopting e-catalogs suggested that fashion innovativeness, information technology innovativeness, and prior experience are driving factors of apparel mobile e-catalogs' adoption.[23] Moreover, the research results showed that 50 percent of the respondents were reluctant to unsubscribe from print catalogs, even when tablet versions of the catalogs were available. Some of the reasons are 1) habitual reasons like "I think sometimes it is nice to be able to flip through a catalog the normal, old-fashion way," 2) prefer to have options like "because I like both of them," and "I like different media," or 3) perceived low values of unsubscribing. The findings suggest that US tablet users are not ready to suspend their use of print catalogs and switch solely to e-catalog versions. Therefore, providing both options to consumers may be a more effective strategy.[24]

Telemarketing

Telemarketing is a direct marketing technique that involves contacting potential customers over the phone to sell them products or services. Companies can use either employees or automated machines to reach out to many individuals at once. In the United States, the telemarketing and call centers industry had a market size of $30.8 billion in 2023.[25] For retailers, telemarketing can be an effective way to create leads and generate sales. In the following section, we will discuss the strengths and weaknesses of this marketing strategy. Although many omnichannel retailers now use short message service (SMS) or text message marketing to engage with their customers, telemarketing remains a valuable option for companies to provide personalized customer services and service recovery in order to gain customer loyalty.

Telemarketing can have several strengths, including:

- Direct communication: Telemarketing provides a direct channel of communication between the company and the prospect or customer. Especially when a prospective customer sends out a query online, it could provide immediate feedback and the ability to address any questions or concerns on the spot.[26]
- Personalization: Telemarketing allows for a more personalized approach, as the representative can tailor the conversation and message to the specific needs and interests of the prospect or customer.[27]
- Cost-effectiveness: Telemarketing can be a cost-effective way to reach a large number of prospects or customers quickly and efficiently, without the need for expensive advertising or marketing campaigns.
- Lead generation: Telemarketing can effectively generate leads and identify potential customers who may be interested in the company's products or services.[28]
- Market research: Telemarketing can also be used for market research, allowing companies to gather information about customer needs and preferences, as well as feedback on their products or services.

Telemarketing can also have several weaknesses, including:

- Intrusiveness: Many people find unsolicited phone calls intrusive and may feel bothered or annoyed by them, especially if they are received during inconvenient times.[29]
- Limited audience: Telemarketing is limited by the number of people who are willing to pickup the phone or engage in a conversation, and it may not be the best method for reaching younger or tech-savvy audiences who prefer other channels.[30]
- Negative perception: Telemarketing has developed a negative reputation in some circles due to aggressive sales tactics, scamming, and unethical behavior by some companies.[31]
- Language barriers: Telemarketing can be difficult in multicultural markets, where language barriers can pose a challenge to effective communication.
- Time-consuming: Telemarketing can be time-consuming and require a significant investment in resources, including staffing, training, and equipment. It may also need a lot of follow-up and persistence to convert leads into sales, making it less efficient than other marketing strategies.

Text Marketing

Text marketing is when companies contact consumers via text messages. There is often a higher response rate with text marketing because of how often consumers use their cell phones. The text message marketing solution was built to drive 18.5 percent of online revenue. There are several phone plans that companies can utilize to send text messages to customers for $0.01 to $0.05 per text, which can be more cost-effective.[32]

Text marketing can include short message service (SMS) and back-and-forth messaging, which allows recipients to respond to brief customer service questions and provide the company with information about their preferences. Additionally, retailers can send a link to a company website via text message where recipients can learn more about a product or sales event or opt-in to receive mobile offers. Push notifications are another method that can be used, where the recipient receives alerts from the company directly to their mobile device. For instance, an order confirmation or delivery notice.[33] Figure 2.1 is an example of how Coach uses SMS marketing to provide coupon codes and automated personalized product alerts to their customers.

Direct Selling Methods

In 2021, direct selling across the United States generated $42.7 billion in retail sales, and 7.3 million entrepreneurs in the United States sold products or services through direct selling channels. According to the direct selling association, direct selling provided a personalized buying experience for 44.6 million discount buyers and preferred customers.[34] Figure 2.2 provides some key stats of the direct selling industry. Terminology related to direct selling includes:

- Direct sellers are those who build a business full time (30 or more hours/week) or part time (fewer than 30 hours/week) and sell products/services to consumers and may sponsor people to join their team.
- Discount buyers are those who are eligible to purchase, sell, and sponsor, but are product lovers, only purchasing products/services they personally enjoy and use at a discount.
- Preferred customers are those who have signed a preferred customer agreement with a direct selling company where they may be eligible to pay wholesale prices for products/services. They are not eligible to sell products/services to others, and they are not eligible to earn.

Face-to-face direct selling includes individual contact, party plan and group sales, and pop-up stores. In the following section, we will discuss each of them in more detail.

Individual contact selling is typically conducted in person, through door-to-door or one-on-one presentations. However, with the rise of online marketing, it is also possible to conduct single-level direct sales virtually. In this type of sales, the salesperson earns their income from commission sales and occasional bonuses provided by the company whose products they are selling. The direct sellers/consultants focus on building relationships with their customers and selling products directly to them.

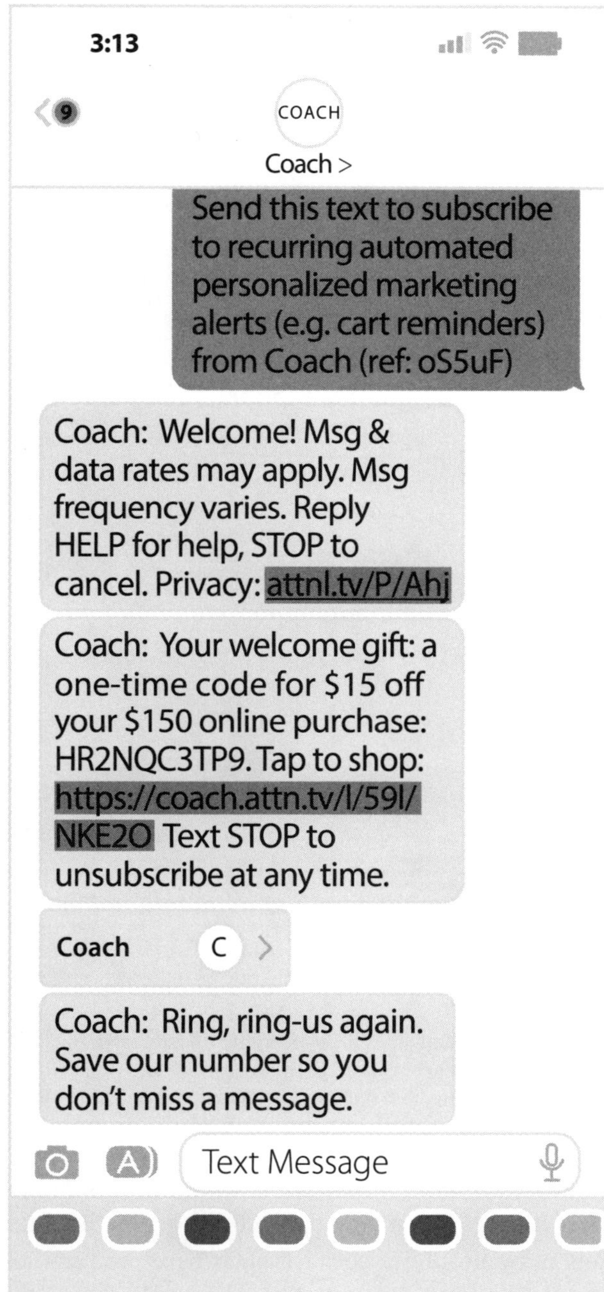

Figure 2.1 Coach uses SMS marketing to provide coupon codes and automated personalized product alerts
(*Source*: Catherine Jai)

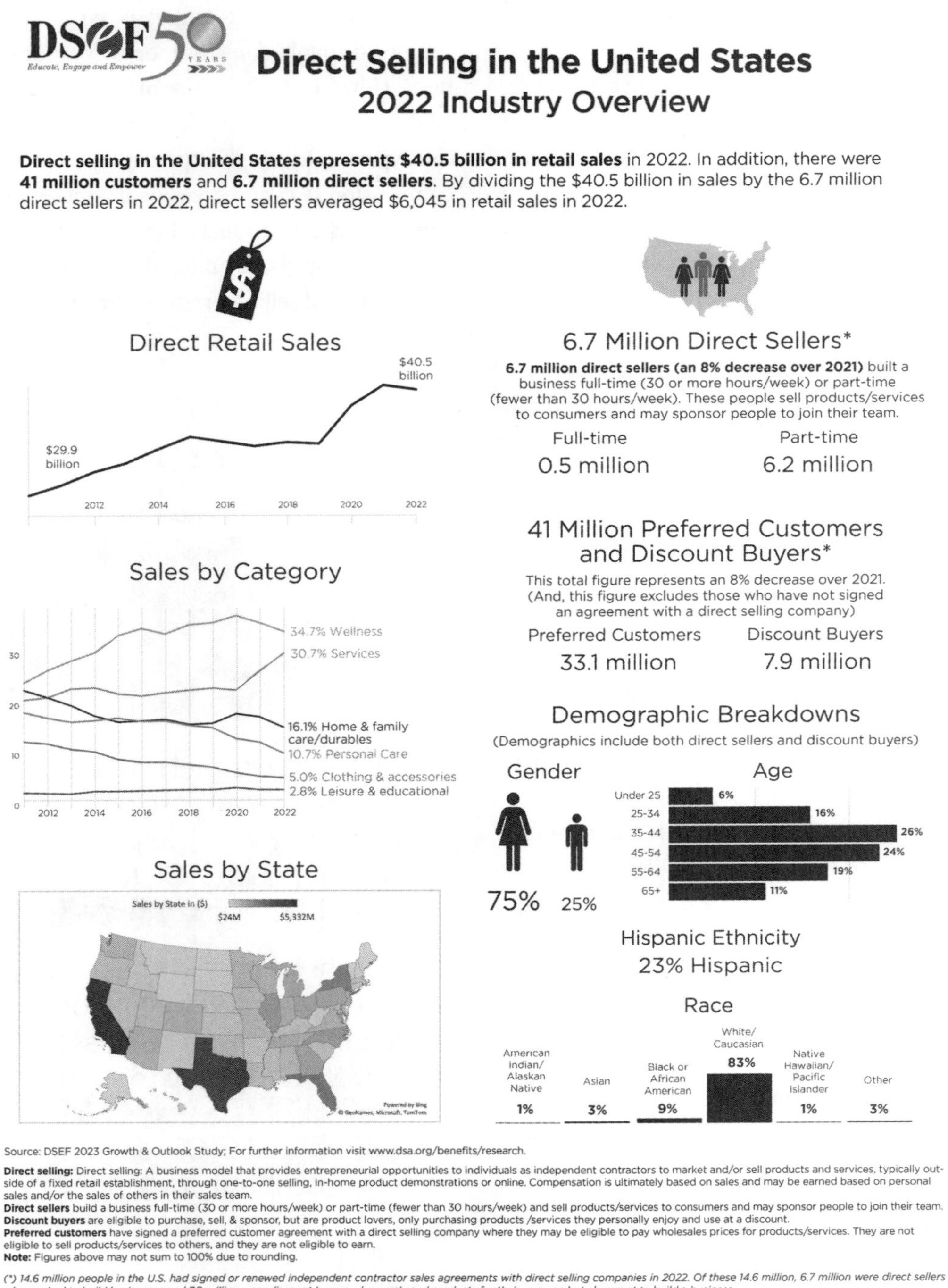

Figure 2.2 Infograph—Direct Selling in the United States 2021 Industry Overview
Note: Figures above may not sum to 100% due to rounding.
(*Source*: DSEF 2023 Growth & Outlook Study; For further information visit www.dsa.org/benefits/research)[35]

Party plan and group sales is another technique for direct selling. The main approach for generating sales leads is by hosting a social event where products are offered for sale. Following this model, salespeople use the opportunity to create future business by asking customers if they would be interested in hosting similar selling parties. Examples that use this approach are Avon and Mary Kay, which frequently host social events to promote their products and attract new sales representatives. In addition to making one-on-one sales, they also use the party plan sales model to expand their sales network.[36] This technique is still being used by direct sell brands like Pampered Chef and LuLaRoe.[37]

A **pop-up shop** is a temporary retail space that is typically used to introduce a new product line, test a new market, or generate awareness for a product or cause. Pop-up shops are evolving and taking on greater importance as brands lean into direct-to-consumer efforts and retail real estate firms see it as a robust driver of traffic. Pop-up stores are typically set up in areas with high foot traffic, such as busy streets, malls, and city centers. The practice of using pop-up shops is sometimes called "flash retailing." For pure-play retailers, pop-up stores are being used for experimentation as well as to connect brands and consumers in an authentic way. Potentially, if the responses are well-received in the area, retailers may establish a physical presence in target locations. Pop-up stores have also become a popular strategy for luxury brands to provide customers with unique and memorable experiences. For instance, Hermès opened a pop-up laundromat concept store in Amsterdam where customers could dye their treasured scarves for a fresh new look. Louis Vuitton and Supreme collaborated on a pop-up store project in Paris and New York, which featured a sold-out collection. Chanel also launched its "Coco Game Club" for a limited time in a rooftop space at Galeries Lafayette in Paris during the summer, providing an exclusive arcade-like space dedicated to beauty and showcasing its new "Red Coco" collection.[38] Figure 2.3 shows the opening of a Louis Vuitton's pop-up store in Paris, announcing their collaborative project with Nike "Air Force 1" by designer Virgil Abloh.[39]

Television Retailing

Television retailing, also known as TV shopping or home shopping, is a form of direct response marketing that involves selling products or services through a television program or channel. The concept involves showcasing products on live or pre-recorded television shows, where viewers can call a phone number or go online to place an order. The products are typically advertised through product demonstrations, testimonials, and other sales techniques to persuade viewers to make a purchase. Television retailing became popular in the 1980s with the launch of channels like the Home Shopping Network (HSN) and Quality Value Convenience (QVC). Today, there are many TV shopping channels and programs that offer a wide range of products, including fashion, beauty, electronics, and home goods. This form of retailing is popular among consumers who enjoy the convenience of shopping from home and the ability to see a product in action before making a purchase. The market size, measured by revenue, of the Cable Shopping Networks industry was $5.2 billion in 2023.[40]

Figure 2.3 Opening of ephemeral pop-up store Louis Vuitton and Nike "Air Force 1" by Virgil Abloh at Quai De La Megisserie in Paris

Infomercials

Infomercials are long-form advertisements that are typically designed to sell a product or service. They emerged in the 1950s when television entered the US household living room, yet they did not gain popularity until 1984 when the FCC lifted the advertisement's time limit. Following one of the most well-known theories in marketing, the Attention-Interest-Desire-Action (AIDA) model, infomercials are characterized more as a complete sales presentation rather than an exposure/awareness campaign typified by the common commercial.[41] The AIDA model contains four distinct components, including:

- Attention: capturing the customer's attention and awareness toward the ad stimuli/product,
- Interest: raising the customer's interest and curiosity by highlighting the features and benefits of the product,
- Desire: stimulating desire and demonstrating how the product is superior to competitors,
- Action: implementing calls to action toward purchasing the product.

Companies such as Target, Apple Computers, and Volvo have been successful in generating significant sales using this type of selling technique. They are often presented in the form of a TV program or a video that provides in-depth information about the product or service, including its features, benefits, testimonials from satisfied customers, and a direct call to action (usually a toll-free phone number, a website, or text code to place an order).[42] Research has found that infomercials are more effective when employing expert comments, celebrity endorsers, product comparisons, and bonus offers to encourage viewers to make a purchase.[43] Generally, informercials are often used for products that require a more detailed explanation or demonstration, such as exercise equipment, kitchen appliances, or beauty products.

While television is still an incredibly powerful medium, parts of an omnichannel marketing plan live on websites, social media, streaming platforms like Hulu and HBO Max, or on radio. Today, infomercials usually last 3 to 30 minutes, depending on where they are aired. On YouTube, generally, the infomercials are 3–10 minutes long, while on television, late-night infomercial ads can go beyond 30 minutes.[44] With the viewing habit changes and interactive media such as interactive television and live streaming, infomercials nowadays are multimedia, multi-platform advertising products. More information about how omnichannel retailers conduct promotions on live-stream selling will be discussed in Chapter 7, Promotion in the Omnichannel Environments.

Home Shopping Channels

The home shopping industry blossomed in the United States in the 1980s. The Home Shopping Network (HSN) was founded in 1982 by Lowell Paxson and Roy Speer. It was the first television shopping network of its kind, dedicated solely to selling products through a televised platform. HSN, QVC, and ShopHQ, formerly known as ShopNBC, are well-known channels in the United States.[45]

The Covid-19 pandemic has had a significant impact on home shopping businesses such as HSN and QVC, as it has with many other retailers. With more people staying at home due to lockdowns and social distancing measures, there has been an increase in demand for online shopping, and HSN and QVC have seen a surge in their sales. However, the pandemic has also caused disruptions in their supply chains, resulting in delayed shipments and inventory shortages. In response, HSN and QVC adapted their business models by increasing their online presence and investing in their e-commerce capabilities. Despite the supply-chain challenges presented by the pandemic, HSN and QVC have been able to continue operating and serving their customers through their television and online channels. After the pandemic, the parent company of HSN and QVC, Qurate Retail Group, reported that they gained 2 million new customers, online traffic rose 36 percent, and e-commerce revenue rose 19 percent, to $2.2 billion, underlining people's desire to buy from home.[46] Consumers nowadays can not only watch the shopping programs on TV, but also use their website or free apps for iPhone and Android.

Electronic Retailing

US e-commerce sales reached $1.03 trillion in 2022, passing $1 trillion for the first time ever,[47] and e-commerce was expected to surpass 20 percent of total retail by 2024.[48] By 2025, the global e-commerce fashion industry is projected to grow to $2.25 trillion.[49] The rapid increase of omnichannel practices has been largely pushed by the pandemic. During 2020–2021, amid the beginning of the Covid-19 pandemic, consumers and retailers readily adopted new digital and omnichannel shopping behaviors such as curbside pickup and home delivery. According to McKinsey & Company's report, the Covid-19 pandemic stimulated ten years' worth of the penetration rate just three months into the pandemic.[50] Therefore, retailers are facing higher expectations for a post-pandemic marketplace.

Forrester, a market research company, predicts that digital sales in the clothing category will reach 47.5 percent by 2024 in the United States.[51] One thing to keep in mind, though, is that this forecasting may not apply to other industries. Physical retail stores still maintain a firm position and are expected to account for three-quarters of total retail sales in 2024.

As consumers increasingly adopt online purchasing and interaction with retailers through multiple channels that retailers/brands operate, there is a strong demand for a tailored experience based on knowledge learned from an individual consumer via the multiple touchpoints (e.g., website browsing, email sign-up, etc.). In the following sections, we will discuss the digital presence of omnichannel retailers, including company websites, online marketplaces, mobile applications (apps), and social media accounts. Table 2.1 lists the 2022 NRF Top 100 Apparel/Jewelry Power Players.

Company Websites

Retail is a process in which businesses sell relatively small quantities of products and services to individual consumers. Therefore, one of the major goals of choosing online presences is to maximize online transactions.

Table 2.1 NRF Top 100 Apparel/Jewelry Power Players

COMPANY	2021 RETAIL SALES (BILLIONS)*	SALES PER STORE (MILLIONS)	STORES
TJX Companies^	$28.74	$11.67	2,462
Macy's	$23.68	$41.54	570
Ross Stores	$18.89	$9.83	1,923
Kohl's	$18.50	$15.72	1,177
GAP	$13.92	$6.48	2,147
Nordstrom	$13.74	$39.83	345
Burlington	$9.34	$11.28	828
J.C. Penney Company	$8.94	$13.37	669
Dillard's	$6.38	$25.50	250
Signet Jewelers	$6.14	$2.72	2,256
Victoria's Secret	$5.17	$6.41	807
Hudson's Bay	$4.50	$31.91	141
American Eagle	$4.34	$4.61	941
Lululemon	$4.06	$12.53	324
Urban Outfitters	$3.69	$6.72	549

*Includes online sales related to respective retailers.

^ Excludes HomeGoods.

Source: NRF's 2022 Top 100 list—Apparel/Jewelry

Brands/stores want to build their online presences that can reach a broader audience beyond their physical location, expanding their customer base and sales potential. Additionally, having a website establishes credibility and legitimacy for the retailer by showcasing their products and services, customer reviews, and important business information. Reflecting on your own experience, have you heard about your family or friend mentioning a brand name, and you went to their website to check out their products and also form a first impression of the brand by looking at their website?

Websites provide retailers with a cost-effective way to market their products through promotions and communication with customers. Websites are also available 24/7, providing customers with constant access to browse and purchase products, ultimately increasing revenue. Finally, websites offer valuable data and insights into customer behavior and preferences, allowing retailers to optimize their products, marketing strategies, and website design to increase sales and better serve their customers. Nowadays, a brand's website is not just a place for customers to complete transactions but also an anchor point to establish its legitimacy in the online world and earn consumer trust. A retailer's website also presents the opportunity to sell products exceeding their geographical locations.

Online Marketplaces

Online marketplaces are defined by two criteria: 1) there are many sellers and buyers on the platforms, and 2) buyers can complete transactions without leaving the site. Omnichannel retailers utilize online marketplaces as one of the channels on which to sell. One of the major benefits of selling on an online marketplace is the pre-existing customer bases that the online marketplaces have. eBay, Amazon, and Etsy are examples of online marketplaces. These online marketplaces are trusted by hundreds of millions of shoppers, and, therefore, provide a great platform for brands to sell their products as third-party sellers. Many online marketplaces also offer third-party sellers opportunities to promote their products to shoppers, such as Amazon Advertising, and options to outsource order fulfillment, such as FBA (Fulfilled by Amazon).

Marketplaces by Users

Marketplaces may be classified based on the targeted users on their platforms such as: **business to consumer (B2C)**, business to business (B2B), consumer to consumer (C2C), or peer to peer (P2P).

Business-to-consumer (B2C) marketplaces mainly focus on bringing shoppers and brands together. New retail marketplace concepts like Showfields, Neighborhood Goods, Bulletin, etc. offer an aggregated physical place for the direct-to-consumer (D2C) concepts to showcase their brands without a long-term leasing commitment (Figure 2.4).

Shopify announced Shop as the online marketplace to connect shoppers with the D2C brands. Shop is a mobile shopping tool that streamlines shopping and order functions on both the business and consumer end of transactions. Through implementing features of Arrive (an order tracking service) and powered by Shop Pay (Shopify's payment service), Shop provides an improved checkout process, transparent order tracking abilities, and exposes new product discoveries to consumers. Users can provide their shopping history and payment information so that future browsing consists of accurate recommendations and an easier checkout process. Because of the increasing importance of maintaining returning customers to remain profitable, Shop curates a feed providing in-app recommendations that recommends businesses to existing customers based on purchase history and who the user follows. Once businesses begin using the app, the functions are automatically implemented and usable by consumers with no extra costs or changes required by the business, nor does the business manage the technical details of administering these changes. Shop consolidates all tracking and order information from various stores/channels within a user's email inbox into one place in the app, providing a live map feature and notification options. Shop significantly improves the online shopping experience, with stores seeing up to 18 percent improvement in conversion rates among existing customers, providing accurate product recommendations to suit each user and creating the optimal channel for cart-to-home businesses to grow.

Etsy, started in 2005, quickly grew from a simple freelance website-building project to a massive online marketplace operating across the world. Using the C2C model, Etsy's original mission was to empower talented and authentic artisans through their emphasis on the "anti-consumerism" and "anti-mass production" image. The loyal following and continuous growth that these principles attracted can be attributed to several factors. In order to acquire sellers in Etsy's early stages of development, teams were sent to visit local art and craft shows across the United States to recruit established sellers with quality products to join the marketplace. Etsy's business model was superior to their main competitor eBay, both economically and in terms of the relationship with their sellers that placed emphasis on the well-being and success of each seller. Etsy's rapid initial growth took place alongside the growth of social networking, allowing the company to leverage the functions and benefits of social networking, which caused word of mouth and SEO channels to soar and benefit them immensely.

a b

Figure 2.4a and b The Showfields stores featuring startup brands (a) Laine London, and (b) Mersi in Georgetown, Washington, DC (Courtesy of Catherine Jai)

Marketplaces by Focus—Horizontal versus Vertical

Horizontal marketplaces try to provide a platform that serves as a one-stop-shop experience. The focus of the horizontal marketplaces is to offer various product types to all different types of customers. They want to be the one-stop shop for many consumers and offer the platform to all different types of sellers. Examples of horizontal marketplaces are eBay, Amazon, and AliExpress.[52] Figure 2.5 shows that, on average, over half of the Top 500 retailers sell products on Amazon by various merchant types.

Vertical marketplaces focus on selling products within a specific segment or to an identified niche market. For instance, a vertical marketplace may focus on (re)selling luxury products, handmade crafts, or a single product category like sneakers. The major characteristic of this type of marketplace is that instead of trying to sell everything to everyone, they develop their product vertically by offering specialized services and high-quality products. This approach enables the marketplaces to create a sense of community and intimacy between the sellers and buyers. Etsy, The RealReal, and StockX are examples of vertical marketplaces.

StockX became popular by introducing an innovative stock-market-like transaction interface for luxury and limited-edition sneakers. During the 2020 Cyber Weekend sale, the company had 10 million visitors and saw a record-breaking one-trade per second.[53] In recent years, the newly formed marketplaces tend to be more interest-focused. For instance, Craftsvilla is a marketplace that sells only regionally with a focus on ethnic Indian fashion; and GoTrendier is a second-hand fashion platform that targets Spanish-speaking users.

Marketplaces by Management Approach

In terms of management approach, different marketplaces have different levels of management involvement in site operations. It can range from fully managed to partially or even unmanaged (Table 2.2). Usually, a fully managed marketplace would charge a higher fee (listing or transaction fee) because there are a lot of management efforts going into the website maintenance and/or operations. Some examples of fully managed marketplaces are The RealReal and ThredUp. The fully managed marketplaces take the responsibility of verifying the product quality, managing inventory, and shipping. On the other hand, Etsy and eBay fall closer to the other end of the spectrum where it has little to no management. These unmanaged marketplaces are mainly used as a public online place for buyers and sellers to meet and make transactions. The customers' trust is mainly built on the previous reviews and sellers' ratings.

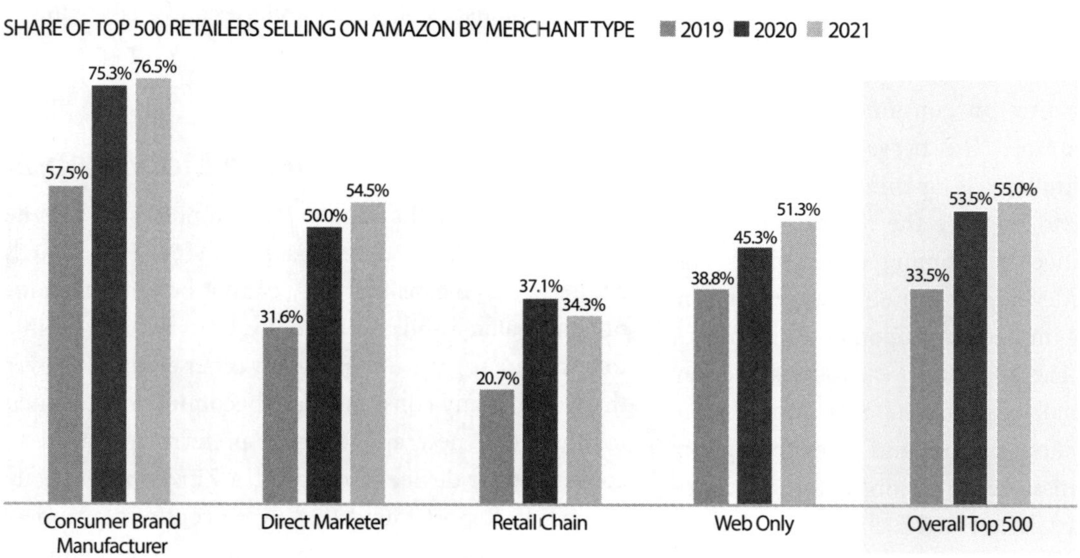

Figure 2.5 Share of Top 500 retailers selling on Amazon
(*Source*: https://www.digitalcommerce360.com/product/top-500/)

Table 2.2 Online Marketplaces by Management Level

	UNMANAGED	FULLY MANAGED
Marketplaces	• Etsy • eBay • Craigslist	• The RealReal • Luxe • Thredup
Features	• Peer to peer transactions • Trust comes from reviews and ratings • Lowest transaction fees	• Intermediate transactions • Marketplace handles the whole operation process • Superior customer experience

Mobile Apps

Globally, people are spending more time on their mobile phone.[54,55] As the world of e-commerce continues to grow in both size and significance, mobile commerce has become a standard for success in the retail industry in order for businesses to remain competitive and satisfy the wants and needs of a new generation of consumers. Native mobile retail apps have played a critical role in the success of omnichannel retailing, as data has shown a strong correlation between app usage and purchases among customers. Consumer research found that the top drivers of downloading retail mobile apps are coupons, loyalty programs, and product search features. According to an eMarketers, more than 70 percent of US mobile app users claim to at least "occasionally" or "frequently" use their mobile apps while shopping in-store.[56]

Strengths of Shopping Mobile Apps

Research has found that shopping gamification is one of the main motivations driving shopping engagement and indirectly impacting on consumers' intention to buy using a mobile app. The pervasive, interactive, and ubiquitous technology is opening up the debate on how to use ICT to improve the retailer–customer relationship to enhance the shopping experience.[57] For instance, Nike has developed a mobile app that can recognize customers immediately upon entering brick-and-mortar stores. The app allows customers to scan a product to find availability in the area, provides an in-store mobile checkout option, and gives the option to reserve products in-store for try-ons before purchasing. Mark Parker, the CEO of NIKE, claims that the app provides "seamless, frictionless shopping," and Nike continues to expand and improve their business model to stay ahead of the competition.

The pros of developing an app for retail business include the following:

- Better customer experience: You can provide a better shopping experience by fully utilizing the special features that a mobile device can provide, such as a camera, voice call, texting, and click-to-call functions.
- Efficient: App loading time is faster than mobile sites, and customers can use the app in offline mode.
- Maintain customer relationships: App allows you to keep in touch with clients no matter where they physically are, send them reminders, and build efficient loyalty programs, rewarding the most loyal customers.
- Apps increase customer retention and loyalty, helping to provide sales support.
- Vast analysis capabilities: You can quickly catch the statistics of user's purchases and analyze the data about how they shop and use your app.

Weaknesses of Shopping Mobile Apps

Probably one of the biggest disadvantages of mobile apps is that their content is not indexed by search engines. This means that they cannot be optimized for organic traffic—and consequently, users will not be able to find your app via Google or any other engine. All over the world, many consumers are becoming less inclined to download new applications, preferring instead to conserve their device resources.[58] A Zipwhip 2019 State of Texting Report found that 61 percent of consumers would not install a new application to communicate with a business. Other weakness of using mobile device for selling include:

- Limited storage space: Mobile apps take up storage space on users' devices, which can be a turnoff for customers who are reluctant to download apps due to limited storage on their device.
- Development and maintenance costs: Developing and maintaining a mobile app can be expensive, especially for smaller retailers with limited resources. This can be a significant barrier to entry for some businesses.
- Need for updates: Mobile apps require updates to fix bugs, add new features, and improve user experience. However, users may not always update their apps, leading to compatibility issues and decreased functionality.
- Platform limitations: Mobile apps are often designed for a specific operating system (e.g., iOS or Android), which can limit the potential customer base for retailers who only offer an app on one platform.

Social Media Accounts

Since its debut, social media has generated three fundamental shifts in the marketplace. Social media accounts enable brands and customers to connect in ways that were not possible in the past. Such connectedness is empowered by various platforms, such as social networking sites (e.g., Facebook), microblogging sites (e.g., X, previously Twitter), and content communities (e.g., YouTube), that allow social networks to build from shared interests and values.[59] The global pandemic that began in 2020 inevitably changed the landscape of social media usage. Due to the social-distancing restrictions, many people switched to social media to maintain social interactions. Among all the social networks, Facebook currently sits at more than 2.79 billion monthly active users, followed by YouTube (2.29 billion users), WhatsApp (2 billion users), Instagram (1.29 billion users), WeChat (1.22 billion users), and TikTok (732 million users).[60]

One recent marketing report forecasts that the global social commerce industry could grow three times as fast as e-commerce, from $492 billion in 2021 to $1.2 trillion by 2025. Gen Z and millennial consumers are predicted to lead growth. According to the report, these two generational cohorts will account for 62 percent of global social commerce spending by 2025.[61] For omnichannel retailers, it is inevitable that social media be utilized to meet, serve, and care for their customers. With more than 71 percent of consumers more likely to consult social media prior to making a buying decision and more than 57 percent of beauty and fashion companies using influencers as part of their marketing strategies, influencer marketing is allowing consumers to be part of a brand's development.[62]

Usage and Reach

In the United States there is a growing share of Americans (over 80 percent) who say they use YouTube, followed by Facebook and Instagram. Figure 2.6 shows social media platform adoption in the last ten years among US adults. Although Instagram, Snapchat, and TikTok have less than 50 percent of the average adoption rate, they have an especially strong following among young adults.[63]

In 2020, TikTok became the first US social platform to launch live shopping capabilities. TikTok partnered with Walmart for an hour-long live stream where TikTok users could buy Walmart fashion items featured by creators. The duo did another live stream in 2021 after reporting the that first event had seven times more views than expected and grew Walmart's TikTok following by 25 percent.[64]

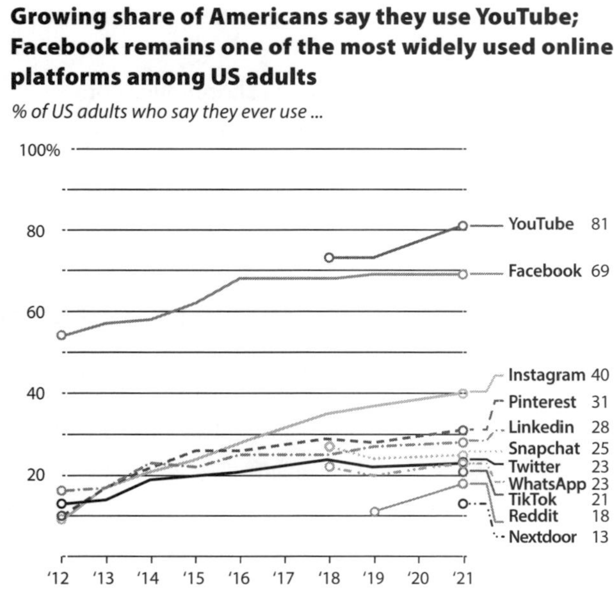

Figure 2.6 Social media platforms adoption in from 2012 to 2021 among US adults
(*Source*: Pew Research, Social media use in 2021, https://www.pewresearch.org/internet/2021/04/07/social-media-use-in-2021/)

Strengths of Social Media for Shopping

- Increased exposure: As people increasingly spend more time on social media, it provides an enormous amount of exposure for products and services. Brands can showcase their products on social media platforms, which can be shared and spread through viral marketing.[65]
- Customer engagement: Social media platforms are a great way for brands to engage with their customers. Customers can ask questions, provide feedback, and receive personalized recommendations. Brands can also use social media to create a sense of community around their products and services.[66]
- Personalization: Social media platforms use algorithms to collect data on user behavior and preferences. This data can be used to provide personalized product recommendations to customers, increasing the likelihood of a purchase.[67]
- User-generated content: Social media platforms are a great way for brands to leverage user-generated content. User-generated content can be in the form of product reviews, photos, or videos, and can help build trust and credibility for the brand.[68]
- Influencer marketing: Social media influencers have a significant impact on the purchasing decisions of their followers. Brands can collaborate with influencers to showcase their products and reach a wider audience.[69]
- Convenience: Social media shopping is convenient for customers as they can make purchases directly from the platform without having to leave the app or website. For instance, Instagram launches payment-in-chat feature for businesses.[70]

Weaknesses of Social Media for Shopping

While social media can be a great platform for selling products, there are also some downsides to consider:

- Platform dependency: Social media platforms can change their algorithms[71] or policies[72] at any time, which can impact a seller's reach and visibility. This can make it difficult to build a consistent customer base or create a stable source of revenue.[73]
- Competition: Social media platforms are crowded marketplaces with many sellers and brands vying for attention. It can be difficult to stand out and gain traction without a strong marketing strategy or established brand reputation.[74]
- Trust: Social media platforms can be susceptible to cyberattacks and data breaches, which can put sensitive customer information at risk. This can lead to a loss of trust and reputation for the seller.[75]
- Negative feedback: Social media platforms provide customers with a public platform to share their opinions and experiences with a brand or product. Negative feedback or reviews can harm a seller's reputation and make it more difficult to attract new customers.[76,77]

CASE STUDY 2.1

How Nordstrom Personalizes Customer Experiences with Omnichannel Strategies

Our customer strategy focuses on providing a seamless and high-quality experience across all Nordstrom channels.

– *Nordstrom Annual Report, 2016, p. 7*

Nordstrom has long been recognized in the retail industry as an innovator and trailblazer, bringing new ideas and formats to market in an effort to best meet the needs of its customers. The upscale department store chain earned the No. 1 spot in Total Retail's 2022 Top 100 Omnichannel Retailers report.[78] According to the report, consumers that engage across the Nordstrom banner, the Rack banner, online, and in-store spend 12 times more than single-channel customers. This isn't a phenomenon that's exclusive to Nordstrom. Omnichannel shoppers are overwhelmingly retailers' most loyal (and profitable) customers. Erik Nordstrom, CEO of Nordstrom, said in the report, "[o]ur focus on serving the customer through our interconnected model with Nordstrom and Nordstrom Rack, a scaled digital platform and a strong store fleet positioned us to capitalize on demand from customers."

Nordstrom's omnichannel strategy focuses on their customers by providing a differentiated and seamless experience in a digital world by bringing all of their assets together in each market to serve customers when, where, and how they want to shop. To achieve this goal, Nordstrom has three major components in the supply chain network: 1) fulfillment centers, 2) distribution centers, and 3) omnichannel centers. The fulfillment centers primarily process and ship orders to the customers. The distribution centers primarily process and ship merchandise to stores and other facilities. Last but not least, the omnichannel centers fulfill both customer orders and ship merchandise to stores. Nordstrom online purchases are primarily shipped to their customers from their fulfillment centers but may also be shipped from the Nordstrom stores, distribution centers, or omnichannel centers. Nordstrom in-store purchases are primarily fulfilled from that store's inventory, but when inventory is unavailable at that store, it may also be shipped to customers from their fulfillment centers, distribution centers, omnichannel centers, or from other Nordstrom stores. Their first large-scale omnichannel center, which opened in 2020, is in Riverside, California. The omnichannel center mainly supports the West Coast region. In addition, they also opened a smaller local omnichannel hub in Torrance, California in 2019 to support the greater Los Angeles (LA) market as part of their market strategy. The hub has a highly curated inventory that serves the specialized needs of the LA market.

As for its strategy going forward, Nordstrom is prioritizing technology investments in supply chain and merchandising capabilities that are at the core of its omnichannel strategy. These include further improvements to its buy online, pickup in-store (BOPIS), and curbside pickup programs, which were exceedingly popular among Nordstrom's customers—and profitable for the retailer. According to Erik Nordstrom, the click-and-collect channel is, in fact, the most profitable touchpoint for Nordstrom.

Nordstrom's business strategy is to deliver a differentiated and seamless experience, which consists of the integration of our digital and physical assets, the development of new supply chain capabilities, and the timely delivery of products.[79] They also expand their inventory flexibility through alternative partnership models, including strategic brands, wholesale, vertical brands, concession, dropship, and other strategies. Below are some examples of the omnichannel integrations Nordstrom offer:

- Mobile apps: Their name apps are available in Apple's App Store and Google Play. Using the app, customers can manage their wish list, find items new to them, see product ratings and reviews, track their orders, redeem rewards, and receive alerts when their favorites drop, come back in stock, or go on sale.
- New store format: To help bridge the gap between online (web, app, social) and offline shopping channels, Nordstrom has opened small-format "Local" stores that provide convenient services for shoppers in New York City and Los Angeles. The Nordstrom Local stores serve as service hubs for online order pickup and returns, express alterations, free styling help, among other offerings.[80]
- Pop-up events: Launched in October 2013, Pop-In@ Nordstrom is an ongoing series of themed pop-up shops that transitions every four to six weeks to offer a new shopping experience and batch of new, often exclusive merchandise.[81]
- Social media integration: Nordstrom presented on social media accounts on Instagram, TikTok, Pinterest, X, Facebook, Snapchat, YouTube, and LinkedIn. For instance, they have integrated Pinterest directly into their stores. They first did this by highlighting their most popular items on Pinterest with in-store displays. In 2018, Pinterest launched the "Pincode" feature to let shoppers scan a Pincode while in-store, then be taken to a Pinterest board such as "gifts under $50" curated by Nordstrom and browse other gift suggestions on the board.
- Livestream: In addition to their blog, The Thread, and email subscriptions, in March 2021, Nordstrom launched Livestream Shopping, marking the next evolution of virtual experiences and digital shopping capabilities. Customers can browse upcoming events and sign up at www.nordstromrsvp.com/nlive. During each Livestream Shopping event, customers can shop for products available at Nordstrom.com and participate in a live chat.[82]

- The Nordy Club: the Nordy Club is Nordstrom's loyalty program, with options to apply for a retail store card, debit card, or Visa credit card. Customers can use their rewards points in-store, at Nordstrom.com, Nordstromrack.com, or through the Nordstrom app.[83]

Another noteworthy point is Nordstrom Media Network, which allows their brand partners to directly connect with their customers through on-site and off-site media campaigns to drive traffic, sales, and engagement. Nordstrom Media Network (NMN) is an advertising program enabling brands to share their stories with Nordstrom and Nordstrom Rack customers via on- and off-site media campaigns. More retail promotion strategies will be discussed in Chapter 7.

Discussion Questions:

1. Have you shopped in Nordstrom before? If there is one near you, go to the store and find out if there are more omnichannel services they offer in-store that are not mentioned in the case.
2. Search for the most recent Nordstrom's 10K (annual report) and identify the various retail channels that Nordstrom operates.
3. Visit Nordstrom's website live stream page, www.nordstromrsvp.com/nlive, to sign up for a virtual event or watch a recorded live stream video of your interest. Write down what interested you most in the live-stream event and how many different retail touchpoints were used (e.g., website, social media, chat, telephone, stores, etc.).
4. Inspect Nordstrom's return policy (located at the footer area on their website) and summarize the return policy that involves their omnichannel services and if there is anything they can improve to serve customers better.
5. List all the social media accounts that Nordstrom operates. List your favorite account(s) and explain why they interest you.
6. Download Nordstrom's mobile app and list the five most useful features and provide a brief explanation of why they can help to facilitate customer experiences.

Career Opportunities

Job Titles	Key Responsibility
Assistant Digital Stylist (Luxury Department Store)	The digital stylist's job is to provide our best e-commerce customers' wardrobe consultations, head-to-toe styling, behind-the-rope access to merchandise, and on-demand personal shopping for any/all of their fashion needs, delivered more quickly and conveniently. Our goal is to make the customer feel like a true VIP at every step of their shopping journey. The individual will work forty hours a week. The position will be supporting a team of lead stylists in building long-term relationships with clients through excellent customer service while becoming their trusted style confidantes. This position requires: • Someone that is strong operationally and can find the best solutions for given problems • Someone that needs little direction and can work independently to solve problems • Flexible, detail-oriented, and able to multi-task with little direction **Knowledge/Skills/Abilities** • Professional and enthusiastic team player, with a demonstrated commitment to customer service excellence • Assist several lead stylists with client communication, outfit recommendations, and operational support • Ability to work well with internal business partners such as our call center and our stores • Ability to work independently to resolve internal and external customer questions and concerns • Experience working in a fast-paced environment • Styling, fashion, and/or fashion retail experience is required • Any additional duties and responsibilities including projects, tasks, and activities as required

Summary

In this chapter, we have surveyed various retail formats available to fashion/lifestyle brands, as well as the major stakeholders involved in the omnichannel retailing arena. The main components of omnichannel retailing include brick-and-mortar stores, direct marketing, direct selling, television retailing, and various e-tailing methods such as selling on company websites, mobile apps, and social media accounts. Each selling method has its strengths and weaknesses that retailers evaluate as they make omnichannel decisions. In 2022, US e-commerce sales surpassed $1 trillion for the first time ever, reaching $1.03 trillion, and e-commerce was expected to surpass 20 percent of total retail in 2024. By 2025, the global e-commerce fashion industry is projected to grow to $2.25 trillion.[84] The rapid increase in omnichannel practices is largely driven by the pandemic. During 2020 to 2021, amid the beginning of the Covid-19 pandemic, consumers and retailers readily adopted new digital and omnichannel shopping behaviors such as curbside pickup and home delivery. Nordstrom is an excellent example of a full-line department store that has grown with technological advances and consumer habit changes, transforming into a top omnichannel retailer. In order to deliver a differentiated and seamless experience, omnichannel retailers need to consider the resources they have in hand and invest in both physical and digital platforms, along with supply chain and information system integrations.

Key Terms

Assortment
Business to business (B2B)
Business to consumer (B2C)
Catalog marketing
Category killer
Consumer to consumer (C2C)
Deep discount store
Diffusion lines
Direct mail marketing
Direct marketing
Direct sellers
Direct selling
Discount buyers
E-catalog
Email marketing
Face-to-face direct selling
Factory outlet store
Full-line department store
Full-line discount store
Horizontal marketplace
Individual contact selling
Infomercials
Limited-line department store
Multi-level marketing
Native mobile retail apps
Off-price retailers
Online marketplaces
Party plan and group sales
Peer to peer (P2P)
Pop-up shop
Preferred customers
Pyramid schemes
Social media accounts
Specialty store
Telemarketing
Television retailing
Text marketing
Vertical marketplaces
Warehouse clubs

Reflection and Discussion Questions

1. Reflecting your own shopping experience, give two examples of omnichannel retailing integrations.
2. What impacts did the Covid-19 pandemic have on the retail industry? In your observation, what has changed since then?
3. What three tactics mentioned in this chapter do you believe are most relevant to the success of omnichannel retailers if they would like to target the following groups: 1) college students; 2) parents with young kids (age 13 and below) at home. Please justify your choices.
4. Search on the internet or the National Retail Federation website to find out the most recent news about how retailers invest in technology to promote their omnichannel integration and services.
5. Do you think physical stores will continue to be relevant in creating retail experiences? In your opinion, what kinds of experiences should retailers consider bringing into their stores?
6. How have discount stores evolved? Do you think discount retail formats will be feasible in the present economy?
7. What are some features that social media platforms now offer to facilitate online shopping? List as many as you can.
8. Reflecting on your experiences as a consumer, what category killers serving your community are still viable, and which have gone out of business?
9. What factors make a category killer stay afloat or even thrive as a competitive business?

CHAPTER 3

Omnichannel Customer Experience

Learning Objectives

Upon finishing this chapter, you will be able to:

- Identify the five stages of the customer journey and describe their characteristics
- Appraise the factors of promoting omnichannel customer experiences and give examples
- Assess the factors that inhibit omnichannel customer experiences and give examples
- Develop omnichannel retailing strategies by applying the customer journey mapping process
- Justify the goal of omnichannel customer experience in facilitating the customer purchase cycle

In Chapter 1 we discussed how omnichannel retailers put consumers at the center of the retail operation. As a result, it is imperative to understand how consumers make a purchase decision and how retailers can help consumers navigate through their shopping journey by providing appropriate information and services at the right time. In this chapter, we will introduce the five-stage shopping journey in the consumer decision-making process. We will discuss the critical factors to promoting omnichannel customer experiences and the factors that will prevent omnichannel customer experiences. Furthermore, you will learn how to identify the problems in delivering an omnichannel customer experience by applying the steps of customer journey mapping.

A Customer's Journey in Five Stages

Reflect on your last shopping experience. What did you buy? Where did you buy it? What is the name of the retailer/brand you made the purchase from? How did you pay for the product? How long did you wait for the product to arrive? Were you happy with the purchase? If not, why? At first glance, when someone talks to you about purchasing something, you probably have the mental image of a person standing in front of the shelf in-store, looking at their mobile phone screen to evaluate a product before proceeding to make a purchase.

A purchase decision is more than just making a transaction. It consists of five stages, namely, 1) awareness stage, 2) evaluation stage, 3) purchase (conversion) stage, 4) postpurchase stage, and 5) retention stage. In the following sections, we will examine the nature of the consumer decision process and how retailers can provide an omnichannel shopping experience throughout the shopping journey.

Awareness Stage

The first stage to start a shopper's journey is awareness. A potential customer may not be aware that a product/solution exists for their need/problem. The objective for omnichannel retailers at this stage is to evoke consumer awareness that the brand/retailer offers a solution or a superior solution to their need/desired state (such as being beautiful or professional).

At the **awareness stage**, retailers should focus on educating potential customers about their new product offerings or present the existing products as a new solution. The traditional media content to evoke customers' interests and awareness includes television ads, billboards, newspaper/magazine ads, radio, or word of mouth. In the online environment, omnichannel retailers can offer things like shareable photographs, blog posts, social media posts, videos, e-catalogs, podcasts, etc. Depending on the consumer segments and their intended contact points with the retailers, different content materials may be developed to maximize the effectiveness of the content. For instance, retailers can develop a shopping-tips email for back-to-school sales targeting parents who have school-aged children, or a short TikTok video or Instagram Reel targeting teenagers on what to wear for the first day of school. In this stage, consumers may conduct a search online or ask people who have experienced similar purchase problems before. Therefore, commercials, search ads, YouTube/video ads, and customer reviews are also important tools for omnichannel retailers to use to engage potential consumers at this stage.

Evaluation Stage

Once potential customers become aware of the product/retail offering, they may enter the second stage: evaluation. In the **evaluation stage**, potential customers will determine whether they want to purchase the product. Many factors influence customers' evaluation of a product.

Usually, the higher the product price, the more effort consumers may put into this stage. For new customers, omnichannel retailers can use consistent content across different channels to build customer trust. At this stage, a potential customer is looking for content that can persuade them that buying the product from the retailer is a superior choice. Therefore, the goal is to help eliminate consumers' doubt about making the purchase. Identifying the pain points that prevent a customer from making a purchase could be useful for identifying effective content at this stage. For instance, if consumers can't make a purchase decision because they do not know what size to order, then in addition to a size chart, retailers can offer the height and weight of the model and the size they wore in the product photo to help the consumer evaluate the product. Research has shown that video also has a better effect on online product evaluation.[1] Blogs and articles about how to choose a product or style can be an effective way to assist customers in making a choice as well. Omnichannel retailers could utilize content such as emails, customer reviews, user-uploaded photos, and product comparison charts, among others to help consumers in their evaluation phase.

Purchase (Conversion) Stage

The **purchase (conversion) stage** is when consumers take the desired action, such as completing a transaction, signing up for an email list, or booking an appointment. This stage is crucial for omnichannel retailers because it's when consumers feel confident in a product or service and are ready to take action. To ensure a successful transaction, it's essential to provide information related to shipping/delivery options, payments, and return policies. The goal is to prevent potential customers from encountering any obstacles as they navigate the checkout process.

In a store environment, customers should be able to make purchases in-store, pickup products in another store (in case of stock-outs), or receive free delivery to their homes. For online purchases, customers can **buy online, pickup in-store (BOPIS)**, have them delivered to their homes, or ship them to another location. To facilitate a smooth transaction, omnichannel retailers should consider two key points. First, their customer-facing interfaces (e.g., store, website, app, catalog, etc.) should have a clear call to action. Second, the purchase process should be as simple as possible by providing customers with the necessary information such as shipping options, delivery time, etc. before they proceed with a transaction.

Online calls to action can include buttons like "add to cart," "checkout now," "share with," "like on social," etc. These calls to action can also be used to measure content outcomes and help businesses reach their goals. To assist customers in completing their transactions, omnichannel retailers can conduct consumer research, such as focus groups, to find out what information is needed during the conversion stage. This information can help them develop content that addresses identified pain points from the customer journey analysis (which will be discussed later in this chapter). Simplifying the purchase process for customers will increase the likelihood of successful transactions.

Finally, sometimes customers are just not ready to pay yet. In that case, more and more retailers offer "My Favorites" or "Save for Later" functions so that customers can put the products they are not ready to purchase in the list as external memory to help them organize the things they plan to buy.[2] This way, the products will not sit in the shopping cart and take up the product counts from your inventory. In Chapter 4, we will discuss in more detail of how to improve the efficiency of the checkout process.

Post-Purchase Stage

In the **post-purchase stage**, consumers will perform a post-purchase evaluation and see if they are satisfied with the purchase. If they are satisfied with the product, they may not have any reactions. However, if they are not satisfied with the product, they may complain to the retailers or return the product. For omnichannel retailers, they should send a follow-up email to ask their customers if they are satisfied once the products or services are delivered. They may also invite customers to write a review for them to provide positive word of mouth for them. **Purchase dissonance**, also known as buyer's remorse, is a psychological state that occurs when a person feels regret or uncertainty after making a purchase.[3] It is a feeling of dissatisfaction or unease that arises after a person has decided to purchase a product or service. This can happen for various reasons, such as feeling that the purchase was too expensive, the product does not meet expectations, or there are better alternatives available. Omnichannel retailers can help to reduce customers' purchase dissonance by using the following strategies:

- Offer post-purchase communication: Following up with customers using emails after purchase to ensure satisfaction and offer assistance can help reduce the likelihood of purchase dissonance. By showing customers that the retailer is committed to their satisfaction, they are more likely to feel confident about their purchase decision.
- Encourage customer reviews: By encouraging customers to leave reviews about their purchase, retailers can provide social proof and help reduce customers' uncertainty about a product. Positive reviews from other customers can reassure potential customers that they are making a good

decision and reduce the likelihood of purchase dissonance.

- Provide customer support: Having a reliable customer support team can help customers with any issues they may have with their purchase. This can help reduce the stress and uncertainty that can lead to purchasing dissonance.

Retention Stage

Research from the Harvard Business Review showed that the more touchpoints a customer uses, the more they end up spending.[4] If businesses can keep customers within their ecosystem, seamlessly moving from touchpoint to touchpoint, then the customer's overall expenditure is likely to be even higher. Therefore, in the **retention stage**, omnichannel retailers can fully integrate their ecosystem to offer free services, send out promotional incentives (e.g., discount codes, free samples, etc.), offer cross-sell recommendations, send out re-order reminders or re-engagement to encourage customers who have not visited the website/store recently to do so.[5] Omnichannel retailers also use loyalty programs to encourage repeat purchases. Below are some examples of omnichannel loyalty programs.

- Amazon Prime: Amazon Prime is a paid loyalty program that offers free two-day shipping, free try-before-you-buy service for fashion items, free games, access to streaming of movies, TV shows, ad-free podcasts, and music, as well as discounts on products.[6]
- Sephora Beauty Insider: Sephora Beauty Insider is a loyalty program for customers of Sephora. Members can earn points for purchases, which can be redeemed for products or other perks, such as free shipping, exclusive offers, and access to beauty classes and events.[7]
- Starbucks Rewards: Starbucks Rewards is a loyalty program that rewards customers for purchases at Starbucks locations. Members earn stars for each purchase, which can be redeemed for free drinks, food, and other perks.[8]
- The Nordy Club: The Nordy Club is a loyalty program for customers of Nordstrom. Members earn points for purchases, which can be redeemed for Nordstrom Notes, which can be used to purchase products at Nordstrom locations or online.[9]
- Target Circle: Target Circle is a loyalty program offered by Target. Members can earn rewards, including discounts on purchases, free shipping, and early access to sales, by making purchases at Target locations or online.[10]

Factors Promoting Omnichannel Customer Experience

To promote omnichannel customer experience, there are several factors that retailers need to focus on. They are consistency, convenience, agility, relevance, and services. We will discuss each factor in the following sections.

Consistency

Consistency is essential for creating a unified brand presence that consumers can trust. However, achieving consistency is challenging and requires attention from top leadership. To build consistency throughout the nonlinear (meaning bouncing back and forth among different channels) omnichannel customer journey, retailers have to focus on the integration across products, prices, promotions, and information regarding orders, logistics, and customer services.[11]

Customers expect consistent product and service offerings across all channels, as well as consistent support across online, offline, and social touchpoints. However, many companies still operate in silos, which creates friction in the customer journey.[12] Departments often work independently, designing and managing their touchpoints differently and adhering to different standards and metrics, leading to issues with ownership and responsibilities.

To deliver a consistent omnichannel experience, companies must focus on end-to-end processes, policies, guidelines, and restructuring teams to collaborate effectively. Therefore, it is essential to ensure that customer-facing departments communicate and collaborate effectively, including marketing, product development, digital or web support, and information technology (IT).

Convenience

Consumers are often pressed for time, and as a result, convenience has become a critical aspect of delivering a positive customer experience. With the convenience of online shopping and the ability to compare prices from a wide range of retailers, customers have become accustomed to having products readily available with minimal effort. Therefore, it's important for businesses to identify ways to save customers time, reduce their effort, and make the buying experience as seamless and effortless as possible. Some omnichannel services that offer convenience to consumers include: BOPIS, cross-channel inventory visibility, store-based fulfillment, cross-channel return, etc.

Amazon is a great example of a retailer using convenience to distinguish themselves from other retailers. For instance, they created the Amazon Prime program, which provides free shipping within two days or less, eliminating the need to go to a physical store. Amazon also offers the try-before-you-buy service for fashion items like clothes and shoes to reduce consumers' uncertainty. By focusing on speed and simplicity, Amazon has been able to stand out in a highly competitive retail landscape.[13]

For fashion retailers, H&M offers a "scan and buy" feature on their mobile app, allowing customers to scan product tags in-store and purchase items online. This feature is useful for the situation when customers can't find their size in-store or want to know if an item is available in more sizes and colors. They also offer in-store returns and free shipping for online orders over a certain amount.[14] US Department store Macy's offers a "Style Crew" program where customers can connect with personal stylists online or in-store.[15] Macy's also offer buy online, pickup in-store, and curbside pickup options, as well as same-day delivery in select locations.

Nowadays, customers expect convenience to be a given. They want to be able to view the same pricing online and offline, have the option to buy online and pickup in-store or vice versa, and have easy return and refund processes. Investing in convenience can be a significant competitive advantage and lead to customer loyalty and repeat business.

Agility

Forty-six percent of US consumers have switched brands or retailers recently.[16] New digital channels and e-commerce activities have surged during the pandemic, and their popularity will likely endure. For example, we observed ten years' worth of growth in US e-commerce penetration during the first ninety days of the Covid-19 pandemic.[17] New entrants with the best digital offers and those retailers that provide an integrated customer experience are capturing the majority of growth, putting pressure on incumbent retailers regarding profitability and customer service.

New frontiers of technology, such as artificial intelligence (AI), augmented reality (like filters used in the mobile app), and new social platforms (such as Discord, TikTok, etc.) for customers, will push retailers to react based on how customers use and interact with them. An agile approach allows retailers to pivot and adjust their strategies in real-time to meet the needs and expectations of their customers across multiple channels. This includes the ability to launch new products or services quickly, optimize the customer experience across all touchpoints, and respond to customer feedback and data insights. Without agility, retailers may struggle to keep up with the competition and deliver the seamless experiences that customers expect in today's omnichannel landscape. For example, Nike has been using technology to enhance the customer experience and streamline operations for years.

During the pandemic, Nike accelerated their investments in e-commerce and launched new features such as virtual try-ons for shoes and apparel. Within two months after the national shut down (shelter-at-home order from the federal government) in the United States, they launched a new service called "Nike Fit," which uses augmented reality to help customers find the perfect size and fit for their shoes.[18] With Nike's agile approach, their direct-to-consumer sales were up 32 percent, and digital sales were up 84 percent in the first year of pandemic, while most retailers' sales suffered from the low traffic in physical stores.[19] Another example is Target. Target has been a leader in omnichannel retailing for years, and during the Covid-19 pandemic, they quickly pivoted to offer new services such as curbside pickup and same-day delivery. They also ramped up their e-commerce capabilities, including expanding their product assortment and improving their website and app.

Relevance

Market research showed that people are 40 percent more likely to spend more than planned when they identify the shopping experience to be highly personalized.[20]

The new consumer expects interactions to be real-time, highly personalized, and tailored to buying preferences, transaction history, and user behaviors. Consumers would share personal details and are comfortable with brands collecting personal data in the name of creating a personalized customer experience. Data analytics can really boost personalized experience. Retailers can use data mining to identify which offers to make to which customers with a full explanation as to why. By using predictive analytics with generative AI like ChatGPT, omnichannel retailers can deliver custom-tailored messages to meet your customers' individual needs.[21] Using advanced statistical methods, omnichannel retailers can utilize all data insights to further increase the effectiveness of customer segmentation. **Customer segmentation** means grouping customers based on their homogeneous values or characteristics. Hence, retailers will be able to build more relevant content based on what the customer wants to receive.

Omnichannel retailers must utilize data to not only gain a clear, value-based understanding of their customer base internally but also to create a highly personalized customer experience externally. In addition to utilizing data, more and more retailers are collaborating with social media influencers to engage their customers. For instance, Emma Chamberlain is a social media personality who made the top 25 most influential people on the internet by *Time* magazine in 2019.[22] During the pandemic, PacSun, a lifestyle brand designed for designed for teens and young adults, partnered with Emma Chamberlain to promote mental health. Customers were encouraged to participate in this self-reflection journey by taking mirror photos and writing realizations about themselves, the world, and their intentions for 2021, which they shared on social media using the #InMyPac Spring Campaign. This concept was further amplified in all of the retailers' 400 stores via window displays, dressing rooms, and PacSun's social media, with a virtual reality (VR) lens launched on Snapchat in March 2021.[23] Customers were encouraged to post their photos on Instagram using the hashtag #pacverse, and these photos would be featured on PacSun's website with a call to action button "Buy Now" to increase their sales, a strategy that PacSun uses to maintain its relevance to their customers by featuring their customers. PacSun also collaborated with influencers and content creators across various social media platforms, such as Instagram, YouTube, and Snapchat, to create sponsored posts and campaigns that drove traffic to their website and physical stores.

Because of its strong social media presence, strategic partnerships, and focus on the brand's strategy, PacSun ranked #5 in investment bank Piper Sandler's "Taking Stock with Teens" Spring 2023 report.[24] The retailer also achieved the #1 spot in the women's brand category and moved up from #5 the previous year, overtaking competitors such as Adidas and Hollister.[25]

Services

In Chapter 1, we discussed various omnichannel shopping experiences, including:

- Buy online, pickup in-store (BOPIS)
- Buy online, ship from store
- Buy online, ship from a fulfillment center
- Buy in-store, ship from the store or another store
- Buy in-store, ship from a fulfillment center
- Use loyalty credits to buy online and in-store
- Having a store locator and in-store stock status features on the website and mobile apps
- Make an in-store appointment online
- Buy online, in-store returns

Good customer experience can help retailers, especially for omnichannel retailing that aims to deliver a seamless shopping experience to customers through excellent services—meaning that online and offline are effectively one continuous experience. Very few people walk into a retail store without having done their homework. Omnichannel shoppers usually start their shopping journey on their phones. They would be following some brands, and they go into stores with a purpose. To achieve this goal, omnichannel retailers can offer self-service tools on their website or mobile app. Self-service tools include a community forum, chatbot, live chat, email support, voice calling, etc. In the meantime, omnichannel retailers also need to empower their employees to provide superior services by investing in training and technology that helps them deliver personalized experiences to customers across channels. For example, retailers can provide their employees with mobile devices that enable them to access customer data and make real-time inventory updates, making it easier for them to help customers find what they need. Retailers can also offer training programs that help employees develop soft skills such as active listening, empathy, and problem-solving, which are essential for delivering exceptional customer experiences. Another way that omnichannel retailers empower their employees is by giving them the flexibility to work across channels. For example, employees can be trained to provide support via chat, email, phone, or social media, depending on the customer's preference. This approach allows retailers to offer seamless, consistent experiences across channels, which is critical to building customer loyalty.[26]

Finally, retailers can empower their employees by creating a culture of continuous improvement. By regularly soliciting feedback from employees and customers and by investing in tools that help them analyze this feedback, retailers can identify areas for improvement and implement changes that make it easier for employees to provide superior services. This approach not only benefits customers but also helps retailers attract and retain top talent.

Factors Inhibiting Omnichannel Customer Experience

Now you know what factors can improve omnichannel customer experience. Next, we will discuss what factors may inhibit omnichannel customer experience. Unfortunately, these are all very common reasons preventing a retailer to deliver a well-rounded and friction-free omnichannel customer experience. These factors are inability to connect the dots using data, inability to meet customer expectations, and ineffective marketing strategy. We will discuss these in more detail below.

Inability to Connect the Dots Using Data

Marketers face a tough time integrating data from different channels to create a seamless customer journey. When different communication channels within a company, such as email, texting, and social media, operate independently of each other, it can create confusion and lead to inconsistent customer experiences. If a company's messaging is inconsistent across different channels, it can lead to a lack of trust in the brand. A survey by eConsultancy shows that managing data across different channels is one of the major challenges that marketers face while planning an omnichannel marketing strategy.[27] The inability to connect the dots prevents them from creating a personalized experience for the customer.

Inability to Meet Customer Expectations

Thanks to retail giants like Amazon and Nordstrom, and streaming services providers like Netflix and YouTube, customers nowadays expect hyper-personalized recommendations wherever they go. The one-size-fits-all experiences have vanished over the past decade, and a customer wouldn't think twice before switching to a competitor's website if the experiences are not up to their expectations. In order to meet customers' expectations, omnichannel retailers have to think like a customer—an art that many retailers have yet to master.[28] To deliver the right message at the right time, compelling content is pivotal to the success of an omnichannel marketing strategy. An ineffective content strategy is bound to make a campaign a failure.

Customers now use multiple media, such as social media, mobile apps, websites, etc., to interact with fashion brands. These channels may also serve different roles in different stages of a buyer's journey. For instance, if a customer sees an ad on their social media feeds about a certain product, they will expect, by clicking that ad, they will be taken to the product page instead of the homepage of the website. If they complete a transaction on the brand's website, they will receive confirmation through their emails. Failing to make these cross-channel connections for your customers will inhibit the omnichannel customer experiences.

Ineffective Marketing Strategy

Marketers realize the potential of omnichannel marketing, yet most of them fail to put together an effective strategy. Most customers suffer because of the disjointed experience offered by the brand due to poor strategy. Some of the major causes of ineffective marketing strategies[29] include:

- Being reactive instead of proactive
- Not using analytics to measure the success of your campaigns
- Not dedicating the resources needed to develop and execute an ongoing strategy

- Spending too much time on the wrong channels
- Not monitoring your competition
- Great ideas with a lack of follow-through or accountability

According to market research, the retail industry spent the most among other industry categories on advertisements and marketing activities from 2017 to 2022.[30] However, many large companies still have information silos and organizational structures preventing the implementation of omnichannel services.[31] To add to these woes, the proliferation of new channels, such as social media and mobile apps, makes implementation even more challenging. By shifting the brand focus from channels to customer experiences, understanding your buyer's persona, and segmenting your buyers, you will be able to deliver the right message to the right user through the right channels.

Investing time and money in ineffective marketing will make a brand irrelevant to specific segments of users, and that would mean potentially losing out to your competitors. To understand your buyer's persona, identify the touchpoints that they use to interact with your brand and make your content relevant for every buyer and channel. In the following section, we will discuss how to create a customer persona and map the journey to develop practices to deliver omnichannel customer experiences.

Customer's Journey Mapping Steps

Customer purchase journey describes the process a customer goes through to achieve their consumption goals with your company. Using a customer journey map, you can identify the different stages your customers go through when interacting with your company. Table 3.1 is a template of a consumer journey map and provides examples of consumer goals, actions, touchpoints and changes, customer thoughts and emotions, pain points, and opportunities for omnichannel retailers to improve in the consumer decision process. The vertical columns in the table represent the consumer decision process, starting from the awareness stage, consideration stage, product acquisition stage, customer service stage, and retention stage (how to make them come back and repurchase from you). The rows are the consumer factors that influence their ways of interacting with you as a retailer. These factors include customer goal(s), customer actions (what will they do?), touchpoints and channels, the thoughts or emotions they may have, any pain points (what is difficult for them to achieve their goal), and ideas of ways to solve the pain points for your customers. Going through the customer journey map will help you decide and find concrete ways to acquire, retain, and grow your customers.

Step 1: Create a Customer Persona

After identifying target customers' interests and concerns during the purchase journey, omnichannel retailers need to create appealing and relevant solutions to address those interests and concerns. Highly relevant and entertaining content will enable retailers to drive website traffic, engagement rate, and sales. How can they create relevant and appealing content? There are several strategies that retailers can use. First, build your buyer persona; second, find content ideas; and third, create content using modern technologies.

Here are different ways to build a buyer persona. For instance, Figure 3.1 describes a buyer persona template. Doing some internal and external research to fill in the blanks in the template will give you a good portrait of your buyer persona. Another online marketing platform, HubSpot, also has a step-by-step interface to help marketers create buyer persona and share them with people within their business. The key components included in the buyer persona are 1) demographic information such as name, age, gender, education, and income; you may obtain this information from your existing customer profiles or from market research; 2) professional status such as job title, level of the job, and type of industry. Think about how this buyer works. Ask questions like what they use in their jobs or how do they prefer to communicate in their work/personal life to help you determine the best channels to position your content to the buyer; 3) psychographic information such as their professional and personal goals. These kinds of details will help you to determine what they might be worried about, and you will be able to create specific solutions for them. If your business wants to emphasize beliefs or values such as a healthy lifestyle or sustainability, defining the beliefs and values of your target customers will be crucial for developing effective content to communicate with them.

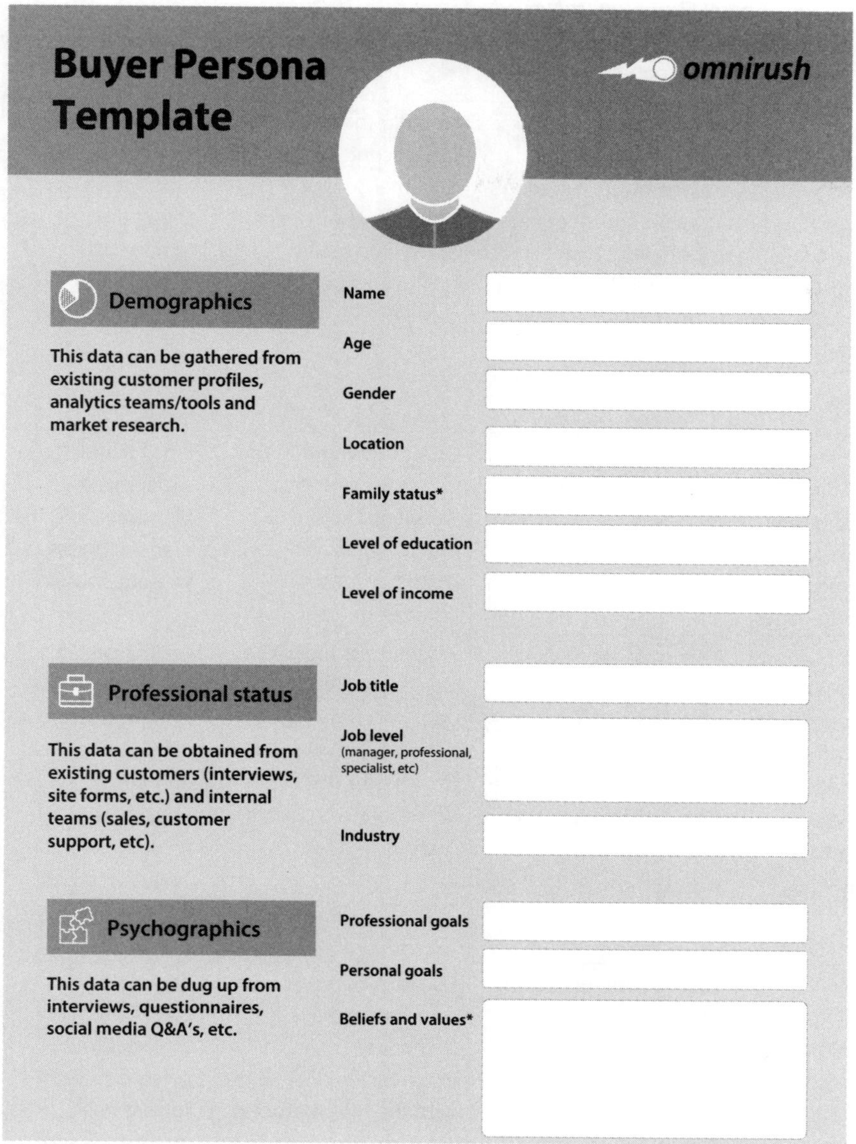

Figure 3.1 Buyer persona template (*Source*: Adopted from Semrush.com)

Table 3.1 How to Map a Consumer's Journey for Apparel Shopping

	Awareness	Consideration	Acquisition	Service	Retention
Customer Goals	To find stylish and affordable clothing options for an upcoming event.	To narrow down clothing options and evaluate their suitability for the upcoming event.	To make a final decision and complete the purchase of the chosen outfit.	To receive the purchased outfit in a timely manner and ensure it meets their expectations.	To continue a positive relationship with the brand and potentially make future purchases.

Table 3.1 How to Map a Consumer's Journey for Apparel Shopping, *continued*

	Awareness	Consideration	Acquisition	Service	Retention
Customer Actions	Browsing online fashion blogs, searching for outfit inspiration, and exploring social media fashion pages.	Reading product reviews, comparing prices and styles, and creating a shortlist of potential outfits.	Adding the selected clothing item to the shopping cart, entering payment and shipping information, and confirming the order.	Tracking the order status, contacting customer support for inquiries or issues, and trying on the outfit upon delivery.	Signing up for loyalty programs, subscribing to newsletters for updates and promotions, and following the brand on social media.
Touchpoints & Channels	Instagram, Pinterest, fashion websites, and online fashion communities.	Online clothing stores, fashion forums, review websites, and social media shopping pages.	Websites, apps, and in-store purchases.	Order tracking portals on the e-commerce website or app, email notifications, and customer service hotlines.	Email newsletters, social media platforms, and the brand's official website or app.
Customer Thoughts/ Emotions	Excitement and curiosity about discovering the latest fashion trends and outfit ideas.	Feeling cautious about making the right choice, looking for reassurance from others' experiences, and seeking validation for their purchases.	A sense of accomplishment and excitement about finally getting the desired outfit, along with anticipation for its arrival.	Anxiousness regarding delivery, satisfaction upon receiving the package, and the desire for a hassle-free return or exchange process if needed.	Feeling valued as a customer, looking forward to exclusive offers, and appreciating personalized recommendations based on past purchases.
Pain Points	Difficulty in filtering through the overwhelming amount of fashion content online.	Difficulty in finding trustworthy reviews and dealing with conflicting opinions, as well as the fear of making the wrong purchase.	Concerns about security and privacy during the payment process, shipping costs, and potential delays in delivery.	Delays in delivery, receiving damaged or incorrect items, or experiencing difficulties with the return process.	Too much communication or irrelevant offers can lead to customer annoyance and potentially opting out of loyalty programs or unsubscribing from newsletters.
Opportunities to Improve	Providing personalized fashion recommendations based on the customer's style preferences to streamline their search process.	Providing detailed product descriptions, real and virtual try-on options to enhance confidence in the decision-making process. Offering chat support or expert advice for personalized assistance.	Ensuring a seamless and secure checkout process, offering transparent information about shipping costs and delivery times, and providing order tracking options to enhance the overall shopping experience. Offering various payment methods and easy returns can reduce barriers to completing the purchase.	Providing accurate and real-time order tracking information, ensuring careful packaging to prevent damage during transit, and offering easy and convenient return or exchange procedures. Prompt and helpful customer support can also enhance the overall post-purchase experience and customer satisfaction.	Tailoring communication, offering exclusive discounts or early access to new collections for loyal customers, and seeking and acting on customer feedback can help continuously improve the customer experience.

Table 3.2 **Buyer Persona and Content Creation Worksheet**

Pain Points and Challenges: This data can be gathered from internal information such as sales, customer support, events and interviews, questionnaires, social media, Q&As, etc.	
• Biggest struggles and pain points	
• Obstacles in the way of overcoming the challenges	
• Irrational and rational fears (if applicable)	
Influences and Key Information Sources: These insights can be taken from market and competitor research, as well as existing customer profiles.	
• Preferred blogs, social networks, and sites	
• Favorite media (digital and print)	
• Key influencers and thought leaders	
• Favorite events, conferences (online/offline)	
Purchasing Process: This data can come from internal teams like sales, customer support, social listening, analytics, etc.	
• Role in the purchase decision-making process	
• Potential lifetime cycle	
• What stops them from making a purchase?	

(*Source*: Adopted from Semrush.com)

Step 2: Choose a Journey to Map

Now, you have used the customer journey table to identify the pain points and challenges your buyers could face. In this stage, you can develop a more specific connection between your buyer persona and the content they need. Table 3.2 provides a template to identify the particular pain points and challenges of this type of buyer. By listing the buyer's key information sources such as preferred social media networks, digital and print media consumption, influencers followed, and if there are any online or offline events they like to visit, you can determine what channel to choose for positioning your marketing content. Finally, include the persona's purchase process profile, such as the consumer role they serve in the purchase decision process. Are they both a user and buyer of the product or just a buyer of the product. How frequently do they buy the product or services (potential lifetime cycle).

Collecting this information will help you to deliver the relevant content to the right person at the right time.

Step 3: Create Practices to Deliver the Omnichannel Customer Experience

There are many practices that omnichannel retailers can offer to their customers, which we discussed in Chapters 1 and 2. In this section, we will take a consumer relationship management perspective to illustrate some practices omnichannel retailers use to create a seamless and engaging customer experience.

Personalized Recommendations

Personalized recommendations may be one of the most fantastic perks of email or SMS marketing to any business, especially for the omnichannel fashion retailer, due to the greater diversity in customers' styles, body types, size differences, and other preferences. It is a process of recommending products and services to a particular customer. It requires a good understanding of the target customers through customers' online browsing history or email click data through tracking cookies. Customizing an email marketing message, campaign, or newsletter is similar to how mass customization creates made-to-order products and services specifically for individual customers.

When personalizing recommendations via email, you may consider one or more combinations of the following critical matters: a) interactive by answering questions or coupon codes that one can use, b) animated GIF or graphics, c) audio or video content, d) episodic contents based on prior engagement with the customers, and e) dynamic content blocks.

Rescuing Abandoned Carts

Let's admit it. Just about all of us browse our favorite shop's mobile app and place clothes or items in the shopping cart, then forget about it. Some say this is a great way to calm the nerves with free retail therapy. However, when we put the omnichannel fashion business hat on, we need to remind the customers of the abandoned cartful of clothes and shoes and encourage them to execute their purchase by rescuing abandoned carts.

Reminder emails can be effective in notifying shipping, cost reductions, discount codes, and/or updating the customers on how popular those pieces are. Statistics showed that about 43 percent of all shopping cart abandonment emails had been opened. In addition, the average click rate of such abandoned shopping cart emails is 21 percent, and the average conversation rate of those emails is about 8.24 percent (although this rate varies by industry, equipment, and recovery strategy).[32] This provides an excellent opportunity for marketers to create savvy abandoned shopping cart emails in time to resonate with the audience and increase conversions.[33]

Engaging Current Customers

As discussed previously, it is key for email marketers to engage current customers in meaningful ways, reach out to target customers, and ensure their emails will be opened.

Tips for engaging customers to read email:

1. The marketer should communicate value in the subject lines to encourage the customer to open and not categorize you as spam.
2. One should personalize the content and offers by including the customer's name in the subject line.
3. Carefully segmenting your email lists using customer demographics, geography, purchase history, and website browsing behavior will pay off by avoiding mistargeted emails.
4. Create calls to action that convert the customers from lookers into buyers.
5. Make sure to optimize your email marketing using responsive design for mobile devices.
6. Most email platforms offer the marketing automation function. Utilize this function to organize and create more relevant and personalized email campaigns.

Re-Engage Past Customers

As a part of global consumer trends, in general, consumers are interested in money-saving opportunities. Approximately 61 percent of customers use coupons, while about 97 percent of people are looking for a deal before purchasing online.[34] All this means deals, discounts, and even coupons are an excellent idea to re-engage these customers and get them to spend money on your business again.

When re-engaging former customers, marketers should be much more thoughtful about the frequency and contents of their email marketing campaign. Regardless, there is a reason why we call these customers "past," hinting that they used to be the ones who were relatively active with your business. On this occasion, marketers should offer a personalized email with well-crafted content, including straightforward questions on the frequency and type of email communication the customer prefers. Of course, gently remind your past customers of the great benefits or transactions they may enjoy. For instance, H&M communicates with their former customers and how to re-engage with the customer base with a special discount offer.

Step 4: Measure the Outcome

Key performance indicator (KPI) is a series of measurements that help a business determine if they are achieving their goals. For omnichannel retailers, KPI can be varied depending on the different types of channels that they operate. One important and unique characteristic that an omnichannel retailer has is that the customers can jump across different channels to complete their customer journey. For instance, a potential customer may have seen an online ad about how to care for a cashmere sweater, clicked on the ad, and read the blog. While reading the blog, she sees a photo of an influencer wearing your company's new seasonal product and clicks on the influencer's photo, leading to the Instagram page. After browsing several outfits, the customer clicks on one of the hyperlinks of the outfit, which leads her to your website product page, and she makes a purchase. She was happy that she found another new color of denim that could accompany her cashmere sweater. Good content creation helps incrementally move a potential customer toward a purchase, even if it means they are navigating different channels. Customer journeys may not happen all at once, so expecting one single piece of content to move a shopper through the shopper's journey is unrealistic. That's why it's imperative to vary the types of content and to have a comprehensive content strategy centered around your business goals.

When it comes to choosing KPIs to evaluate your business goals, there is the **SMART principle**, which stands for selecting a Specific business goal; the goal should be Measurable and Achievable and be Relevant to overall business objectives. Most importantly, the KPIs need to be Time-phased. For instance, you should specify if the KPIs are evaluated by day, week, month, etc. Digital KPIs are online metrics that measure success across different online marketing channels. Some basic KPI examples for omnichannel retailers are pay-per-click (PPC), conversion rate, customer lifetime value (CLV), return on investment (ROI), etc. **Pay-per-click (PPC)** is the pre-negotiated cost that a brand agrees to pay for each click ad received.

Conversion rate is the percentage of visitors who become customers. **Customer lifetime value (CLV)** represents the total revenue a business can reasonably expect from a single customer account throughout the business relationship and is a function of average annual revenue per customer divided by the average lifespan of a customer (average years that a customer continues to purchase from a brand).[35] There are some specific KPIs pertaining to different channels of omnichannel retailing. We will discuss those specific KPIs of online advertising, social media marketing, and email marketing in the following chapters.

Since different departments in a company may have different business goals, they may look at different indices as their KPIs. For instance, the sales and marketing team may like to monitor total sales, average order value, and conversion rate by product category, while the content team would look at the total traffic, top landing pages, page views, conversion rate by page, etc. For the management team, they may want to see the monthly sales growth, total customer engagement, total number of visits, and total sales by products and costs of new customer acquisition. Table 3.3 provides an example of different target KPIs for different teams in omnichannel retailing.

Return on investment (ROI) is the monetary return a retailer gets back from an investment. ROI is an important indicator for retail upper management when deciding where to allocate operation and marketing budget. In the following chapters, we will discuss more about the ROI in different channels and how to use ROI to evaluate the outcomes of retail businesses. The concept can be expressed by the following calculation formula:

$$[(\text{Sales generated} - \text{Money invested}) \div \text{Money invested}] \times 100.$$

In summary, omnichannel retailers must establish SMART goals and clearly identify the KPIs that will be used to measure the omnichannel customer experience. By having measurable outcomes, managers can make the necessary changes to enhance the customer journey.

Step 5: Make Necessary Changes to Improve the Customer's Journey

Omnichannel retailing focuses on providing a seamless shopping experience for customers across all channels, including brick-and-mortar stores, online platforms, social media, mobile apps, etc. To improve a customer's shopping journey, retailers must make necessary changes to enhance the customer experience.

One key strategy of omnichannel retailing is to integrate the different channels and provide consistent messaging and branding throughout. By ensuring that the product information, pricing, and promotions are consistent across all channels, the customer is more likely to have a positive experience and form a long-term loyalty to the brand. By collecting data on customer preferences,

Table 3.3 Different Departments and Their Targeted KPIs

SALES AND MARKETING TEAM	CONTENT TEAM	MANAGEMENT TEAM
• Total sales • Average order value • Conversions • Conversion rates • Conversion rates by product or category • Total number of engaged visitors • Conversion rates by demographics • Customer lifetime value • Lead value	• Total traffic • Traffic by source • Top landing pages • Page views • Engagement rate per page/video • Conversion rate by page	• Month-over-month traffic, sales, or list growth • Total customer engagement • Conversion rate • Total sales by product category • Cost of customer acquisition

purchase history, and behavior, retailers can offer personalized recommendations and promotions tailored to the individual's needs and preferences. For example, a clothing retailer could use data to suggest outfits based on the customer's previous purchases or offer discounts on products that complement the customer's current wardrobe.

According to Harvard Business Review, there are four key capabilities that are essential for creating successful customer journeys. These capabilities include 1) automation to ensure smooth navigation through each step of the online path, 2) personalization to create a unique and customized experience for each customer, 3) contextual interaction to engage customers and guide them through the journey, and 4) journey innovation to continually enhance and extend the journey and promote customer loyalty. Furthermore, the most successful companies have a specific organizational structure that includes a chief experience officer who oversees a strategist with a focus on customer journeys, as well as a journey product manager. The journey product manager is responsible for leading a team of designers, developers, data analysts, marketers, and other professionals to create and maintain exceptional customer journeys. They are also accountable for the journey's ROI and general business performance.[36]

Overall, by implementing these strategies, retailers can improve customers' shopping journeys, increase customer satisfaction and loyalty, and ultimately facilitate the so-called "Buy, Own, and Repeat" cycle.[37] During the global pandemic, many fashion businesses created omnichannel services such as BOPIS or online purchase return in-store in order to enhance omnichannel customer experiences. In the next chapter, we will discuss strategies of how to implement omnichannel strategies for fashion brands.

CASE STUDY 3.1

Omnichannel Retailing by Creating Engaging Online Content

Ralph Lauren is no stranger to creating digital content to engage their customers. They have made shoppable movies, animated storybooks, and interactive store windows to impress their customers. In 2020, Ralph Lauren partnered with Snapchat to create a virtual wardrobe for Bitmoji, an application of Snapchat in which users can create avatars of themselves. Ralph Lauren offered twelve branded Ralph Lauren customizable items in the virtual wardrobe that were also shoppable through Ralph Lauren retail stores and through Snapchat collaborations. In two months, over 10 million users dressed their avatars in Ralph Lauren outfits and tried on the collection more than 250 million times.[38] Patrice Louvet, CEO of Ralph Lauren, said they have leveraged web analytics to inform their business strategies, including shifting towards delivering unique consumer experiences in the context of D2C format instead of wholesale.[39]

Moreover, during the 2020 pandemic, most retailers had to close or limit their store operation hours. Ralph Lauren offered an immersive virtual store experience that featured their flagship stores in Hong Kong, New York, Los Angeles, and Paris.[40] Consider a screenshot of the virtual store experience on their website featuring their physical store in West Broadway, New York. Customers can use the navigation sign on the floor to move inside the virtual store and click the product images in an immersive view to see the product details or check out the product on the Ralph Lauren website. They also rolled out a virtual shoppable game with its signature Polo Bear, called The Holiday Run. In the game, the Polo Bear races to a Ralph Lauren store to collect holiday gifts and find new products. The game can be downloaded globally on Ralph Lauren's website and through Instant Games on Facebook Messenger.

Discussion Questions:

1. Do you like Ralph Lauren's approach to using digital content to engage their customers? Why or why not?
2. What type(s) of customer do you think Ralph Lauren developed this content/campaign for?
3. Go to Ralph Lauren's website or social media channels and examine their content. Can you give some examples of the content strategies we have discussed in this chapter?
4. Define a target customer persona for Ralph Lauren and give an example of the customer's shopping journey.
5. If you were the marketing director of Ralph Lauren, what other strategies/campaigns would you develop for them? Why?

CASE STUDY 3.2

Adidas Group Uses Emails to Assist Customers' Shopping Journey

Adidas is a multinational athletic corporation that designs and manufactures footwear, clothing, and accessories. Let's learn about how they use emails to assist their customers through their omnichannel shopping journey. Adidas Group (Adidas-Salomon AG back then) acquired Reebok for $3.8 billion in 2006. With net sales of €23.64 billion in 2019 and €19.84 billion in 2020,[41] they are the largest sportswear manufacturer in Europe and the second largest in the world after Nike. This company sets a guiding business strategy of "'Owning the Game' for the period until 2025" through "increasing brand credibility, elevating the experience for our consumer, and pushing the boundaries in sustainability."[42]

Now, let's have a close look at their email marketing strategy to appeal to new subscribers. Once you sign up to subscribe to their emails and newsletter, you receive a welcome email as a new subscriber. In that email, the company informs the subscriber that they have unlocked enough points for an exclusive product with an opportunity to customize their shoes.

The following email Adidas sends is a request for the subscriber to personalize their email and product preferences. This is another step they are taking to request more details from their subscribers to understand their needs and wants. In this second email, they do not miss an opportunity to promote their mobile app by providing a link to download it. Adidas clearly understands and is eager to track the customer's browsing behavior to personalize the product offerings to the customer via email or push notifications via mobile app.

After a customer makes a purchase in any of their omnichannel touchpoints, Adidas sends an email two weeks later asking for feedback on the product. The company continues to send emails that match the stated preferences for specific deals to the store. Adidas never misses any opportunities to gather and learn about their customers. Also, by asking for the customer's feedback, they gently let the customer know that they are interested in the post-purchase satisfaction of the shoes or apparel that the customer bought. This is an excellent example of utilizing automated email communication, which clearly shows a human touch.

Another excellent example of Adidas' take on re-engaging with customers is through rescuing abandoned carts by email communication. They sent an email reminder with a dollop of humor with a headline saying, "*Is your Wi-Fi okay?*" The message is fun and quirky. Along with their wit, they also share the reviews posted by fellow community members to generate cross-selling opportunities for their products.

Discussion Questions:

1. How does Adidas use email marketing to deepen their understanding of their customers?
2. Discuss the effectiveness of the timing of email communication with their customers.
3. Are there other ways to engage customers when they abandon their shopping carts?

Career Opportunities

Job Titles	Key Responsibility
Assistant Digital Merchandiser /	Pre-Season Planning: Partner with Merchants to understand overall product strategy and launches per season. Ideate on digital shop experiences in alignment with Brand priorities and financial plans. **Daily responsibilities** Performs daily optimizations to Digital Store based on performance (via Digital KPIs), Brand updates, and product sell through optimizing product pages and updating navigation to improve key performance metrics of Digital store. Accountable for product launching on the site on time and with all applicable selling information (Images, Copy, Color Names, etc.) and ensures it is merchandised and searchable in all equivalent locations cross- site. Liaises with Planning and Merchants to understand impacts of inventory shifts to floor set and other updates in strategy and sell performance from test reads, customer feedback or store learnings. – Champions digital evolution within category (new technology and site enhancement testing, etc.). – Pulls reporting and performs analysis to make recommendations for the future to the Manager. – Supports Manager in executing, troubleshooting, and optimizing offers in collaboration with peers and develops the customer experience strategy. – Maps the shopper's journey through the shopping funnel. – Partners with Marketing team to validate daily email distribution and linking strategy, attending email strategy meetings, and flagging discrepancies and making recommendations. – Collaborates with Digital Site Operations Production partners for daily business needs. **Qualifications** 1–3 years of Retail experience within a Digital merchandising/e-commerce function Bachelor's degree or equivalent experience required Must be proficient in Microsoft Excel Team player/Detail oriented/Ability to collaborate up, down, and across the organization; Highly motivated; Consistent in work ethic; Fashion sense; Commitment to quality; Open to learning

Summary

Omnichannel shopping has become a standard in retail, but technology and innovation are pushing the evolution even further. Moving from multichannel retail to an integrated omnichannel approach has led to a smoother and more efficient shopping experience for customers. The next stage of the journey is to move towards a fully functioning omnichannel retail ecosystem. Putting consumers at the center of retail operations is essential for omnichannel retailers. To achieve this, it's imperative to understand how consumers make purchase decisions and how retailers can help them navigate their shopping journey. In this chapter, we introduced the five-stage shopping journey in consumers' decision-making process, discussed the key factors for promoting and preventing omnichannel customer experiences, and have shown you how to identify problems using customer journey mapping.

The five stages of the omnichannel consumer experience are awareness, evaluation, purchase (conversion), post-purchase, and retention. To provide a great omnichannel experience, consistency, convenience, agility, and relevance are crucial. Integrating data from different channels is a challenge for marketers, as without it can lead to inconsistent experiences and a lack of trust.

Meeting customer expectations and creating effective strategies are also key factors in enhancing omnichannel customer experience. Therefore, identifying touchpoints and understanding buyer personas is crucial for omnichannel retailers to deliver personalized interactions. Using a customer journey map, retailers can identify the different stages customers go through when interacting with the company. By implementing these strategies, retailers can improve customers' shopping journeys, increase customer satisfaction and loyalty, and ultimately facilitate the "Buy, Own, and Repeat" cycle.

Key Terms

Average lifespan of a customer
Awareness stage
Buy online, pickup in-store (BOPIS)
Chief experience officer
Conversion rate
Customer journey
Customer lifetime value (CLV)
Digital KPIs
Evaluation stage
Key performance indicator (KPI)
Online calls to action
Pay-per-click (PPC)
Post-purchase stage
Purchase (conversion) stage
Purchase dissonance
Rescuing abandoned carts
Retention stage
Return on investment (ROI)
SMART principles

Reflection and Discussion Questions

1. How can omnichannel retailers effectively use traditional media and online platforms to create awareness about their brands and products?
2. In your opinion, what content strategies can omnichannel retailers use to build trust with new customers during the evaluation stage? Please give an example.
3. The placement of the call to action can have a significant impact on its effectiveness.

Please go online and look for places where customers are most likely to see the call to action and design it accordingly. Some possible placements to consider include:

- homepage of the website
- checkout process
- social media channels
- email marketing campaigns

4. How has the pandemic affected consumer expectations of convenience in the omnichannel customer experience?
5. In your opinion, which of the three factors discussed (consistency, convenience, agility) do you think is the most important for building customer loyalty? Why?
6. Have you ever had a positive or negative experience with an omnichannel retailer? How did their consistency, convenience, and agility (or lack thereof) impact your experience?
7. Do you think that retailers should prioritize investing in new technologies (such as AI, augmented reality [AR], etc.) to enhance the omnichannel experience, or focus more on improving the consistency, convenience, and agility of their existing channels? Why?
8. What are the key components of a buyer persona, and why is it important to create one?
9. Explain how a retailer can find ideas of content to develop a more specific connection between their buyer persona and the content they need.
10. What are the different stages of the consumer decision process in a customer journey map, and why is it important to identify them?

PART 2

Omnichannel Operations

In Part 2, the operational side of the omnichannel retail business will be introduced in Chapters 4 to 8. We delve into the intricacies of implementing omnichannel strategies within the retail landscape. This part also provides a holistic view, covering cross-channel integration, supply chain management, promotional techniques, and customer service approaches specifically tailored for the omnichannel environment. Comprising five chapters, Part 2 offers valuable insights into how omnichannel retailers navigate the dynamic world of modern commerce.

CHAPTER 4

Implementing Omnichannel Strategies

Learning Objectives

Upon finishing this chapter, you will be able to:

- Assess the basic and additional operational considerations for an omnichannel retailing website
- Estimate the factors involved in implementing e-commerce and brick-and-mortar channels
- Explain the process of choosing an appropriate digital platform for omnichannel presences
- Identify the important considerations of using a mobile website or a mobile application
- Devise how businesses integrate brick-and-mortar stores, websites, social accounts, mobile applications, and catalogs to provide omnichannel services

In this chapter, we will discuss how retailers expand their retail presence into the online and offline channels from two angles. First, we will examine the different approaches to how a brick-and-mortar store could expand their reach to the online environment. For instance, how to establish various online presences such as websites, mobile apps, and social media accounts. Following that, we will discuss how emerging direct-to-consumer (D2C) retailers may start their business online and then decide to expand their reach to brick-and-mortar stores as a sustainable growth strategy.

Traditional Retailers Migrating into E-Commerce Websites

Since the 1990s, the growing use of personal computers and internet penetration has moved most single-channel brick-and-mortar retailers to develop their websites in order to take online orders. Building a website is much easier now than it was just a decade ago. For most omnichannel retailers, it is more important to keep their websites updated so that customers can find the current products they want and return for new products and inspiration. For new designer brands or startups, many e-commerce website builders offer user-friendly interfaces for brands to create their websites from pre-existing templates. For instance, direct-to-consumer (D2C) brands have chosen website designs from numerous templates created for various business types and goals. These templates vary in terms of content width, header layout, navigation design, logo placement, overall usability, and user experience. In this section, we will discuss the basic and additional operation considerations for omnichannel retailing websites, should a retailer choose an in-house or third-party platform to develop their websites. Moreover, we will discuss the three dimensions of evaluating a website to see if it delivers good consumer experiences, namely, appearance, usability, and speed.

Basic Operation Features

An omnichannel retail website should include 1) selling and logistic integration such as shopping cart, shipping services, payment services, and **point of sale (POS)** systems and 2) marketing integrations such as **search engine optimization (SEO)** tools, email marketing tools, social media integration, and coupons, to allow the retailers to sell on multiple channels and deliver a seamless customer experience. Depending on the customer volume your company serves and your budget, there are different types of platforms you can consider. Shopify (www.shopify.com), Wix (www.wix.com), and Big Commerce.com (www.bigcommerce.com) are some examples of these website building/hosting platforms. Table 4.1 is a comparison of some top retail website-building platforms regarding transaction fees, sales features, abandoned cart recovery features, number of products on the lowest pricing plan, payment options, etc. The price of using these platforms can be less than $30 per month, which is an economical solution for startup D2C brands.

Additional Operation Options

For additional operation functions, some website platforms incorporate third-party apps such as product sourcing, channel analysis features to let omnichannel retailers analyze their online traffic, social sharing to help with the customer decision and create buzz, counting down timer to create a sense of urgency, etc. Other special features on Wix.com include offering multilingual sites that can help business owners grow their businesses in different countries by creating multiple sites. The Shopify Lite program allows brands to sell their products directly on Facebook, without even creating a website. Consumers will not be forced to leave the Facebook Messenger app to make purchases. It also allows brands to provide automated customer support through the Facebook Messenger app. Retailers who use website hosting sites like Big Commerce, Salesforce Commerce Cloud, and Shopify can also promote shoppable content on the trendy social media platform TikTok.[1]

In-House versus Third-Party Platform Development and Operation

There are pros and cons to creating your website either in-house or via a third-party platform. Developing your site in-house gives you more control over its design and functionality. However, it can be more expensive and time-consuming than using a third-party platform. Using a third-party platform can be more cost-effective and quicker to set up. However, you may have less control over the design and functionality of your site. For small stores that are just trying to reach their base customer directly, this is a great way to start their business without investing too much in building and maintaining the websites. If you decide to build a website from a pre-made template, the prices of the themes can vary from a few bucks to a couple of thousand dollars, depending on the aesthetics and functionality. You may also hire a professional to build a website for you. Many website builder platforms offer suggestions for professional website builders on their platforms.

Ultimately, the decision depends on your business needs and resources. If you have the budget and expertise to develop your site in-house, it may be the best option for you. If you're looking for a more cost-effective solution or don't have the resources to develop your site in-house, a third-party platform may be a better fit.

Select a Website Domain Name

After choosing a platform to host your website, you need to select a domain name. A domain name is like the physical address of your store. It should be easy to remember, concise, and represent your brand. Avoid using a name that is long, hard to spell, or too close to another brand. If your domain name is long or too hard to spell, you won't be able to acquire much direct traffic. If your domain name is similar to another brand, people might mistake your brand for a knockoff. This similarity could lead to legal issues like trademark infringement. If your brand is a service brand that provides services in a certain area, you can include the location of your brand and domain name to increase your website ranking in the search results. To make sure your domain name is user-friendly, try to type it out on different types of devices (e.g., PCs, laptops, mobile phones) to see if there are any unexpected inconveniences. For instance, people find that domain names that include the dash(-) symbol or numbers increase the difficulty of typing as it will require users to switch to a second keyboard with numbers and symbols on mobile devices. Finding a good domain name is not an easy job, and it usually requires a solid amount of effort, but the earlier you decide on your domain name, the better, as you will be able to include the domain name in all your marketing materials.

You can use tools like LeanDomainSearch (https://leandomainsearch.com/) to find out if your domain name has been registered. If the brand name you have in mind has already been registered, you may use the domain name generator function to find a website domain name. If your company is located in the United States, you may also use the Trademark Electronic Search System (TESS), http://tmsearch.uspto.gov, to perform a basic word mark search to see if your brand name has been registered with the United States Patent and Trademark Office (USPTO). It is usually more difficult trying to fit a domain name with an existing business. Given the fact that most consumers now conduct an online search before they make a purchase, for a new company that is choosing a name for their business, consider registering a domain name at the same time. If you would like to know more about the different types of trademarks and their strength, see Chapter 9, Table 9.1 Types of Trademarks in Order of Strength of Mark.

Considerations When Building a Website

There are three major dimensions when it comes to building a website. The first dimension is appearance, the second dimension is usability, and the third dimension is speed. We break down the factors and importance of each dimension in the following section. We also provide some useful online tools below for you to implement when you design (or re-design) your website presence. Next, we will first discuss the appearance dimension.

Appearance

Appearance is a very important element of website design, as it is the first dimension that consumers see and process, thus setting the tone for how the brand is perceived as a whole. A well-designed website with high-quality visuals can convey a trustworthy perception, while an overly crowded website with low-quality images may drive customers away from the site. The homepage, also known as the main page, is the initial page the user is brought to when visiting a website. The homepage address only contains the domain name (e.g., www.Amazon.com). The goal of the homepage is not only to welcome customers to the website, but also to entice them to dig deeper into the website's content. A worthy homepage can create a respectable first impression of your brand. The major product/service categories should be displayed on the homepage's main navigation

Table 4.1 Selected Website Builder Platforms and Features

WIX	SHOPIFY	BIG COMMERCE
Starting Price: $27/month	Starting Price: $29/month	Starting Price: $29/month
Transaction Fees	Transaction Fees	Transaction Fees
2.9%+$0.30	2.9%+$0.30	None
Free plan or free trial	Free plan or free trial	Free plan or free trial
Free plan	3-day free trial, then first months for $1/month	14-day free trial
Abandoned cart recovery	Abandoned cart recovery	Abandoned cart recovery
Yes	Yes	Yes
Bandwidth	Bandwidth	Bandwidth
Unlimited	Unlimited	Unlimited
Storage space	Storage space	Storage space
20GB–50GB	Unlimited	Unlimited
Number of products on cheapest plan	Number of products on cheapest plan	Number of products on cheapest plan
Unlimited	Unlimited	Unlimited
Payment options examples	Payment options examples	Payment options examples
Paypal, Wix Payments, Stripe, Square	Shopify Payments, Paypal, Klarna	Paypal, Square, Stripe, Klarna

(*Source*: adapted from https://www.websitebuilderexpert.com/ecommerce-website-builders/best/)

and remain in the same position as the user navigates across different pages within the website. Following conventions on website design and keeping consistency (across different web pages and devices) are two essential aspects of evaluating a website's appearance.

Website Convention

In English and most phonetic language-speaking countries, people read from left to right and top to bottom. Therefore, the website convention typically places the brand logo in the top left corner or center position of the page to catch the eye of the consumer. Moreover, the navigation bar is usually placed at the top or left-hand side of the page. However, for countries whose language reads from right to left, such as Arabic or Hebrew, the logo and navigation bar should be aligned to the right side of the page. Following the convention of web design can help your consumers quickly navigate your website without having to waste time and effort learning how your website works. While creativity in website design is beneficial, if the designer's effort to be creative diminishes the effectiveness of the website by not following conventions, users may have trouble navigating the website.

Consistency

Color scheme: Color scheme is the first visual indicator of a website's quality. As the business grows, you may add more product pages to your website. A common error made by many companies is that, as they add new elements to the newly developed web pages, they forget to update the previously created pages (such as contact information, return policy, etc.) containing older visual elements. When multiple employees are responsible for maintaining the website design, it is likely that someone may use an old visual element or make the addition of a new visual element with slight differences by accident. It is essential that these visual elements are defined in one central place, such as a team-accessible folder, and used consistently across the website.

Images and page layout: Without the ability to examine products physically, images and videos are important tools for customers to quickly learn about your product. Avoid having different product pictures or photo styles from page to page. The positioning of the page layout needs to be consistent across all product categories on your website. Create a layout template and keep your website design within these barriers for all pages.

For example, if the product name and description are arranged on the right side of the page, do not abruptly change it to the left side of the page. Consistent product images in terms of size, style, and quality can convey a sense of trust, and consumers may feel confused if they see inconsistent images or page layouts.

Navigation: Consistency in the position of a website's navigation tools presents an important anchor to help customers stay on track with their shopping tasks. According to a study by the user design research firm Nielsen/Norman Group,[2] navigation buttons are more important for a mobile interface than for a desktop interface. A navigation button is an icon used on a mobile website that, when clicked, opens to reveal a navigation menu. It is commonly represented as a stack of three horizontal bars resembling a hamburger. Therefore, hiding navigation buttons like hamburger menus decreases content discoverability by 21 percent on a desktop computer and may evoke a feeling of frustration that causes consumers to feel lost on the website. Most consumers today have developed an expectation of where the navigation tools should be on web pages and how to interact with them. The best practice regarding navigation placement in web design requires that brands maintain internal consistency of navigation tools (like always floating on the top of the window) to increase the predictability and perceived ease of use.

Consistency across Devices—Mobile-First Design versus Responsive Design

It is hard to deny that we are moving into a mobile society. In 2016, mobile users surpassed desktop users. Globally, approximately 55 percent of total internet traffic comes from mobile phones, and people are spending more time on mobile devices. In 2019, around 80 percent of worldwide users accessed their social media via mobile phone only, while only 2 percent of users used solely their laptop or desktop computers to access social media platforms.[3] With this trend, Google has announced that they will fully use a "mobile-first" indexing method as the default ranking algorithm from September 2020.[4] They will provide search ranking results for all sites based on the mobile content of their websites. Therefore, for any website that wants a higher search result ranking, the mobile-first design is essential for delivering the best search engine optimization (SEO) results.

First introduced by Luke Wroblewski in 2009, **mobile-first design** is the strategy of building your website for mobile devices before developing the desktop version. Mobile-first design is based on a strategy called progressive enhancement, which suggests that it is easier to begin with a simple prototype, in this case, a mobile page, and continue to add and adjust content to conform to the larger and more complex device formats such as desktops or tablets, rather than vice versa. When using the mobile-first strategy to create a website, the first step is to carefully analyze the website content and structure the website to deliver the best user experience on mobile devices. This may require a significant amount of time and preparation in the production of the first design; however, you will be able to determine the essential content and functions needed for your website, and effectively deliver a valuable user experience through mobile devices by using this process. Once the mobile version is completed, you may add additional layers of design to satisfy the needs of users who are viewing the website on larger screens. For companies who expect the majority of their website traffic to come from mobile devices, the mobile-first design approach is the most suitable and effective strategy to be implemented.

The pros of mobile-first design include the ability to access more web users, as well as its potential to be more cost-efficient. As the majority of internet browsing now takes place on smartphones, the mobile-first design allows a website to embed phone features such as camera access, texting, and direct calling. The mobile-first design proves to be more cost-efficient because it typically costs less than developing mobile apps. The cons of mobile-first design are that the desktop experience may not be optimized. For example, if your website contains a heavy amount of content (like blogs, heavy product specification information, etc.), or the majority of your customer base uses a desktop to access your website, then the mobile-first design may not be suitable for your business. Figure 4.1 illustrates examples of mobile-first design and responsive design on various sizes of screens.

Responsive design is also called adaptive design. First coined by Ethan Marcotte, a web designer whose clients include *New York Magazine*, the Sundance Film Festival, and Google, in 2010, responsive design is a technique that suggests automatically adjusting a website design based on the size of the user's screens.[5] It allows a company to create one website with the ability to be adjusted in order to suit the format of various devices and browsers. Therefore, companies don't

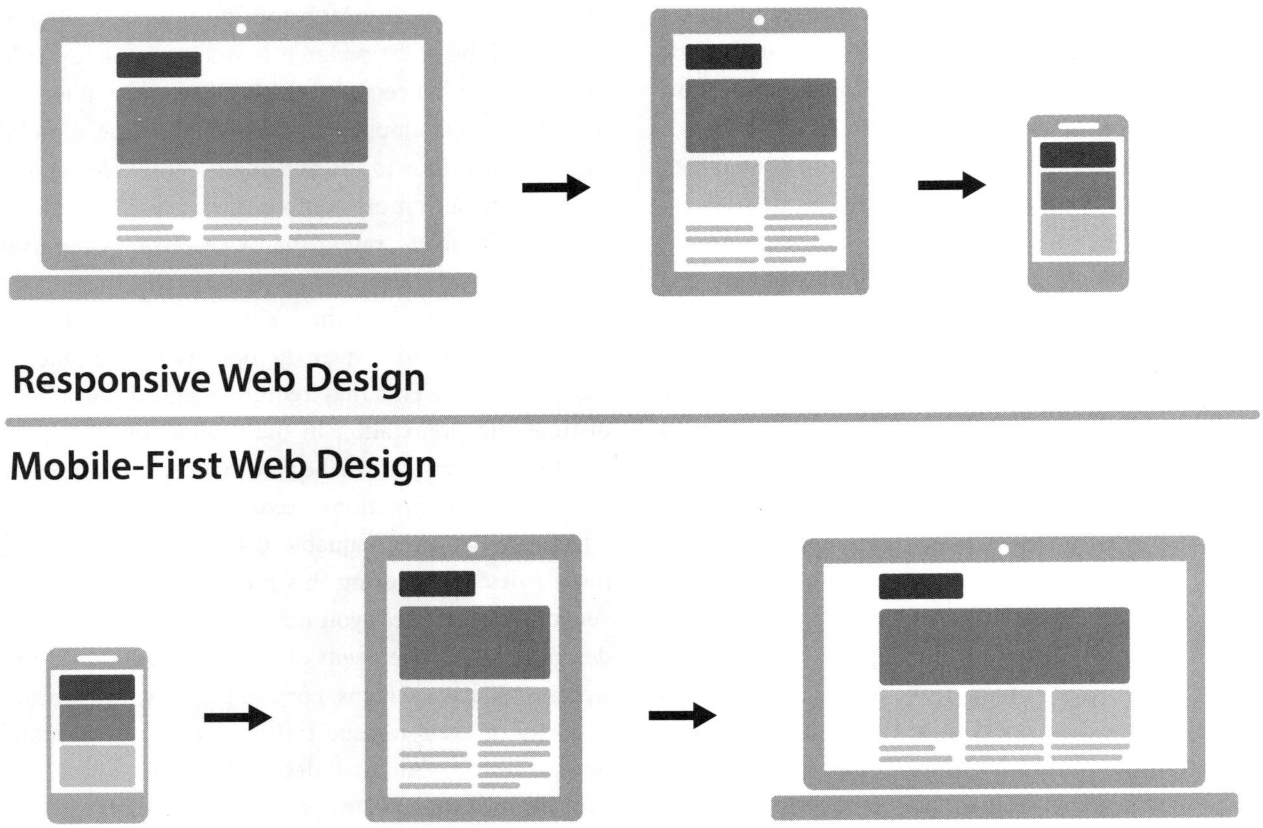

Figure 4.1 Example of responsive design and mobile-first design

need to maintain two versions (a desktop version and a mobile version) of their website. The design philosophy of responsive design is called graceful degradation, meaning that retailers build a website that works in the newest browsers but falls back to a simplified version in older browsers—although it is not as good as the original version, it still delivers essential content and functionality. This is a great approach for when it is unknown what devices customers will use to access the website or when the business must have a desktop website for B2B customers since most B2B business transactions are conducted on desktop or laptop computers. Given the important role of mobile devices today, even if the responsive design approach is used to develop a website, checking for the proper display and functionality of a website on various mobile screens remains crucial.

There are three main pros of using the responsive design method, including cost efficiency, capacity for complex transactions, and suitability for information-heavy content. Responsive design tends to be more cost-effective than mobile-first design, as it requires fewer website content analysis efforts than mobile-first design. In addition, responsive design can better accommodate complex calls to action, such as an order that requires multiple entry information (e.g., body measurements and text). Responsive design is a more suitable alternative for information-oriented websites, as your customers may feel it will be more enjoyable to browse your website from a desktop device if the site contains large quantities of information. However, the downside of using responsive design is that the mobile experience may not be fully optimized on mobile devices. For example, a virtual signing tool on a smart device or taking a photo and uploading it to a customer review will be much easier on mobile devices.[6]

Which Design Strategy Should You Choose?

It depends. Before you make the decision to use responsive versus mobile-first design, you should ask yourself two questions: what devices (personal computer [PC] or mobile) do my target customers use to access my website, and what device can deliver the best shopping experience for my customers? You should then choose the design method that can deliver the best **user experience (UX)**, providing customers with the ability to find information quickly, easily search for the products they want, and be able to pay as smoothly as possible. Most consumers won't be able to tell if a website is created using a responsive design or mobile-first strategy, but they will know if the website delivers an enjoyable and seamless shopping experience. If 80 percent of your targeted customers use a desktop to access your website, then you should prioritize optimizing your website experience for desktop users. Most website hosting platforms nowadays provide website analytics reports to give you information regarding how and when your customers access your websites. If you choose to host a website by yourself, applying analytics application, such as Google Analytics, to your website will be useful. There are industry statistics that provide benchmarks for how general technology usage stands among your target market, such as site traffic overview, the traffic sources by device types (desktop versus mobile) and countries, the demographics of site audience, etc.

You may ask what you should do if your website has a 50/50 split on device usage. Look into the trends of device usage among your target market and determine what your business plans to achieve in the next three to five years. Many e-commerce industry reports release yearly or quarterly reports on technology usage and forecasting among different demographic groups (e.g., Gen Z or European market). Last but not least, conducting a consumer focus group to interview your customers and asking them to identify the pain points when they use your website is a great way to directly gather useful information. This leads to our next key principle of website design: Usability.

Usability

Website usability is defined as the level of ease and accessibility presented to visitors upon browsing and interacting with a website. It evaluates how efficient and effective the website is at communicating information with its customers and is often seen as a necessity for retail businesses. Additionally, since retail businesses involve monetary transactions, a retail website must provide a safe and easy process for customers to complete their online transactions in order for retailers to appear legitimate and useful from the consumers' perspective. Therefore, in the following section, we will discuss how to evaluate website usability from the perspective of facilitating consumers' shopping journeys. Retail website usability can be evaluated by using the following approaches: 1) intuitive interface, 2) creating effective visual hierarchies, 3) customer segment, and 4) checkout process.

Intuitive Interface

Studies[7] show that people form a first impression in 500 milliseconds (0.5 seconds) when they are brought to a homepage. The area on the screen that is initially visible before scrolling down on the page is called the "above the fold" area or the "upper fold" area. This area should answer three key questions for your customer: What are you offering? Is there something for me? What do you want me to do next (or "call to action")? Everlane is a direct-to-consumer (D2C) company known for its commitment to transparent pricing and ethical manufacturing. They effectively use their above-the-fold area to answer these three key questions. As shown in Figure 4.2, a website lists the main product navigation in the top-left corner (what their site offers). In the center of the page is their main promotion of the day ("Your sweatpants will be jealous") followed by their famous transparent pricing ("Starting at $48") to answer the second question—Is there something for me? The "Shop Now" button placed directly below provides a clear call to action for visitors.

A simple and minimalist design avoids unnecessary distractions and reduces the cognitive burden of processing too much information at one time. Formatting web content into clearly defined areas not only supports a quick scanning of the content on the website, but also makes the shopper interact with your website more intuitively. By facilitating the product evaluation process, the chance of converting shoppers to buyers is significantly increased. Burberry, a British luxury fashion brand that are renowned for their iconic trench coats and plaid pattern, also utilizes this principle to design their product pages.

Effective Visual Hierarchy

Many fashion websites use a clean page design to convey an elegant brand image and easy-to-navigate user interface (UI). A clear visual hierarchy can guide your customers to quickly navigate your page and find

Figure 4.2 Example of a good homepage design

what they want. For example, French luxury fashion brand Louis Vuitton effectively uses a short video to make the primary message (e.g., new seasonal collection) stand out. Louis Vuitton's iconic LV monogram graces a wide range of products, including luxury bags, leather goods, ready-to-wear, shoes, perfumes, watches, etc. The top portion of the webpage contains the header area. A well-designed header area should include a search box, access to the shopping cart, account login, store location search, etc. The bottom of the page contains the footer area. In the footer area, you can include information related to your company policy, contact information, return policy information, and hiring information. Conducting a website analysis of your major competitors will provide an accurate set of example information to build from when determining what needs to be included in the footer area. Supporting images and short videos are also beneficial in efforts to capture the attention of consumers and evoke positive emotions. In addition, presenting two to three call to action (CTA) buttons (e.g., Discover the campaign, Shop the collection) on the home page will encourage customers to explore more.

Relevancy—Customer Segments

Customers visit websites with their goals in mind. As mentioned at the beginning of this chapter, you need to have a clear idea of who your customers are and what their goals consist of when they come to your website. Interviewing your target customers and creating a customer persona can help in designing a more effective retail interface that fulfills different types of customers' shopping goals in the various stages of the consumer journey (we discussed this in Chapter 3). For example, Vans, a California skateboarding and lifestyle brand, knows that their customers wear their shoes for different kinds of activities and have preferences for different styles of their shoes. Therefore, on their homepage navigation, they have not only the traditional product categories by gender and age (e.g., women, men, kids, etc.), but also options to shop by activity (skate), style (classic), and special services (custom shoes) (Figure 4.3).

Checkout Process

On the other hand, there are certain checkpoints that are known to create a bad shopping experience and should be avoided whenever possible. Globally, e-commerce brands have lost $18 billion to abandoned shopping carts.[8] Marketers have been interested in finding out the reasons why customers will spend time putting products into their shopping cart, then end up abandoning them entirely. A study analyzed 41 cart abandonment reports and found that nearly 70 percent of shoppers abandoned their shopping carts.[9] That means that, on average, seven out of ten people who have spent time shopping on a site and selecting products to add to their shopping cart end up leaving the sites without purchasing anything. A

Figure 4.3 Example of website design by customer segments

recent market report showed that 18 percent of US online shoppers abandoned their shopping cart in the three months analyzed because the checkout process was too long/complicated.[10] Therefore, ensuring that your shopping channel implements an easy and seamless checkout process is one of the most important factors of usability. Figure 4.4 lists the reasons for cart abandonments during the checkout process. A January 2019 survey of online shoppers worldwide revealed that 41 percent of shoppers had abandoned an online shopping cart when the cost of delivery turned out to be higher than anticipated, making it the most common reason for doing so. Notably, nearly 28 percent of the participants said the item was out of stock, which could be avoided if the inventory system could update the information timely so that no shopping time is wasted on picking an already out-of-stock product. This data provides a checklist for retailers to see if they are losing business from a bad checkout experience.[11]

Speed

Speed is a very important factor regarding conversion rate and search ranking. According to Yahoo research, website traffic may be increased by 9 percent if the page load time is reduced by 0.4 seconds. Amazon.com found that a 1-second delay in website speed could cost them $1.6 billion in sales each year. For mobile devices, research shows that 53 percent of mobile site visits are abandoned if the load time exceeds 3 seconds. It is suggested that a website load time should be lower than 1.3 seconds, which is why testing is important to implement prior to launching your website.

Moreover, Google search engine takes bounce rate and conversion rate into account when generating ranking results (SEO efforts). **Bounce rate** is the percentage of visitors to a particular website who only viewed one page divided by all the visitors. **Conversion rate** is calculated as the number of visitors to a website that completed a desired goal (a conversion) out of the total number of visitors.

Website Speed and Conversion Rate

While a slower loading rate loses traffic and sends customers away, it also hurts the conversion rate. As you can imagine, the quicker the loading speed, the more likely the consumer will be to complete their shopping task. Walmart, one of the top omnichannel retailers in the world, saw a 2 percent increase in conversions when they improved their website speed by 1 second.[12] According to Google, a 1-second website speed improvement can increase conversions for mobile users by up to 27 percent.[13] This means that a faster website yields more sales.

Page speed affects SEO. Improving page speed also improves the total traffic and therefore, the conversion rates subsequently.[14] A website ranking will be penalized

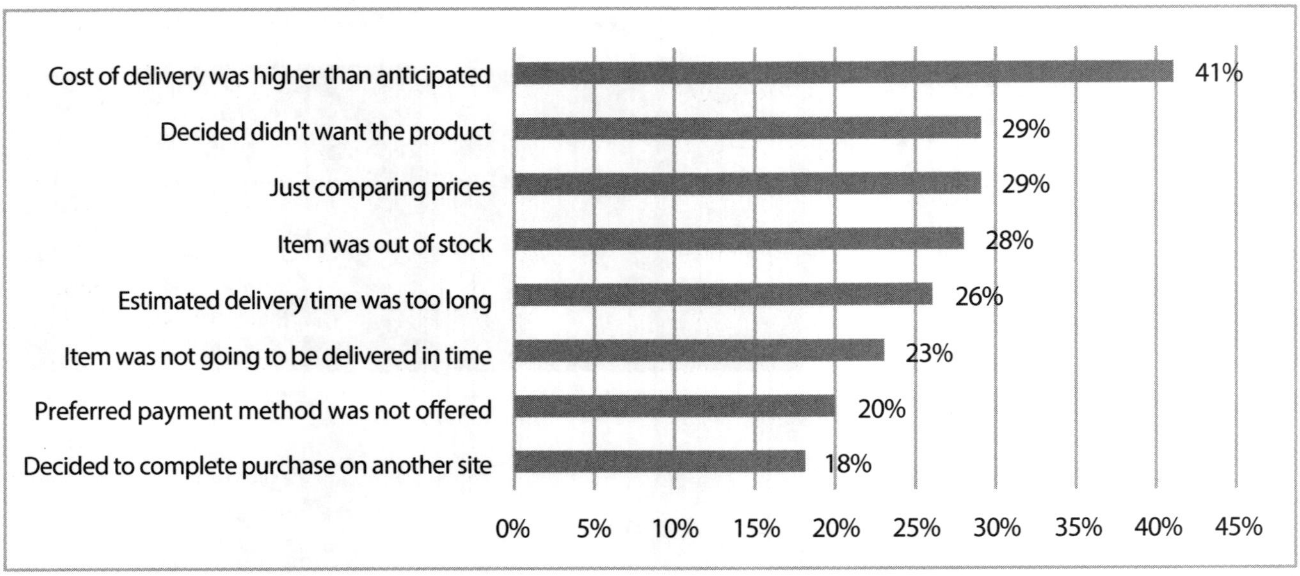

Figure 4.4 Primary reasons for digital shoppers worldwide to abandon their carts during checkout
(*Source*: Statista, 2023)[11]

with a higher bounce rate if caused by a slow loading speed. After the website is developed, it is crucial to perform site speed tests to determine whether the website is performing to its full potential regarding efficiency. If the load time of a website is taking too long, the following ways may improve the loading speed.

How to Optimize Website Loading Speed

Images, files, codes, scripts, and plug-ins are common causes that lead to a slow loading speed, and images are typically the primary cause. There is a trade-off relationship between image quality and loading speed. Images that are larger in size and higher in resolution create a bigger data file, and as size and resolution increase, so does the load time. Resizing the images to be smaller or compressing the files before updating the images can improve load time if images are the leading cause. However, experimenting on which combinations will keep load time low while still presenting a pleasant/quality image is highly encouraged. Google PageSpeed Insights (https://developers.google.com/speed/pagespeed/insights/) is a tool that can be used to help website developers evaluate their website speed and provides directions on how the website can be improved. It produces reports on the performance of a page on both mobile and desktop devices and provides suggestions for how to fix a page's leading issues. For international retailers, Pingdom Tools (https://tools.pingdom.com/) lets you test your website speed in various geographic locations, including most major cities in other countries.

Fashion Retailers to Your Fingertips via Mobile Apps

Leveraging mobile apps in omnichannel retailing provides a multifaceted advantage by seamlessly integrating online and offline experiences. This approach enhances customer engagement, fosters brand loyalty, and drives business growth. Reflecting your personal experience: do you share your mobile with your family or friends? Probably not, correct? With 24/7 accessibility, personalized user experiences, and direct marketing channels, mobile apps contribute to a streamlined purchasing process and real-time updates. They also serve as a powerful tool for loyalty programs and offer a competitive edge through data analytics. By embracing mobile apps, omnichannel retailers create a cohesive and convenient shopping journey, ultimately strengthening customer relationships and establishing a robust presence across diverse channels.

Native Mobile Apps versus Mobile Website

While both native mobile apps and mobile sites can be accessed on mobile devices, they are accessed through different routes. Consumers can pull out a mobile site via browser apps such as Safari, Chrome, Opera, etc. For mobile apps, they will need to download the apps from an Apps Store (iOS system) or from Google Play (Android system) before using the apps.

Native Mobile applications (apps) have some advantages over mobile websites. First, it's easier to offer a personalized experience in mobile apps. Customers can answer some initial questions when they download the apps, and then the content of the app will be customized based on their preferences. Mobile apps also have the advantage of utilizing features that are unique for mobile devices, such as contact lists, cameras, GPS, measurements, compass, etc. Retailers can also provide functions like personalized recommendations, back-to-stock alerts, sharing favorite items with friends on social media, SMS texting, etc., on mobile apps. Omnichannel retailers can track engagement in the app and provide geographic-specific content in real-time such as store suggestions and product suggestions based on the local weather. If retailers are able to offer the right product at the right time, their conversion rate will increase.

Second, apps allow retailers to send out notifications. There are two types of notifications: in-app or push notifications. An **in-app notification** is the notification sent when a customer opens the app; **push notifications** are sent whether a customer opens the app or not. Since customers can choose which type of notifications they would like to receive, it's considered less intrusive. Moreover, according to Accengage's Push Notification Benchmark Report,[15] mobile notification has high reaction rates—a 10.7 percent push notification reaction rate on Android devices and a 4.9 percent push reaction rate on iOS devices. Since brands can monitor their customers' engagement in the app, personalized notifications can be sent out based on customers' app usage patterns (choosing times/days in a week when customers are likely to interact with the apps).

However, mobile sites have some advantages over native mobile apps. First, developing a mobile app can cost more than a responsive mobile website. Depending on what mobile devices your customers use, you may need to develop mobile apps for both Android and Apple's iOS platforms. In addition to the development fee, Apple App Store charges a $99 annual developer fee, and Google Play charges a one-time fee of $25. Second, a mobile site presents a broader reach than an app as it does not require the steps of searching the app name and downloading the app on mobile devices before using it. Third, it is easier to do search engine optimization (SEO) and promote your brand via search ads. For small retailers, if your business objective is to offer an interactive shopping experience and you want to use uniquely engaging features to drive your customer loyalty, then you should choose the native mobile app approach. If your goal is to reach a wide range of people and you want to increase your brand visibility, then a mobile website would be a better choice. Table 4.2 lists the advantages that mobile apps and mobile sites have over each other.

Examples of Mobile Applications in Omnichannel Retailing

In the following section, we will discuss how ASOS, Nike, and Sephora used their mobile apps to provide engaging shopping experiences, easy check out process, and cross-channel services.

ASOS

Augmented reality (AR) is a technology that superimposes a computer-generated image on a user's view of real environment. ASOS is a British online fashion and beauty retailer known for its wide selection of trendy clothing, accessories, and cosmetics. ASOS tested an AR experience called Virtual Catwalk on its 100 ASOS design products using their mobile app.[16] The feature allows ASOS customers to view an augmented video of models

Table 4.2 Mobile Apps Versus Mobile Sites

ADVANTAGES OF MOBILE APPS	ADVANTAGES OF MOBILE SITES
• Better performance • Personalized experience • Leverage device capabilities • Can be used offline • Great for services that require regular uses	• Cost-effective • Broader audience reach • SEO and brand visibility • Great for public communication and marketing endeavors

wearing the products and walking in the customers' real surroundings. During the trial, more than 150,000 ASOS customers tried "Virtual Catwalk" (Figure 4.5). Warby Parker, a US direct-to-consumer eyewear brand, utilized AR technology to let customers virtually try on their sunglasses via their smartphone camera.

The Nike App

Nike has introduced a mobile app[17] that can recognize customers immediately upon entering brick-and-mortar stores. The app allows customers to scan a product to find availability in the area, provides an in-store mobile checkout option, and gives the option to reserve products in-store for try-ons before purchasing. Mark Parker, the CEO of NIKE, claims that the app provides "seamless, frictionless shopping," and Nike continues to expand and improve their business model to stay ahead of the competition.

Sephora

Through market research, Sephora found that their customers commonly search for information about customer reviews, tips for using the beauty products, and recommendations from social influencers when they shop in stores. Since 2016, Sephora has launched the Sephora retail mobile apps such as Sephora: Makeup and Skincare, Sephora Corporate Events, etc. to provide shoppers with the latest trends and new releases of beauty products, exclusive offers and deals, and virtual try-on for eye, cheek, and lip makeup products. Sephora customers can redeem their points for Beauty Insider Cash or samples via the app.

Figure 4.5 ASOS launched an augmented reality feature, Virtual Catwalk, on their mobile app
(*Source*: https://www.theindustry.fashion/asos-steps-into-augmented-reality-with-virtual-catwalk/)

Social Commerce: Social Media Platforms for Selling Products

According to a Sprout Social report, 68 percent of consumers made at least one purchase directly from social media in 2021. Facebook Shops, Instagram Shopping, and TikTok Shopping are some of the most popular social media platforms for omnichannel retailers.

Facebook

Facebook is the most used social media platform in the world, with roughly 1.79 billion monthly active users. In 2023, Facebook accounted for over 53 percent of all social media traffic in the United States.[18] Facebook's appeal is not only based on its wide audiences but also on its strong mobile integration and Facebook Messenger app. Facebook provides specific tools exclusively for Business pages to help improve results (https://www.facebook.com/business/m/facebook-business-page).[19] There are several ways to sell on Facebook:

- Facebook Shop: If you have an e-commerce website, you can use Facebook Shop to integrate your products directly into Facebook. This allows users to browse and purchase your products without leaving the platform.
- Facebook Live: You can use Facebook Live to showcase your product or service in real time. This allows potential buyers to see your product in action and ask any questions they may have. You can also offer special promotions or discounts to viewers.
- Facebook Marketplace: This is a free platform that allows you to buy and sell items with people in your local community. You can create a listing for your product or service, set a price, and negotiate with potential buyers. Facebook Marketplace is a great option for selling physical products such as clothing, furniture, and electronics.
- Facebook groups: You can join or create a Facebook group specifically for your product or service. This allows you to connect with potential buyers who have a specific interest in what you are selling. You can also use Facebook Groups to answer questions and provide customer service.

Facebook's Page Insights tool can help brands understand the people who are following and taking action on their page. This analytical tool provides additional insight into who your target audience is and the content engagements. For omnichannel retailers who mainly use Facebook and Instagram for social media marketing, Facebook also offers a tool called Business Suite (www.facebook.com/business/facebook-business-suite) to manage Facebook, Instagram, and Messenger accounts in one place. Retailers can also run various personalized ads targeting audiences with similar demographics or habits to the brand's current customers (Facebook calls this feature Lookalike Audience).[20]

As mentioned in Chapter 1, online live-streaming shopping has been popular in the Asia Pacific area for several years, and US consumers are recently following suit. ASOS, a British online fashion brand, went live with "100 layers of ASOS," a short contest between ASOS staff members where they had 30 minutes to create a look for their models—using 100 layers of ASOS clothing to dramatic effect to engage their followers.

Instagram

As one of the leading social networks worldwide, Instagram is an important platform for omnichannel retailers. Accordingly to Pew Research, 78 percent of US adults use Instagram, which makes the platform especially important for the companies who target the millennial and Gen Z population.[21] Starting as a photo-sharing social network service, Instagram offers opportunities for fashion brands to reach their current and inspired customers, manage their reputation, and positively shape their brand image on social media. In 2020, Instagram introduced the Instagram Shop feature, which allows users to purchase items without leaving the app (i.e., Instagram Checkout). Brands can curate a list of shoppable products directly accessible through the "View Shop" button on their Instagram profile page.

In addition to Shop, brands can use Instagram's Posts, Reels (short-form-video), Stories, Highlights, and IGTV (long-form-video) to engage with their fan communities. Aware of this opportunity, almost all fashion, beauty, watches, and jewelry brands (96 to 98 percent) have an Instagram account.[22] For instance, Chanel, the French high-fashion powerhouse, is the leading luxury brand on Instagram, with 59.8 million followers as of January 2024.[23] Louis Vuitton—with 55.2 million followers as of January 2024, is the second most-followed luxury brand. Gucci, known for its horse-bit loafer and Italian leather goods, is the third most-followed luxury brand with 52.3 million followers on Instagram.[24] Dior, Dolce & Gabbana, Prada, Versace, Burberry, and Michael Kors also have a strong presence on the platform, as all these luxury brands have over 16 million followers on Instagram.

As a social media, Instagram is not only valuable for fashion and beauty brands; it is also a powerful platform for celebrity endorsements and engaging social influencers. Singers such as Ariana Grande, Selena Gomez, Beyoncé, and television personalities and socialites Kylie Jenner and Kim Kardashian West are some of the most followed Instagram accounts worldwide.[25] Instagram has an active US audience of 127 million monthly active users.[26] With so many celebrity influencers and users, Instagram is also a perfect platform for social media influencer marketing. We will discuss more details about social influencer marketing in Chapter 7.

TikTok

The social media platform TikTok, an app whose content revolves around 15- to 60-second videos and a loyal following of teens, has experienced an explosion in popularity in recent years. It has 65.9 million monthly active users in the United States. In 2020, TikTok became the first non-Facebook mobile app to reach 3 billion downloads globally. Although TikTok is still in the early stages of monetization, brands have been using hashtag challenges and user-generated content to create buzz and go viral. According to Vogue, "Fashion and beauty brands have drawn billions of views by sponsoring hashtag challenges that encourage users to submit video responses."[27] The same article notes that there is some evidence from an independent brand awareness study that TikTok videos lead to better brand recall. TikTok has become one of the most crucial areas for brands to understand and utilize to successfully reach today's teenage consumers.

MAC Cosmetics launched its first TikTok campaign, a hashtag challenge called #YouOwnIt, in 2019 during the New York Fashion Week. The result was a stunning 1.5 billion views in six days, the highest amount recorded for a TikTok campaign over a similar period. Fashion brands that have seen success on the platform include PrettyLittleThing (1.6 million followers) and Fashion Nova (2.6 million followers). PrettyLittleThing has relied on the authentic and relatable content that has made TikTok so popular. Their feed is almost entirely user-generated content. As TikTok encourages brands to loosen creative control and lead with authenticity on the platform, PrettyLittleThing posts videos of customers featuring their clothes in fun and inventive ways, and it has helped the brand to grow its following to 1.6 million. User giveaways, outfit challenges, look books and influencer marketing are the most commonly used ways to grow audiences on TikTok. In August 2021, TikTok and Shopify announced a partnership that would bring shopping capabilities to the video-sharing app in a move that leverages its highly specific algorithm.[28] The collaboration presents a great opportunity for fashion retailers and influencers to capture the sales opportunities on this popular platform. Case Study 4.2 discusses TikTok, its young audience, and fashion brands.

Pinterest

Pinterest has a monthly active user base of 335 million, with 88 million in the United States alone. The platform is used primarily as a discovery platform for refining and discovering personal styles. In terms of demographics, Pinterest has a predominately female audience (US: 70 percent; worldwide: 76 percent) and 45 percent of US consumers whose household income exceeds $100K are on Pinterest.[29] A recent Pinterest study suggests that people on Pinterest are "slow shoppers," claiming 35 percent of them are more likely to take a week to make purchase decisions and spend two times more per month than people on other platforms.[30] Many users come to Pinterest with long-term purchase intent, such as redesigning their living rooms, planning significant events like weddings, preparing holiday shopping list, etc. Market research showed that 48 percent of users used Pinterest to find/shop for products, which is much higher than other social media platforms (Figure 4.6).[31]

There are several ways to sell on Pinterest:

1. Create a Pinterest business account: First and foremost, you need to create a Pinterest business account to showcase your products and services. This will enable you to access Pinterest Analytics, Promoted Pins, and other features that can help you grow your business on the platform.
2. Optimize your profile and upload your catalog: Pinterest provides a shopping solution for brands to upload their product catalog and the ability to feature products on the profile. You want to ensure that your profile is complete and optimized for search. Use keywords in your profile description, business name, and board titles to make it easier for users to find you.
3. Create boards: Organize your products into boards to make it easier for users to navigate and find what they're looking for. Use clear and descriptive board titles and descriptions, and make sure your boards have high-quality, visually appealing images.
4. Use rich pins: Rich pins automatically sync information from your site to your Pins. They help you add more info directly to the Pin to makes it easier for users to learn about your products and make purchasing decisions.
5. Run Pinterest ads: Pinterest offers several advertising options, including Promoted Pins, Promoted Videos, and Carousel Ads. These can help you reach a wider audience and drive more sales.

Social Media Activities on Select Social Networks by US Social Media Users, Nov 2018

% of respondents

	Instagram	Facebook	Snapchat	Pinterest	Twitter
Viewing photos	77%	65%	62%	57%	39%
Watching videos	50%	46%	50%	19%	32%
Sharing content with everyone	49%	57%	47%	21%	33%
Sharing content with one to one	33%	45%	49%	13%	20%
Networking	25%	36%	20%	11%	29%
News	19%	38%	15%	9%	54%
Finding/shopping for products	10%	14%	4%	48%	7%
Promoting my business	7%	6%	4%	4%	7%

Note: n=2,500
Source: Cowen and Company, "Facebook: US Ad Buyer Survey and Consumer Survey Highlights; Model Update," Jan 10, 2019

245232 www.eMarketer.com

Figure 4.6 Pinterest users have a higher intent to find/shop for products on the platform
(*Source*: eMarketer, https://content-na1.emarketer.com/pinterest-is-the-talk-of-shoptalk-as-it-eyes-ipo)

Physical Presence: Brick-and-Mortar Stores and Kiosks

Different from the traditional retailer that involved many middlemen like wholesalers and distributors, **Direct-to-Consumer (D2C or DTC) retailers** utilize internet platforms to directly sell products/services to individual consumers (Figure 4.7). A decade ago, digital-first was the key success means for direct-to-consumer brands to start their businesses. But as the retail landscape has evolved over time, what brands are focusing on to promote growth has also evolved. Many D2C retailers disrupt the existing retail market by offering arguably "the best product" with a minimalist design and cheaper cost. Moreover, they also exploit the power of social media and influencer marketing to create a fan community that shares their brand values and beliefs, hence increasing customer loyalty.

The benefits that the D2C brands offer to consumers include: 1) personalization, 2) convenience, and 3) exclusivity. For instance, companies like Warby Parker (eyewear retailer), Glossier (beauty/makeup retailer), Everlane (apparel/accessory retailer), and Allbirds (shoe retailer) are successful examples of D2C brands emerging from the past decade. According to eMarketer,[32] D2C sales will account for 24.3 percent of total e-commerce sales in 2020. Stitch Fix uses AI to select products for their customers based on their answers to a series of style preference questions. The Interactive Advertising Bureau (IAB) listed Stitch Fix as a market disrupter that generated over 100 million dollars in revenue in 2019.[33] In the following sections, we will discuss the factors of consideration for online D2C retailers to open physical locations or touch points to offer omnichannel services to their customers. These include location and consumer demand, costs, using brick-and-mortar stores as showrooms and warehouses and using digital kiosks in stores.

Box 4.1 Retail Like a Pro

Pinterest has added guides for businesses on how to promote products on the platform (https://business.pinterest.com/en-gb/). Brands can create Standard Pins, Video Pins, and Idea Pins. A standard pin is a vertical static photo (2:3 ratio) with a superimposed logo. Brands can use up to 100 characters for the title and up to 500 characters for the description. Clear titles and descriptions will help Pins get discovered in search. A Video Pin can be used for organic content or video ads. For organic content, Pinterest recommends videos between 15 seconds and 1 minute long. For video ads, 6 to 15 seconds works best. Use text overlay or captions to help tell your story because not everyone watches videos with sound on, so do not rely on audio or dialogue to convey important information. Same as the Standard Pin, you can use up to 100 characters for your title and up to 500 characters for your description. An Idea Pin is a multi-page canvas to share your ideas. Use video(s) on the first page and plan to tell a complete story about you (and your brand). The Ideal Pins are designed to help you grow your audience.

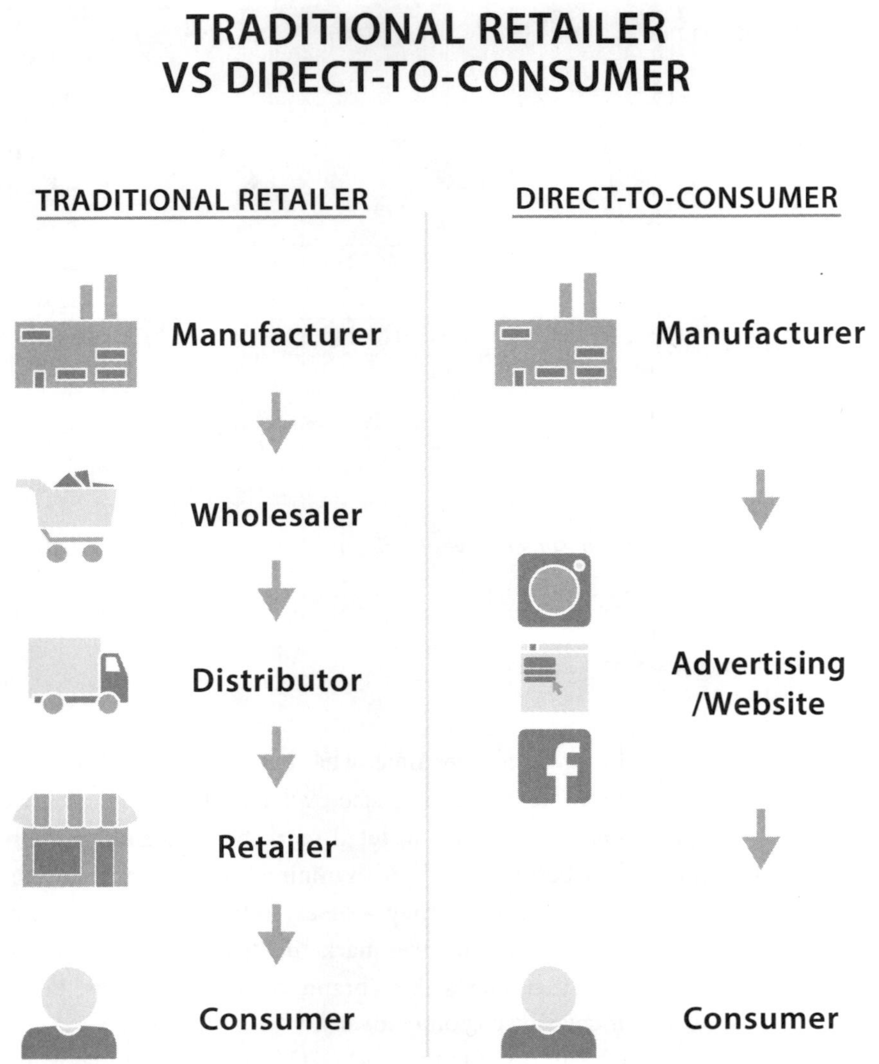

Figure 4.7 Traditional retailer versus direct-to-consumer retail
(*Source*: https://us.hitachi-solutions.com/blog/direct-to-consumer-retail/)

Location and Customer Demand

When it comes to picking a physical store location, customer demand is the most important deciding factor for omnichannel retailers. Some digital-native D2C brands are expanding their distribution by opening brick-and-mortar stores, pop-up stores, or creating partnerships with traditional brick-and-mortar retailers. Since 2019, Warby Parker has opened over 100 stores in the United States and Canada. Many D2C brands that have opened brick-and-mortar stores found the customers who interact with their brand in the physical store have lower return rates and more repeat purchases compared to the customers who only purchase from them online.[34]

The same trend of opening physical stores is not just for small/medium-sized D2C brands. Online retail giants like Amazon also joined the game after being a pure-play for more than ten years. Amazon started in 1994 as a virtual merchant. After years of pure online operation, they opened their first physical store called Amazon Books in 2015.[35] In 2017, the company bought Whole Foods Market for $13.7 billion, bringing over 460 stores under its management. This acquisition quickly gave Amazon the physical presence they need as an omnichannel retailer. As of 2023, Amazon operates close to 600 physical stores in the United States, the majority of which are locations of grocer Whole Foods Market. Amazon also operates Amazon-branded stores, including Amazon Style (clothing, shoes, and accessories), Amazon Go (cashier-less convenience stores), and Amazon Fresh (grocery). Amazon customers can do pickup and returns in all these locations.[36]

Costs

When omnichannel retailers open physical stores, they need to consider several cost factors. One of the most important factors is rent. Retailers should also consider the cost of hiring employees, utilities, insurance, marketing, and advertising. In addition, retailers should consider the cost of inventory management and logistics. Opening physical locations can be costly for omnichannel retailers. In the previous chapter, we discussed Macy's small community store approach to save up the operational cost of big stores. Nordstrom, in recent years, also set up warehouse centers and their neighborhood stores (Nordstrom Local) to facilitate cross-channel logistics and customer services.

To save on the rent, brands can investigate the locations that are in a less expensive neighborhood. For instance, retailers can look for locations in neighborhoods that are up-and-coming or that may be slightly outside of prime retail areas. These neighborhoods may offer lower rent prices while still providing a good level of foot traffic and visibility. Another example of D2C retailers that save on rent is by setting up their store on the second floor of a main street. Glossier is a beauty brand that started as an online-only retailer and has since expanded to open physical stores in major cities like New York and Los Angeles. In New York City, Glossier's flagship store is located on the second floor of a building on Lafayette Street in the trendy SoHo neighborhood. By setting up their store on the second floor, Glossier is able to save on rent compared to ground-level retail spaces in the same area. Despite being located on the second floor, Glossier's store is still highly visible and attracts customers through its eye-catching pink exterior and Instagram-worthy interior design. The store also has a buzzer system at street level that allows customers to easily gain access.[37] By leveraging their strong online presence and social media following, Glossier is able to drive foot traffic to their physical store despite its second-floor location. This approach allows Glossier to save on rent while still providing customers with a unique and engaging brand experience.

Brandy Melville is another clothing brand that targets younger shoppers and has a "cult" following on social media. The brand has opened stores across the United States and Europe, with many of their stores located on the second floor of buildings in popular shopping areas. By setting up their stores on the second floor, Brandy Melville is able to save on rent and provide a more exclusive and intimate shopping experience for their customers. The brand also uses social media influencers and targeted advertising campaigns to drive foot traffic to their physical stores. The brand's popularity on social media helps to create a sense of exclusivity and encourages customers to visit their physical stores to experience the brand in person.

To save money, many fashion brands use pop-up stores to promote featured collections or test new store concepts in a new market.[38] For example, Coach launched their first London pop-up store, which focused on repairs, upcycling, customization, and leather care as part of its (Re)Loved circular program.[39] Banana Republic, an upscale clothing and accessories retailer owned by The Gap, unveiled its first Home store in Los Angeles as a pop-up store before they opened another home store in New York. The company, which has a number of brand pop-ups in L.A., also wanted to test the location, "We also offer our new BR Home collection in several existing retail stores, including San Francisco and the larger Bay Area, San Diego, Chicago, Seattle, Denver, Dallas, Houston, and Miami," said Sandra Stangl, president and chief executive officer of Banana Republic.[40]

For D2C fashion startups, like PH5 and House of Sunny, having pop-up stores is a great entryway for meeting their customers. PH5, a knitwear brand, opened their first pop-up store in New York City in 2023.[41] Indie brand House of Sunny has opened a pop-up shop in the heart of Soho, London, to promote its mid-century modern design brand image. The brand first gained its fame in 2021, when Kendall Jenner wore its knitted Hockney dress and posted on Instagram. House of Sunny hopes to expand its consumer base with their new pop-up store in central London.[42]

Showrooms and Fulfillment Centers

Omnichannel retailers can use their physical stores as both showrooms and fulfillment centers to enhance the customer experience and streamline their operations. By using their physical stores as showrooms, retailers can provide customers with the opportunity to see and try on products before making a purchase, while also using the space as a warehouse to fulfill online orders and manage inventory. For example, Reformation, a women's clothing brand, is another example of a D2C brand opening physical stores as showrooms. Reformation opened its first physical store in Los Angeles in 2013. The brand's stores are designed as showrooms where customers can try on clothing and receive styling advice. Omnichannel retailer Nordstrom uses Nordstrom Local stores to serve as a showroom for customers to try on clothes and accessories, pickup online orders, and get alterations done.[43] Bonobos is a D2C men's clothing brand that opened its first physical store in 2012. The brand's Guideshops are designed as showrooms where customers can enjoy some beer, try on clothing, and receive personalized styling advice from Bonobos Guides (a special name for the service personnel in their stores). The Guideshops also serve as mini fulfillment centers where customers can place online orders and have them shipped directly to their home. During the 2019 pandemic, many fashion brands quickly changed their logistic process and started to fulfill online orders from stores.[44]

In-Store Ordering and Digital Kiosks

Retailers can use digital kiosks and ordering in-stores to provide omnichannel services that allow customers to seamlessly transition between in-store and online shopping experiences. Digital kiosks can provide customers with self-service options to browse and purchase products, while ordering in-store allows customers to place online orders for in-store pickup or home delivery.

- Nike: Nike has introduced Nike Fit, a digital kiosk that uses augmented reality to help customers find the perfect shoe size. Customers can use the kiosk to scan their feet and receive recommendations for shoe sizes and styles.
- Sephora: Sephora has introduced digital kiosks in its stores that allow customers to try on makeup virtually using augmented reality. Customers can see how different makeup products and shades look on their skin before making a purchase.
- Home Depot: Home Depot has introduced a mobile app that allows customers to browse and purchase products online, as well as a feature that allows customers to order products online for in-store pickup. Customers can use the app to scan products in-store and receive recommendations for related products and accessories.
- Target: Target has introduced a mobile app that allows customers to scan products in-store and place orders for home delivery or in-store pickup. The app also includes features like price comparisons and product recommendations.

By using digital kiosks and ordering in-store, omnichannel retailers can provide customers with a more personalized and convenient shopping experience. These omnichannel services can help to increase customer satisfaction and drive sales while also improving operational efficiency.

CASE STUDY 4.1

Italian Direct-to-Consumer Brand Disrupted the Handcrafted Footwear Industry

Handmade Italian leather shoe company Velasca proves to be a prime example of innovative business strategies at their best. Co-founders Enrico Casati and Jacopo Sebastio successfully disrupted the retail market in 2013 with the launch of their D2C (direct-to-consumer) business model that substantially cuts costs and is specifically catered to the needs of each individual consumer. Initially focusing on building their online presence and conducting solely e-commerce sales directly to consumers, Velasca was able to eliminate multiple layers of distribution to produce the highly sought-after quality of handmade leather shoes for a fraction of the standard cost. The founders of Velasca strived to create and maintain strong and honest relationships with each production company, and the trust between both parties served as a cornerstone for their success. Velasca then focused its media and marketing efforts on sharing their story and presenting their business as "not just another discount site." As Velasca continued to grow, Casati and Sebastio saw the potential in other channels and began to explore in-person sales, beginning with occasional pop-up shops and eventually opening their first permanent retail store in Milan in 2015. Velasca has only grown since, opening stores in London, Paris, and Rome, but continues to hold their connection with the customer as their number one priority.

(*Source*: Adapted from https://www.shopify.com/blog/velasca-dtc)

Discussion Questions:

1. Do you think the D2C business model will continue to thrive on the market?
2. Research Velasca's website (https://www.velasca.com/) and find out its brand image. Apply the three principles of evaluating a website: appearance, functionality, and speed to analyze Velasca's website. Summarize key points in each dimension and discuss.
3. In which countries and cities does Velasca have brick-and-mortar stores? If they want to expand into more countries/cities, where would you suggest to them? Why?
4. What other retail channels do you think Velasca should expand into in addition to their website? Why?

CASE STUDY 4.2

TikTok, Its Young Audience, and Fashion Brands

Launched in September 2016, TikTok is one of the top ten most-used social networks in the United States, with 26.5 million monthly active users. ByteDance, a Chinese technology company that runs several popular social networking apps, owns TikTok. Worldwide, it has been downloaded more than 1 billion times. According to app analytics tracker Sensor Tower, TikTok's popularity in the United States peaked in December 2018, and continues to grow, becoming the first non-Facebook mobile app to reach 3 billion downloads worldwide. In addition to the United States, TikTok is also available in more than 150 markets and in 50+ languages.[45]

In terms of the TikTok users' demographic profiles, 62 percent of US TikTok users are aged between 10 and 29. In 2024, a report showed that over 33 percent of US adults currently have an account on TikTok—for Gen Z, the percentage jumps to 71 percent. For omnichannel retailers who want to target young audiences, TikTok can be a very attractive platform. A study showed that around half of TikTok users (15 percent of all adults and 36 percent of Gen Z) had made purchases based on content viewed on the platform, which makes the platform a very effective channel to help omnichannel retailers to raise their brand awareness and increase sales. TicTok partnered with Walmart for an hour-long live stream where TikTok users could buy Walmart fashion items featured by creators. The duo did another live stream in 2021 after reporting the first event that had seven times more views than expected and grew Walmart's TikTok following by 25 percent.

Many fashion retailers work with TikTok influencers on promoting their products. For example, Fendi, an Italian luxury brand, launched its account on TikTok in 2020. It was looking to increase its awareness and engagement on this new channel. They launched a campaign with @sabrinacarpenter called "F is for…" to play on their values of family, freedom, friends, future, and fearless. They ran five separate weekly ads that each corresponded to one of the five values. The ads directed users to Fendi's profile so they could follow the brand. The campaign resulted in 15k new followers and over 4 million video views.

At the other end, marketing on TikTok can seem random and fun. Morgan Presley (@morganpresleyxo), a TikToker who has 4.4 million followers, started the #GucciModelChallenge on TikTok. She featured a voice-over on how to look like a Gucci model and went viral. Presley's on-point description of a "Gucci model" is based on Gucci Creative Director Alessandro Michele's signature granny-chic aesthetic for the brand. Within a short time (around a month), the hashtag #GucciModelChallenge had around 21.9 million views on TikTok.[46] Moreover, Gucci did not take offense to it; instead, they acquired the voice-over by @morganpresleyxo. Moreover, Gucci selected some TikTokers' posts to be included as part of an upcoming project with Gucci. Gucci also linked the fun voice-over directly to the official Gucci account on TikTok. Search #GucciModelChallenge to watch some hilarious posts.

Despite trending hashtags like #TikTokmademebuy, one survey found the US shoppers are hesitant to pay for products directly on social sites. In turn, retailers miss out on the click-through and conversion data that are owned by the social sites. It's a big barrier to success for the business model. Meanwhile, live stream sales on marketplaces could avoid the trust issue and information barrier. As they operate as retailer media platforms, Amazon Live (live streaming by the largest US-based online marketplace) and Alibaba's Taobao Live (live streaming channel by the largest Chinese-based online marketplace) keep buyers on their sites all the way through the sale. Amazon continues to grow its live stream efforts launching Amazon live in India.[47] Meta, on the other hand, has scaled back its focus on shopping. It halted live shopping on Facebook in October 2022, and removed the shop tab from Instagram's navigation bar in March 2023.[48]

Discussion Questions:

1. Do you think TikTok will continue to be popular among the younger generation such as Gen Z? Why or why not?
2. Why do you think TikTok has become so popular? Do you follow any brands on TikTok?
3. What makes TikTok unique when compared to other social media platforms such as Instagram or Snapchat?
4. Considering your answer above, what does this say about Gen Z as consumers?
5. In your opinion, will this kind of branded hashtag challenge continue to be successful on social media? Is TikTok the only home for this kind of hashtag challenge?

Career Opportunities

Job Titles	Key Responsibility

Product Manager, Global Omnichannel Fulfillment (Ship from Store)	The Product Manager, Ship from Store, maintains and communicates the product vision, strategy, and road map for their product area(s). They are responsible for discovering, delivering, and optimizing omnichannel products and capabilities that fundamentally transform how our consumers can find, purchase, and enjoy beauty products across our global portfolio of brands. This is a key role that works collaboratively with brands, business partners, solution architects, data, and delivery teams spanning Online, Stores, Supply Chain, Retail Operations, and more. You'll help shape our culture and our people and be an ambassador for Global Omnichannel across the company's global organization.
	
	Global Omnichannel is a fast-growing team and this role has significant growth opportunity.
	
	Qualifications
	
	• BA/BS in related field or relevant experience, MBA a plus
	• 6+ years' work experience in management consulting, product management, e-commerce operations, or similar
	• Experience with supply chain/logistics in e-commerce or consumer products a plus
	• People who are successful in this role demonstrate:
	  ○ Strong project management skills and "owner" mentality; ability to marshal resources and key stakeholders and drive a project through to completion despite setbacks
	  ○ Strong problem-solving skills; outstanding quantitative and analytical skills, including P&L development and understanding of key drivers that drive profitability in a multi-channel retailer
	  ○ Ability to prioritize effectively
	  ○ Excellent communicator with ability to build strong cross-functional relationships, to understand incentives, and to ensure alignment in a matrixed organization
	  ○ Executive presence with high business IQ
	  ○ Ability to work on several projects simultaneously and to thrive in a project-based, matrixed environment with a closely intertwined team
	  ○ Strong attention to detail and results orientation; high work ethic and persistence to drive an initiative to completion; a "roll up the sleeves" attitude towards tackling a challenge
	
	The anticipated base salary range for this position is around $100K to $160K. Exact salary depends on several factors such as experience, skills, education, and budget. Salary range may vary based on geographic location. In addition to base salary, this position is eligible for participation in a highly competitive bonus program with possibility for overachievement based on performance and company results as well as participation in the share incentive plan.

(*Source*: Adapted from https://jobs.elcompanies.com/estee-lauder-companies/jobs/234851?lang=en-us&src=JB-10400)

Summary

From traditional brick-and-mortar stores to D2C online retailers, operating multiple channels is imperative to meet consumers wherever they are. This chapter provides a comprehensive overview of essential features and dimensions for evaluating a website, discerning the difference between a mobile application and a mobile site, the importance of social media platforms for retailers, and factors to consider when opening physical locations. For omnichannel retailers, expanding their physical and online presence is crucial for business growth. A website's visual appearance, structure conventions, clear navigation, and consistency across devices are vital dimensions for creating a user-friendly experience that can boost sales. Social media platforms like Facebook, Instagram, and TikTok are constantly innovating to offer retailers ways to build online communities and drive sales. With more consumers spending time on social media, brands need to effectively utilize these platforms to promote products, engage with followers, and optimize social media marketing campaigns. Furthermore, we discuss the factors retailers should consider when deciding to open physical locations or touchpoints. These questions cover topics such as cost factors, strategies to reduce costs, and ways to ensure a seamless transition between online and physical channels. By carefully considering these factors, retailers can make informed decisions about their physical presence and enhance their overall retail strategy.

Key Terms

Augmented reality (AR)
Bounce rate
Call to action (CTA)
Color scheme
Consistency
Conversion rate
Direct-to-consumer (D2C)
Domain name
Graceful degradation
Homepage
Images and page layout
In-app notification
Mobile-first design
Native mobile applications (Apps)
Navigation
Point of sale (POS)
Progressive enhancement
Push notification
Responsive design
Search engine optimization (SEO)
User experience (UX)
Visual hierarchy
Website builder platforms
Website convention
Website usability

Reflection and Discussion Questions

1. What are the two main categories of features that an omnichannel retail website should include, and why are they important?
2. What are some pros and cons of creating a website in-house versus using a third-party platform, and how should businesses make this decision?
3. Why is choosing the right domain name important for a website, and what are some considerations to keep in mind when selecting one?
4. What are some tools businesses can use to find out if a domain name is available, and what should they do if the name they want is already taken?
5. What are some examples of visual elements that should remain consistent across a website, and why is consistency important?
6. How does following website convention help users navigate a website more easily?
7. How does responsive design differ from mobile-first design, and what are the advantages and disadvantages of using responsive design?
8. How can a well-designed homepage create a good first impression of a brand, and what are some key elements that should be included in a homepage's main navigation?
9. Why is it important to check for proper display and functionality of a website on various mobile screens, even when using responsive design?
10. Why is it important for omnichannel retailers to have a presence on social media platforms like Facebook, Instagram, and TikTok?
11. How can retailers use Facebook's Page Insights tool to better understand their target audience?
12. What are some of the ways brands can use Instagram to connect with their followers and promote their products?
13. Pick a social media platform that you think will be appropriate to promote to 1) Gen Z; 2) Millennials; and 3) Gen Alpha and provide your rationale.
14. What are some of the challenges that retailers may face when selling their products on social media, and how can these challenges be addressed?
15. What factors should omnichannel retailers consider when deciding to open physical locations or touchpoints?
16. What are some cost factors that omnichannel retailers should consider when opening physical locations, and what are some strategies that can help reduce these costs?

CHAPTER 5
Cross-Channel Integration

Learning Objectives

Upon finishing this chapter, you will be able to:

- Identify the components of cross-channel planning and development
- Understand the need for synchronization of business functions across channels
- Investigate solutions to common cross-channel problems
- Address marketing strategies from a cross-channel perspective
- Examine customer relationship management in fully integrated omnichannel retail environment

In this chapter, we will look at one of the most fundamental goals of omnichannel retailers: cross-channel integration, which refers to connecting channels within the omnichannel context to create a seamless customer experience. Omnichannel retailers gain critical and invaluable intelligence about their customers' preferences, interests, and shopping behaviors by collecting valuable information on their customers. Retailers can access their customers' demographic, psychographic, and geographic information, product preferences, and shopping and return patterns using integrated customer database systems. We start with the fundamentals of cross-channel integration planning and development.

Cross-Channel Integration Strategies

Consumer behavior, market growth, and business–consumer interactions are all being strongly influenced by technological advancements and ongoing digitization in the retail industry. Businesses are trying to support these advancements by offering multiple integrated channels. By combining all customer contact points into a harmonized and seamless experience, the omnichannel retail strategy has revolutionized the retail sector.[1] Especially, the fashion industry more clearly understands the value of the cross-channel shopping, omnichannel shopping, recently also known as "Phygital," being the driver of higher revenue and higher margins through direct purchase from the retail e-commerce platforms, and greater loyalty. This explains why pure e-tail brands open up physical store fronts as an additional channel for their customers. For instance, Warby Parker has physical stores in metropolitan cities to get customers to really experience their offerings by trying on frames in person. Moreover, traditional brick-and-mortar retailers are heavily investing their effort on digital channels.[2]

Before the Covid-19 pandemic, many fashion retailers, especially small businesses and local boutiques, saw omnichannel integration as a burden, rather than a proactive strategy to entice their consumers.[3] However, larger retail brands/corporations had already incorporated the omnichannel presence in their retail strategies prior to the pandemic. During the pandemic, many small fashion retailers faced the critical need to further harness their omnichannel strategies and implementations at the next level.

Omnichannel retailers must unlock the value of cross-channel shopping through personalization available on their various channels, not discounts or promotional efforts. Omnichannel retailers strive for integration of the multiple channels they operate rather than isolation of each channel. Customer-centric retailers provide a consistent shopping experience across all channels of communication with their customers. To unlock the value of cross-channel shopping the retailer should build useful and valuable company databases by capturing information on their clients. To access their databases and identify shopping patterns, product preferences, demographic, psychographic, and geographic information, retailers use centralized systems. They can offer more services and provide better customer experiences through their online and offline stores, physical or digital catalogs, mobile commerce systems, or any other wireless device they use to efficiently reach customers. We'll begin with the basics of cross-channel integration.

For the past 20-plus years of operation of e-commerce channel in the United States and around the globe, e-commerce has rooted down in the everyday shopping landscape of contemporary consumers. They use various channels to meet their product/service information search and/or acquisition needs. Among many, convenience in accessing product information at their own pace or with no limit on geographical location has led to the greater success of omnichannel retailers' e-commerce channels. Successful retailers are those that not only offer the multiple selling channels available, but also encourage customers to use and shop on all of them.

Several facets must converge to result in a superior harmonized and seamless omnichannel strategy and its performance. The omnichannel fashion business must develop an overarching omnichannel integration strategy to include all channels rather than treat each channel individually. They should also select the relevant technologies to enable their business to support all channels adequately. In order to keep monitoring and tracking their performance, they should adopt performance measurement tools. The fashion business must cultivate executives who buy into the omnichannel philosophy and its holistic approach to the operation of all channels. Lastly, but not least, omnichannel businesses need to educate and develop their sale associates and client advisors to embrace the online channels as opportunities for furthering customer service as well as generating increased sales.

Cross-Channel Integration Levels—Semi- versus Fully Integrated

Chapter 1 introduced organizational structures for omnichannel retailers. Fashion business companies should also consider internal operational structures that encourage teamwork and collaboration for maximum effectiveness. Communication between the core business and other channels should be open, well-organized, and accessible to all participants.

There are three types of structures in an omnichannel retailing structure: semi-integrated, fully integrated, and independent formats. **Semi-integrated structures** share some but not all operational and informational tools across channels. The majority of the retailers polled used a semi-integrated team structure. For example, merchandising and pricing in a core brick-and-mortar business may differ from the company's online store, or some divisions may be run separately or partially integrated. Omnichannel businesses are rarely fully integrated, and when they are, they are typically large global retailers. Fully integrated structures are those in which all key business functions and information are shared across channels.

Independent structures are those in which all operating channels operate independently, and information is not shared between them. This format is commonly used by smaller retail businesses. Each approach has advantages and disadvantages. Decision-making and response times, for example, may be faster in independent organizations than in fully integrated larger companies. Brand consistency across channels is likely to be more effective in fully integrated companies than in those with independent structures. From a historical perspective, independent structures were very common in the early days of online selling, 1996 to 2001. Semi-integration took place roughly between 2002 and 2006, and fully integrated teams has emerged since then. All versions are present in the marketplace, but it is expected that in the future more robust organizations will utilize global, fully integrated team structures.[4]

Significance of Cross-Channel Synchronization

To reach the pinnacle of omnichannel service, careful planning and management are required. The brand must be consistent across all channels. To operate complex merchandising and distribution systems, appropriate technology is chosen. Inter-company, inter-channel, and supply chain communications networks must encompass all dimensions.

Cross-channel collaboration is critical because it has an impact on brand equity, sales, and profits. Online shopping today is what window shopping was to past generations. Both experiences aim to bring customers to the point of sale, but the path to completion is changing. Cross-channel customers spend 30 percent more than single-channel shoppers, but many retailers have yet to achieve optimal operating conditions that allow them to maximize revenue growth while satisfying their customers. Customers today are altering the nature of retailing. Their expectations are high for consistent merchandise selection and customer service across channels.

According to retail strategy researchers,[5] single-channel or semi-integrated retailers evolved their decisions and processes as they moved towards implementing an omnichannel strategy. The retailers faced numerous challenges in shifting from a single channel strategy to an omnichannel strategy. In fact, it was almost impossible to evolve directly from a siloed strategy to omnichannel strategy without levels of transition periods or stages. Moreover, through their transformative process, most businesses experienced "omnichannel strategy-related challenges" such as organizational, cultural, managerial, marketing, and resources. Initially, these challenges were a high priority while implementing omnichannel integration. Subsequently, they experienced "development-related challenges" such as retail mix, information systems, and customer relationship management.[6] In addition to these challenges, it is crucial for the businesses to understand what their omnichannel shoppers are expecting the businesses to deliver. In the next section we will examine possible solutions to the cross-channel collaboration issues.

Solutions to Cross-Channel Collaboration Problems

As retailers look into cross-channel options, a number of problematic issues can occur. Finding methods for businesses to build on their current strengths as they expand their customer contact and service offerings is difficult, time-consuming, and requires significant financial and human resources. Key factors include technological infrastructures, implementation expenses, and a number of operational and facilitation problems. Four major areas of worry are highlighted in the discussion that follows, along with possible fixes for typical cross-channel problems.

Synchronizing Information Technology

When managing their company across channels, retailers can easily access facilitating technologies. The abundance of businesses that display their goods and expertise at retail trade shows indicates that this business area has undergone more new development than any other. In reality, the abundance of resources might be one of the factors contributing to retailers' struggles in locating the best solutions for their problems.

Retailers of all sizes can use integrative software, but some find it challenging to explain their needs to software providers. The merchandising efforts of multichannel retailers are not always in sync with the planning schedules. For instance, if many of their customers live in Australia, where the winters are opposite to those in the northern hemisphere, catalog and online retailers offering wool sweaters might find it challenging to estimate inventories for their online stores. The choice of the suitable inventory planning software takes global climate variation into account. The integration problem has been overcome by some businesses.

Sharing Customer Data among Various Channels

Long before the days of omnichannel retailing, retailers were gathering data on their consumers. Most have a ton of information, though not all of it is pertinent to the current order. Information can be gathered with ease in-store using a mobile point of sale (POS) device (see Figure 5.1) or online transactional activities, but it can be more challenging to use it effectively. The advantage belongs to retailers who manage databases and take advantage of them. We are conscious that laws and privacy concerns restrict retailers' ability to collect certain kinds of sensitive data or information without the consent of the customer. Chapter 9 goes into detail on customer privacy and data security. The most useful datasets contain data that was gathered using opt-in methods. Customers anticipate receiving value in return when they give retailers their confidential information.

Figure 5.1 A mobile POS device not only supports the transactional process but also assists collecting email addresses from consumers

Once customer data is gathered it should seamlessly flow between the channels through electronic data interchange to use the data to its fullest to benefit the organization and supply chain partners and, in turn, to serve the customers more effectively.

Implementing Customer Service Procedures

Even in the omnichannel retailing era, it is imperative to continue cultivating new customers in the brick-and-mortar store environment where those customers seek direct product trials of fashion items and prefer the human touch in their customer journey. Within their omnichannel integration strategy, retailers can embrace 360-degree customer service procedures to serve the customer in whichever channel they encounter the products/services more effectively.

It is imperative to have frequent training sessions and continued development to enable staff to keep up with cross-collaborative efforts. Sales associates, in particular, need to be agile with the new information technologies and the kind of customer interface that encourages cross-channel shopping and interactive service. The established practice of teaching new hires multiple selling techniques should be supplemented with cross-channel suggestion selling tactics and in-store order fulfillment practices.

New compensation policies are required to promote the complete participation of the in-store and online sales associates. Innovative retailers pay commissions to sales associates on products that were extensively browsed in-store, even though the transaction may have been finished online with the aid of cross-channel business technology systems. Similar to this, a purchase made online but fulfilled in-store may be fully or partially credited to either section.

For instance, Best Buy, the largest consumer electronic retailer in the United States, does not pay commissions to its sales associates, but it does give store credit for online orders that the store fulfilled and delivered to customers' homes. Prior to this change, stores could only receive credit if a consumer used an in-store kiosk or picked up an item in-store that they had ordered online. By employing this strategy, retailers avoid the perception that the internet channel cannibalizes their sales. As new policies are created, it is anticipated that decisions that are appropriate to the retailer's goals, operational strategies, and accounting practices will fluctuate.

Technology-savvy customers have no problem finding information or customer service assistance online. However, not all customers fall into this category. Although many individuals are comfortable initiating product searches or accessing inventory information online, others need more confidence in a self-help environment. Customer support needs are more significant when returning products to the retailer. Even though many omnichannel retailers are equipped with chatbots and frequently asked question pages on their websites, customer service, through 1-800 calls, will likely be around for a while.

Embracing Changes

One of the most challenging aspects of putting a new plan into action is changing ingrained mindsets and getting them onboard with the new plan. While some corporate cultures are more receptive to innovation, others are more change resistant. Therefore, business owners need to think creatively and outside the box to come up with fresh ideas and answers. Although these developments are a part of the answer, technology solutions help retailers integrate data, merchandising, and delivery functions. In a perfect world, retailers would take the finest assets from the most successful channel and apply them to streamline operations in others. The key objective is to create a synergy among the various channels that the business operates and, in turn, boost overall sales and profitability.

Successful omnichannel retailers make proactive plans and keep an eye out for changes in the retail landscape that offer opportunities for growth of the business, redesign of the products, customer experience and/or operation, or outreach to new customers. As mentioned earlier, omnichannel integration is a process of evolution rather than revolution. Thus, the business needs to take the time to smoothly migrate into the new plan with the majority of the key personnel onboard.

Online shops and brick-and-mortar stores are no longer seen as separate entities. One of the top objectives in retailers' growth strategies is cross-channel integration. The carefully chosen suitable marketing strategies will determine how well the overall multichannel experience will turn out. The end result is to develop long-lasting customer loyalty across all platforms.

Integrated Marketing Strategies

As fashion companies discover efficient methods for implementing and operating omnichannel businesses, the traditional marketing strategy elements of product, price, place/channels, and promotion need to be updated. When creating integrated marketing strategies, factors like branding, product pricing and selling, fulfillment optimization, successful sales promotions, and customer support programs are taken into account.

Developing Brand Equity across Channels

It is imperative to stress the importance of the fashion industry as a brand and creating a lasting, recognizable image in the minds of target customers. Here we discuss ways that omnichannel retailers are extending their brand equity across channels. It is easy to identify retailers that recognize the benefits of brand management from physical stores to catalogs to online e-commerce site. Victoria's Secret implements a consistent theme of their brand image using colors, type font, style, model selection, and visual merchandising techniques across stores, internet, and catalog channels. From their existing business involving a mail-order catalog started in 1977 (until the cancelation of catalog circulation in 2016), it was by chance that Victoria's Secret migrated to an e-commerce channel. Since the company launched its website in 1999, traffic on the internet was encouraged to directly place orders online instead of mailing or calling in as well as to watch their famous online fashion shows. Since then, it has become common practice for them to tie an event like a fashion show with their merchandise presentation theme, catalog covers, in-store displays and graphics, online video, and email advertisements. The distinctive brand image of Victoria's Secret is clearly communicated and experienced by consumers and visitors to their stores and website. Viewers immediately know they are at Victoria's Secret and not at Fredericks of Hollywood, an American lingerie brand founded in 1944 and closed in 2015 due to bankruptcy, or elsewhere. That is the power of brand image and diversification.

Another illustration comes from the UK-based fashion retailer Oasis Fashion, one of the 13 brands owned and run by Boohoo Group plc, a British online fast fashion retailer, targeting older teenagers to customers in their early 30s. Along with operating more than eighty physical stores in the UK and more than ninety retail sites globally, Oasis Fashion also runs an online e-commerce site. They not only seamlessly integrated the two retail channels, but they also made it easier for customers to interact with and experience their fashion brands. The trending products from store sales data close to the target customers are displayed in a carousel on the product pages of their online e-commerce sites. They also included an "inspiration exhibit," which is a collection of user-generated styling drawn from the business's @OasisFashion Instagram account, which has over 420,000 followers. Additionally, they set an excellent example for social commerce by showcasing shoppable designs and fashions on Instagram Shopping. Additionally, the customer can add an object to their shopping bag on their mobile app and then later purchase it online or in-store. The customer can locate the closest store where they can find the item in their size using the "Find in Store" function of the mobile app. In the same year, their omnichannel integrated approach along with other strategies led to a 45 percent increase in profits.[7]

Merchandise Selling and Pricing Strategies and Practices

Merchandising is the fundamental key function of a retail business. Sourcing and presenting the right goods at the right place, at the right price, at the right time is a core concept of merchandising. Merchandising involves the selection and procuring of goods, research, and development of new private label products, planning of an assorted array of goods catering to target customers, and allocation of such goods to the various channels of the retail organization. Selling the merchandise cannot occur unless sufficient buying power and expertise are present and systems compatible with the complex needs of omnichannel businesses are in place. Pricing strategy is based on science and art and it can vary greatly by type of business and channels used.

Cross-Channel Selling: Products

In order to offer the consistency of the product assortment across the channels, fashion businesses should be equipped with inventory management and fulfillment solutions that can integrate all inventories and orders through a harmonized system. The system will automatically update all touchpoints on a real-time basis. For instance, "ShopifyPlus" enables the company with key functions such as inventory and order management, fulfillment, and customer service through store, catalog, and online channels. It allows the company/business to have direct access to the real-time inventory level across all channels.[8]

Assortment allocation

In the context of a fully integrated omnichannel business environment, product assortment to brick-and-mortar store level is important. This is because each retail location of omnichannel integration performs as a distribution center to fulfill customers' orders. The inventory level in a particular store is no longer only for the customers who come to the store to shop for the items. The store will frequently support the fulfillment needs of the other stores in the region or across the country or even across the ocean. Therefore, the accurate prediction of the assortment needs in each region and down to store level will be critical to satisfy the customers' needs and prevent a stockout situation, but also to fully support the organizational level's fulfillment needs through a maximum level of agility and minimal level of shipping costs.[9]

In-store inventory versus e-commerce inventory

At times, an online only merchandise mix may reach a greater customer base than the business serves in the brick-and-mortar based channels. Extended sizes available online could bring substantial traffic to the online channel while giving flexibility at store level in terms of their management of the inventory. Through an in-store kiosk or mobile POS device, the sale associates can easily locate products and have them shipped to the customer's home. In this way, e-commerce inventory housed in the key distribution centers or key retail stores can support the overall omnichannel business to function smoothly.

Online search of in-store inventory

This is one of the most sought-after features among omnichannel shoppers. It is usually available to the sales associate through their own POS system to locate goods from other stores. There is an exemplary case in the luxury fashion retail landscape. For instance, Louis Vuitton's global website serves to ship its products to a total of thirty-three countries in four continents: the Americas, Europe, Asia, and Oceania. The website gives full access to the inventory of each and all products down to a specific store, a city, and country on all of its products. It is much easier for them to have control over the information because they are a vertically integrated company that only sells through their own retail locations. Their retail distribution strategies gives a huge advantage to customers and to their employees when it comes to the online search capabilities of their in-store inventory.[10]

Pricing Techniques

Online retailers certainly added more dynamics to seasonal sales practices in the retail industry. During the Covid-19 pandemic, the world of retail experienced the hardship of getting the proper shipments supplied from their global sourcing partners. In 2021, retailers intentionally purchased less to support their business functions, which in turn, impacted their pricing strategies as well as promotional activities. For instance, a smaller number of items were put on to the sales floor and lower markdown percentages prevailed in both physical and online channels.

Because it was so simple to compare prices online, customers were more conscious of the need to buy wisely and look for the best deal. Consumer price awareness is increased during economic crises like the recessions of 2020–2023 and 2008–2009. Offering unique goods that are not frequently found at competing retailers may be one of the strategic moves made by fashion retailers to avoid price war issues and gain a competitive edge.

All merchants must consider pricing, which is both a science and an art. Retailers can establish and maintain prices across all their operating channels by being aware of a variety of price setting variables. Additionally, some channels can be strategically used to sell off their stock in order to get ready for the new season and create a fresh appearance for the retailer. Managing healthy/profitable pricing and balancing the variety of products go hand in hand. Most retailers attempt to keep pricing uniformity across all channels when they add new ones.

Effective Distributional Strategies and Practices

Fulfillment solutions lead the way when it comes to providing renowned customer service. Often answers to complex distribution problems emanate from the acquisition of new technologies. In this section, we will discuss customer expectations on distributional strategies and practices and fulfillment strategies.

Customer Expectations

Ordering items online to pickup in-person was adopted and practiced in fashion retail for almost two decades, yet it received a spotlight during the pandemic. This feature is also known as "buy online, ship to shop." For instance, in the earlier omnichannel retailing days circa 2000s, American Eagle Outfitters started their Buy Online Ship to Store program to enhance their customer experience. This was not only for their convenience but also a profitable way of bringing their customers into stores to pickup their purchases. This practice has been adopted by an endless number of the global or national chain fashion retailers. In addition, the vast majority of them also offer the free returns option in stores. This is another great tactic to have customers visit the retailer to complete their transaction and to have a chance to browse the merchandise.

Contemporary omnichannel shoppers anticipate their ways to utilize online coupons or other promotions in-store and vice versa. Allowing this practice may be much easier for the fully integrated, national chain omnichannel retailers. Synchronizing the customer database between online and brick-and-mortar channels would be a prerequisite to make this happen.

Omnichannel shoppers are savvy in their product search online. Some of them cannot find their sizes or styles in-store and they turn to the online counterpart to find what they need. For instance, Ann Taylor has been listening to these needs from their target customer. As of February 2023, they offer over 300 styles as Online Exclusives on their e-commerce site. Having these online exclusive items widely available on their website brings greater impact to their customers and loyal customers visit their website to extend their shopping journey.[11]

As General Data Protection and Regulation (GDPR) in the EU puts more pressure on US-based retailers, more and more customers increasingly voice their preference to have an explicit opt-in to provide completely cross-functional customer relationship management data to retailers. As we write this textbook in 2023, many of the leading retailers are putting more emphasis on consumer privacy and data protection and they update their privacy policy.[12]

The true beauty of omnichannel retailing is that there is no limit to geographical locations and no limit on day and time to browse and purchase products. Even though consumers understand that the retailer may need to update their e-commerce sites, they really demand the around-the-clock availability of the e-commerce site with relatively fast browsing speed. These will put more pressure on the retailer's IT team to make sure they are bandwidth and memory ready to handle the number of the shoppers at a given time and day.

Fulfillment Strategies

With omnichannel shopping, customers can make purchases through a variety of sales channels—online using a laptop or mobile phone, in brick-and-mortar stores, or at wholesale distributors—while enjoying a seamless, all-encompassing shopping experience. For companies that manufacture consumer goods, including direct-to-consumer enterprises like retail, this new standard has significant ramifications. These businesses must take on the challenge of providing excellent customer service across all sales channels if they want to survive, and they must modify their supply chains appropriately. However, because most companies' supply chains precede the advent of omnichannel, it can be challenging to add the recently demanded capabilities on top of legacy systems.[13]

For instance, the apparel company Anthropologie, one of Urban Outfitter's brands with a very strong performance, had mixed results when it refined its integration systems. In the beginning, the company discovered that keeping its stores and direct business on distinct systems enabled the company to expand quickly. Anthropologie's direct operation consists of catalogs and online shops. Employees have a difficult time watching channels because different information technology systems use stock-keeping unit (SKU) numbers with different numbers of digits. As a result, a salesperson might not understand what a client wants if they have seen a dress online because the SKUs and product descriptions vary between systems. In addition to looking for a unified technology platform, Anthropologie wants a closer interaction between its various departments.

Promotional Strategies and Practices

Retail sales promotion experts frequently use a wide range of media for advertising, sales promotion strategies, and direct marketing techniques to reach consumers. The retail fashion business, like all other sectors, now has more dynamic promotional strategies thanks to the internet and mobile technology. The way that consumers consume information has also drastically changed. Social media platforms like Facebook, Instagram, and TikTok, among many others, have an impact on how users perceive advertising and the part that influencers play in their decision-making. Indeed, promotional efforts are entering a brave new world.

In 2007, for the first time online advertising captured a greater market share than radio advertising.[14] Fast forward to the 2020s, digital advertising spending has surpassed all other media. The projected overall US media spending by media types is shown in Table 5.1. Additionally, it is anticipated that by 2025, worldwide spending on digital advertising will surpass $1 trillion. Digital ads were the most sought-after advertising medium in 2020, with marketers spending over $142 billion on them. As you can see, the majority of the media advertising money was spent on digital advertisements.

Consistent Cross-Channel Exposure

It may sound obvious, but it is crucial to reiterate the launch of the promotional campaign and having the promoted line available in-store and across all channels. As the fashion business is getting bigger and more complex, such standard practice may need a lot of coordination and planning among the various departments and divisions. When a retailer advertises the latest,

Table 5.1 Projected US Total Media Ad Spending by Media (in billions)

MEDIA CHANNEL/ YEAR	2019 (PRE-PANDEMIC)	2022	2023	2024	2025
Digital	$132.46	$220.93	$250.18	$278.53	$304.17
—Mobile	$87.30	$150.16	$170.33	$189.83	$207.50
TV*	$70.59	$67.88	$67.20	$66.53	$65.86
Print	$15.41	$8.47	$7.79	$7.25	$6.75
—Newspaper*	$7.96	$3.92	$3.60	$3.36	$3.13
—Magazine*	$7.45	$4.55	$4.19	$3.89	$3.62
Radio**	$13.90	$11.88	$11.82	$11.76	$11.71
Out-of-home	$8.65	$7.18	$7.34	$7.44	$7.54
Directories*	$1.19	$0.64	$0.58	$0.52	$0.48
Total	$242.19	$316.98	$344.91	$372.04	$396.52

Note: *excludes Digital; **excludes off-air radio and Digital
(*Source*: eMarketer, 2021. https://forecasts-na1.emarketer.com/584b26021403070290f93a2f/5851918b0626310a2c186b4c)

greatest electronic gadget online, that item had better be available on the brick-and-mortar selling floor concurrently. This careful and strategic coordination between the merchandising team and the marketing/promotion division is the key to synchronize the entire cross-channel experience. In order to prevent any hiccups in relation to synchronization between the channels, the fashion retailer must pay a great amount of attention to detail and coordination of extensive inventory information flows and execution.

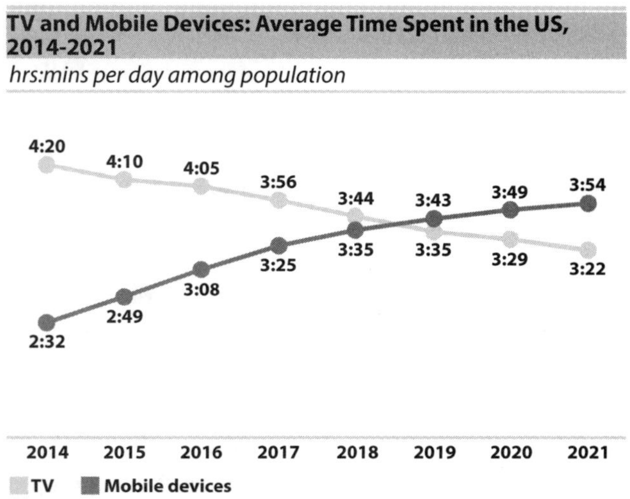

Figure 5.2 TV and mobile devices: average time spent in the United States from 2014 to 2021
(*Source*: emarketer.com)

Contemporary Media Trends

As consumers' lifestyles become more diverse and amplified by the availability of on-demand media content, the less viewers are tied to TV broadcasting, and the more into their on-demand programs available through the streaming subscriptions. Also, consumers spend more and more time on their smartphones and/or tablets than any other media such as TV. When watching TV, the TV is connected to the internet as SmartTV or with a streaming stick or device such as a Roku stick, Fire TV Stick by Amazon, Apple TV, among many others, so the streaming services can be shown on their TV.

North Americans spend an average of 3 hours and 15 minutes per day on their phone.[15] As shown in Figure 5.2, eMarketer (2019) projected that by 2021, time spent on mobile devices would outweigh the time spent watching TV. For instance, they predicted that people would spend 3 hours and 54 minutes per day on mobile devices on average, while they would spend 3 hours and 22 minutes per day watching TV.[16]

Personalization

Due to streaming services and numerous user-generated contents, increasingly consumers are expanding their consumption to cater for their individual interests. There is a great example in the United States: Under Armour, one of the global fitness apparel and footwear brands, dedicated their effort to create a cross-channel shopping experience catered to their end customers.[17] It combines its social presence, influencer marketing with admired athletes, and in-store content and interactive engagement with its "UA Shop" lifestyle-based custom shopping app, and its Connected Fitness community.

Their app gives users a customized experience based on information about them, such as their favorite athletes, exercise routines, and past purchases. For instance, its collaboration with several apps enables the delivery of information about users' fitness activities and locations based on connected fitness trackers. They consequently get tailored product recommendations based on that information.

The UA Play application, which enables users to scan barcodes throughout the store to learn about product details and obtain additional useful content, is one of the other marketing strategies. This is an additional method of tying the networks together and luring viewers to every channel for a memorable experience. As a result, their stores, websites, apps, and social media platforms have seen an increase in traffic and user interaction.

Social media advertising

Web 2.0 technology is the second generation of World Wide Web technology that enables individual users to interact and collaborate with each other on the web. The Web 2.0 technologies allow users to post text, photos, videos, and tag, comment, and interact with other users on the platforms in real-time. It is important to mention that Web 3.0 is on its way to the retail world. The term, Web 3.0, is defined as a new iteration of the World Wide Web technology that incorporates the decentralization, blockchain technology, and token-based economies. The definition was given back in 2014.[18] In this book, we define **social media (social networks)** as a group of internet-based applications that build on the ideological and technological foundations of Web 2.0 and allow the creation and exchange of user-generated content.[19] The popularity of smartphones grew in the 2010s, and social media usage has become one of the most popular activities when people use the internet. In 2021, there were 3.48 billion users on social media globally. Eighty-two percent of the population in the United States (233 million people) had at least one social media account.[20] The average count of social media apps among worldwide internet users is 8.5.[21] On top of that, the average social media user spends around 145 minutes a day scrolling different platforms—plenty of time for businesses to get in front of the eyes of potential customers and spread the message about their brand.[22] Therefore, social media has become an essential part of omnichannel retailers' marketing plans.

Social media advertising refers to the advertising and marketing promotional practices that use social networks to increase brand or company awareness or promote particular products, which eventually lead to sales. For many fashion brands, social media platforms have become one of the most effective marketing channels in the past decade. Most brands nowadays operate multiple social media platforms, such as Facebook, Instagram, YouTube, Twitter, Snapchat, etc., to reach different segments of customers and engage with customers in real-time. For example, founded in 2004, Facebook now has more than 2.7 billion monthly active users worldwide[23] and counts for two-thirds of social media users among US adults.[24] However, Gen Z consumers appear to prefer video-first social platforms like Snapchat, TikTok, and YouTube. Thus, brands should invest in building customer relationships on the social media platforms that their target customers use.

As of July 2021, Nike had more than 164 million followers on Instagram (https://www.instagram.com/nike/). Consider the number of people that a post on Nike's Instagram account can reach, which is more than the total population in Germany (83 million people), France (67 million), or the United Kingdom (66 million).[25] Consumers can interact with a brand and other consumers using text, photos, and videos. This communication format lets consumers no longer be limited to a passive role in their relationship with a brand, and brands can provide immediate response to improve customer serviceability.

Figure 5.3 illustrates the social media presence of the top fifteen most popular luxury brands. All of these luxury brands have accounts on Facebook, Instagram, YouTube, and Twitter to communicate with their followers. Depending on each brand's social media strategies, these luxury brands may also select various platforms such as Pinterest, SnapChat, or TikTok to reach their intended target markets/audiences. Figure 5.3 also demonstrates social media strategies among different luxury brands. On the right half of the table, you may find some foreign social media platforms. Asia is a significant revenue source for many luxury brands. That's why brands like Rolex, Versace, Valentino, and Omega invested in major social media platforms in Asian countries (e.g., WeChat, Weibo, Line, Kakao Talk, etc.). WeChat and Weibo are two major social media platforms in China that have 1.24 billion[26] and 313 million[27] monthly active users, respectively. Kakao Talk is popular in South Korea and Line is popular in Japan and Taiwan.

			Social media platforms																		
Ranking	Brands	Category	Facebook	Instagram	Instagram Beauty	YouTube	Twitter	TikTok*	Tumblr	LinkedIn	Snap Chat	Pinterest	Gucci Podcast	Foursquare	WeChat	Weibo	Youko	Spotify	Line	Kakao	Xiaohongshu
1	Gucci	Fashion	●	●	●	●	●	●	●	●	●	●	●								
2	Chanel	Fashion	●	●		●	●			●											
3	Hermès	Fashion	●	●		●	●			●											
4	Dior	Fashion	●	●		●	●	●	●												
5	Louis Vuitton	Fashion	●	●		●	●	●		●	●	●		●							
6	Rolex	Watch	●	●		●	●			●		●			●	●	●				
7	Tiffany	Jewellery	●	●		●	●			●		●									
8	Prada	Fashion	●	●		●	●	●		●								●			
9	Versace	Fashion	●	●		●	●	●		●		●			●	●					
10	Armani	Fashion	●	●		●	●														
11	Valentino	Fashion	●	●		●	●				●	●			●	●		●	●	●	●
12	Balenciaga	Fashion	●	●		●	●	●													
13	Cartier	Jewellery	●	●		●	●					●									
14	Burburry	Fashion	●	●		●	●	●		●											
15	Omega	Watch	●	●		●	●					●			●	●	●				

Figure 5.3 Summary of social media channels used by luxury brands
(*Source*: Authors)

Social media also changes the relationships between brands and their customers. By looking into the users' profiles, brands can develop a better understanding of their consumer base and implement targeted ads to reach new customers. For instance, Facebook has a Lookalike Audience tool to help retailers to reach new customers who have similar characteristics with their existing customers. Oftentimes, social media can even recast the customer relationship, transforming the customer into an ally or an enemy, not just an audience. For example, many dissatisfied customers now choose to post complaints on the brands' social media account even if they can just return the unsatisfactory products. According to Cotton Incorporated's 2021 Sustainability & Health and Wellness Survey, over a third of consumers (39 percent) say they will take to social media to complain if a specific brand does not hold up.[28] Therefore, social media platforms have become the cornerstone of most fashion brands' marketing strategies.

To summarize, some of the most impactful benefits of social media for fashion retailers include:

- Cultivate brand image and increase brand awareness
- Build consumer relationships
- Increase cross-channel traffic
- Provide immediate response to improve customer serviceability
- Implement targeted ads to reach new customers

Email marketing and advertising

Email marketing is prevalent to any retailer regardless of their distribution strategies. As consumers, we receive numerous emails from retailers every day. There are more than 5.6 billion active email accounts worldwide that are owned by 3.9 billion email users who check them regularly. A joint study by Shop.org and Forrester Research found that 85 percent of retailers in the United States already regard email marketing as one of the most effective customer acquisition strategies, especially for start-ups and small businesses.[29] For every $1 spent on **email marketing**, $38 in revenue was generated, with an average ROI of 122 per cent.[30,31] Thus, retailers consider email marketing as the most effective way to attract potential customers.

One of the most significant advantages of email marketing is cost-effectiveness, compared to mainstream marketing and promotional channels such as print or media ad placements. First, the email marketing's cost-effectiveness is directly associated with the extremely high return on investment mentioned above. Second, email marketing also allows retailers to target specific demographic and psychographic segmentations. Based on those segmentations, they could curate personalized, targeted messages and connect their marketing channels to create a cohesive buyer's shopping journey. Third, the global ubiquity of the internet and email account users allows retailers to easily reach a global audience. Fourth, email marketing can increase **engagement rate** and deepen brand awareness with potential customers, new customers, and repeat customers via creating personalized and customized experiences. Fifth, email marketing offers retailers a testing opportunity to capture valuable customer data to gain more exciting and meaningful customer contact points. Finally, email is perhaps the most accessible and most convenient marketing platform to share information through the power of automation. For example, Tommy Hilfiger's welcome email communication makes you feel like part of an exclusive club. It includes clear images without confusion, just a 20 percent discount code, and a call to action.[32]

The ubiquity of retailers' email communication does have the possibility of presenting some challenges to consumers. They form their perceptions of email communication as negative (e.g., spam or unwanted) or positive (e.g., valuable, attractive, interesting). According to research conducted by Janrain and Blue, almost all consumers (96 percent) have received less targeted information or promotions. The most common types of mistargeted email content include:

- Over 70 percent of customers said the business does not understand the consumer's needs
- Closer to one-half of customers reported that they received mixed information across different communication methods
- About 40 percent of customers reported that misunderstanding is about one's demographics

All these errors can have a severe adverse effect on the brand's advertising campaigns. After receiving non-personalized or mistargeted emails, consumers reported actions such as automatically delete emails (68 percent unsubscribe from emails (54 percent), classify emails as "junk" or "spam" (45 percent), becomes less willing to buy products (29 percent), lessen the frequency of visiting the website (13 percent), and no longer see the website (10 percent).[33]

There are various useful email platforms that can help the fashion business owner to implement their email marketing campaign in a more efficient manner. While you are obtaining the email list, you, as the fashion retail business owner/employee, ought to examine the proper platform for email marketing efforts for your organization. There are more than a dozen major platforms for email marketing campaigns. Many of them are relatively well known through their strong performance and adoption in the marketplace. The most popular email marketing platforms available for fashion entrepreneurs and corporates include Constant Contact, SendGrid, Drip, ConvertKit, AWeber, GetResponse, MailChimp, among others.[34]

Online banner and search advertising

Like any newly established store, once a retailer builds its online presence, the next step is to advertise to let your target market know about your retail business. In this chapter, we introduce commonly used platforms in the online advertising industry, as well as different pricing mechanisms. We will also discuss the online advertising market, the different types of online advertisements, the different players involved in the online advertising ecosystem, and how omnichannel retailers can utilize online advertising to promote their businesses.

For the retail industry, advertising has been an important means to increase traffic and sales. According to eMarketer, among the different industries in digital ads spending, the retail industry spent over $35 billion and ranked the highest among the various industries on digital ad spending each year (Figure 5.4). Along with consumers' changing media consumption patterns, digital ads play an essential role for omnichannel retailers to succeed in the competitive business environment.

The search engine advertising market was built and globalized mainly by Google in the past two decades. Google launched its famous search ads platform, Google AdWords, in 2000. Since then, ad sales have comprised Google's primary revenue source. Google Ads (formerly, Google AdWords) is a self-service advertising program that enables retailers to purchase individualized and affordable keywords to display ads on the google.com search results page (SERP).[35] Since its debut, Google has grown its online ads business to a $147 billion empire. As of October 2020, Google accounted for almost 90 percent of global desktop search traffic.[36] One of the main factors behind the success of Google Ads is its ability to allow individual retailers to purchase carefully selected keywords that target potential customers, regardless of budget. Once a Google Ads program is implemented, when a consumer enters the same keywords or phrase that a retailer targeted, the retailer's ad will be served if their bid is the highest among all the ads bidders (i.e., other retailers/businesses on the platforms) and will be charged at the price of the second-highest bid plus one cent. In contrast to traditional TV or print ads, this

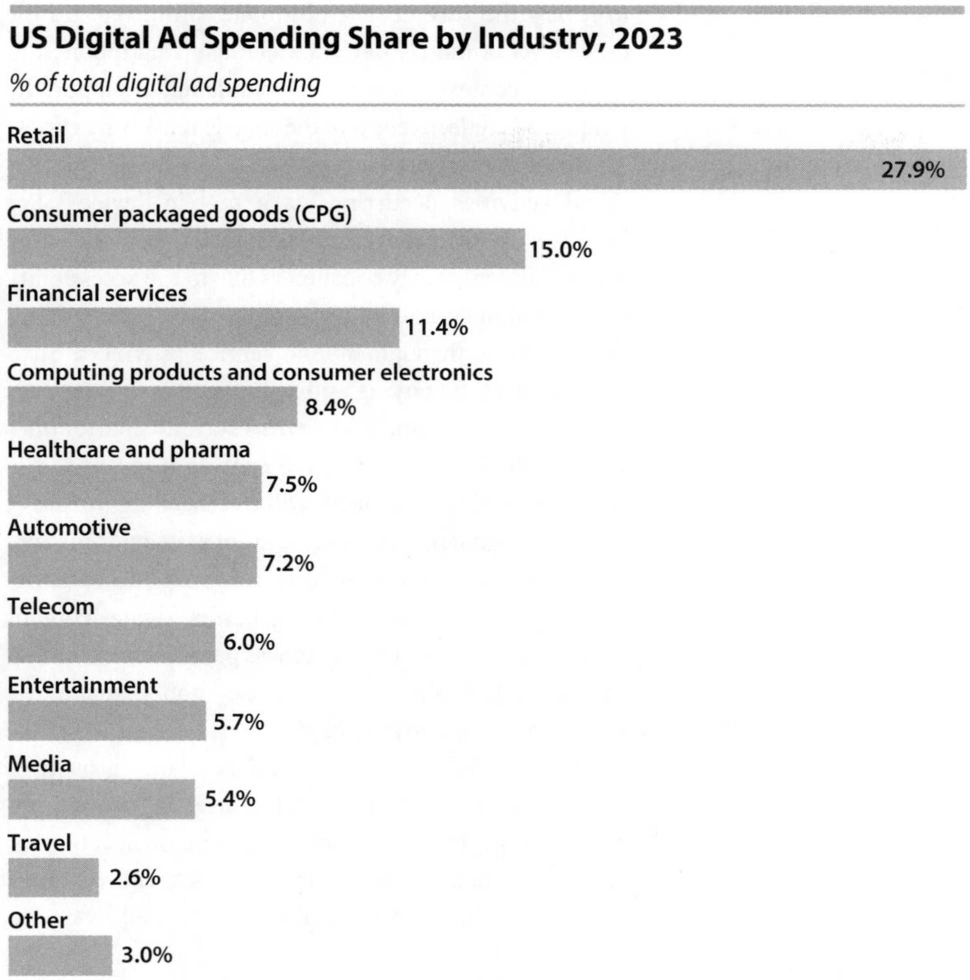

Figure 5.4 Retail industry tops the digital ads spending (*Source*: Insider Intelligence/eMarketer, 2023. https://www.insiderintelligence.com/content/us-digital-ad-spending-by-industry-2023)

innovative and automatic platform sends ads to pre-qualified customers that have already shown interest in the products/services that the retailers are selling to the retailer's website. Another distinct difference between the traditional and the online ads platform is that a retailer will not be charged unless someone clicks on the link. This is called a **pay-per-click (PPC)** pricing mechanism. If done right, **search engine marketing (SEM)** can drive more new website visitors than any other online advertising method. Moreover, it enables more precise targeting of ready-to-purchase customers. For instance, search keywords like "where to buy cowboy boots" show a higher purchase intent than "cowboy boots."

As of September 2021, Google had a market share of 87 percent in the global search-engine market, followed by Microsoft's Bing with 7 percent. Baidu, the biggest search engine in China, has less than 1 percent, as the majority of its users are limited to China.[37]

Ever since the introduction of Google Search in 1997, the worldwide desktop market share of all search engines has been somewhat skewed. The company has also expanded its services to email services, productivity tools, enterprise products, mobile devices (e.g., Android phones), and other ventures. Around 80 percent of Google's revenue is generated through online advertising (Figure 5.5). In 2020, Google's revenue of $181.69 billion was one of the highest for tech companies in the world, and occupied over half of the total search ads market in the world.[38]

Cross-channel promotion

Cross-selling refers to "making a recommendation adjacent to the original product or selling an additional product or service to a customer."[39] The further product/service recommendations are often related to what your customers have already bought. Understanding the customer purchase history or browse history, therefore, is crucial to market the alternative or related products via email marketing and social media marketing.

	2021	2022
Google Search and other	$ 148,951	$ 162,450
YouTube ads	$ 28,845	$ 29,243
Google Network	$31,701	$32,780
Google Advertising total	**$ 209,497**	**$ 224,473**
Google other	$ 28,032	$ 29,055
Google Services total	**$ 237,529**	**$ 253,528**
Google cloud	$ 19,206	$ 26,280
Total revenues	**$ 257,637**	**$ 282,836**

Figure 5.5 Revenues stream breakdown by Alphabet, a parent company of Google (in millions)
(*Source*: Alphabet, Inc. (2022). 10-k form. https://abc.xyz/assets/9a/bd/838c917c4b4ab21f94e84c3c2c65/goog-10-k-q4-2022.pdf

Furthermore, cross-selling can be adopted in other areas. For instance, fashion marketers can suggest the relevant products or related categories to your customers in a reminder email about the abandoned cart or through push notification on a mobile app or even the products can be suggested on the website or mobile site during the customer's next visit. Carefully collected digital shopping behavior can be very handy when you are creating cross-selling opportunities for your business.

In addition to the reminder email about the abandoned cart, an order confirmation email is another fantastic opportunity to generate the cross-selling of the related products that you carry in your retail business. More than two-thirds of online shoppers open their order confirmation email. The order confirmation email may be the perfect way to strategically present the relevant products or services that may be useful to your target customers.

Location-based marketing campaign

Before we discuss the location-based marketing and its campaign strategies, we need to define what it means. **Mobile marketing** refers to two different marketing methods—one method is marketing on or with a mobile device (such as a mobile phone). In contrast, the other (more traditional) method is marketing "on-the-go," or **location-based** or **proximity marketing**, which will be covered in detail later in the chapter. It is helpful for us to review the current state of mobile commerce and the usage level of mobile devices, especially smartphones, in the global context. These are the foundation to support the ubiquity and effectiveness of the mobile marketing effort.

Mobile commerce is defined as business transactional activities occurring via a mobile device.[40] For instance, mobile commerce has penetrated the daily lives of contemporary consumers due to the accessibility of smartphones and other mobile devices and wireless networks through mobile service providers. Such activities include buying and selling goods and services through wireless handheld devices such as smartphones and tablets. Mobile commerce enables users to access online shopping platforms without needing to use a desktop computer. Some examples of existing initiatives and services include mobile gaming, mobile banking, electronic tickets and boarding passes, digital content purchases and delivery, contactless payments and in-app payments, location-based services, mobile marketing and coupons, and loyalty cards.

The Covid-19 pandemic accelerated the growth of mobile commerce and will have a lasting impact on consumer payment and retail transactional activities. The way companies and brands interact with consumers through their devices will continue to add value to customers.[41]

In 2021, the number of smartphone users reached approximately 3.67 billion, accounting for more than 48 percent of the world's population. The number of smartphone users is projected to reach 7.51 billion by 2026.[42] China, India, and US are the countries with the most smartphone users.[43] The latest research shows that 56 percent of children between the ages of 8 and 12 own a mobile phone, 40 percent of Americans will give their children a mobile phone by the age of 10, and 98 percent of Gen Z own a smartphone.[44]

Compared with sales in 2019, consumers spent an average of 30 percent more time on mobile shopping apps in 2020. According to Statista's Digital Market Insights (2024), the revenue from m-commerce sales reached an estimated US$1.7 trillion in 2023, accounting for over half of all retail e-commerce sales. With over 80 percent of visits and 66 percent of orders coming from mobile devices, mobile devices were the main global drivers of retail website traffic and transactions.[45]

Location-based marketing refers to a marketing strategy reaching customers in the right place at the right time with the right message and experience. In this marketing strategy, promotional message/content, selection of medium to reach customers, and services offered to the customers are adapted to a particular customer's current physical location. This marketing strategy is powered by retail technologies such as Bluetooth, GPS, RFID, Wi-Fi, and Beacon.

Location-based marketing is one of the best ways to bring traffic to your location and increase brand awareness. This marketing strategy utilizes geographic location data for advertising and acquiring new customers while improving services for their existing audiences. It involves much less investment yet provides immediate feedback to the campaign. Since location-based marketing uses the customer's opt-in process, it allows the business and location-based marketers to easily segment the target market based on geographic location and demographic information and offer much more **personalized content**. With the nature of the location-marketing occurring in the specific environment with much detailed context about the customers, it does improve the impulse buying behavior in the marketplace. Finally, location-based marketing is not only a marketing implementation tool but is also an excellent data collection tool on customers' market behavior.[46] Below we will discuss the different types of location-based marketing in detail.

Social-Local-Mobile (So-Lo-Mo) marketing refers to a marketing strategy micro-targeting prospects and consumers whenever, wherever, with contextually relevant content, information or promotion that is designed to be shared on social media platforms. This marketing strategy utilizes a social mobile app which can be downloaded and used by the potential customers. Through this social mobile app, the business can track the consumers' physical location and allow customers to input information (e.g., check-ins, posts, status updates, ratings and reviews, etc.) and to receive information (e.g., store hours, products and services, ratings and reviews, coupons and promotions of nearby businesses).

Proximity marketing This involves targeting potential consumers with personalized advertisements based on their interests and enticing them to make a purchasing decision in the immediate future. This marketing is possible due to beacon technology, which was first introduced by Apply iBeacon in 2013. Beacons are small wireless transmitters that use low-energy Bluetooth technology to send signals to other smart devices nearby. They are one of the latest developments in location technology and proximity marketing. In the retail or other commercial space, a beacon device operated by batteries repeatedly broadcasts out an identifier, which is a unique ID number that a mobile device recognizes as unique to the beacon. When a mobile device picks up this identifier, then the beacon will carry out programmed functions within proximity. Usually, we can find this technology placed in strategic locations in a retail environment such as aisle or point-of-sale. It can send mobile alerts with product information, reviews, and deals or rewards to the consumers/mobile device owners when they approach a specific area. In addition, customers may receive the in-store text message or location-based app messaging as a part of the location-based marketing campaign. All in all, the mobile marketing effort is on the rise, as shown in Figure 5.6.

Customer Relationship Management

A company's customer base is one of its most significant assets. And this is true for fashion businesses due to the industry's maturity, the proliferation of brands, and declining brand loyalty among consumers. This asset deserves strict management and supervision. **Customer relationship management** (CRM) refers to a strategic management of acquiring new customers, retaining the current customers, and nurturing preferably life-long interactions with customers. The core of this strategy is to invest time and concerted resources in deepening the relationships with the current customer base and prospects with the aim of retaining their customers as

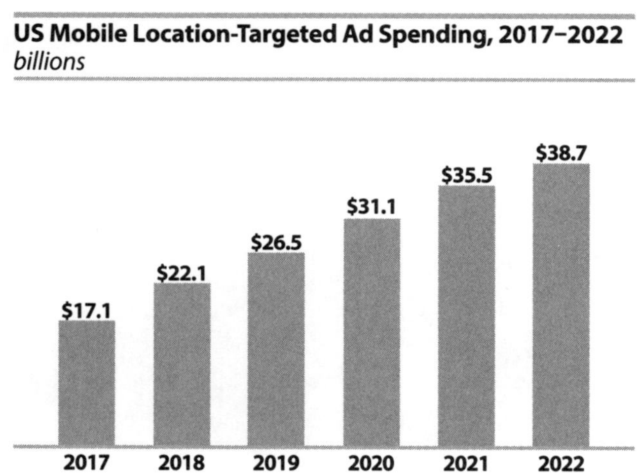

Figure 5.6 US location-based mobile ad spending, 2017–2022
(*Source*: eMarketer.com)

long as possible and increasing their loyalty toward the business. The company's relationship with its customers encompasses direct interactions with customers, such as sales and service-related processes, and the analysis of customer trends and behaviors, among others. Ultimately, CRM enhances the customer's overall experience with the business by delivering memorable shopping journeys and customer service. By doing so, the business can expand the **customer lifetime value (CLV)**, which is defined as a total worth of a customer to your company/brand over the entire period of the customer–company relationship. This is based not just on a purchase-by-purchase basis but also on a holistic relationship such as customer experience during their lifetime relationship with the company. To understand CLV, a company regularly gathers feedback from the customer at all key touchpoints. Thus, CLV contributes to better understanding the existing customer and maintaining a great relationship with them because it is more cost-effective than acquiring new customers. CLV is also supported by the 80–20 rule that 80 percent of the total contribution/revenues come from 20 percent of the customer base that is considered loyal to your company/organization.[47]

Any business can hugely benefit from CRM using advanced software and retail technology to build and operate the customer base. Such CRM software enables fashion businesses to manage all of their interactions with their existing and potential customers. This technology may synchronize browsing and purchasing data with marketing automation and email marketing systems. As of 2020, there were more than 3.9 billion active users worldwide. Businesses can use email marketing and CRM platforms such as Salesforce together to organize contacts, automate activities, and store customer data.[48] CRM software offers a more personalized customer experience through the data collected with various touchpoints with customers. Such technology also monitors which marketing pieces each contact has received and opened. This technology tremendously helps the marketing campaign effort of the omnichannel fashion business with recruitment and retention of the customer base.[49] According to Split Base (2021), 40 percent of all luxury purchases are affected by the customer's digital experience.[50] For example, Canada Goose's email opt-in form is an excellent example of a form that offers a benefit ("get exclusive access to products, experiences and more") without providing a discount. Through well-thought-out CRM, fashion retailers may build long-lasting customer loyalty toward their business and product offerings.

CASE STUDY 5.1

Location-Based Marketing Campaign Powered by Beacon Technology

Macy's has long been the center of the department store experience. For more than a century, it has been America's one-stop-shop for clothes, shoes, cosmetics, jewelry, appliances, and furniture. As e-commerce was fast climbing up the sales revenues, Macy's made a big decision to become the first retail chain that incorporated beacon technology into their 444 stores in the United States This technology is a geo-mapping system that—through a smartphone's Bluetooth technology—can provide real-time information on how customers are interacting with Macy's at the department level. Based on customers' in-store and online purchasing and browsing histories and their current location in the store, Macy's can push marketing collateral and offer promotions on products in nearby departments to the Shopkick app on their phones.

In 2016, Barneys New York adopted the beacon in its flagship store in Manhattan's Chelsea neighborhood. The luxury department store has launched an iBeacon platform and its mobile app to alert users when new content is uploaded and help customers navigate the store. As part of this location-based marketing campaign, when a user opens the Barneys New York app, they will see two prompts: the first to allow push notifications, and the second to enable Barneys to use a customer's location to determine whether they are in or near a Barney store. Once a user grants access, they receive notifications based on inventory in their mobile shopping bag or wish list and recommended internal publications based on what the user recently opened at Barneys' The Window.[51]

As of 2019, Nordstrom, Neiman Marcus, and Alex and Ani are included in the omnichannel fashion retailers that have adopted beacon technology. In addition, Lord & Taylor, Saks, and Uniqlo have also adopted location-based marketing through "smart mannequins" created by University Display, a global mannequin company. These smart mannequins are equipped with beacons inside their mannequins and send a signal to anyone within a 100-foot range of the store to increase foot traffic. Shoppers can instantly see the details of an outfit or purchase any of its components right from their phones. This technology has been widely used by big-box mass merchants such as Target and Walmart.[52]

Discussion Questions:

1. How will location-based retail technology further improve the consumer journeys in brick-and-mortar stores?
2. Discuss other examples from the fashion retailers that you have used personally.
3. What is your position on opt-in marketing strategy using location-based marketing?
4. List the pros and cons of beacon technology and share them with the class.

Career Opportunities

Job Titles	Key Responsibility
Marketing Coordinator	• Implement marketing initiatives with retail partners to build short- and long-term sales. • Develop marketing programs with marketing director, including trunk show activations, social media takeovers, brand ambassador programs. • Train retailer partners on how to leverage the retail portal to increase share of voice, which is a measure of market share of the brand at a given time. ○ Assist retailer partners with digital visuals. ○ Manage all operational aspects of trunk shows. ○ Inspect retailer website compliance. ○ Implement retail marketing programs with all US retail partners, making sure they receive all marketing material and follow up for proper implementation. ○ Manage and execute all marketing, advertising, and promotional activities to our retail partners. ○ Achieve business objectives through effective Marketing & PR strategies. ○ Generate new marketing ideas and opportunities to ensure business success. **Qualifications** • Bachelor's degree in Business, Marketing, Communications, or a related discipline. • 2–3 years' progressive management experience with a combination of corporate retail, visual merchandising, product merchandising, operational marketing, and wholesale sales. • Strong project management skills, attention to detail, and the ability to meet aggressive deadlines and manage multiple projects simultaneously. • Must have excellent interpersonal and written/verbal communication skills; ability to thrive in a cross-functional environment. • Proficiency with Microsoft Office applications (Excel, Word, and PowerPoint, Photoshop, etc.). • Experience developing cross-channel marketing campaigns. • Marketing experience targeted to a variety of different consumers with a strong understanding of cultural trends is preferred. • Superior verbal and written communications skills. • Appreciated previous titles: Marketing Coordinator, Marketing Assistant.

(*Source*: https://accurservices.com/job/marketing-coordinator-luxury-fashion/)

Summary

In modern omnichannel retail companies, brick-and-mortar store, e-commerce website, mail-order catalog, and other direct marketing divisions are no longer separate from one another. All omnichannel retailers prioritize cross-channel cooperation and integration. Omnichannel organizational structures benefit retailers in a synergistic way among the various channels they operate. Semi-integrated, fully-integrated, and independent structures are three prevalent types. The successful omnichannel retailers have been working toward fully integrated organizations and operate their businesses internationally without border or geographical limits.

Integration among the channels comes with challenges including synchronizing information technology, sharing customer data among various channels, implementing customer service procedures, and embracing changes. Integrated marketing strategies accompany changes in developing brand equity across channels, merchandise selling and pricing strategies, distributional strategies and practices, and promotional strategies and practices. Among other things, the consumer media consumption pattern has led to significant changes in promotional strategies. Without question, retailers spend most advertising dollars on digital advertising including social media advertising, email advertising, and online banner and search advertising.

Contemporary consumers are price conscious and digitally savvy. Cross-shoppers are people who buy across a variety of price points and retail channels. They prioritize convenience over all else and feel at ease making purchases online or through other channels at their own pace and choice. Designing and managing omnichannel organizations that meet or surpass customer expectations requires effective organizational leadership.

Key Terms

Beacon
Cross-selling
Customer relationship management (CRM)
Customer lifetime Value (CLV)
Email marketing
Engagement rate
Fully integrated structures
Google Ads
Independent structures
Location-based marketing
Mobile commerce
Mobile marketing
Pay-per-click
Personalized content
Proximity Marketing
Semi-integrated structures
Search engine marketing (SEM)
Social-local-mobile (slo-lo-mo) marketing
Social media advertising
Social media (social networks)
Web 2.0

Reflection and Discussion Questions

1. Organizational structures have changed since the advent of e-commerce, moving from independent, pure play sites to more complex, completely integrated structures. Which organizational model will eventually control the bulk of omnichannel retailers? Explain why.
2. Which of the barriers/challenges to cross-channel integration do you think retailers need to address first? Provide a couple of solutions to the issue you've chosen.
3. When it comes to cross-channel shopping and service choices, customers have high expectations. What fulfillment options are required to make the option of placing an online purchase and picking it up in-store a reality? In your answer, draw on your personal experience.
4. As new technologies are developed, more people are using alternative media. What is the current state of ads on social media platforms? In your response, make a case for the benefits and drawbacks of this advertising platform.
5. If internet banner advertising is waning in effectiveness, what is taking its place? In your response, go over two alternatives or prospects.
6. All marketing strategies must include customer relationship management (CRM). How does CRM help omnichannel businesses improve their customers' multichannel experiences?
7. In light of technological advancements, how are recruitment, placement, and training methods changing? What components of the hiring procedure won't likely alter entirely?
8. When compared to catalog retailers, what important factors influence the profit and loss of online retailers? Should retailers look at the performance of the business as a whole or regard each channel as a separate profit center?

CHAPTER 6

Omnichannel Supply Chain and Logistic Management

Learning Objectives

Upon completion of this chapter, you will be able to:

- Compare and contrast supply chain management strategies in multichannel and omnichannel retailers
- Understand the logistical challenges of building an omnichannel supply chain
- Give examples of consumer experience with an omnichannel logistic system
- Describe types of fulfillment systems
- Assess the impact of returns and recent market benchmarks
- Identify strategies to use return management data to improve business decisions

In this chapter, we will discuss the differences between supply chain management strategies in multichannel retailers and omnichannel retailers. An integrated database/platform is essential for delivering an omnichannel consumer experience that is cohesive and convenient across different contact points. Moreover, data must be available across ordering/inventory systems, fulfillment, and return systems. Finally, the product return data should be communicated with product, marketing, sales and fulfillment departments for future business improvements.

Figure 6.1 Overview of the supply chain management

Multichannel and Omnichannel Supply Chain Management Differences

In the field of supply chain management (SCM), omnichannel SCM solutions are often used interchangeably with multichannel SCM solutions. In addition, retailing and marketing professionals often use these interchangeably, which can cause confusion as well, as they are not. From the consumers' point of view, both types of supply chain operations seek to provide multiple transactional channels to consumers. However, understanding the elements of omnichannel versus multichannel supply chains is essential to win the market competition in the plethora of emerging brands and retailers in the fashion industry. In this section, we will discuss how these differ.

What Are the Differences?

Omnichannel SCM may appear similar to multichannel SCM in respect to serving consumers across different transactional channels. Both multichannel and omnichannel retailers provide customers with many touchpoints or channels to support the customers' browsing and purchasing experience. **Omnichannel SCM** refers to "a set of process to effectively and efficiently integrate suppliers, manufacturers, distribution centers, distributors, and retailers so that products are produced and distributed through collaborative planning of demand, production, logistics, and inventory deployment" (p. 8).[1] The end goal is to achieve customer desired value and satisfaction while minimizing the total cost for the business through a synchronized and collaborative planning process. As shown in Figure 6.1, SCM oversees the entire pipeline of the products from concept to consumer.

In the optimized omnichannel retail environment, each store or location performs as a warehouse or distribution center through their online platform to order products and ship to store or to the customer's mailing address.[2,3] The key advantage is full integration among the supply chain partners and components across all channels—online, mobile, brick-and-mortar store, social shopping, and others. As result, this fully integrated supply chain structure offers a seamless customer experience from information seeking, browsing, purchasing, and returning or exchanging the purchased item. This can make the customers' shopping journey much smoother and more convenient, with consistency and reliable services 24/7 with no geographical limitations.[4]

Recall the previous example of consumers shopping at businesses utilizing multichannel sales. Unlike the drawbacks of multichannel sales, omnichannel SCM solutions give consumers the flexibility to ship items from e-commerce sites to their home or brick-and-mortar store locations for them to physically pickup the items from the store. Moreover, consumers may opt to complete purchases online and in storefronts simultaneously, and if an item is unavailable in the store, consumers can order from their smartphone or through the in-store kiosk or sales associate's mobile device.

This is the omnichannel shopping experience, a constant flow of products and customer services between all sales channels seamlessly. Consumers that have the freedom to purchase items while still making in-store purchases and vice versa are more likely to complete their purchases. Similarly, if consumers run into any of the potential roadblocks in multichannel-exclusive supply chains, they are likely to abandon their shopping carts for other competitors.

Rather multichannel supply chains predated omnichannel. Multichannel SCM soared in response to the rise of e-commerce in the early 2000s. **Multichannel SCM** refers to offering additional transactional channels to consumers which allow them to access product information and purchase goods without geographical and temporal limitations.[5] For instance, fashion retailers with existing mail-order catalogs had an advantage at the beginning of the multichannel supply chain based on their know-how and well-established mailing lists. Some examples include J. Crew, Lands' End, and Victoria's Secret, among many others. These retailers added e-commerce sites to their existing channels—physical stores and mail-order catalogs—and made a much smoother transition into the multichannel supply chain compared to traditional brick-and-mortar retailers.

Retailers adopting multichannel supply chains tend to develop organizational silos that focus solely on serving one channel, and each channel remains separate from one another, with its own department, warehouse, and transportation solutions. For instance, the online catalog is different from items stocked in physical stores, and pricing may differ. Each store has its own stock, often jealously guarded, and the organization's online store is a separate entity from retail stores. Unfortunately, a disconnect grows between multiple retail channels, increasing costs and reducing visibility across the multichannel supply chain of a company. Until the mid 2010s, this is typically what happened to many department stores including Saks Fifth Avenue which operated Saks Direct versus Saks Stores. Moreover, many of the retailer's outlet stores still operate as separate entities and they do not accept returns from the full-price retail stores and vice versa. Instead, they offer store merchandise credit to encourage the customers to spend the fund at the outlet stores (e.g., Polo Ralph Lauren outlets).

Logistical Challenges of an Omnichannel SCM

Omnichannel SCM sounds ideal for fashion retailers. However, it is not that easy to implement because it does present some logistical challenges to be managed and overcome. **Logistics** is defined as the entire process of planning, implementing, and controlling the efficient flow of materials and products, services, information, energy, people, and other resources that move into, through, and out of a firm (in both the public and private sectors) to the customers.[6] To maximize the firm's profit, optimizing the logistics is necessary. Ideal logistics involves the positioning of resources at the right time, in the right place, at the right cost, at the right quality, while optimizing a given performance measure and satisfying customers amid a given set of constraints. Logistics adds value to the supply chain process when inventory is strategically positioned to achieve sales.

As shown in Figure 6.2, there are many nodes or supply chain partners involved in the logistics systems. A logistics system refers to a network of organizations, people, activities, information, and resources involved in the physical flow of the products from supplier to end-user/customer. It consists of five facets: a) order management, b) inventory, c) transportation, d) warehousing, material handling, and packaging, and e) facility network. An omnichannel supply chain does present many challenges, including managing the flows of products across multiple channels, aligning inventory and delivery, coordinating with suppliers, manufacturers, and third-party logistic providers, connecting in-store purchases and pickups with online orders and even international orders. And lastly, managing the information and communication among logistical partners and sub-systems.

The first major logistical challenge for the omnichannel retailer is *inventory visibility*. When the business has many channels to coordinate, it is naturally difficult to track inventory spread across multiple distribution centers and retail locations, compared to single or multichannel SCM cases. The second challenge is *potential disconnection between supply chain partners*. When different warehouses and distribution centers operate on various systems, communication can be interrupted, and the logistical flow can be weakened. An omnichannel system will not work correctly if different systems do not communicate with each other. Therefore, the omnichannel retailer should ensure the compatibility among the various systems or unify the systems throughout the channels, warehouses, and point of sale (POS). The third challenge is *speed of delivery of the order to the end user*. Ensuring speedy order fulfillment and delivery is one of the most critical parts of selling across channels. When omnichannel customers buy online, they expect to receive order confirmation within a few hours and to receive the order at their choice of location within a few days at most. *Returns management* would be the fourth major challenge in omnichannel SCM. When a company is establishing an omnichannel logistics system, processing order returns is a crucial consideration. If the company cannot provide a simple return to the company using multiple options—in-store or via mail using pre-paid label or self-label, it is likely to lose future orders. This is not a choice for the business anymore, it is a must from the omnichannel shoppers' expectations and demands. The final challenge is the *cost of operating multiple channels.* Omnichannel seems like it should command higher profit margins. However, this is only possible when you have the volume of sales simultaneously occurring seamlessly via multiple channels. The fact is that each channel comes with operating expenses. Storing, packaging, and delivery of inventory from multiple sites costs money.[7]

Focus on the Consumer Journey

In order to unlock the financial gains through omnichannel SCM, the retailer must focus on the consumer journey at every touchpoint. According to McKinsey and Company's report, customer expectations in service journeys in the era of omnichannel retailing fall into three categories: a) *speed and flexibility*, represented as minimum processing time, responsiveness, and needs-based service, b) *reliability and transparency*, including proactive outreach and communication, and c) *interaction and care with* comprehensive competence, empathy, and personal attention.[8] As shown in Figure 6.2, when

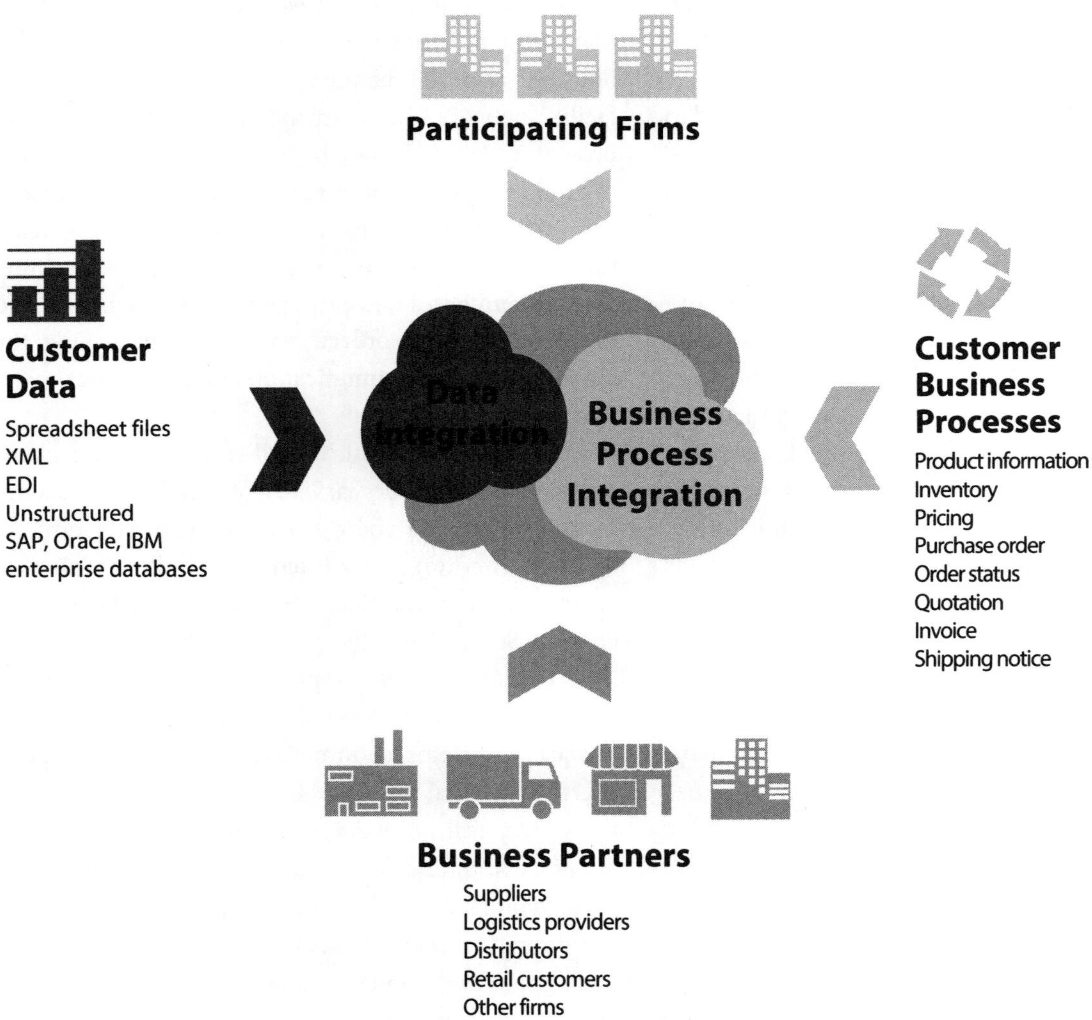

Figure 6.2 Cloud-based supply chain
(*Source*: Catherine Jai)

multiple network partners are involved, often retailers adopt a cloud-based logistics platform to continuously communicate and collaborate with the different parties. Through real-time shared information about the location of the inventory, dispatch of the shipment, delivery updates, and customer preference and sales data, among others, all parties involved in the logistics operations can be on the same page to harmoniously and effectively support the customer journey and business's goals.

First of all, the retailer ought to offer the customer shopping options through any channel: pickup in-store, or have products delivered to home or other locations (e.g., click and collect). A Pittsburgh-based American omnichannel retailer, American Eagle Outfitters offers "Buy Online Ship to Store (BOSS)," which is a smart strategy to bring the online shoppers to the physical stores to get the instant gratification of trying on and additional shopping needs met.

Needless to say, digital channels have completely transformed the ways that customers prefer to shop. Beyond the expectation that information and services will be accessible with a few keystrokes, customers have also become accustomed to engaging with companies through multiple channels. Many customers, for instance, use different channels to gather information on products and to make a purchase. Social media and chat are also rapidly gaining channel share. However, many companies have subpar digital capabilities that actually increase customer demand for engagement. Indeed, organizations that attempt to migrate customers to digital channels before they are fully ready can trigger the "**boomerang effect**," in which customers can keep coming back to a company multiple times in an effort to resolve a problem.[9]

Real-time inventory tracking helps both the customer and the business. From the customer's perspective, this would allow them to avoid abandoned carts and streamline shopping, while businesses could gain the ease of visualizing their inventory online as well.[10,11] For instance, Louis Vuitton, one arm of the number one global luxury conglomerate Louis Vuitton Moët Hennessey (LVMH), offers a centralized inventory visualization to both online customers and their customer advisors. When you enter your postal code, their e-commerce site shows the locations of their physical store that has the items. In the physical store, the customer advisor looks up the inventory in the same manner that the customer would do on the mobile tablet to assist their customers.

The Goals of Omnichannel Logistic System

In this section, we will discuss the goals of the omnichannel logistic system in contrast to traditional retailers' logistical practices. In the days of implementing traditional warehousing methods, a retailer would divide the supply chain by product type. In contemporary omnichannel warehousing and fulfillment centers, you would experience the warehouse and fulfillment centers organized and operated in a way to accommodate the disassembly and assembly services for different goods. This is to increase the *responsiveness*: in other words, satisfying customer requirements in a timely manner. In addition, due to the innate characteristics of omnichannel retailing, the customers can shop for the products anytime and anywhere through the multiple modes of the shopping channels. Therefore, multichannel logistic systems do not suffice to meet omnichannel customers. The omnichannel logistic systems are to be flexible and agile to fulfill the order seamlessly and promptly. Figure 6.3 presents a logistics operation flow chart to visualize the back-end of the omnichannel retail logistics. For instance, Amazon is soaring its expansion of fulfillment centers to mid-sized cities to speed up their fulfillment lead time, optimizing the logistics system. Office supplies and commonly purchased items on Amazon are available to be delivered next day through their own fulfillment trucks and part-time employees. This is only possible due to their 110 active fulfillment centers in the United States and 185 centers globally.[12]

Omnichannel logistic systems will clearly maintain visibility of all inventory: knowing where the product is is an essential requirement for omnichannel distribution, and the company needs to have real-time visibility of all stock keeping units (SKUs) located in the fulfillment centers or physical stores. This is to *reduce the variance* and possible delay in customer order processing. Once the fulfillment has been completed regardless of the channel that the order was placed, the omnichannel retailer must utilize their customer behavioral data and artificial intelligence to deepen their analytics about the customers regarding order fulfillment, delivery, and exchanges and returns. Insights into the customer's data in relation to logistical areas can support better strategizing of the customer journey all together. Through various facility network members (also known as supply chain members), omnichannel retail logistics systems

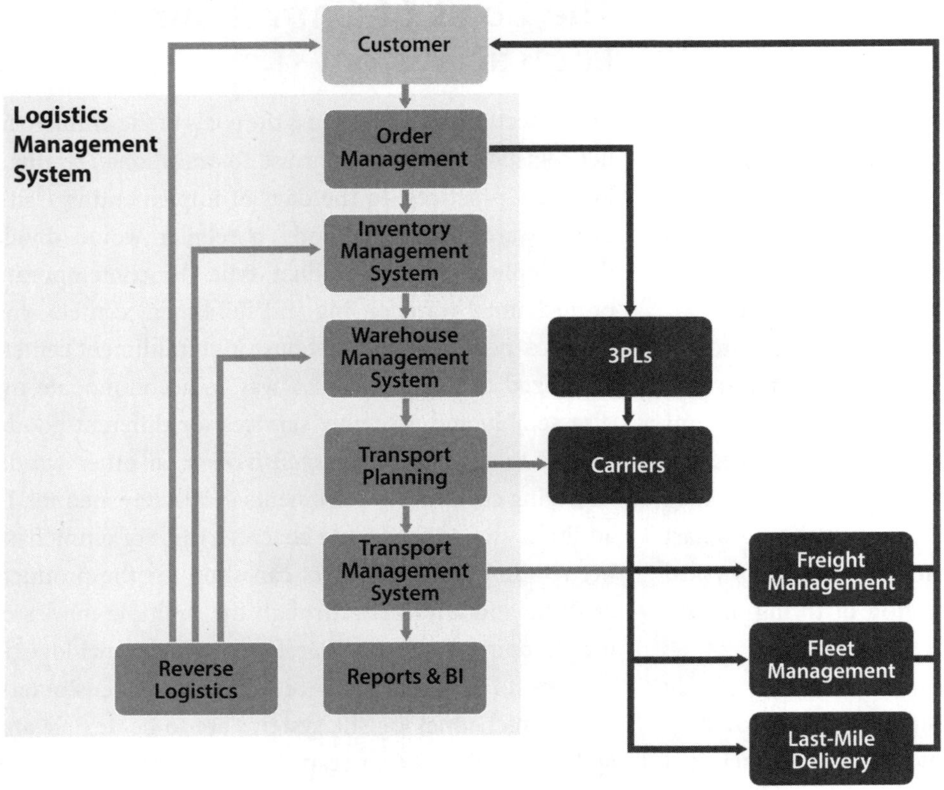

Figure 6.3 Logistics operations flow chart

aim to *reduce the inventory* on hand in their custody; thus, they control asset commitment and increase inventory turnover rate.[13]

Omnichannel logistic systems aim to ensure an efficient operation. Especially for labor-intensive sorting and packaging operations, the retailer can *minimize labor costs* by utilizing a smart warehouse management system (WMS).[14] For instance, Nordstrom is working with Attabotics, offering an automated cube storage and retrieval system, and Tompkins Robotics with an automated product sorting capacity, at its distribution center in the San Jose area to optimize labor costs and speedy deliveries of products to consumers. The cosmetics are stocked on row after row of shelving to fulfill online orders for the West Coast as well as to help stock its stores in the area. With the adoption of these robotics in the warehouse, they aim to get closer to customers and avoid extended shipping and fulfillment delays. Moreover, those robotics technologies require 90 percent less space than other alternatives, which allows the company to be nimbler and stock more inventory.[15] When possible, omnichannel logistic systems will aim to *consolidate the shipment* to save on transportation cost per each order received. Transportation cost is directly related to the type of product, size of shipment, and distance traveled. On average, more than 60 percent of each logistics dollar is spent on transportation. Another goal of the omnichannel logistics management is to *maintain high quality* of the products and services. When product quality fails after delivery of the order and replacement is necessary, logistical costs rapidly accumulate. Logistical costs, once expended, cannot be reversed or recovered. Therefore, commitment to zero-defect order-to-delivery performance is a main goal of omnichannel logistics.[16] Last but not least, the logistics system must *support the product life cycle* and contribute to the sustainability effort of the business, as consumer interest in this area is rapidly growing.

Delivering a Unified Consumer Experience: Data

In this section, we will discuss how omnichannel retailers can deliver a unified customer experience through a seamless logistics management system and flawless communication with partners and customers. Once again, the critical advantage of omnichannel SCM can be the synchronized collaboration among the channels and facility network members through a continuous process and communication. The frictionless flow of data regarding product inventory, fulfillment process, order management including order automation, and return process is imperative to enable the logistics system to work efficiently and harmoniously. Figure 6.4 exhibits the flow of the information within the integrated logistics system. Light gray rectangles indicate inbound logistics and warehousing management, medium gray rounded rectangles indicate the inventory management system, and medium gray rectangles indicate the fulfillment system and outbound logistics. In warehouse or distribution centers in the United States, radio frequency identification (RFID) is commonly used to expedite the logistical and communication process with parties involved in the flow of the inventory. For instance, Lululemon, the world leading athleisure brand, fully operates its stores with RFID technology to locate the inventory in the backroom quickly and assist the customers with the ordering process to ship to their mailing address or store pickup.

Product Inventory System

In the fashion industry, *inventory control* can be broadly defined as the activity of checking and monitoring the inventory level of products at all SKUs. A **product inventory system** is a method used to manage and locate inventory. The inventory control software can help fashion retailers manage product (re)ordering by monitoring all aspects of the inventory quantity on the shelves, storage rooms, and warehouses. In the omnichannel supply chain context, this inventory control will also monitor the inventory levels in all physical stores operated by the fashion retailers in addition to the warehouses, **third-party logistics (3PL)** fulfillment centers, and/or distribution centers. Figure 6.5 shows the various facets that inventory management oversees.

Especially, small- and medium-sized retailers should consider an inventory management system with POS integration. An inventory management system is an excellent way for small- to medium-sized retailers with multiple transactional channels to keep their inventory accurate. With the integration of POS, the inventory

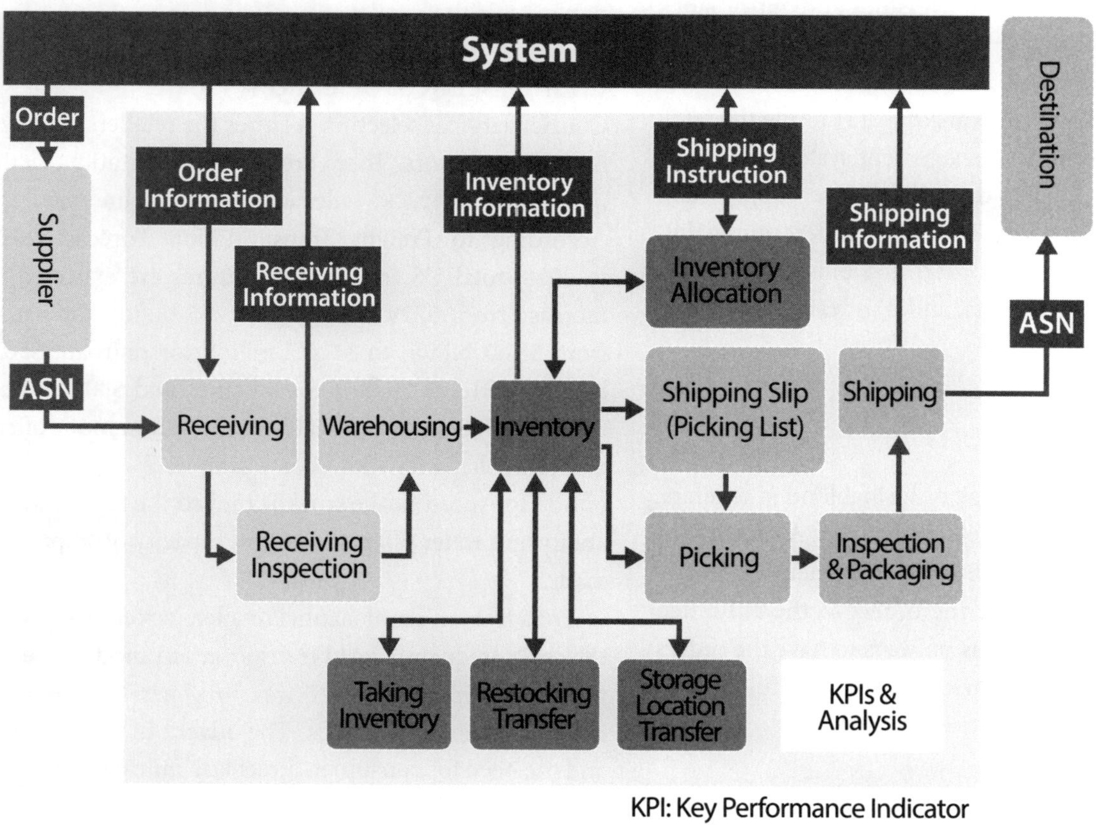

Figure 6.4 Information flow within the integrated logistics system

Figure 6.5 Overview of product inventory management

management system is automatically updated every time a customer makes a purchase, thereby improving real-time accuracy of inventory level for the business.

In addition, a product inventory management system enables the business to avoid overstock and out-of-stock situations by tracking inventory levels. By reducing the inventory level, the retailer can lower their asset commitment and overall total costs of running the retail business. The inventory management systems do many other functions crucial to the omnichannel supply chain including a) tracking sales processes, orders, and deliveries, b) generating work orders and bills of materials, c) organizing inventory data, and d) offering security of transactional data.[17,18]

Fulfillment System

The order fulfillment strategy is the lifeblood of retailers, especially in an omnichannel supply chain. A **fulfillment system** refers to the organized management of receiving, processing, and delivering orders to the customer. In this section, we will focus on ways to have the orders fulfilled—in-house fulfillment, outsourced fulfillment, and third-party logistics providers.

In-House Fulfillment

In-house order fulfillment is when an order is processed and fulfilled by the business itself, without seeking assistance from outside the business. The significant advantage of keeping order fulfillment in-house is complete control of the fulfillment process. Your team picks and packs the products from your shelves, and you use a freight carrier that you have selected on the basis of price, delivery speed, and reliability. The business has full control over package/order handling, shipping accuracy, and on-time delivery rates. In addition, the business may be able to manage the returns quicker, thus happier customers. This fulfillment option is ideal for companies with highly customized products with low order quantities or only seasonal shipments because in-house fulfillment requires well-trained employees, warehouse technology, and management software in place. All three requirements need upfront allocation of resources to make this work including warehouse rent, warehouse equipment, labor, utilities, insurance, shipping materials, warehouse software and staff training, and shipping costs.[19]

Outsourced Fulfillment

Outsourced fulfillment is when the process of storing the inventory, shipping the order out to the customer, and order/refund processing is handled by an organization outside the retailer.

Courier services selection

Courier services selection requires the retailers to weigh on various factors. There are five transportation methods including truck, railroad, water, pipeline, and air. According to Freight Transportation Forecast 2017 to 2028, total US freight expenditures are expected to increase from $719 billion to $1,245 billion for truck, from $81.3 billion to $120.2 billion for railroad, $56.1 billion to $163.54 billion for pipeline, and $30.5 billion to $54.6 billion for air.[20] Each transportation mode offers different characteristics. For example, air is the best option for speed, while truck is ranked the top for availability and water offers the largest capacity of shipment/load.

For a fashion omnichannel retailer, parcel services are the most frequently used transportation mode to reach the customers. Parcel services in general present an important part of logistics. The advent of e-commerce and the need for consumer-direct last-mile delivery have significantly increased demand for package delivery services. Packages are regularly transported by using the line-haul services of rail, truck, and air.

Federal Express (FedEx) was the first widely recognized air package services provider established in 1973. United Parcel Service (UPS) was founded in 1907 and started with specialized service—contract delivery of local shipments for department stores. Today, UPS offer more than 20 different service options regionally, nationally, and globally. Among those, UPS Supply Chain Solutions® provides value added services to a large account to expedite the shipping and handling lead time. For instance, UPS offers inbound, warehousing, outbound, and returns management.[21] The UPS Supply Chain Solutions facility stocks Nike shoes at its warehouse in Louisville, Kentucky, and processes orders hourly. All related communication and financial administration are handled by a UPS call center. In addition, United States Postal Service (USPS) introduced a new service called "If it fits it ships" in 2010, which offers one flat rate for any shipment between two US domestic locations using the size—not weight—of the package. In addition, free-of-charge boxes are offered to the customers, thus adding convenience to the micro-sized businesses (e.g., Etsy) and peer-to-peer (P2P) sellers (e.g., Poshmark, a social commerce platform with over 80 million users who can buy and sell from fashion to home goods to electronics).

In today's omnichannel supply chain environment, FedEx's "Smart Post" exhibits a great collaboration with USPS. This service utilizes FedEx assets for original pickup, regional sortation, and line haul operations while utilizing the USPS for its vast reach to every address in the United States for final-mile delivery. This is an example of a strategic partnership that combines the strengths of both companies to achieve a win-win parcel service offering.

When an omnichannel retailer is to select a courier service for its business, there are several facets to examine including ease of service (frequency of pickups), area coverage (local, national, international), fee structure, service guarantees, order trackability, proof of delivery, package security, and compatibility with inventory management software/technology.[22]

Third-party logistics

Third-party logistics (3PL) refers to an outsourcing of one or more functions of logistics services. Most common 3PL services are warehousing and fulfillment of the order. Companies that use 3PL services outsource 69 percent to warehouses and 81 percent to domestic transportation. When inventory is not on the move between locations it may have to be stored for some time in the warehouse or distribution center. Warehousing is the activity related to receiving storing, and shipping materials to and from production or distribution locations. Beyond those functions, 3PL providers can offer inventory management, transportation, and returns management. A common example is a manufacturer using "Fulfillment by Amazon" (FbA) to process their online sales from top to bottom. Imagine you are a small business owner selling your products on Amazon. If you choose the FbA option, then you will send the products to Amazon's fulfillment centers. Then, Amazon would catalog and store the products. When the order is received, Amazon would pick and pack your products and ship your products out to the customer and provide order support, including returns management (see Figure 6.6).

The advantages of using 3PL service include a) access to 3PL delivery and fulfillment optimization, b) reduced overhead (e.g., warehouse rent cost, fulfillment team payroll cost), c) easier management of internationalization through a 3PL global fulfillment network, and d) ease of set up of logistic solutions. However, 3PL comes with some disadvantages including a) lack of customer service support, b) steep set-up fees, c) limited control over package and order processing, d) possible quality-control problems, and e) possible complications regarding returns management that could frustrate customers.[23,24]

Drop shipping

Drop shipping refers to a fulfillment option completed by a wholesaler or manufacturer. To fulfill an order through this option, the retailer needs to forward orders to the wholesaler or manufacturer. As shown in Figure 6.7, drop shipping may appear similar to 3PL to the customer. In the case of drop shipping, the retailer does not keep the items it sells in stock. Instead, when an item is sold, the retailer purchases it from a third-party supplier. The supplier may be a manufacturer or a wholesaler that procures products from manufacturers to sell to drop shippers. In the drop shipping fulfillment option, the supplier handles all orders and ships them to customers. The retailer acts as an intermediary to collate the orders from the customer, and then pass the order information to the supplier. The retailer is only billed for the products sold. The major advantages of drop shipping include a) being free from the responsibility

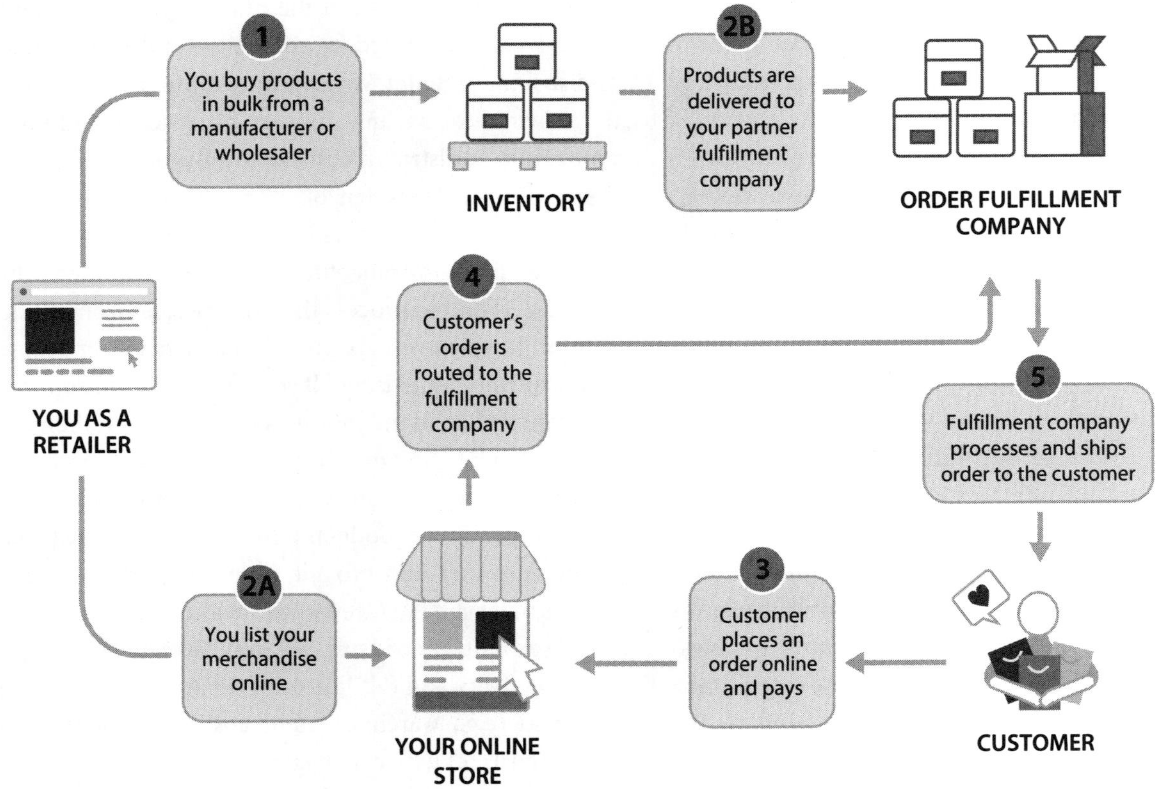

Figure 6.6 Overview of operation of order fulfillment completed by a 3PL provider

Figure 6.7 Drop shipping operation flow

of fulfillment, b) starting and running a business with less capital to acquire the inventory, c) freedom to test products, d) capacity to offer broader product assortment, and e) option to afford higher risks, and higher returns on untested products. However, this fulfillment option also bears some disadvantages such as a) dependence on external parties (wholesalers or manufacturer), b) limited profits compared to other options, c) lack of control over the entire fulfillment process.[25,26] For instance, this fulfillment option is very popular among e-commerce startups and department stores (e.g., Bloomingdale's) to minimize inventory risks and costs while increasing the merchandise assortment level.[27]

Order Management and Automation with POS Integration

Order management refers to the process of getting a customer's order from your possession to their hands. It needs to be fully synchronized with the warehouse and inventory management systems to update information in all aspects and to be able to proceed with further processing steps almost immediately. An order management system is a software platform that can track your sales, orders, fulfillment, inventory, and the process of linking them together. The system can help companies adopt an order automation, which is when software automatically manages new order details that are sent from an e-commerce site to a warehouse.

Many of the order management and order automation software are not integrated with a Point-of-Sale (POS) system. The POS is a key to document, process, and complete the sales transactions between the business and the customer. In 2020, the value of mobile POS transactions was more than $1 billion, and 54 percent of enterprises have used mobile POS to process transactions. For stores that use mobile POS systems, 79 percent of them are small- and medium-sized brands with annual sales revenue below $10 million, while 21 percent are large enterprises.[28] As the omnichannel logistics system advances, it is more and more common to see the one-stop supply chain software solutions available.

For instance, let's review how Brightpearl, one of the fulfillment management software options, works for omnichannel retailers. Their omnichannel solution aims to consolidate all logistical systems into one management software from receiving inventory, orders, warehouses, shipping, and fulfillment. These activities are all managed in one single system. As soon as an order is placed, picked, packed, and shipped, the retailer is updated on the status. Based on the replenishment activities, invoices are issued, and inventory levels and accounts are automatically updated. They offer a seamlessly integrated workflow in relation to an overall logistics system. In addition, this fulfillment management software is compatible with e-commerce platforms including Amazon, eBay, Walmart, Shopify, BigCommerce, and Magento (Adobe commerce) as well as shopping and fulfillment vendors such as ShipStation, DHL, UPS, and FedEx, among others. Notably, it enables "Fulfillment by Amazon" (FbA) on orders from other e-commerce platforms, such as Shopify, Big Commerce, Magento, eBay, and others.[29]

Logistics Management Systems

For larger fashion companies, an **enterprise resource planning (ERP)** tool with a WMS integration is the way to go. The ERP system integrates all back-office functions to create a master data environment including locations of each component and inventory. It also updates the status of the order placed to replenish inventory for the business. As a part of integrated logistics management system (shown in Figure 6.8), WMS automates the warehouse processes to ensure proper supervision of goods from entering the warehouse (receiving, also known as **in-bound logistics**) to leaving the warehouse (transporting, also known as **out-bound logistics**). ERP with robust WMS makes it easy to manage clothing inventory for omnichannel fashion retailers. When an order is received, the WMS processes the order and updates the inventory management system. Using the **Distribution Order Management (DOM)** system, the retailer may be able to optimize the fulfillment, so orders arrive to customers on time while incurring the lowest cost. DOM system processes the order routing, order splitting, shipping, inventory forecasting, reordering, and inventory management. The **Order Management System (OMS)** allows the retailers to consolidate all orders received from various transactional channels and synchronize the order information with other fulfillment service providers. Lastly, **Transportation Management System (TMS)** platform/software provides the retailer visibility into day-to-day transportation operations and streamlines the shipping process to make it easier for businesses to manage and optimize their transportation operations, whether they are by land, air, or sea. TMS also provides trade compliance information and documentation and ensures the timely delivery of freight and goods.[30] For instance, Oracle offers platforms and software solutions to manage SCM and manufacturing.

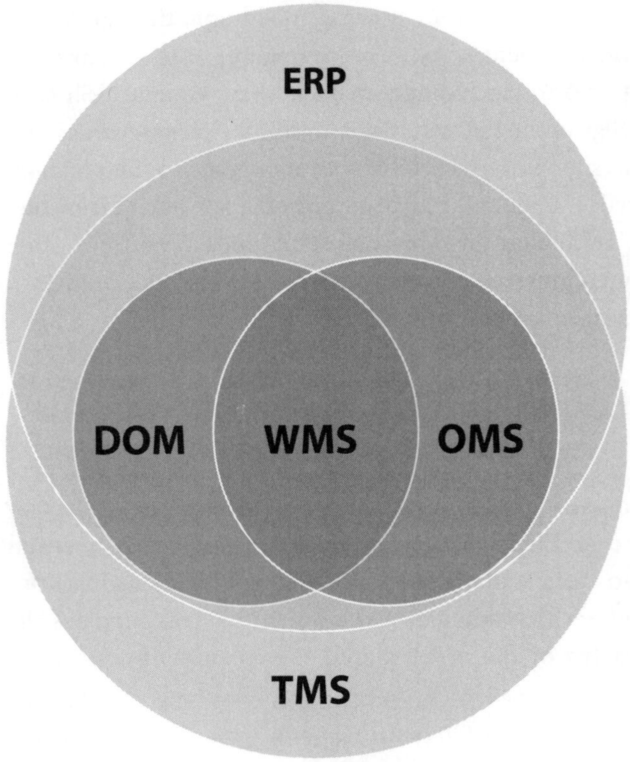

Figure 6.8 Integrated logistics management systems
(*Source:* the author.)

Returns Management Systems

Consider how consumers may feel frustrated when confronted with businesses using multichannel solutions, instead of omnichannel ones. Product purchased online can only be shipped to a consumer's address. Items purchased in the store may have different prices from online sales. Meanwhile, promo codes from emails or online deals may not be accepted in brick-and-mortar stores. As a result, consumers become frustrated and face many different obstacles to completing orders when products are not available in their channel of choice. These issues may continue when it comes to the return process for customers and return management for the business. **Returns management** refers to the reverse logistics and order management process that can help the omnichannel retailers improve their customer's shopping experience.[31] **Reverse logistics** is a way to handle the return, reuse, recycling, or disposal of products that make the reverse journey from the customer to the supplier. All in all, the return management process is part customer support, part (reverse) logistics, and part inventory management. In the next section, we will have a deep dive into the reasons why consumers return their fashion purchases.

Top Reasons for Returns

According to an academic journal article by Bernon, Cullen, and Gorst (2016), return rates for online retailing can be double those for stores. They suggest that omnichannel returns management—network configuration and returns management processes—has yet to fully mature.[32] As shown in Figure 6.9, over 10 percent of the 2020 retail sales in the United States were returned. The returned merchandise is worth $428 billion.[33] In an

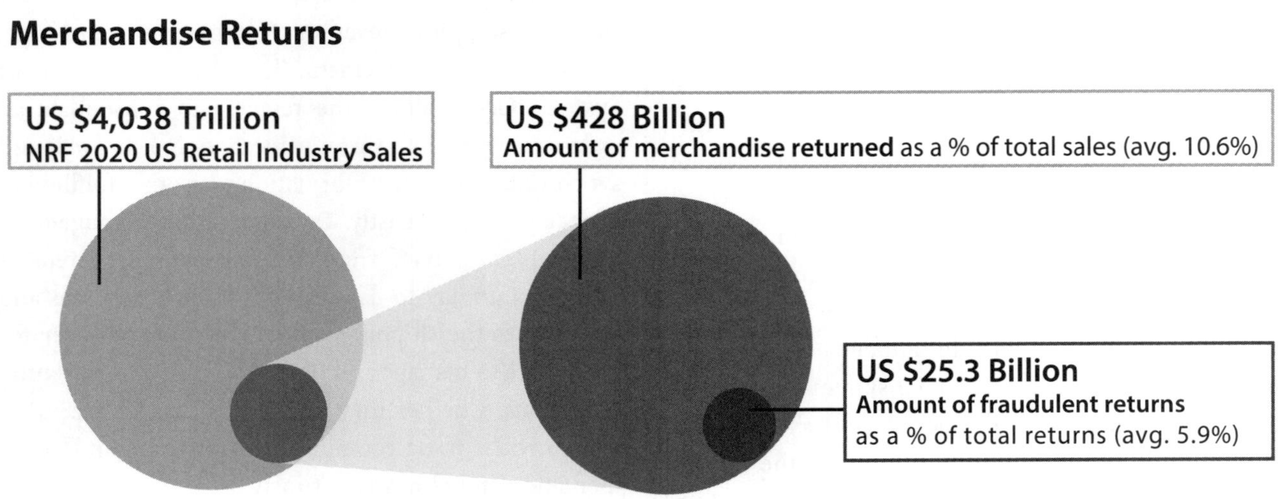

Figure 6.9 Overview of retail returns: Merchandise returns and fraudulent returns
(*Source*: https://www.merchantfraudjournal.com/return-fraud-how-merchants-lost-25-3b-in-fraudulent-returns/)

article by *Vogue Business* (2022) the NRF were cited as reporting that in the beginning of 2022, US consumers were predicted to return more than $761 billion worth of clothing.[34] This is substantial because returned merchandise adds logistical costs to the business.

There are many reasons why merchandise is returned to the retailers. More than 56 percent of the customers mentioned that there were some mistakes in the order or delivery which include: a) wrong product delivered (fulfillment error), b) damage or defective items, or c) product does not match the site representation. In addition, issues with product quality and issues with size and fit are also frequently cited. Other reasons for returning products were change of mind or late arrival of delivery.[35, 36] To address the critical needs in managing the apparel returns, McKinsey & Company conducted a Returns Management Survey and found which companies currently offer shopping tools to their customers and how effective each tool is to reduce returns[37] (see Figure 6.10).

One of the critical issues in returns management can be bracketing and return fraud/wardrobing.[38] **Bracketing** refers to the practice of buying a number of different sizes or colors of an article of clothing with the intention to return most, if not all, of the items. Some shoppers deliberately overbuy and then return unwanted items. This practice can impact inventory levels and create possible temporary stockout situations. The more significant issues are caused by **wardrobing**, which are not new issues for omnichannel retailing per se. Wardrobing refers to a fraudulent activities that occur in both a traditional retail context and omnichannel retail context, where customers have purchased items with a clear intention to wear/use the items for a special occasion only to return the worn-out product for a refund later.[39] According to National Retail Federation (2020), 5.9 percent of the total returns, approximately $25.3 billion, were categorized as fraudulent returns.[40] With e-commerce allowing for no direct or in-person contact

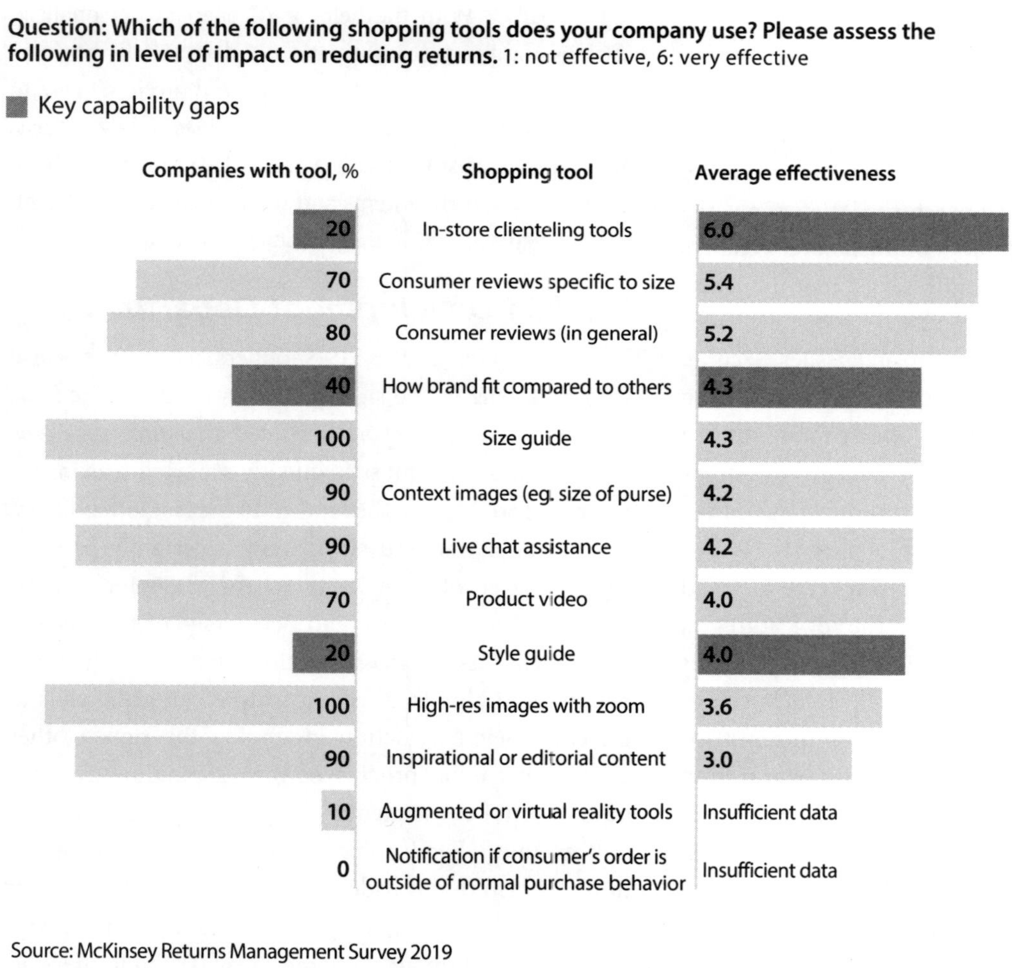

Figure 6.10 Shopping tools and their effectiveness in reducing apparel returns from the customer
(*Source*: https://www.mckinsey.com/industries/retail/our-insights/returning-to-order-improving-returns-management-for-apparel-companies)

for the return process, it has increased the tendency of this return fraud.[41] These unethical consumer return behaviors do hurt the fashion retailers' bottom line, especially when they offer free shipping and returns.

Benchmarks of Returns, Refunds, and Costs

Returns occur quite frequently in the fashion industry, especially when products are purchased without trying them on first. Clothing returns can increase fees and reduce revenues for online retailers, including the cost of sorting and redistributing the merchandise once it has arrived at the supplier's return center (inventory costs). In addition, customer support for the return process is a contributing factor to the business's bottom line. If the business offers free return shipping and handling, then it will erode the bottom line as well. And because the clothes may be outdated or unattractive by the time they are returned, online sellers may have to discount the price to promote the returned items.[42]

Another factor influencing prevalent return rates in the fashion industry may be generous return policies. Yet, omnichannel retailers should be mindful to set up their benchmarks of returns, refunds, and costs, to adequately minimize the business impact of returns.[43] Before putting restrictions on a return policy, omnichannel retailers could first consider supporting the customer's journey. First, offering detailed sizing charts and measuring guides can defray the fit- and size-related issues. Second, the retailer should offer an alternative product during the return process to convert the return for refund to exchange to have another opportunity to meet the customer's expectation. Offering alternative product choices can be facilitated by the use of artificial intelligence (AI) or machine learning (ML). Third, offering very detailed product descriptions and highlighting the key features on the product page can reduce the guessing game that your customer may experience. In addition, as a business, purchasing fraud protection and implementing a stringent ban against serial returners is another option. Last but not least, the omnichannel retailer should work with the return policy that supports their business operation. Approximately 8–10 percent of purchases are returned to brick-and-mortar retailers, totaling billions of dollars each year. Online retailers usually experience double or triple the returns (in dollar amounts) than physical retailers do. Therefore, a generous return policy is critical to building brand reputation and customer loyalty, but the return policy must be carefully designed not to burden the company. In addition, there is evidence that handling returns well would build loyalty at the consumer level.[44] For a retailer with a fashion forward assortment, having a 90-day free return policy may impose a greater risk because that merchandise is "perishable." When it comes to fashionable merchandise, timing is of the essence for success, and returned merchandise may not be sellable beyond a certain window.

Connecting the Data Back to Related Departments

Over the years, capturing and analyzing data has helped fashion companies better understand, target, and attract customers. From a business perspective, data allows companies to see changes in their business. In particular, it can be aggregated to view the overall trends of multiple business units, which is especially important for brands operating globally.[45] With the help of AI-enabled personalized settings and product information, today's retail customers can understand the situation better and are less likely to buy the wrong clothing. In turn, this does reduce returns and improves customer satisfaction.[46] Let's look into how to connect the returned items and reasons for returning with various departments at the omnichannel retailer.

Product Development Department

In fact, 46 percent of 3,519 shoppers around the world who took part in the survey of Narvar's 2019 *The State of Online Returns Report* indicated that incorrect size, fit, or color are the most frequently reported reasons for returning products to the retailer. In the fashion industry, not having a standard sizing system certainly presents another layer of complexity to the shopping experience and contributes to high percentage of returns and subsequent loss on gross margin. Product development departments should consider using AI and ML tools to increase their satisfaction in finding the right clothes because even the process of repackaging returns can have harmful consequences for your shoppers and your bottom line.[47] For instance, True Fit™ is a personalization platform that is widely adopted by over 200 fashion online retailers globally including Macy's, Lane Brant, Asics, Under Armour, to name a few. True Fit offers an AI-driven size, fit, and style recommendations based on the customer's entry of body measurements, body shape, age, and usual sizes that the customer wears from specific brands. True Fit™ is known for maintaining their Fashion Genome™ database from over 200 million registered members. To learn more about this technology, visit https://www.truefit.com.

Marketing Department

About 14 percent of Narvar's survey participants reported that they returned a product because it did not match its description or photo as depicted on the website.[48] This presents a wonderful opportunity for the retailer to pay greater attention to the accuracy of the product description and other relevant information on the website. Fabric hand information can be very useful as well, especially for customers who are tactile-oriented or sensitive to certain textural elements of a garment. Marketing departments could also solicit product reviews from prior purchasers to share their experience verbally and visually with the potential customers regarding fit, sizing, and much more. Naturally, in the omnichannel retail environment, customer reviews are one of the most convincing ways online retailers can build trust and confidence among their target audiences to reduce returns. Research shows that 88 percent of customers trust user-generated reviews.[49] Moreover, customer engagement of sharing their photos can pan out greatly to reduce returns as well. For instance, Boden, Mod Cloth, Rent the Runway, and Amazon are inviting their customers to share their photos wearing the purchased items.[50] On Boden's website, the retailer asks the customers to submit photos of themselves showing how they style their Boden pieces. Boden makes sure that customer photos are conveniently hyperlinked to the product page. The customer photos are displayed in each product page as well as the retailer's gallery. The retailer also runs a "Boden by You" as a part of the Instagram stories to feature "real" customers. For the photo gallery of Boden styled by everyday consumers, check out the user submitted photos on their Instagram tagged @boden_clothing (https://www.bodenusa.com/en-us/boden-by-me-gallery).

Payment Department

More than three-quarters of Narvar's survey participants reported that convenience is the priority when choosing a retailer. On top of that, 81 percent of shoppers want frictionless cross-device e-commerce experiences among website, mobile site, mobile app, and shoppable product pages on social media platforms, etc.[51]

Nearly 50 percent of customers who cannot use their preferred payment method will give up their purchase. In other words, the best option for retailers is to accept as many payment methods as possible. The good news is that if you have a flexible POS system, taking other payment methods is not a big obstacle: 41 percent of the respondents reported that they frequently use cashless (e.g., mobile payment), while 97 percent of respondents switched to credit and debit payments. By 2025, eMarketer forecasted that approximately 125 million consumers who are 14 years of age or older would use proximity-based mobile payments in the United States for in-store retail purchases.[52]

Fulfillment Department

More than 20 percent of Narvar's survey participants said that the reason for return was that the item was damaged, broken, or no longer functional. This is a crucial area that fulfillment departments should prevent by looking into ways to solve the problem. In addition, about two-thirds of shoppers want to know the return policy before clicking the buy button. Close to three-quarters of the respondents said their return experience would affect their purchasing goods from online retailers again. The 47 percent of shoppers reported that they would not buy goods if they had to pay for the return shipping fee. This trend is most apparent among millennial consumers.[53,54]

When we consider the reduction in physical stores among fast fashion retailers in order to strengthen their business operations, returning items to a store may not be a valid option for customers anymore. For instance, Inditex, which owns ZARA, announced it closed 1,200 stores while opening 450 stores worldwide between 2020 and 2021. H&M also plans to close 350 stores and open 100 stores in the midst of the lease negotiation of 1,250 stores at the global level in 2020 due to the pandemic. This trend was accelerated by the Covid-19 pandemic and spread to other sectors of the fashion industry. For instance, the major US conglomerate GAP Inc. also announced its plan to close over 300 Gap and Banana Republic stores by 2023. Moreover, Macy's declared that it would further reduce their retail perimeter by closing 125 stores by 2024.[55] These factors present a challenge for the omnichannel fashion retailer as they attempt to work the return shipping cost into the price of the product, while still providing sustainable products at a reasonable price point with Millennials in mind.

CASE STUDY 6.1

How Policy Issues and External Factors Affect Omnichannel Retailer's Supply Chain

The Covid-19 pandemic posed significant challenges for supply chains globally. Multiple national lockdowns slowed or even temporarily stopped the flow of raw materials and finished goods, disrupting manufacturing as a result. However, the pandemic has not necessarily created any new challenges for supply chains. In some areas, it brought to light previously unseen vulnerabilities, and of course, many organizations have suffered staff shortages and losses due to Covid-19. But overall, it has accelerated and magnified problems that already existed in the supply chain.

The following are some findings from a survey that Ernst & Young LLP conducted in late 2020. The respondents were 200 senior-level supply chain executives at organizations across many sectors, including consumer products, retail, life sciences, industrial products, automotive, and high-tech companies in the United States with over $1 billion in revenues. In the aftermath of severe disruption from the Covid-19 pandemic, the survey found that enterprises in the United States plan to shake up their supply chain strategies to become more resilient, collaborative, and networked with customers, suppliers, and other stakeholders. To do that, they will increase investment in supply chain technologies like AI and robotic process automation while retraining workers.[56]

According to a Harvard Business Review article (2020), temporary trade restrictions and shortages of medicines, critical medical supplies, and other products have highlighted weaknesses in companies' production strategies and supply chains almost everywhere.[57] Therefore, manufacturers worldwide have been bearing more significant political and competitive pressures to increase their domestic production, increase employment opportunities in their own countries, and reduce or even eliminate their dependence on sources deemed risky. For instance, supply chain professionals at Jabil, a Florida-based manufacturing service company, reported that the pandemic disrupted 78 percent of supply chains—more than any other event in the last decade.[58]

In addition, the pandemic exposed loopholes in the global supply chain, rapidly increasing border controls, confusing customs regulations, and reducing long-distance transportation and timely fulfillment capabilities. This shows the need for greater transparency and rapid hub capabilities to ensure business continuity.[59]

Moreover, supply chain professionals anticipated that needs identified during the pandemic along with the national interests on high-tech, healthcare, and pharmaceutical organizations would significantly impact future supply chain decisions on those sectors. This involves looming demands at the national level, such as vaccines and personal protective equipment (PPE), and the result of ongoing economic problems such as the United States–China trade war or Brexit. At the same time, a strong customer demand for low price over domestic sourcing and production was noted by supply chain professionals. Such product sectors include retail and fashion industries which particularly experience ferocious price competition.[60]

During the Covid-19 pandemic, 92 percent did not halt technology investments. This speaks to the value of a digital supply chain in helping enterprises navigate disruptive forces and respond faster to volatile supply and demand. Some 47 percent of all companies reported that the pandemic had affected their workforce. Although many employees are required to work from home, other employees (especially in a factory environment) must adapt to physical separation, contact tracing, and more PPE. Industrial products and high-tech manufacturing companies are investing heavily in technology to reduce employees' exposure in labor-intensive industries to Covid-19.

Discussion Questions:

1. What are the key takeaways from the Covid-19 pandemic for supply chain managers?
2. What are the possible options for supply chain professionals to minimize risk in terms of global sourcing?
3. How would the lessons learned from the pandemic influence the reshoring strategies among the major manufacturers or retailers?

Career Opportunities

Job Title	Key Responsibilities and Qualifications
Senior Director of Operations and Logistics Portfolio	The Senior Director will drive key programs within the Operations & Logistics portfolio. This role will lead diverse cross-function team members to execute complex and strategic programs. We are looking for a leader who has experience building program management functions and can oversee end-to-end execution across multiple parallel program workstreams, including risk management, issue/conflict resolution and dependency management. The ideal candidate for this position will be seasoned in program management with strong leadership skills, communication skills, and expertise with digital and technology transformation. This person will have substantial, demonstrated experience in an agile and program model structure. This role requires a candidate who is strong at building relationships across functions to align strategies and drive execution. This person will be a strategic problem solver with an ability to prioritize multiple and competing priorities while driving a plan to execution. This individual will play equal parts problem solver and doer, tackling the roles of strategist, operator, influencer, and delivery specialist, and create an inclusive team environment that inspires a diversity of perspectives and bold ideas. WHAT WILL YOU WORK ON? You will be asked to lead the elevated programs driving the digital transformation of Nike and in doing so be comfortable consistently assessing tradeoffs and manage delivery across multiple workstreams. You will be responsible for the end-to-end timely, on-budget technology execution of the Technology program, actively engaging key business and technology portfolio partners to ensure opportunities, risks and issues are understood and addressed. You will co-create and help develop product dashboards, portfolio reporting and analysis activities. WHO WILL YOU WORK WITH? You will partner with senior and executive level internal partners to cultivate collaboration, strategic alignment and integrated planning and execution across all functions. You will have close partnership with the Portfolio, Product, Finance, Technology, and Strategy functions of Global Technology, in addition to the leaders of Global Technology teams. You will work closely to coordinate with other Technology teams on dependencies across the portfolio. **Qualifications** - Bachelor's degree or Master's (preferred) or equivalent experience. - 10+ years of Technical Program Management experience; self-motivated, with a high sense of accountability, urgency, and drive. - 8+ years of experience, including previous experience with Inventory & Order management, warehouse management, transportation, Logistics, and Customer Service Technology. - 8+ years of people management experience leading global teams. - Proven track record in leading large-scale technology programs in inventory, logistics, fulfillment, order management and operations to improve supply chain efficiencies and effectiveness. - Experience leading large program management efforts including establishing effective governance structures, cross functional coordination, and executive stakeholder management and reporting. - Strong relationship-building skills and experience working closely with senior executives and cross-functional partners to deliver key strategic initiatives. - Experience running and executing multi-million-dollar budgets across multiple technology platforms and business areas. - Strong oral and written communication skills and ability to challenge the status quo. - Ability to deal with ambiguity and work in a dynamic, results-oriented matrixed environment. - Experience in defining and delivering Portfolio reporting that provide strategic insights and holds cross-functional leads accountable for delivering results.

	– Provide input on the full funnel integrated planning, resource & capacity planning and execution for the technology team by partnering with business, strategy, and finance teams. – Manage external vendors, contracts, relationships, and technical requirements to continue to develop and enhance the operations & logistics platform. – Delivery experience using Agile and Waterfall methodologies. – Deep experience with tools such as Aha! JIRA, Confluence, and Planisware

(*Source*: https://fashionunited.com/fashion-jobs/sr-director-program-management-operations-and-logistics-portfolio-san-francisco-1340607)

Job Title	Key Responsibilities and Qualifications
Global Supply Planning Manager/ Lead	WHO WE ARE LOOKING FOR We are looking for an end-to-end supply chain expert to create and deliver reliable supply plans to serve our consumers while aligning to inventory objectives! The manager/lead is consumer focused, process and critical metric driven, and is comfortable using data and sophisticated analytics to drive and influence cross-functional partners with clear and compelling insights, options and recommendations. The successful candidate instills trust, acts with courage, embraces and leads change, communicates vision and purpose, fosters collaboration, cultivates innovation, and ensures accountability. WHAT YOU WILL WORK ON If this role is for you, you will be working with Nike's Global Apparel and Accessories Supply Planning team. Your responsibilities will include day-to-day management of a gender-dimension within our Apparel business, working on initiatives to improve our supply planning capabilities and decision-making, and playing an active role in creating a dynamic culture of respect and inclusion. You will serve as a point of escalation within your team to support cross-gender and cross-classification efforts to shape supply in support of maintaining a healthy supply outlook. WHO YOU WILL WORK WITH This is the Nike matrix: You will engage and collaborate with global and geography product, merch, planning, analytics, sourcing, and manufacturing teams … essentially an end-to-end supply chain role to ensure supply is positioned for our most critical product and demand priorities. You will partner with Nike Tech and analytics teams to gain insights and build sustainable capabilities to improve the speed and quality of our decision-making. Additionally, you will connect within our team to share and receive best practice insights as we relentlessly work to improve our operational excellence and contributions to fuel Nike growth. **Qualifications** – Bachelor's degree and minimum of 6 years directly relevant work experience. Alternatively, Master's degree and 4 years of directly relevant work experience. – Excellent written, spoken, and visual communication skills. – Flexibility in switching from strategic to tactical and operational levels of thinking and working. – Outstanding interpersonal, influencing, and facilitation skills with the ability to work both cross-functionally and cross-culturally, specifically building positive relationships between key players and immediate team. – Validated analytical skills, working with large data sets and building executive stories. – High proficiency with Excel (pivot tables, formulas, macros). – Tolerance for a sophisticated, ever-changing, and dynamic work environment. – Ability to demonstrate good decision-making in ambiguous circumstances. – Contribution on strategic initiatives as well as continuing process improvement projects. – Experience preferred with Tableau, Cognos, SSAS, MMX, SAP. – Experiences preferred in supply/inventory planning and management, marketplace planning/buying, merchandising, demand planning, financial planning.

(*Source*: https://fashionunited.com/fashion-jobs/global-supply-planning-manager-lead-beaverton-1375829)

Summary

Today, the omnichannel supply chain is essential due to the fast-changing nature of the retail industry, and it holds great potential for all businesses regardless of its size. However, most companies continue navigating its waters to find the best way to build a seamless, integrated experience for customers. In this chapter, we examined the difference the multichannel SCM and omnichannel SCM systems. Ultimately, omnichannel is going to become the new gold standard in retail. In this chapter we discuss the omnichannel SCM and logistics systems that are crucial to make this transformation possible for the retailers. The omnichannel supply chain and logistics systems thrive based on the integrated system where the data flows among the supply chain members. Logistics management systems comprise inventory system, fulfillment system, and order management system where customer support shines through status of the ordered or returned products/services. Due to the experiential nature of fashion and the importance of sizing and fit, returns management is highly important to minimize the business impact of the returns.

Key Terms

Boomerang effect
Bracketing
Consumer journey
Distribution order management (DOM)
Drop shipping
Enterprise resource planning (ERP)
Fulfillment system
In-bound logistics
In-house order fulfillment
Logistics
Logistics system
Multichannel supply chain management (SCM)
Omnichannel supply chain management (SCM)
Order automation
Order management
Order management system (OMS)
Out-bound logistics
Outsourced fulfillment
Product inventory system
Returns management
Reverse logistics
Third-party logistics (3PL)
Transportation management system (TMS)
Warehouse management system (WMS)
Warehousing
Wardrobing

Reflection and Discussion Questions

1. What are the differences between multichannel supply chain and omnichannel supply chain management?
2. What are the similarities between multichannel supply chain and omnichannel supply chain management?
3. What are the challenges that omnichannel retailers are facing in terms of logistics?
4. Describe the ideal logistics systems for an omnichannel fashion retailer.
5. Explain the importance of data in relation to the customer experience/journey management.
6. What are the benefits of 3PL over in-house fulfillment option?
7. What are the benefits of drop shipping in relation to inventory management?
8. What are the strengths that an integrated logistics management system would bring to an omnichannel retailer?
9. Based on the top reasons for returns covered in this chapter, what are possible ways to minimize the business impact of returns/refunds?

CHAPTER 7

Promotion in the Omnichannel Environments

Learning Objectives

Upon finishing this chapter, you will be able to:

- Appraise the various promotion strategies of offline touchpoints that involve omnichannel channels and give examples
- Evaluate the various promotion strategies of online-line touchpoints that involve omnichannel channels and give examples
- Plan content marketing strategies for different consumer decision stages
- Develop a plan for an appropriate content type in promoting omnichannel customer experiences
- Evaluate the outcomes of omnichannel promotions

Omnichannel retailers, who operate both physical brick-and-mortar stores as well as online presence, can leverage their multiple touchpoints with customers to promote their products. The goals of promotions for the omnichannel retailers include: 1) increase brand awareness and loyalty across different channels and platforms; 2) create a seamless and consistent customer experience that matches their preferences and needs; 3) boost sales and conversions by offering personalized and relevant offers and incentives; 4) enhance customer retention and satisfaction by providing timely and effective support and feedback, and 5) optimize marketing campaigns and strategies by measuring and analyzing data from multiple sources.

Omnichannel Retailing Touchpoints Dynamics and Customer Experience

In the following sections, we will first discuss offline touchpoints, including brick-and-mortar stores, print media, and pop-up and experiential events. Next, we will move to the online touchpoints, which include promotions on search engines, social media channels, and through emails.

Offline Touchpoints

Offline touchpoints like brick-and-mortar stores, print media, and pop-up events play a pivotal role in omnichannel retailers' promotional strategies. In physical stores, strategic displays and trained staff boost in-store promotions and enhance customer experiences. Print media, including newspapers and magazines, serves a broad audience, with advertisements featuring quick-response (QR) codes for seamless online engagement. Pop-up events and experiential marketing create interactive brand experiences, fostering word-of-mouth recommendations. These offline touchpoints not only contribute to local visibility and community engagement but also serve as bridges, seamlessly connecting customers between physical and digital realms in an omnichannel approach.

Brick-and-Mortar Stores

Omnichannel retailers can utilize their brick-and-mortar stores to promote their online products through in-store promotions such as signages, flyers, or displays that highlight their online offerings. For example, they can use in-store signages or posters with QR codes or URLs that lead customers to their online store, where they can browse and purchase products that are not available in the physical stores. Moreover, consumers also can use smartphone apps to compare prices or download a coupon to use when they check out.

In the meantime, by offering the "buy online, pickup in-store" (BOPIS) option, you can encourage customers to visit the store, where they may be enticed to make additional purchases while they pickup their online orders. For example, the store associates at Buckle, an American jeans and youth clothing retailer, will place extra items in the fitting room when customers come in to pickup their orders and try on their online orders to cross-sell other companion products. Another way to promote inside physical stores is to use proximity marketing technology. As mentioned in Chapter 5, omnichannel retailers like Macy's, Nordstrom, and Neiman Marcus adopted beacon technology in their location-based campaigns to send out push notifications to customers' mobile devices. These push notifications can also include online customer reviews, which can help customers make their purchase decisions. Other examples for omnichannel retailers to promote their goods use QR codes and mobile apps. For example, you can place QR codes on product tags or signs that customers can scan with their smartphones to access the product catalog on the online store, where they can learn more and make a purchase (Figure 7.1). You can also promote your mobile apps in-store, which can provide an easy

Figure 7.1 Fashion brand Uniqlo uses in-store signage with QR codes to promote their use of recycled polyester (left) or online collections (right)
(*Source*: Catherine Jai)

way for customers to shop online and enjoy customized product suggestions. This type of in-store promotion broadens the depth of the product offerings in-store. **Endless aisle** is a term used to describe a marketing and sales technique by which retailers can provide in-store customers with the opportunity to order products that are either not normally sold in the store or that are currently out of stock. It's also known as "buy in-store, ship to customer."

Omnichannel retailers can enhance their customer experience by incorporating online user-generated content into their physical stores. To achieve this, they can utilize digital signage in their store, to display their social media feeds in the physical store (shown in Figure 7.2). This will enable them to direct in-store customers toward their online offerings and create a seamless shopping experience. By leveraging brick-and-mortar stores to promote online products, omnichannel retailers can create a seamless shopping experience for customers across different channels, increase online sales, and drive traffic to online stores while utilizing the physical presence of the stores.

Print Media

Similar to in-store display, omnichannel retailers can use print media to promote their products online by integrating digital elements into their print advertising, such as QR codes or website URLs. There are various ways in which print media can be utilized for omnichannel

Figure 7.2 Specialty retailer chain Boxlunch displays user-generated social media content at their Columbia, MD store
(*Source*: Catherine Jai)

promotions, such as direct mail, catalogs, brochures, newspapers, magazine ads, and more. These types of promotions also contribute to the retailer's presence, and we have previously examined catalogs as an example in Chapter 3. For instance:

- Direct mail: Retailers can use direct mail campaigns to reach potential customers through print advertising. Direct mail pieces can include postcards or letters with special promotions or discount codes that are exclusive to the online store, encouraging customers to make a purchase online. The direct mail piece can also include website URLs or QR codes that take customers directly to the online store or mobile app. For instance, Louis Vuitton launched an interactive digital campaign called "LV Pass." The campaign involved using QR codes placed on print advertisements and billboards. When scanned with the LV Pass app, users could unlock exclusive content, such as behind-the-scenes videos, interviews with designers, and interactive 3D models of products. This campaign merged traditional print advertising with digital interactivity, offering a seamless and engaging experience for customers.[1]
- Catalogs and brochures: Omnichannel retailers can distribute print catalogs or brochures that showcase their products, with QR codes or website URLs that direct customers to their online store to make a purchase. These print materials can include high-quality images, product descriptions, and pricing information that entices customers to visit the online store.
- Packaging inserts: Retailers can include print inserts in their product packaging that promote their online store. These inserts can include special promotions or discount codes that are exclusive to the online store, as well as website URLs or QR codes that direct customers to the online store.
- Newspaper and magazine ads: Retailers have the option to use print ads in newspapers and magazines to promote their products online. By including website URLs or QR codes in the ads, customers can be directed straight to the online store. These ads can feature captivating headlines, product images, and calls to action to inspire customers to visit the online store.

Pop-Up and Experiential Events

Omnichannel retailers can set up pop-up and experiential events to sell their products in several key steps: omnichannel retailers can host in-store product demonstrations or events that showcase their products. For example, brands can set up demo stations or displays where customers can try out or interact with products, and provide information on how to purchase those products online. Organizing a memorable pop-up or experiential event necessitates meticulous planning, excellent execution abilities, and responsibility. The steps involved are outlined below:

1. *Define the event objectives*: Retailers need to first establish clear objectives for their pop-up or experiential event. This includes identifying the specific goals they want to achieve, such as increasing brand awareness, driving sales, capturing customer data, or launching a new product. Defining the event objectives will help guide the planning and execution of the event.
2. *Choose the right location*: The location of the pop-up or experiential event is critical to its success. Retailers should carefully select a location that aligns with their target market, brand image, and event objectives. Factors to consider include foot traffic, visibility, accessibility, local regulations, and cost. Popular locations for pop-up events include shopping malls, high-traffic areas in urban centers, or trendy neighborhoods.
3. *Design an engaging experience*: The key to a successful pop-up or experiential event is to create an engaging and immersive experience for customers. Retailers should carefully design the event space to reflect their brand and product offerings and create a unique and memorable experience that encourages customers to interact with the products and make purchases. This can include creating attractive displays, interactive product demos, unique installations, or engaging activities that align with the event objectives and target audience.
4. *Coordinate online and offline channels*: Omnichannel retailers should ensure that their pop-up or experiential event is fully integrated with their online channels. This includes creating a seamless customer journey from online to offline and vice versa. For example, retailers can use digital signage or QR codes at the event to drive customers to their website or social media accounts, where they can learn more about the products, make purchases, or engage in online activities related to the event.
5. *Leverage technology*: Technology can play a crucial role in enhancing the customer experience at a pop-up or experiential event. Retailers can use technologies such as interactive displays, virtual reality (VR) or augmented reality (AR) experiences, mobile apps, or social media walls to engage customers, provide personalized recommendations, or capture customer data for future marketing efforts. Leveraging technology can also create a sense of innovation and excitement, driving customer interest and participation.
6. *Promote the event*: Retailers need to promote their pop-up or experiential events to generate awareness and attract customers. This can include using various marketing channels, such as social media, email marketing, online advertising, influencer collaborations, and PR efforts to create buzz and generate interest. Retailers should also use the event location as a marketing asset, leveraging its unique features and attractions to create promotional content that will drive attendance and engagement.
7. *Measure and optimize*: After the event, it's important for retailers to measure the success of their pop-up or experiential event against the predefined objectives. This can include tracking sales, customer footfall, engagement metrics, customer feedback, or online interactions related to the event. Based on the results, retailers can identify areas of improvement and optimize their approach for future events.

By carefully planning and executing their pop-up or experiential events and integrating online and offline channels, omnichannel retailers can create a unique and memorable experience for customers that drives engagement, sales, and brand loyalty (Figure 7.3).

Figure 7.3 VANS hosted pop-up events for their VIP customers in Taipei, Taiwan, to make branded wooden speakers in one of their retail locations in a department store
(*Source*: Catherine Jai)

Online Touchpoints

In this section, let's dive into the topic of promotions from the perspective of online touchpoints. These touchpoints include websites and apps, search engines, displayed ads, social media channels, email, and third-party review sites and mentions. Prior to the rise of internet commerce, many of these online touchpoints were not available to retailers and consumers. As they are relatively new, these online touchpoints are essential promotion tools for omnichannel retailers.

Website and Apps

The key to delivering an omnichannel customer experience that excels is being seamless, and websites serve as a pivotal point for omnichannel retailers to deliver the omnichannel customer experience. A Google & Nielsen survey found that three out of four mobile searches trigger additional user actions. Whether these actions are a store visit, a phone call, or further research, they can have a valuable outcome for a business. Customers should be able to tell no difference between applications and touchpoints. It's important for all aspects of your business, including your website, live chat, social media channels, and physical stores, to be consistent and aligned with each other. Therefore, when it comes to conducting promotions on websites and apps, it's imperative to consider how to make the website and apps well connected with other touchpoints.

Search engine optimization (SEO) is the practice of optimizing your web content so that search engines such as Google or Bing can recognize your online channels. As a result, when a customer searches for your product on search engines like Google, your website will show up on the first page of the search results.

Reflecting on your experience of searching for a product/service online, how many pages of results do you usually go over? If your answer is one or two pages, you are with most of the search engine users.[2] Because very few people go through more than two pages of results, the goal of SEO is to help move the ranking to the first page of search results. **Search engine results pages (SERPs)** are a search engine's response to a keyword(s) query. Using Google as an example, when someone searches a keyword, Google will return numerous pages of search results. Most search engines present the paid-ads content first (top area of the results page). The SEO strategies we will be talking about in this chapter will focus on how to optimize the website ranking within the organic search results (see an illustration of the paid and organic search results in Figure 7.4).

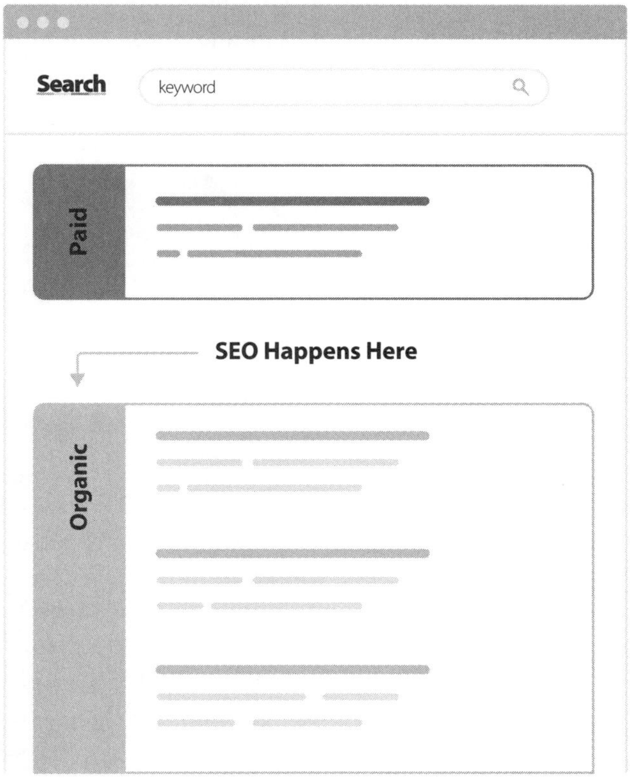

Figure 7.4 SEO is an approach to improve a website's ranking for targeted keywords within the organic search results (to be rendered)

Onsite SEO is the practice of optimizing your own website elements in order to rank higher in the SERP. It is arguably the most controllable aspect of SEO to omnichannel retailers because it's your own website and content. There are several practices that are commonly used to improve ranking in search engine results. In this section, you'll learn what Google values in search results, how to research and select keywords relevant to your business, and how to develop a specific SEO strategy for fashion retailers. The first step of onsite SEO is to provide a sitemap (Figure 7.5) of your website for search engines to crawl. **Crawling** is a term describing the process of search engines like Google send a bot to the internet to "read" the webpages and index the content for future search. To ensure that your page gets crawled (and indexed with search engines), you can have an XML sitemap uploaded to Google Search Central to give Google the roadmap for all your new content.[3]

Mapping Keywords to Different Tiers of Webpages (Using Shopper Intentions)

As shoppers progress through their buying journey, their information needs change. Customers who have already selected a specific brand and style, such as a Burberry trenchcoat, may be seeking a better deal. They may search using keywords such as "discount," "sales," or "deals," in addition to the brand and style. Retailers should ensure that these search terms are incorporated into the product page's headings or titles, so that search engines like Google can rank the page higher and customers can quickly find what they're looking for.

Here is another example, if a college student is looking for a holiday gift for their mom, then the search keywords may be as general as "holiday gifts for mom," "2025 holiday gift ideas," etc. Or, if they know their mom's gardening hobby or exercise interests, the search keywords may become "gardening clothes," "gardening clothes for sale," etc. At this stage, the customer is in the awareness stage in the shopping funnel and exploring possible solutions for their shopping goals. Therefore, retailers need to identify what the shopper's intentions are and make sure there is an appropriate webpage with keywords that match those intentions. SEO-friendly content that is easily searchable online not only drives traffic, but also brings value to your audience. Moreover, it will improve the website's overall visibility.

Major Strategies to Maximize Your Product Relevance for Search Engine

As a omnichannel retailer, what are some strategies you can implement to maximize your website relevance for the search engine and help your customers to find you? We provide several strategies.

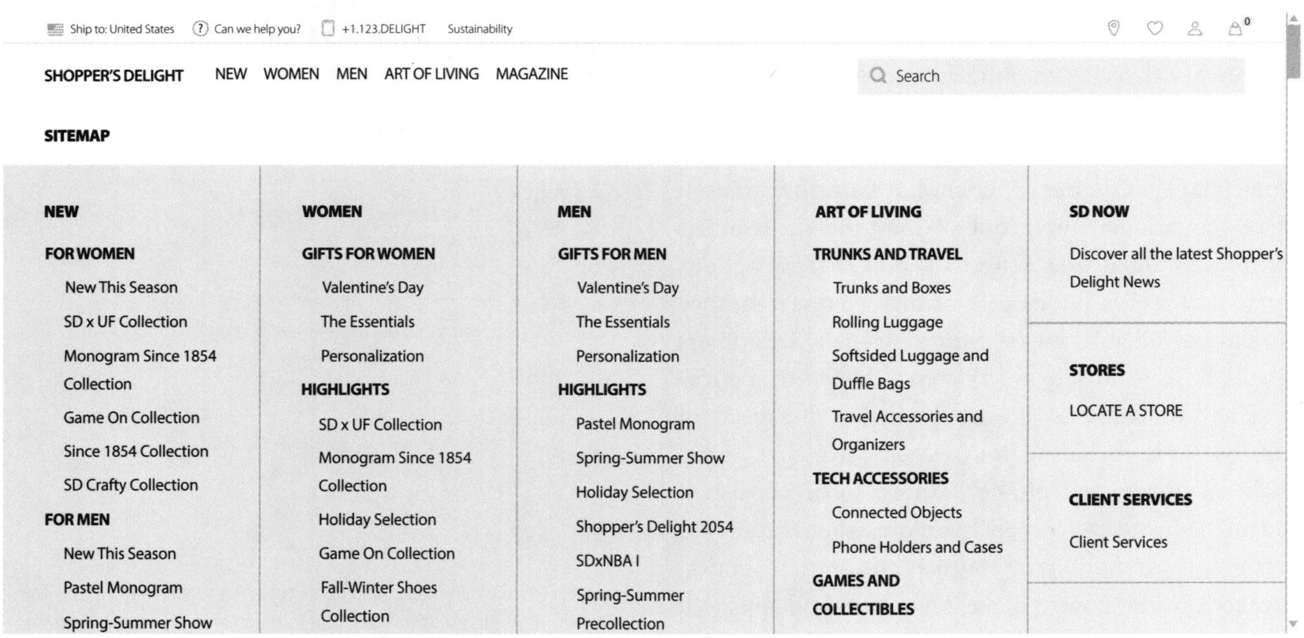

Figure 7.5 Example of a site map

Optimize the website for mobile devices

As discussed in Chapter 4, it is advisable to adopt a mobile-first design to enhance your search result ranking. Given Google's mobile-first indexing and the fact that nearly 60 percent of internet traffic occurs through mobile devices, it is best to have a website that provides a single URL version to users across various devices as a sound SEO strategy.[4] Google provides an online tool for businesses to test if a website is mobile-friendly by providing a URL or code (https://search.google.com/test/mobile-friendly). The free tool tests how easily a customer can navigate the website on a mobile device.

Optimize the images properly

Images play a very important role in providing important product information and helping a customer evaluate a product. Adding descriptive titles, captions, filenames, and alt text for images displayed on the website to improve the SERP. **Alternative text (alt text)** is the descriptive text which conveys the meaning and context of a visual item in a digital setting, such as on an app or web page. Remember that a consumer is less likely to come to your website if your webpage shows on the tenth page of their search results. Adding descriptions to product images can help a search engine to better match the content on the site with a search query. For example, a product image named "Double-Breasted Blazer" would be a better choice than "product1357246," because the file name reflects what type of product image it is. As a result, when someone searches the keyword "women's blazer," the webpage with the descriptive product name will be ranked higher in the SERP. Adding high search volume keywords in the image file name and alt text with the product photos can improve the visibility of your product images and will improve the SERP rankings as well. Although regular site visitors may not see this information during their browsing experience, these images and information are important for a search engine to decide the ranking of the research keywords and the page.

Create more pages, reducing duplicate pages from indexing

In the eyes of a search engine, a website that has more unique pages indicates that they have more unique products/information per search query; therefore, the search engine would prioritize a website that has more pages over a website that has fewer pages. For an omnichannel retailer, it is recommended to integrate product descriptions, blogs, customer reviews, and social media content to draw more attention from your viewers with more web pages. Thus, the fresh set of content boosts the SEO of your page. On the other hand, you need to make sure that you are adding value to the pages. Do not create duplicate pages with the same/similar product descriptions/images. The search engine would lower a website's quality score. It may be unavoidable to have duplicate webpages, for instance, an international brand may have webpages in different languages. Figure 7.6 shows an example of how a retailer can code their main website as a "canonical" page and the foreign language pages as "alternate." This way, Google will know what to index for their search engine and leave out those pages they don't need to index.

Creating shareable content for social media

To reach more people, remember to make your engaging content sharable. We have discussed the importance of content in driving customers to your website in the earlier section of this chapter. Make sure that the website pages you have created are easy to share so that your customers can easily share them on various social media platforms to spread word of mouth. This organic endorsement can bring more traffic to your site, and most importantly, it's free. Most social media platforms have developed ways for brands to embed the "share" icon/buttons on their site.

Search Engine

Search engines play an important touchpoint in consumers' shopping journeys. Omnichannel retailers can use online ads to draw more traffic to their stores or websites. Depending on the marketing goals and omnichannel retailers' branding strategies, you may

```
<link rel="canonical" href="https://example.com/">
<link rel="alternate" hreflang="es" href="https://m.example.com/es/">
<link rel="alternate" hreflang="fr" href="https://m.example.com/fr/">
<link rel="alternate" hreflang="de" href="https://m.example.com/de/">
<link rel="alternate" hreflang="th" href="https://m.example.com/th/">
```

Figure 7.6 Example of coding to guide Googlebot not to index duplicate pages in different foreign languages

create different campaigns for their marketing/sales needs. Here we will use Google as an example since it has the most search volume in the world at the point of this book was written.[5] Google has been a pioneer in online advertising and offers comprehensive ways for brands to manage their campaigns directly on its platforms. Defined by the ad format and its display methods, there are search ads, display ads, video ads, shopping ads, app campaigns, local campaigns, and smart campaigns (Figure 7.7).

Local Campaigns

Local campaigns help to promote store locations across channels such as Search, Display, Google Maps, and YouTube. To use local campaigns, omnichannel retailers need to have an account with Google My Business (https://www.google.com/business/). Google My Business is a free business profile account that can show retail store hours, phone numbers, photos, reviews, websites, etc. Since more and more customers use mobile phones to search for products or stores, local campaigns help customers to find nearby retailers at the right time.

Search Ads

Search Ads (also called paid-search ads) are text-only ads served based on someone's search query. It is a great tool to reach people when they are searching for the products or services you offer. If done right, the search ads can drive sales and traffic for omnichannel retailers. **Keyword Planner** is a tool that helps you identify the best keywords to use based on your customers' interests and purchase intent. Google price keywords based on the search volume. The lower the Google keyword search volume, the cheaper it should be to win an auction and show your ad at the top of the SERP. The exact prices are determined by how many other businesses are bidding on the same keywords.[6]

Display Ads

Display ads are image or video ads on websites partnered with a display network. Display ads can offer a visually engaging tool to drive sales, traffic, and brand awareness. Since the display network involves thousands of websites and apps, it can help retailers expand their reach beyond just people who actively search for the products they sell. Moreover, omnichannel retailers can utilize the displayed ads to "remind" customers of products that they reviewed on their website by using **Remarketing** ads. Remarketing is a technique that follows up with people who have already visited a website or seen the retailer's ads before.

Video Ads on YouTube

Video ads on YouTube refer to video ads embedded in YouTube video content instead of retailers publishing a video campaign through their YouTube channel. Some examples are bumper ads (6-second non-skippable ads), skippable in-stream ads (viewers can skip ads after 5 seconds), non-skippable in-stream ads (15 seconds for increasing brand awareness), etc. Video campaigns are great tools for omnichannel retailers to drive awareness and product considerations. With the right call to action, it can also increase sales. To increase reach, video ads can be displayed even when a video is embedded on another website other than the retailer's site.

Shopping Ads

Shopping ads appear on search results and the Google Shopping tab. Shopping ads are ideal for omnichannel retailers who are looking to increase their sales (see an example in Figure 7.7). For small retail stores, they can also use local inventory ads to promote products available at their physical locations and drive in-store traffic.

App Campaigns

App campaigns can help to promote retailers' apps on many channels. The business goals of app campaigns are usually to drive installs and in-app engagements. The app campaign uses info from the retailer's app to automatically optimize ads across Search, Play, YouTube, Discover, and over 3 million affiliated sites and apps.[7]

Social Media Channels

Fashion retailers rely on social media channels to connect with customers, showcase their products, and increase brand awareness. Utilizing social media channels effectively can generate feedback, drive website traffic, and boost sales. By doing so, fashion retailers can establish a loyal customer base, improve their reputation, and gain a competitive edge. Since we have discussed how omnichannel retailers can use social media channels for selling products in Chapter 4, we will focus on

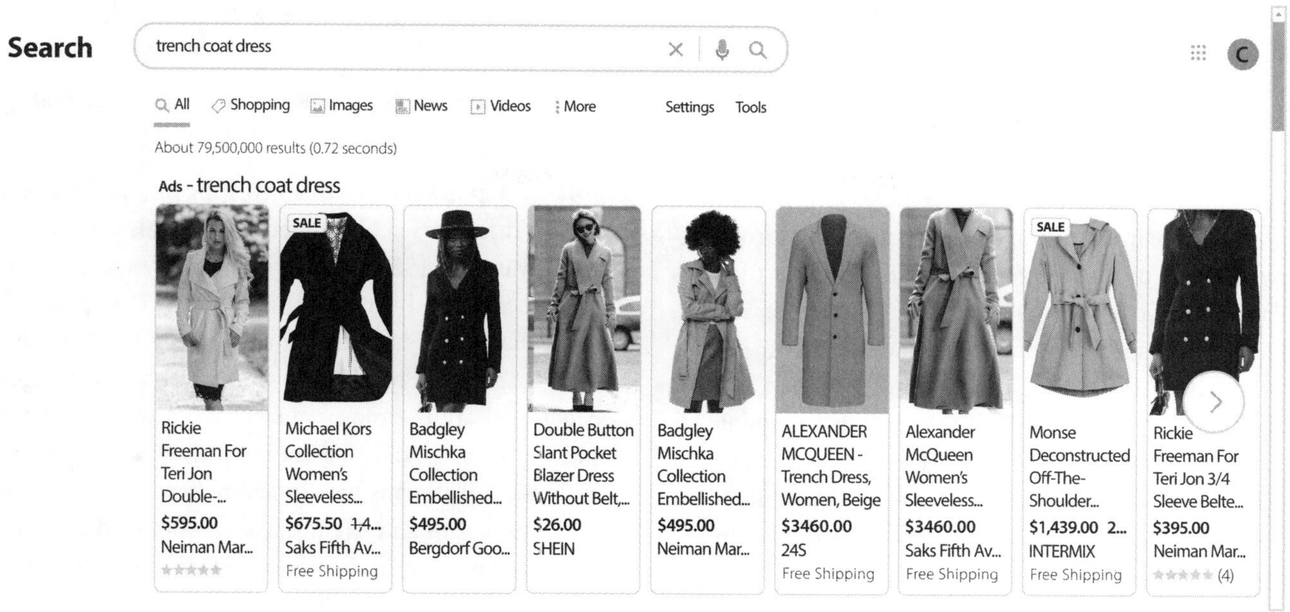

Figure 7.7 An example of shopping ads to search query of "trench coat dress"

general principles of promotions on social media and how to work with social influencers on promotion here. Specifically, this section will cover the frequency and scheduling of social media posts, display ads on social media platforms, and the crucial aspect of including influencer marketing on social media.

Social Media Post Frequency and Scheduling

In terms of the frequency of social media postings, there are no magic numbers applied to different platforms. How often a retailer should post depends largely on its products, social media platforms, and target audiences' preferences. Many omnichannel retailers find that to maintain good visibility among their audience without annoying them, they need to post at least once per day to stay in the news feed. Some market experts have suggested that posting two feed posts per week and two stories per day is ideal for building a following on Instagram.[8] For TikTok, it is recommended to post three–five times per week for starters in order to stay in front of the followers. You can also post as much as you can and track what types of content work best to attract larger audience and engagement. For Facebook, marketers recommend posting between once and twice a day. For X (formerly Twitter), brands can post two–three times per day and no more than three–five times per day. It's also recommended that no matter how frequently you are posting, the best practice is to follow the *rule of thirds*. This means one-third of tweets promote your business, one-third of tweets share personal stories, and one-third of tweets are about informative insights from experts or influencers.[9]

Pop-Up Events on Social Media

Omnichannel retailers increasingly use pop-up events/stores as a vehicle to reach consumers and bring them to physical stores and interact with the products and services.[10]

- Post a heads up to your audience five to ten days out when audiences are most likely to be deciding on plans for their next weekend outing.
- Use trendy, high-quality photography and short videos to attract your audience's attention
- Creating excitement by documenting your event setup process and shoot a video when you have more visitors to showcase a well-attended event atmosphere.
- Hashtag (#) your brand, collaborate brands, events theme, location, products, etc. in the promotional messages

Display Ads on Social Media

One way for brands to increase their cross-channel reach and improve their business goals is by using social display ads. These ads are essentially traditional banner placements that are created by automating popular social media posts. Given that shoppers increasingly use Instagram and TikTok for product research, it's important for brands to showcase their products in action through social content. This type of content is highly sought after and can help improve brand awareness, direct response, and customer prospecting. Brands must therefore consider the role that ads play in their overall social media marketing strategies. Examples of social media ads include static image ads, video ads, carousel ads, story ads, and branded content ads (e.g., Spark ads on TikTok). Branded content ads allow omnichannel retailers to take posts from social influencers on Instagram or TikTok and promote them as ads. More details on influencer marketing are in the next section.

Influencer Marketing on Social Media Channels

In Chapter 2, we explored different social media platforms and analyzed their shopping capabilities. Now, let's delve into how omnichannel retailers can collaborate with social influencers for promotional purposes. As live commerce gains popularity, it's essential for omnichannel retailers to integrate social influencers into their marketing strategy to remain competitive.

Influencer marketing is a practice that employs leading, niche-content creators to improve brands' desired business outcomes. Influencer marketing has become more and more important for online marketing because it promotes positive word-of-mouth and social proof. Social proof is defined as the psychological phenomenon whereby people copy the actions of others because they assume this action is acceptable when others are doing it.[11] Through social influencers, brands may be able to improve their brand/product awareness, increase traffic and sales, attract new customers, etc. **Engagement rate** has been used as an important indicator to measure the effectiveness of social media marketing. It is calculated as total engagements (i.e., the sum of shares, comments, and likes, etc.) divided by total followers, multiplied by 100 percent. For example, if Company A posted on Instagram to its 100,000 followers and received 2,000 likes, 1,000 comments, and 500 shares. This means that their total engagement would be 3,500 (2,000+1,000+500). We can plug the numbers into the equation to the equation below to calculate Company A's engagement rate.

$$\text{Engagement rate} = \text{total engagements}/\text{total followers} \times 100\%$$

$$\text{Company A's Engagement Rate} = 3500/100{,}000 \times 100\% = 3.5\%$$

Market reports showed that investing in visual content will help marketers achieve their social goals. Increasing brand awareness (58 percent), community engagement (41 percent), and growing audiences (35 percent) remain marketers' top goals for social, with more than half of marketers saying video (54 percent) and images (53 percent) are the most valuable types of content for achieving these goals.[12] Therefore, photo/video-focused social media platforms have generated more traffic than others. Instagram and TikTok have maintained a dominant position in terms of social influencer marketing. One of the major reasons that Instagram can assume this leading position in social media marketing is that Instagram has a relatively high engagement rate in comparison to other social media channels. The average Facebook or X (formerly Twitter) user has an engagement rate of only 0.5–1.0 percent. The average Instagram account, though, has an engagement rate of 3 percent.[13] Therefore, in recent market research about influencer marketing, over 90 percent of businesses surveyed cite Instagram as one of the most important channels for influencer marketing.[14] However, there are more and more brands that target Gen Z have their eyes on other social media platforms such as TikTok, YouTube, Snapchat, and Pinterest.

Influencer marketing spending is the payment made to influencers or their representatives to promote products and services primarily on social media and other platforms featuring user-generated content. It excludes non-cash payments such as free products or trips and paid media. The US market for influencer marketing is growing double-digit each year and in 2023 had grown into a $21.1 billion industry.[15] In the following section, we will discuss the types of social influencers and their compensations, the Federal Trade Commission (FTC) guidelines for social media influencers, how to find social influencers, and ways to evaluate the outcome of influencer marketing.

Types of Social Influencers and How to Choose Influencers for Your Business

In the realm of social media, there exist various types of influencers. In this segment, we will shed light on brand influencers and brand ambassadors. A social media influencer is a person who has a dedicated following in a particular niche with whom they regularly interact. As a result, they possess the ability to influence their audiences' purchasing choices. More than 70 percent of marketers claim that influencer marketing provides better quality customers and traffic compared to other sources. Additionally, almost 90 percent of marketers attest that the return on investment from influencer marketing is either comparable to or better than other channels.[16] Moreover, 49 percent of US consumers say they depend on influencer recommendations for their purchase decisions.

A **brand ambassador** is hired by a business to work under contract to help them achieve specific business goals such as increasing brand awareness and boosting conversions and sales. A brand ambassador's contract is typically long term (ranging from several months to even years). Under the contract, the brand ambassadors represent the brand and the lifestyle associated with it and have deep knowledge about the business's products or services. In the context of omnichannel retailing, brands work with social media influencers as their brand ambassadors. Sometimes, brands can also recruit their own followers to be their brand ambassadors. For example, if you are a D2C brand of running sneakers, you have several niche markets that you can target, including marathon runners, casual joggers, trail runners, etc. You can approach influencers in each of these markets on social media. With this approach, your brand can connect with every segment of your audience. In comparison, if you partnered with a well-known Olympic runner, you would reach a broad audience that may not even have an interest in running.

Based on the number of followers, marketers have classified influencers into the following categories (Figure 7.8):[17]

- Nano-influencers: influencers with 1,000–10,000 followers, who usually engage a small and niche audience.
- Micro-influencers are influencers with followings between 10,000 and 100,000, who hold an impressive status with a broader audience.
- Macro-influencers are influencers with followings between 100,000 and 1 million who have earned premier status as social media noisemakers.
- Mega-influencers are influencers with 1 million–5 million followers who have attained followership that puts them in a category similar to celebrities.
- Celebrity influencers are well-known personalities whose fame translates into prestigious social media status with more than 5 million followers. Since celebrities are so well-known, there are many ways to work with them. You may focus on social media, print or online ads, TV commercials, blogs, or other written publications. You can ask the celebrity to pose for pictures promoting your products, explain why their audience members would love your products or services, provide coupons and discount codes, or write reviews telling audience members why they stand by your brand. You may even sponsor an event the celebrity is hosting or attending. For instance, Amazon sponsored Khloe Kardashian's baby shower—with 93.7 million followers on Instagram, a reality TV show, several entrepreneurial endeavors, and a famous family. Amazon was looking to feature their wide range of baby registry and maternity products in the broadcasted event.

Besides categorizing influencers by their number of followers, we can also categorize influencers by the mediums and the area of interest they use to communicate with their followings.

Blogger influencers are the influencers who gained followings from their blog posts. A famous lifestyle blog influencer is Hannah Bronfman of HBFIT.com. Hannah's blog is about health, beauty, fitness, and creating a life that makes you happy and feels good. Between her blog subscribers, social media following, ads, the book she wrote, and the app she created, Hannah has millions of followers who keep up with her life. Her blog features a variety of product, gym, and spa reviews. Blogger influencers often collaborate with brands that fit with the area of interest among their followers.

Key opinion leaders (KOLs) are high-level experts on a specialized topic within a particular field. For example, a KOL might specialize in makeup application, the Paleo lifestyle, or Bikram yoga. If your business is looking to attract audience members in a very specialized field, a KOL is a great option—due to their expert knowledge on a certain topic, KOLs are trusted contributors in their industries and have followers who are also invested in those subjects.

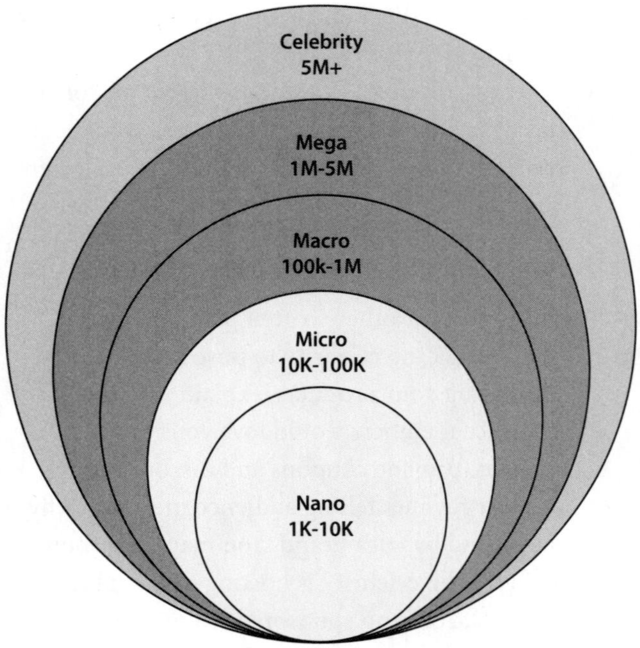

Figure 7.8 Five tiers of social influencers by the number of their followers

While considering how many followers an influencer has is important, brands also need to consider their answers the following questions when it comes to choosing influencers to work with:

- Does this influencer and his or her lifestyle fit our brand image?
- Have they worked with any of our competitors?
- Who is this influencer's current audience?
- Is our target audience active on the platform/channel primarily used by this influencer?
- Can our budget afford to work with this influencer?
- Has this influencer actually used any of our products or services before? Are they a customer?
- Does this person have a personality we want to work with?
- What will this influencer expect from us?

Communicate Brand Guidelines and Expectations with Your Influencer(s)

Once you have chosen an influencer, be sure to share your brand guidelines. Sharing details about your brand voice, tag lines, and language helps create an essential foundation for your collaboration. Remember that even though an Instagram story only appears for twenty-four hours (unless it is a highlight), the influencer who appears in it is still representing your brand and business. In this stage you should also determine whether your influencer will be creating content for your campaign on their own or if you'll be providing the content for them to post. Ensure they have the tools and assets to do so accurately while giving the influencer space to maintain their authenticity and transparency to their followers.

The last part before rolling out an influencer campaign is to finalize the expectation with the chosen influencers. Like any business relationship, it is very important for brands and influencers to both have a clear understanding of the expectations of the campaign. A social influencer contract should include the following elements:

1. How this influencer will be paid or rewarded (money, swag, discounts, coupon codes, etc.).
2. How long you will be working together (i.e., the contract term, renewal, and cancellation policies).
3. How you and the influencer will work with each other (e.g., products information, visual assets, etc.).
4. How the influencer will disclose the material connection with you and ensure compliance with FTC guidelines (more details in the next section).
5. Things to avoid in the influencer's posts, confidentiality, exclusivity, etc.
6. Any other terms of the contract necessary for your specific business to review.

Potential Issues that May Hinder Influencer Marketing

There are other factors that can negatively affect the performance of an influencer marketing campaign. Some of these common issues come from the matter of influencers' authenticity. For instance, brands may select influencers who are not aligned with their brand image or would not normally use the product—therefore, being perceived as inauthentic to their followers. Or, brands may push a rigid script on the influencer, rather than collaborating on a creative approach they feel will resonate with their fans, or influencers may publish blatantly promotional material—hard-selling content that turns off fans.

On the other hand, some common issues are more operational/technical. For instance, brands (especially for smaller startups) may fail to set clear terms and timelines for their agreement. Or they may not set up proper tracking, URLs, or landing pages beforehand, which could cause difficulty in evaluating the outcomes of an influencer marketing campaign. Knowing these negative factors that may hinder your influencer marketing campaign can help reduce wasted time and marketing budget, and the frustration associated with it. We will discuss the government regulation on influencer marketing and how to execute a transparent and authentic influencer marketing campaign in Chapter 9 Ethical and Legal Issues in Omnichannel Retailing.

Email and Text Messages

Do you subscribe to some retailer's email list or sign up to receive text messages (short message service, SMS) to get discounts codes, stay informed on your orders, or receive new product information? When your birthday is coming up, do you expect to receive an email or a text message addressed specifically to you from the retailers? As mentioned in Chapters 2 and 5, email and text message play a vital role in **customer relationship management (CRM)**. In addition, email and text messages are strategic tools for personalized marketing and promotions. According to market research, six out of ten customers say they expect companies to understand their unique needs and expectations and be treated like a person rather than a number.[18] A study about promotional email found that brands can gain a 3 percent boost to the email opening rate and almost trigger a 4 percent increase to spending for the opt-in customers. In other words, when *a retailer* asks a customer for their birthday, *the customer will expect to receive a birthday greeting or coupon code via email or text from the retailer.* With advanced technologies such as automation and machine learning, if their birthday is coming and they did not receive a birthday wish with some discount or gift, they will not feel that you "see" them or want their business. One of the key benefits of CRM emails ot text is their ability to attract non-opt-in customers to visit a company's website through the hyperlinks. By providing engaging products or online experiences, these visitors may be encouraged to opt-in for alerts, creating additional opportunities for communication and building brand relationships. In the following section, we introduce four types of emails/text messages that omnichannel retailers can develop to engage and assist customers' shopping tasks.

Broadcasting Email/Text Message

Broadcasting email refers to a one-time email campaign that you send to a specific group of your customers or subscribers. Since it is sent only once to the broad customer base, it does not require automation or follow-up emails. Such emails include newsletters, promo campaigns, special offers, and featured blog posts, among others.[19] For instance, net-a-porter.com, one of the subsidiaries under Yoox-Net-a-Porter Group, uses a unique blend of bright and light colors to attract the recipient's attention to the curated high-end designer goods they offer on their e-commerce site. This luxury fashion retailer uses the same brand aesthetics in all newsletters and email communication. Their newsletters are well organized to showcase the latest designer fashions to keep up with the edgy and high-end feel of the brand image.

A **broadcasting message** refers to similar text messages as a broadcasting email. It usually has links with the text so that it can redirect customers to other channels such as a website. A simple example of a broadcast text message is "Attention all fashionistas! Our new collection has just launched, and it's (a fire emoji). Head to our website to see what's in store and get your hands on the latest trends. [Website link]."

Transactional Email/Text Message

Transactional emails/text message are typically defined as automated email or text notifications regarding the purchases made via the e-commerce site and in-store retail environments. Moreover, these emails/text are activated when customers perform specific actions such as confirming the shipment of the orders or returns of the ordered products, activating/deactivating an account, starting a subscription, or requesting a password recovery, among others.

Triggered Email/Text Message

Triggered emails/text messages refer to automated emails triggered by an action taken (or not) by a website visitor or a change in a customer's behavior or profile via trigger marketing automation. Usually, businesses use this type of email to offer some opportunities to activate their account. For instance, if the subscriber does not respond or clicks during the purchase cycle, the business will send an email to re-engage them, called a *reactivation email.* In addition, when the shoppers abandoned the shopping carts, the company could send a remarketing email to remind them of the items that the shoppers browsed and placed in the shopping carts. Another type of triggered email/text message is about accessing the customer's account, which mostly involves password updates, email changes, configuration file changes, etc. In addition, businesses do frequently utilize personal events or milestone emails for birthdays, anniversaries, and other landmarks such as special offers or engagements. For instance, on the subscriber's birthday, a birthday wish email is sent by Stitch Fix to a customer. This type of email is triggered by the data provided by the customer.

Onboarding Email/Text Message

When customers sign up for an account or service, fashion businesses can send an **onboarding email/text** to show immediate appreciation for their business. These emails usually welcome new customers, offer instructions on using their product or service, and encourage further engagement and interaction with the company. For instance, Pieces, a Danish clothing and accessory company, sent an onboarding email to a customer to share how to use the services. In the email, they stress the imperatives of basic style, transparent sourcing, and environmental sustainability.[20] Moreover, these onboarding emails can create superb cross- or up-selling opportunities for the business through informing customers about what the business entails. Aerie, a US intimate apparel and lifestyle brand, likes to send short and sweet text messages to welcome new customers, provide discount codes, and redirect customers back to their website. New customers can get a huge deal from Aerie's text coupons, such as 40 percent off.[21]

Third-Party Review Sites or Mentions

Some may call the online promotional strategy of increasing third-party reviews and mentions as **offsite SEO** or **Referral**, because having third-party review sites or mentions may increase a retailer's website credibility. It is essential for small- and medium-sized retailers to implement this strategy to increase website traffic, drive customer engagement, and boost sales. As it involves linking the retailers' websites to reputable external sites, search engines will use the number and quality of these third-party external links to determine the credibility of the retailer's website content for specific search keywords, ultimately influencing the page ranking in a SERP. Moreover, third-party review sites or mentions are important for omnichannel promotion for several reasons:

- *Trust and credibility:* Third-party review sites provide unbiased and independent reviews and feedback from actual customers. This helps build trust and credibility for fashion retailers, as potential customers can rely on the opinions and experiences of others. Positive reviews and mentions on reputable review sites can enhance the retailer's reputation and influence purchasing decisions, especially in the era of online shopping where customers heavily rely on reviews before making a purchase.
- *Social proof:* Third-party review sites or mentions serve as social proof for fashion retailers. When customers see positive reviews or mention a retailer's products or services, it creates a perception that others have had a positive experience with the brand. This can motivate potential customers to trust the brand and be more likely to make a purchase or engage with the retailer across multiple channels, including online and offline.
- *Increased visibility and exposure:* Positive reviews and mentions on third-party sites can increase the visibility and exposure of a fashion retailer. When customers leave reviews on these sites, it creates user-generated content that can be indexed by search engines, leading to higher search rankings and increased organic traffic. Additionally, review sites often have their own audience and followers, which can expose the retailer's brand and products to a wider audience, leading to increased brand awareness and potential customer reach.
- *Integration with omnichannel strategy:* Third-party review sites or mentions can be integrated into a fashion retailer's omnichannel marketing strategy. For example, retailers can use positive reviews or mentions in their email marketing campaigns, social media posts, website testimonials, or in-store displays. This provides consistent and compelling content across different channels, reinforcing a positive perception of the brand and products among customers, regardless of the channel they engage with.

In summary, third-party review sites or mentions are important for omnichannel promotion as they build trust and credibility, provide social proof, increase visibility and exposure, integrate with omnichannel strategies, and offer valuable feedback and insights for fashion retailers. Incorporating positive reviews and mentions from third-party sites into a comprehensive omnichannel marketing strategy can strengthen the retailer's brand image, drive customer engagement, and boost sales.

Using Content Marketing to Navigate Consumers across Channels

Content marketing is a strategy that emphasizes creating and distributing valuable, relevant, and consistent content to attract and engage target customers, which will ultimately lead to sales and customer loyalty. A key difference that makes content marketing different from traditional marketing is that instead of just focusing on promoting products or services, omnichannel retailers use content on different channels to navigate their customers through the shopping journey. Through different channels, omnichannel retailers may reach different types of clientele and build customer relations by providing useful and engaging content. Therefore, when it comes to creating a comprehensive content marketing strategy, omnichannel retailers have to ask themselves the following questions: 1) What type of content do we need to create to engage customers and help them in their purchase journey? 2) How can I measure the success of the content? and 3) Where can we improve our content strategy?

For many retailers, creating content that converts browsers to buyers is the top priority of content marketing. However, it is not the only positive outcome. A comprehensive content marketing strategy can build brand awareness, engage loyal customers, save promotion cost, and attract new customers. Many brands have seen the benefits of using content to build their brand equity and community. Nowadays, customers come to a brand for values and identity, not just for obtaining a product.[22] Therefore, useful (and delightful) content can give customers the value they are looking for and a community that they want to belong to. Revolution Beauty, for instance, became the third fastest-growing company in the UK by using an authentic content marketing strategy. Revolution Beauty appeals to their customers by offering affordable, cruelty-free, and trend-led products weekly. Within five years after launching their business on X (formerly Twitter), they have accumulated more than 1.7 million followers on Instagram and over 3.5 million across its social media accounts. They would reach out to their product users and ask them to take a day or two to create a video for them, and they would compensate them for their time. By doing so, they were able to attract the followers of real product users. They also hire employees who represent their target customers in terms of age, skin tone, and ethnicity, so that they can produce content that their customers can relate to.[23] By using a content strategy that is developed around their real customers and users, they were able to increase their social media engagement and increase organic results without paying a lot of money on their marketing budget. In sum, with well-thought-out content, omnichannel retailers will be able to engage customers in a non-intrusive way, thereby reducing the cost of paying more for ads to increase brand awareness and traffic.

Use Content Marketing to Help Consumer Decision-Making

We discussed the consumer's journey in Chapter 3. When developing content for promotions, retailers can use a **content marketing funnel** (Figure 7.9) in developing the promotions. The funnel describes a process from attracting a new customer to after the customer completes a transaction, including the awareness stage, evaluation stage, and conversion stage. In each stage, consumers demand different types of information to help with their purchase decisions. Therefore, retailers must provide useful and relevant content to help customers navigate through the funnel.

Awareness Stage

A potential customer may not be aware that a product/solution exists for their problem. The objective of the content at this stage is to evoke consumer awareness that the brand/retailer offers a solution to their need/desired state—a need that a product would satisfy or a desired state (such as being beautiful or professional), etc.

At the **awareness stage**, the content at the Top-of-funnel (TOFU) should focus on educating the

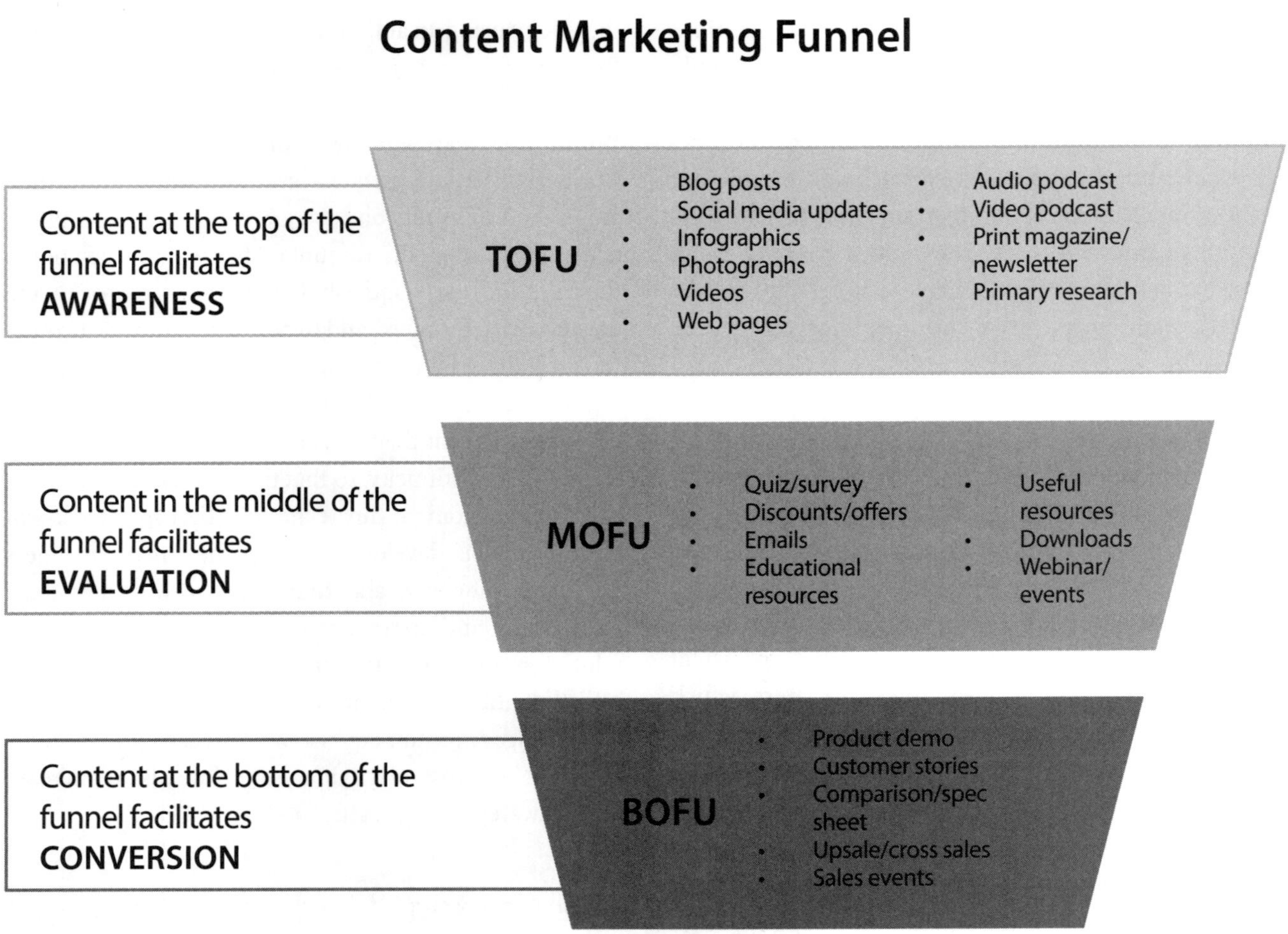

Figure 7.9 Content marketing funnel

potential customers about the product offerings. The major content retailers used in this stage are things like shareable photographs, blog posts, social media posts, videos, e-catalogs, podcasts, etc. For example, Net-a-Porter is a luxury online fashion retailer that offers high-end clothing, accessories, and beauty products. They have an online magazine called *Porter* which features fashion news, style guides, and interviews with celebrities, influencers, and industry experts. For blog posting, Nordstrom is a high-end department store that offers a wide range of fashion and beauty products. They have a blog called "The Thread" which features fashion trends, style tips, and interviews with designers. In addition, listicles (e.g. Top 20 gift ideas for Christmas, Mother's Day, Father's Day, Valentine's Day, etc.) can receive two times more shares than other blog post formats.

Evaluation Stage

Once potential customers become aware of the product/retail offering, they may enter the evaluation stage. In the **evaluation stage**, the potential customers will determine whether they want to purchase the product or not. There are many factors that influence customers' evaluation of a product. The higher the product price, the more effort consumers may put into this stage. For new customers, omnichannel retailers can use consistent content across different channels to build up customer trust at this stage, too. At this stage, a potential customer is looking for content that can persuade them that buying the product from the retailer is a superior choice. Therefore, the goal of the content at this stage is to help eliminate consumers' doubt about making the purchase. Identifying the pain points that prevent a customer from making a purchase could be the very source of identifying what kind of content that needs to be offered on different channels. For instance, if consumers need size information to make a purchase, in addition to a size chart, maybe a retailer can offer the height and weight of the model and the size they wore in the product photo to help the consumer evaluate the product. Research has shown that video also conveys a better effect on online product evaluation.[24] Omnichannel retailers could utilize content such as emails, customer reviews, user-uploaded photos, product comparisons chart, etc. to help consumers in their evaluation phase.

Conversion Stage

Conversion stage is the stage in which consumers make a desirable action (e.g., complete a transaction, enroll in the email list, book an appointment, etc.). For omnichannel retailers, this is the stage when consumers feel confident with a product or service, and they are ready to take action. At this stage, information that is related to completing a transaction and consequential acts such as shipping, payments, and return policy is extremely important for a potential customer to complete a transaction. The goal at this stage is to prevent potential customers from stumbling at any point as they navigate through the check-out process. There are two key questions omnichannel retailers need to keep in mind. First, does the content have a clear call to action? Second, are we making the purchase process as simple as possible?

The calls to action can be buttons of "add-to-cart," "check-out now," "share with," "like on social," etc. These calls to action can also be used to measure the content outcomes later and help you to reach your business goals. In Chapter 3 we discussed ways to improve the efficiency of the check-out process. In this chapter, we will focus on the content that you should provide to customers to reduce their perceived purchase risks and increase their confidence in the purchase. This can be achieved by providing customers with the information they need before proceeding to a completed transaction. One of the best ways to do this is to develop content addressing the identified pain points from the results of your shoppers' journey analyses (details provided in Chapter 3).

For new business, you may want to conduct consumer research such as focus groups to find out how types of information are needed during the conversion stage and make the purchase process as simple as possible. Finally, sometimes customers are just not ready to pay yet. In that case, more and more retailers offer "My Favorites" or "Save for Later" functions, so that customers can put the products they are not ready to purchase in the list as external memory to help them organize the things they plan to buy.[25] This way, the products will not sit in the shopping cart and take up the product counts from your inventory.

How Should Omnichannel Retailers Implement Content Marketing

Major strategies of content marketing include blogging, podcasts, videos, magazines (online or offline), newsletters, etc., in addition to the regular product pages. Among the different types of shoppable content, videos (short- or long-form) are the most commonly used form.[26] Brands use these content for storytelling and promotion to bring traffic to their website or stores and create sales. Moreover, fashion retailers can provide styling tips and techniques in their blog articles to attract and engage their customers. Stories about how the brand started and was advocated for can also help consumers to verify the company's personality. Studies have shown that more consumers are looking for brands that reflect their beliefs and values.[27,28] For example, Everlane, a D2C apparel retailer, established their radical transparent brand image by showing their transparent pricing (a breakdown of their cost of production for each product), what goes into their garment production, and who (and where) produces their products. Moreover, according to market research, more than 80 percent of video marketers say that video has increased traffic to their websites and directly increased sales.[29] Among many ways of converting promotion materials to shoppable content, hyperlinks, tags on photos, and videos are the most common methods to make shoppable content.

For omnichannel retailers, promoting useful and shoppable content across multiple channels, such as websites and social media channels, is a no-brainer. While the shoppable content is entertaining, it will also enable the business to "sell without selling." Recall your own experience using social media. How many times did you find yourself watching the content to check out the products? Most importantly, shoppable content is an implicit way to promote a product to those customers who are not ready to purchase it yet. Consumers usually go through a series of steps to make a purchase decision. Depending on the types of products and how involved they are in the purchase decision, the decision process may vary in terms of time and effort. In the following section, we will introduce types of content a retailer can develop for promotion, and we will discuss shoppable content in more detail.

Types of Content

Evergreen Content

Evergreen content is the content that will continuously be relevant to customers without seasonal effect. Just like its name, this type of content can always be on your website and contributes to consistent traffic to your channels as well. Examples of evergreen content can include a guide about how to select a cosmetic product, color and styling principles, finding your perfect color/size/fit, etc. It can also be educational content, such as how a silk blouse was made, or how to correctly wash your cashmere sweater so that it stays soft and warm. Beauty brands often create educational videos to teach their customers how to use a new eye shadow product or put on a certain style of makeup. Infographics are a great format for this type of information because it is more visually appealing than multiple paragraphs of text. If you do not have the time to create the evergreen content in-house, a curated list of helpful resources can also help too. The links can be used as the offsite SEO, which we have discussed earlier in this chapter.

Seasonal Content

Seasonal content is created for certain holidays, seasons, or events. Keeping a holiday calendar handy and planning ahead is the rule of thumb when you develop seasonal content. Keep in mind that the purpose of the content is to convert your customers from visitors to customers and eventually become loyal customers. Therefore, the seasonal content must make your customers feel that you are providing them with useful or entertaining information. For example, a gift suggestion list for the year-end holiday season for mom/dad/grandparents, what to wear for Valentine's Day, the most popular back-to-school items this year, etc. You should also add a call to action with product links in the content because nothing frustrates a consumer more than seeing something they are interested in and then don't know where to get them!

Shoppable Content (Sell without Selling)

Creating content (images, catalogs, videos) that is shoppable is also getting increasingly popular because it blurs the line between content and commerce.[30] The term **shoppable content** is defined as any form of content whether it's a social media post, image, video, or even a virtual reality game that allows customers to buy the products directly from the content they are viewing in real-time. Many social media platforms now provide methods to tag the product links to social media posts, like Instagram Stories, Facebook Shops, etc. There are also many apps/platforms available for content to be equipped with links and tags. Dior launched an AR campaign for their sneaker, B27. They partnered with Snapchat to create an AR lens that allowed Snapchatters to virtually try on six different pairs of sneakers. This interactive experience enabled users to see themselves wearing the products in real-time using the Snapchat app, enhancing customer engagement and encouraging virtual exploration of Dior's latest offerings. The Lens was promoted via the AR Lens in carousel and the Snap Ad formats, and offered the possibility for users to buy them directly.[31]

User-Generated Content

When it comes to **user-generated content** (UGC), there are several forms that it can take, including likes, ratings, reviews, questions and answers, and user-submitted images and videos. For omnichannel retailers, it can be beneficial to use this content across various channels to provide a unique experience for both online and offline shoppers. This is because consumers tend to trust what other customers say about a product more than the product photos and descriptions provided by the stores. Customer reviews and ratings can provide immediate assistance to potential buyers in making purchase decisions. Clothing retailers, for instance, tend to utilize customer reviews, particularly those that provide information about product fit, on their websites. Retailers must seek permission from social media users to use their content. Once permission is obtained, the curated photo and video content can be embedded with the appropriate product links to boost online sales and enable further ROI analyses. User-generated content is typically employed in retailers' online channels, such as Lookbooks, category page carousels (a slideshow of photos on the website), and email promotions. See an example of the pool retailer can use to label the photo on Pinterest at https://apps.shopify.com/photoslurp-visual-commerce.

For fashion businesses and brands, it is important to test a few kinds of content and track the results to see which piece of content has the most intended effects, whether it's engagements or conversion rate. The key questions for an omnichannel retailer to ask to determine if content is effective are: 1) did our target customers view, interact with, or share the content? 2) is there an increase in sales after viewing or interacting with the content? To answer these questions, you can use online metrics such as total traffic, bounce rate, page views, time on page, conversions, etc. Although we have been talking about different types of content, retailers do not need to adopt all of them. At the end of the day, only the most relevant and useful content will attract and convert customers. In the following sections, we will discuss various key performance indicators (KPIs), the principle of setting up KPIs, and how to evaluate the return on investment (ROI).

How to Measure the Outcomes of Promotions for Omnichannel Retailers

For omnichannel retailers, measuring the outcomes of promotions is crucial to optimize their marketing strategies and maximize their return on investment. Promotions can have different effects on different channels, such as online, offline, or by the internal departments that plan and execute these promotions. By tracking and analyzing the data from each channel, omnichannel retailers can understand how their customers respond to their offers, what motivates them to buy, and how they switch between channels. Measuring the outcomes of promotions can help omnichannel retailers design more effective and personalized promotions that increase customer loyalty and satisfaction.

Conversion and Other KPIs

When a person visiting your website successfully achieves a particular goal or who walks into your physical store and makes a purchase, these desired actions can be referred to as a conversion. This means that a consumer has transitioned from being a mere visitor to becoming a potential lead or even a paying customer. A conversion is essentially the point at which a passive visitor transforms into an active, engaged visitor or customer. The **conversion rate** is calculated as the percentage of visitors who have successfully accomplished the desired goals.

Key performance indicator (KPI) is a set of measurements that help a business to determine if they are achieving their goals. When it comes to choosing KPIs, there are **SMART principles**: select a Specific business goal, the goal should be Measurable, and Achievable, and is Relevant to overall business objectives. Most importantly, the KPIs need to be Time-phased; for instance, they are evaluated by day, week, or month, etc. Digital KPIs are online metrics that measure success across different online marketing channels. Some basic KPI examples for omnichannel retailers are pay-per-click (PPC), conversion rate, customer lifetime value (CLV), return on investment (ROI), etc. **Pay-per-click (PPC)** is the pre-negotiated cost that a brand agrees to pay for each click ad received.

Important KPIs by Channels

For omnichannel retailers, KPIs can be varied depending on the different types of channels that they operate. One important and unique characteristic that an omnichannel retailer has is that the customers can jump across different channels to complete their customer journey. For instance, a potential customer may have seen an ad about how to care for a cashmere sweater, clicked on the ad, and read the blog. While reading the blog, they see a photo of an influencer wearing your company's new seasonal product and clicks on the influencer's photo leading to the Instagram page. After browsing several outfits, the customer clicks on one of the hyperlinks of the outfit which leads her to your website product page, and they make a purchase. The customer was happy that they found another, new color of denim that could accompany their cashmere sweater. The aforementioned example shows good content creation helps incrementally move a potential customer toward a purchase, even if it means they are navigating different channels. As the customer journey may not happen all at once, expecting one single piece of content to move a customer through the shopper's journey is unrealistic. That's why it's imperative to vary the types of content and to have a comprehensive content strategy centered around your business goals.

In a long-term view, **customer lifetime value (CLV)** represents the total revenue a business can reasonably expect from a single customer account throughout the business relationship and is a function of average annual revenue per customer divided by the average lifespan of a customer (average years that a customer continues to purchase from a brand).[32] There are some specific KPIs pertaining to different channels of omnichannel retailing (see Table 7.1). We will discuss those specific KPIs of online advertising, social media marketing, and email marketing in the following chapters.

Table 7.1 Selected Targeted KPIs by Channels

CHANNELS	LEADING INDICATOR	TERTIARY	SECONDARY KPI	PRIMARY KPI
Social Accounts	Followers	Engagement	Site visits	Conversions
Search/Display Ads	Impressions	Click through rate	Conversions	Cost per acquisition
Email	Delivery rate	Open rate	Click through rate	Conversion rate
Text Message	Delivery rate	Click through rate	Unsubscribe Rate	Conversion rate
Referrals	Referrals gained	Site visits	Conversions	Revenue
Content Marketing	Content views/visits	Bounce rate	Content shares	Conversions

Important KPIs by Departments

Since different departments in a company may have different business goals, they may look at different indices as their KPIs. For instance, for the sales and marketing team, they may like to monitor total sales, average order value, conversion rate by product category, etc.; while the content team would look at the total traffic, top landing pages, page views, and conversion rate by page, etc. For the management team, they may want to see the monthly sales growth, total customer engagement, the total number of visits, and total sales by products and costs of new customer acquisition. Table 7.2 provides an example of different target KPIs for different teams in omnichannel retailing.

Evaluating Return on Investment (ROI)

Return on investment (ROI) is the monetary return a retailer gets back from an investment. ROI is an important indicator for retail upper management when deciding where to allocate operation and marketing budget. In the following chapters, we will discuss more about the ROI in different channels and how to use ROI to evaluate the outcomes of retail businesses. The concept can be expressed by the following calculation formula:

$$[(\text{Sales generated} - \text{Money invested}) \div \text{Money invested}] \times 100$$

Throughout this chapter, we have explored a range of promotional techniques for both online and offline touchpoints from the viewpoint of omnichannel retailers. We have also discussed how to utilize diverse content to guide consumers throughout their shopping experience. In addition, we have delved into the various online metrics that are now available and how omnichannel retailers can effectively use different KPIs to measure the success of their promotions in omnichannel environments. By utilizing KPIs, omnichannel retailers can establish expectations and demonstrate that their efforts are positively impacting their businesses.

Table 7.2 Different Departments and Their Targeted KPIs

SALES AND MARKETING TEAM	CONTENT DEVELOPMENT TEAM	MANAGEMENT TEAM
• Total sales • Average order value • Conversions • Conversion rates • Conversion rates by product or category • Total number of engaged visitors • Conversion rates by demographics • Customer lifetime value • Lead value	• Total traffic • Traffic by source • Top landing pages • Page views • Engagement rate per page/video • Conversion rate by page	• Month-over-month traffic, sales, or list growth • Total customer engagement • Conversion rate • Total sales by product category • Cost of customer acquisition

CASE STUDY 7.1

Online Advertising across Channels and Retail Media

In the highly competitive fashion industry, successful retailers must keep up with changing customer preferences and industry trends by implementing effective omnichannel promotions. Failure to do so can result in losing market share to competitors who excel in this area. However, managing omnichannel promotion can be quite challenging, especially when it comes to avoiding potential conflicts between different channels. To deliver an integrated customer experience, retailers must ensure a consistent message and pricing strategy across channels to avoid customer confusion or dissatisfaction. This requires effective coordination and communication between various departments and channels within the organization, as well as a robust data management system to securely collect, store, and analyze customer data from various touchpoints. Bradley Hearn, Product Marketing Manager at ChannelAdvisor, in comments shared in an interview with Retail TouchPoint, said: "a critical component in creating that efficiency comes down to accurate targeting. Leveraging multiple ad types and multiple channels gives you the ability to become more strategic with your campaigns, target consumers across the entire buying funnel, and deliver your potential customers the right product ad, in the right place at just the right time."[33] In addition, measuring the effectiveness of omnichannel promotions and attributing results to specific channels or campaigns can be difficult, requiring robust analytics and reporting capabilities to accurately track and evaluate performance. Therefore, established retailers that have a sizable customer base are well-positioned to offer an advertisement network that offers highly relevant and interest-specific audience with a closed-loop measurement. It is called Retail Media or retail media network (RMN), and it is posited to be a new stream of revenue for omnichannel retailers.

Retail media refers to the advertising activities carried out by retailers on their own platforms, such as websites, mobile apps, and physical stores. It involves leveraging the retailer's customer data, traffic, and digital touchpoints to offer targeted advertising opportunities to brands and advertisers. Retail media allows omnichannel retailers to monetize their platforms by providing advertising space and services, while also enabling brands to reach their target audience in a contextually relevant and engaging manner.[34] This form of advertising often involves utilizing customer insights and analytics to deliver personalized and targeted ad experiences, enhancing the overall shopping journey for consumers. Based on market research, in 2022, global retail media revenue reached $101 billion.[35] Did you know that a significant percentage of retailers are earning over $100 million in revenue from their media networks? It's interesting to note that Amazon dominates the retail media industry, claiming over 75 percent of the US market share. By the end of 2023, Amazon's share was ten times larger than its closest competitor, Walmart (The number was estimated using the 2024 numbers: https://content-na1.emarketer.com/retail-media-search-forecast-trends-2024.). As digital advertising continues to grow with consumers' shopping habits, omnichannel retailers are adopting the retail media business model to monetize their online platforms and capitalize on this trend. This way, retailers can leverage their first-party shopper data and online/offline presence to provide targeted advertising opportunities to brands and advertisers. Retail media allows omnichannel retailers to generate additional revenue streams, enhance customer experiences through personalized advertising, and create mutually beneficial partnerships with brands. The retail media concept aligns with the evolving retail landscape, where retailers transform their digital platforms into advertising channels, enabling them to maximize their reach, engage customers, and create a more integrated and profitable omnichannel business model.

Nordstrom Media Network (NMN) is an advertising program enabling brands to share their messages with Nordstrom and Nordstrom Rack customers via on- and offsite media campaigns. It has 18.8 million social media followers, 32 million active customers, and 1.9 billion annual unique visitors. In 2022, Nordstrom generated $40 million from their Nordstrom Media Network (NMN). Nordstrom said that their offsite touchpoints (including paid social and display ads, YouTube videos, search and shopping ads, and affiliate campaigns) now make up 60 percent of their advertising business. Moreover, Walmart has teamed up with a whole host of platforms, including

TikTok, Snap, Roku, and Firework, to enable offsite, video-based advertising.

Retail media is becoming increasingly popular in Europe as well. Zalando is a prominent European fashion e-commerce platform. They offer a wide range of clothing, shoes, and accessories from various brands. Although Zalando primarily operates as an online fashion retailer, they have recently started opening a few physical stores in select locations. They have developed their own retail media business called "Zalando Media Solutions" to provide advertising and marketing solutions to brands, allowing them to leverage Zalando's customer data and digital channels to reach their target audience. Zalando Media Solutions offers various ad formats, including display ads, native ads, and sponsored product placements, enabling brands to drive brand awareness and conversions among Zalando's user base.[36] With a focus on providing a seamless shopping experience, Zalando claims to offer combined convenience, extensive product selection, and personalized recommendations to cater to the fashion needs of their customers.

According to market research firm Forrester, retailers report a high average retail media margin of 50–70 percent (as opposed to around 30 percent gross margin for department stores). Onsite advertising (those ads displayed on the retailers' site or mobile apps) yields even higher margins of 70–80 percent. Additionally, 25 percent of retailers who participated in the study were earning over $100 million in revenue from their retail media networks.[37] The future of omnichannel promotions is poised to be dynamic and transformative. With advancements in technology, data analytics, and customer targeting, retail media will become increasingly personalized and tailored to individual consumers. Retailers will leverage artificial intelligence and machine learning algorithms to deliver highly relevant and contextual advertising experiences. Additionally, the integration of offline and online channels will continue to evolve, creating seamless omnichannel experiences for consumers. As retailers gain deeper insights into customer behavior and preferences, they will be able to optimize their advertising strategies and drive higher engagement and conversion rates. Overall, the future of retail media holds immense potential for innovative and impactful marketing approaches that connect retailers with their target audience in more meaningful ways.

Discussion Questions:

1. What role does customer support and feedback play in enhancing the effectiveness of omnichannel promotions? How can retailers ensure timely and effective support across different channels, and how can they leverage customer feedback to iterate and improve their promotional strategies?
2. In your experience, what are some best practices for creating a seamless and consistent customer experience across multiple channels in omnichannel promotions?
3. Go to Amazon.com and search for "Burberry," and describe the search results on the site. Do you think retail media is a more effective way to increase traffic and engagement with consumers compared to Google search ads? Why or why not?
4. How does the adoption of retail media benefit fashion retailers in terms of revenue generation and customer engagement? What are some potential challenges they may face in implementing and managing retail media strategies?
5. In what ways can fashion retailers leverage customer data and analytics to enhance the effectiveness of their retail media initiatives? How can personalized advertising and targeting contribute to a more seamless and tailored customer experience?
6. From the consumer's point of view, can retailers strike a balance between monetizing their platforms through advertising while maintaining transparency, data privacy, and preserving customer trust?

Career Opportunities

Job Titles	Key Responsibility
Marketing Specialist—entry-level	**Social media responsibilities**: • Partner and collaborate with cross-functional teams, and customer care partners in regards to day-to-day social content • Own development and execution of all Google Analytics organic link tags for all social channels • Own process to schedule and post content across paid and organic social platforms including: Facebook, Instagram, Pinterest, X (formerly Twitter), YouTube, Snapchat, etc. • Write copy across social channels • Own and manage daily social engagement with followers and community • Own and manage paid social media strategy • Participate in seasonal social/editorial/influencer marketing brainstorms • Assist in local social media shoots • Support user-generated content moderation **General marketing responsibilities:** • Create high level creative and seasonal briefs—website creative, email, organic and paid social • Regularly maintain/update seasonal Marketing editorial calendars • Collaborate with other cross-functional teams to develop and monitor strategic marketing campaigns • Analyze and report on campaign performance. Leverage insights for campaign optimization • Submit and manage all Workfront jobs • Work with Planning/Merchandise teams to ensure product inventory prior to the creation of deliverables • Coordinate shot sheets for digital campaigns/asset creation • Participate in regional and brand marketing meetings/check-ins, as needed **Qualifications:** • Bachelor's degree in Social Media, Communications, Journalism, Marketing, or other related field is highly desired • 3+ years of professional social media or marketing/ communications experience • Strong organizational skills and social-first thinking is a must • Ability to prioritize projects and collaborate with other team members is a must • Strong organizational skills and social/digital-first thinking is a must • A desire to pursue a career in either social media or omnichannel marketing • Knowledge of social media platforms: Facebook, Instagram, Pinterest, YouTube, X (formerly Twitter), and TikTok • Knowledge of Google Analytics • Familiarity with social tools like Sprinklr and Curalate • Knowledge of luxury retail landscape a plus

Summary

Omnichannel retailers can utilize their various touchpoints to promote products, aiming to increase brand awareness, create seamless experiences, boost sales, enhance customer satisfaction, and optimize marketing strategies. Offline touchpoints include physical stores, print media, pop-up stores, and experiential events. In addition to offline touchpoints, omnichannel retailers can leverage a range of online touchpoints to execute effective promotions. Through their website and mobile apps, they can showcase special offers, personalized recommendations, and limited-time promotions to capture customer attention and drive conversions. Online advertising allows them to reach a wider audience and target specific demographics or interests. Social media channels enable retailers to engage customers with interactive content, influencer collaborations, and sponsored posts. Email marketing can deliver personalized promotions directly to customers' inboxes, nurturing loyalty and encouraging repeat purchases. Meanwhile, omnichannel retailers can use third-party review sites and referral programs to increase their SERP ranking and incentivize customers to share promotions with their networks. To ensure an integrated shopping experience, retailers should develop cohesive promotional content that caters to customer preferences and needs, maintaining consistency and seamless navigation across multiple channels. Content marketing differs from traditional marketing by using content across various channels to guide customers through the shopping journey. Omnichannel retailers can reach diverse clientele and foster customer relationships by delivering valuable and engaging content. By integrating these online touchpoints, omnichannel retailers can create cohesive and impactful promotional strategies. Finally, measuring the outcomes of promotions is crucial for omnichannel retailers as it helps evaluate effectiveness, understand customer behavior, optimize strategies, assess ROI, and track progress toward business objectives. It enables data-driven decisions, resource allocation, and continuous improvement in the competitive retail landscape.

Key Terms

Alternative text (Alt text)
App campaigns
Awareness stage
Blogger influencers
Brand ambassador
Broadcasting email/Message
Celebrity influencers
Content marketing
Content marketing funnel
Conversion rate
Conversion stage
Crawling
Customer lifetime value (CLV)
Customer relationship management (CRM)
Digital KPIs
Display ads
Endless aisle
Engagement rate
Evaluation stage
Evergreen content
Google my business
Influencer marketing
Influencer marketing spending
Key opinion leaders (KOLs)
Key performance indicator (KPI)
Keyword planner
Local campaigns
Macro-influencers
Mega-influencers
Micro-influencers
Nano-influencers
Offsite SEO or referral
Onboarding email/Text message
Onsite SEO
Organic search results
Pay-per-click (PPC)
Remarketing
Retail media
Return on investment (ROI)
Search ads
Search engine optimization (SEO)
Search engine results pages (SERPS)
Seasonal content
Shoppable content
Shopping ads
SMART principles
Social display ads
Social media influencer
Social proof
Transactional email/Text message
Triggered email/Text message
User-generated content (UGC)
Video ads on YouTube

Reflection and Discussion Questions

1. How does the integration of online and offline channels impact the effectiveness of promotions in omnichannel retailing? Can you give some examples?
2. How can fashion retailers leverage online advertising to enhance their omnichannel promotions? Reflecting on your recent shopping experience, what are some successful examples of fashion brands effectively using online advertising across channels?
3. What role does personalization play in omnichannel promotions? How can retailers utilize customer data to deliver personalized promotions across multiple channels?
4. How can fashion retailers ensure a consistent brand experience across different channels during promotions? What are the potential risks of inconsistent branding, and how can they be mitigated?
5. What are the key metrics and analytics that retailers should consider when evaluating the effectiveness of their omnichannel promotions? How can they track and measure the impact of promotions across various channels?
6. How can technology and data analytics help retailers optimize their omnichannel promotions? What are the key tools and technologies that retailers should consider investing in?
7. How can social media platforms be effectively utilized in omnichannel promotions? Use your favorite retailer as an example, and consider what are the best practices for engaging customers and driving conversions through social media advertising.
8. With the rise of social media influencers, how can fashion retailers leverage influencer partnerships as a means of promoting their brands and products? What are the potential benefits and risks associated with influencer collaborations in omnichannel promotions?
9. What are the future trends and innovations in omnichannel promotions? How can retailers stay ahead of the competition and adapt to changing customer preferences and technologies?
10. What are some ethical considerations related to omnichannel promotions? Have you seen some recent news discussing this issue? In your opinion, how can retailers balance data privacy/data concerns while delivering personalized promotions?

CHAPTER 8

Omnichannel Customer Service

Learning Objectives

Upon finishing this chapter, you will be able to:

- Describe a framework for customer service planning
- Outline customer expectations regarding service via various channels
- Identify customer service characteristics that are shared by top retailers
- Illuminate strategies that enable effective customer service across channels
- Recognize customer service and customer relationship management

In Chapter 8, specific omnichannel services sought by customers regardless of the channel shopped for and those tied to individual channels are discussed. Chapter 3 described the many changes in customer behavior. Omnichannel customer service requires careful planning and execution—just like other retail strategies to create delightful customer journeys, which in turn, build a lifelong customer relationship with the retailer.

Foundational Elements for Effective Omnichannel Customer Service

Customer service initiatives require extensive planning. Giving current consumers what they want and trying to draw in new ones are two crucial components. Many businesses receive reputable recognition from customers who use their main avenue of distribution. However, as new channels are introduced, it's possible that established strategies won't take into account the different types of customers. There is no one measurement that fits all.

It presents a curious paradox to provide service through one channel, then extend to others. On the one hand, many customers use every avenue a retailer provides for commerce. Their overall experience ought to be seamless and captivating, encouraging lifelong value as well as repeat business. Conversely, when they add channels, retailers must modify their customer support procedures. To please every customer across every channel, at least occasionally, is a difficult job. In this part, we'll first look at some fundamental categories of services before examining a mnemonic tool for making decisions in customer service.

Levels of Omnichannel Customer Service

When it comes to retail service, there are two basic meanings: providing service to customers and offering retail services as a business. The fundamental kinds of service remain the same whether a company is a solely electronic retailer or a multiunit specialty store chain that also runs a catalog and an online store. Customer relationship management is critical in the delivery of services to consumers because it provides an ideology and framework for decision-making.

Macro and Micro Views of Retail Service

The macro perspective examines retailing in the context of retail service companies. A computer repair and installation company, a dry-cleaning establishment, and a hair salon are examples of service companies. The micro perspective examines services delivered to customers via various platforms. Customer services include gift wrapping, in-store jewelry repairs, email follow-up to a catalog transaction, and do-it-yourself learning modules on a home renovation web microsite. Customer amenities are sometimes free and other times paid offerings. Many retailers charge a fee for gift-wrapping, but others include it free with purchase.

Basic/Fundamental and Enhanced Services

There are two types of customer service: fundamental and enhanced. Retailers provide fundamental client services, which are commonly expected by the customers. Fundamental services include generic greetings, department or merchandise finding information, and check-out assistance. Accepting credit cards and handling returns are also basic customer service processes. Customers anticipate and rarely question the availability of these basic or fundamental services.

Below are the expected fundamental services from omnichannel retailers:

- ✓ Looking up in-store merchandise availability while online
- ✓ Using online coupons or promotions in-store or with catalogs
- ✓ Reviewing or confirming in-store events online
- ✓ Browsing online, buying in-store
- ✓ Buying online, picking up in-store
- ✓ Visiting a store, buying from extended inventory via electronic kiosk
- ✓ Comparing prices in-store, placing an order via mobile phone
- ✓ Buying online, returning to a physical store
- ✓ Gift registry available cross the channels

Enhanced services are complete, value-added services provided by retailers. These include, but are not limited to, gift wrapping, delivery, personal shoppers, gift registries, loyalty programs, alteration and installation services, and the availability of computerized kiosks. Saying "good morning" to a customer who has entered a store or "welcome" to a new visitor to a website is a form of fundamental service but greeting that customer by name directly or in print on a website is a form of enhanced service.

Clienteling is the practice of personal shopping in brick-and-mortar stores, which includes providing extensive merchandise help and fashion or technical assistance. Clienteling is carried out by trained sales professionals who maintain detailed records of specific groups of customers with whom they have established a relationship over time. Competitive customer care strategies are built around augmented services. For instance, Men's Wearhouse sales associates engage in clienteling, particularly with professional males who are the retailer's target market. The company's database includes a wealth of information about previous purchases made by customers, which sales associates supplement with personal notations. Some offer wardrobe consultations in their clients' offices, while others directly transport freshly tailored suits to the customer.

All stores provide basic/fundamental services, and higher-end retailers such as Nordstrom, Neiman Marcus, and Saks Fifth Avenue typically provide a high degree of enhanced services. Unsurprisingly, there are exceptions to the generalization that good service levels are only found in high-end stores. Target, for example, is well-known not only for its low prices but also for its excellent customer care. If customers are unable to find a sales associate, one can be called within a minute by pressing a call button or using an internal telephone. If customers require assistance, all team members and leaders are expected to chip in. Many multichannel retailers, such as L.L. Bean, can offer detailed product information that is beyond the purview of average brick-and-mortar sales associates thanks to their carefully developed merchandise and customer information databases.

Customer Relationship Management Practices

Customers' expectations toward customer services have increased at the same rate as omnichannel retailing. Retailers stay competitive by providing more, better, and more meaningful customer services. Customer relationship management (CRM), which was introduced in Chapter 5, is critical in developing customer support strategies. This management practice includes not only basic customer demographic and sales data, but also more significant lifestyle, psychographic, and behavioral data.

Retailers collect usable consumer information using a variety of statistical software and other technological tools. According to a National Retail Federation (NRF) annual survey, 68 percent of retailers who participated in their survey use data mining tools, and 84 percent use Web site statistics. More than half of businesses use CRM software, and 78 percent use data for customer support. CRM philosophy is based on three tenets: know your customer, document customer behavior in a database, and leverage that data to create successful strategies that keep customers satisfied.[1]

Various Payment Options as Customer Service

With the rise of the payment revolution that coincided with the rise of e-commerce, there has been a tremendous change in the use of credit and debit cards in the place of cash and check. In 2005, debit and credit cards accounted for 55 percent of in-store payments. In 2014, online payments in e-commerce were made using credit cards (46 percent), debit cards (32 percent), and alternative payment methods such as Paypal, Amazon Payment, Google Wallet, or PayPal Credit, formerly Bill Me Later. Inevitably, merchants that accept multiple payment types usually experience lower incidences of shopping cart abandonment from shoppers, and higher re-order conversion, which leads to increased sales revenues. In this section, we will discuss the various payment systems available for e-commerce merchants and omnichannel retailers.

There are six payment types that can be used in the omnichannel retail context.[2] The most common and frequently used payment method is credit card, due to the ease of use and security benefits built into the cards. Even though debit cards are often used in e-commerce and are considered a great way to live within a budget, it is equivalent to cash carried in a card format. Prepaid cards contain a preset amount of currency which can be used via brick-and-mortar and online retailers. One of the significant benefits of using a prepaid card is that we cannot overspend on them. Although the adoption rate of prepaid cards is low in the United States, they have gradually become popular in specific market segments. Although not popular today, bank transfer is still considered the primary payment method for e-commerce. Another form of payment used in the e-commerce and omnichannel context is an **e-wallet.** E-wallet is an advanced digital payment method integrated with mobile wallets which refers to the e-wallet system operated via mobile device and app (see Figure 8.1). In the next section, we will delve into the emerging digital payment methods, which have been gaining popularity in recent years.

Mobile payment system

Mobile payment is defined as a payment made for a product or service through a portable electronic device such as a mobile phone or tablet. As shown in Figure 8.1, NFC mobile payments or proximity mobile wallets are contactless payments between a mobile wallet stored on a smartphone and an NFC-enabled card reader. When the distance between the devices is less than two inches, these card readers can wirelessly communicate payment instructions. Magnetic secure transmission payments are also contactless and work like NFC, except they use magnetic signals between the credit card and the card reader or POS. QR (quick response) payments involve QR codes, which belong to consumers and are scanned by retailers, and vice versa, to confirm and authorize mobile payments. SMS payments complete mobile payments via text messages and add a fee to the consumer's monthly phone bill. Mobile bank or peer-to-peer payments do not require a card reader or POS but works by transferring the payment directly from the consumer's bank account to the payee's account.

Venmo, Zelle, Google Pay, PayPal, Apple Pay, and Samsung Pay are strong competitors in this field. The first four are examples of popular peer-to-peer payments. Apple has surpassed all other competitors in in-store contactless payments. The characteristic of Samsung Pay is that it can work anywhere on magnetic stripe cards, although more secure NFC point-of-sale devices have mainly replaced those magnetic stripe cards. Although the PayPal application does not support direct NFC wireless payments made by Apple Pay and Google Pay, it can make payments in multiple stores.[3,4]

Figure 8.1 Contactless payment through mobile payment system

Mobile payment systems have shown considerable advantages in Europe and Asia. Still, they have yet to be adopted widely in the United States. Low utilization of mobile payment systems in the United States affects consumer behavior because consumers would not demand or trust mobile payment systems if not already widely implemented. Thus, low market concentration in banking and well-developed non-cash payment systems can explain the barriers to adoption in the United States.[5]

Other payment systems

E-micropayments refer to small transactions occurring in the e-commerce environment. Since credit card transaction fees can be between $0.25 to $0.35 per transaction plus 2–3 percent of the purchase price and debit cards also hold a fixed rate of more than $0.35 per transaction, many vendors do not see the value of accepting such payment methods for a small purchase under $5 or $10. Also, e-micropayments are popular among minor consumers who do not have credit or debit cards yet. Micropayment can occur by aggregating the charges per download of music and/or e-book and such through Apple's iTunes store. Also, mobile phone service providers may allow a consumer to charge a ringtone download directly to their mobile service bill. For instance, in Taiwan and South Korea, among other Asian countries, a wide variety of purchases via online and vending machines can be made via mobile phone payment.

The "buy now pay later" (BNPL) payment system refers to a micro-loan program issued to the customers. For example, Klarna, Afterpay, and Affirm fall into this category. Over the 2019 holiday season, 44 percent of US consumers mentioned having a wide variety of payment options available on the retailers' sites, including BNPL options, increased their likelihood to spend more money with the retailers.[6]

Biometric payment is a method of payment using various parts of the body. Eye tracking, fingerprint scanning, and facial recognition (see Figure 8.2) are widely used biometric payment methods. For instance, after the entered fingerprint matches the stored fingerprint, the payment will be approved. If the fingerprints do not match, the payment will not be processed. In addition to biometric payments, with the help of AI-driven chatbots

Figure 8.2 Contactless biometric payment through facial recognition

or voice recognition software such as Alexa by Amazon, consumers can quickly obtain solutions to their queries, and in addition, they can use AI-driven tools to place orders.[7]

Optimizing Customer Service

The omnichannel business must understand the levels of customer service they need to offer to their customers across the channels they operate. In this section, we will discuss how to optimize customer service at two major levels—cross-channel services and in-store services. Cross-channel services will focus on the integration and consistency of critical service elements across the channels. On the other hand, in-store services will focus on the direct customer experience based on experiential service components.

Cross-Channel Services

The omnichannel business owner should horn in on the synchronization of the flexible point-of-sale system, loyalty programs, self-service options, personalization, and return process across channels. By integrating these critical service components across the channels, the omnichannel business can offer customers consistency and efficiency in serving their needs regardless of the channels.

Flexible Point-of-Sale (POS) System

In the traditional retail setting, an individual **POS** system is where a sale occurs. The point of sale is the stage where customers are to be effectively served through a smooth and pleasant transactional experience as a part of the customer journey. For example, POS includes your online storefront or a specific cash register in your brick-and-mortar location. A POS system consists of two parts: the hardware and the software. The hardware may include a card reader, cash register, and receipt printer. POS software is responsible for recording the transaction and sending that information along with debit or credit card information for payment processing.[8]

Retailers can integrate similar technology stacks with a contemporary POS system, integrating in-store and online technologies to create a complete omnichannel retail experience. The current POS system provides retailers with a unified platform that can easily bridge the gap between online and in-store. By integrating marketing, sales, and customer service departments, the platform enables retailers to design their omnichannel retail strategy.

It is even more critical for your POS system to become more than a payment platform. In this way, you not only have an integrated payment function that can accept all the payment methods the customer wants (contactless, using their mobile device, etc.), but you should also be innovative. Nordstrom, for example, recently underwent a revolutionary overhaul while keeping the omnichannel experience in mind. They are using software integrated into POS to create customer profiles, including information about their style preferences. That way, they can send product recommendations to customers and alert them to new product launches via their favorite brands. Moreover, they make sure to integrate the same inventory management system on their website and applications to avoid friction.[9] Some of the popular POS systems/platforms include Square, Shopify, Vend, Quickbooks, ShopKeep, Paysafe, Lightspeed, Revel, TouchBistro, and others.

As depicted in Figure 8.3, there are multiple data exchange touchpoints in the omnichannel retailing context. Each touchpoint requires security measures and careful monitoring to ensure stable business operations. POS systems can support this smooth data exchange and integrate various components into a seamless and connected user interface.

For example, **Vend** is one of the most adopted POS systems for online retailers, and is straightforward to use for in-store or online retailing and/or for a business operating multiple locations. Vend's multichannel e-commerce highlights include integrating

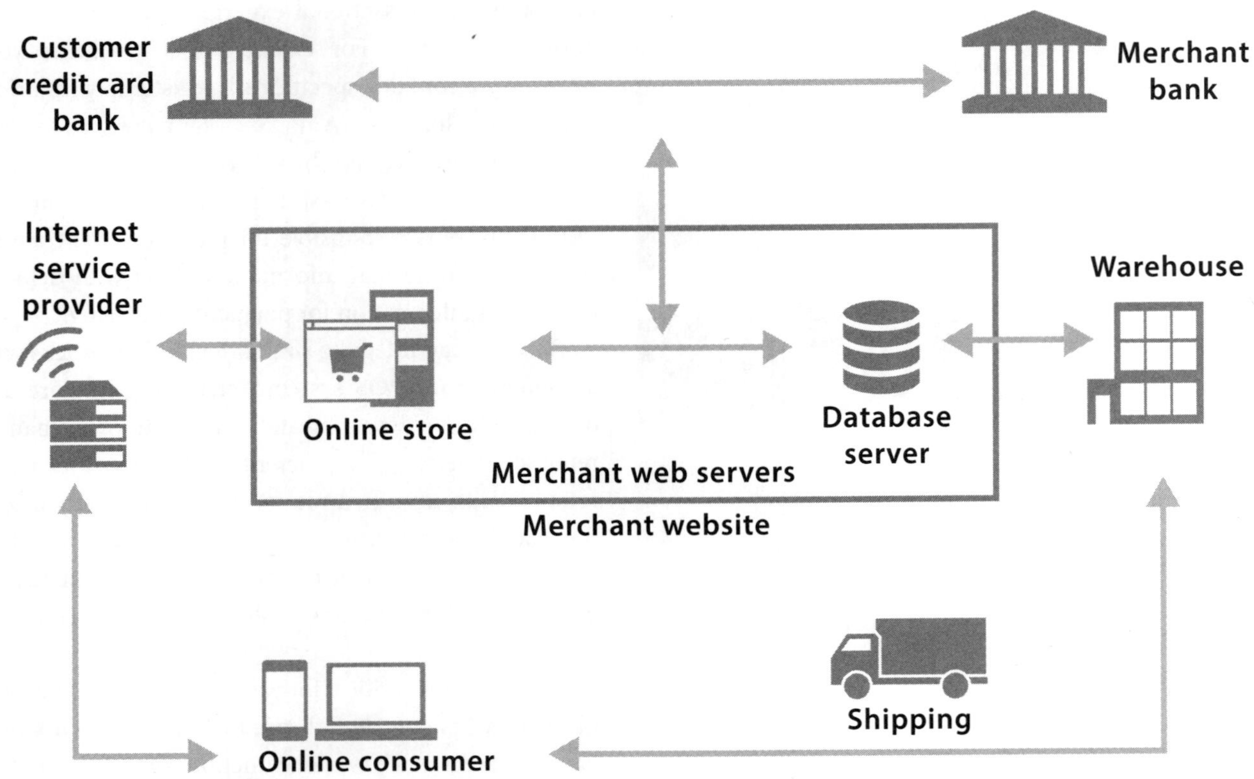

Figure 8.3 Data exchange touchpoints
(*Source*: Author)

WooCommerce, BigCommerce, and Shopify, synchronizing your in-store and online inventory. Shopify is another excellent example of a POS solution for an omnichannel fashion retailer with a physical location and e-commerce site. Shopify fully integrates inventory and sales transactions across physical and online channels, especially multiple online sales platforms. Even the smallest retailers can quickly sell online and offline. One of Shopify's strengths is that online sales channels include the Shopify website, existing websites with Shopify "Buy" buttons, Amazon, Instagram, Facebook Messenger, Facebook Shop, and eBay.[10]

Loyalty Programs

Customers are satisfied when retailers respond to their needs by offering meaningful services and adequate follow-ups in a timely manner. Several examples from the ranks of top performers show how customer expectations and retail delivery are converging. It is becoming increasingly challenging to distinguish services that are clearly cross-channel. This demonstrates that multichannel selling is effective. All sales platforms use loyalty programs, self-service options, and personalization.

Loyalty points earned and redeemed across channels

Customers should be rewarded for their loyalty. There are various kinds of frequent shopper programs in existence, including:

- ✓ Immediate rewards—Make a purchase and immediately receive a coupon for a dollar amount or a percentage off a future purchase.
- ✓ Extra incentives—Credit card holders receive preferential treatment when using their in-store charge during specified time periods, often before a general sale is declared. Customers who choose a retailer-sponsored card are typically frequent shoppers.
- ✓ Targeted promotions—Some retailers explicitly target their high spenders, usually the top 10 or 20 percent of their customer base, for preferred customer shopping days, special events, or gifts.
- ✓ Point systems—The more you spend, the more points you earn per dollar spent. If you are a member of Neiman Marcus' InCircle program and spend thousands of dollars with the store each year, you can earn rewards as simple as a savings coupon or as lavish as a vacation to Tuscany.

- ✓ Credit card points—Retailers that offer Visa- or MasterCard-sponsored universal credit cards may give special cash-back incentives or other point-based rewards for purchases made with the card. Extra points are frequently awarded for buying preselected products.[11]

In 2018, Nordstrom revamped its loyalty program "The Nordy Club" by incorporating its new subsidiaries including HauteLook and Trunk Club in addition to the usual channels such as Nordstrom and Nordstrom Rack. Based on the accrued points, they have four kinds of membership tiers—Member, Insider, Influencer, and Ambassador. Each tier comes with distinctive benefits. Also, they connect their debit and credit card members into this loyalty program by giving extra points per dollar-based spending on those cards.

Most fashion retailers' loyalty program involve a signup bonus (percentage discount on the day of the signup) and earning points based on the dollar amount spending with the retailers (Open Loyalty). They also use store credit cards which earn the customers five times greater points based on their purchases with the retailers and their affiliated retailers.

In the case of Nike's loyalty program, they offer exclusive shoes and gear only to their loyalty program members through their app, SNKRS. Their members also get free shipping on all purchases in the United States and get exclusive deals on their birthday or anniversary. Nike has three other apps to engage their customers including Nike App, a shopping app that keeps the customers updated with the latest products, Nike Run Club app, and Nike Training Club app, which provides hundreds of workouts for various fitness levels with a wide range of styles, lengths, and intensity levels along with nutrition tips and wellness guidance from Nike trainers.

With the average North American household participating in twelve loyalty programs, many best-of-breed retailers are revamping their retention efforts to stick out from the crowd. Nordstrom recognized that giving frequent customers cash back on purchases wasn't enough to foster the elusive quality of "loyalty." Instead, Nordstrom's new program allows customers to plan private shopping excursions to Chicago or San Francisco, as well as access to a 24-hour fashion emergency hotline. According to Michael Greenberg, vice president of marketing at Loyalty Lab Inc. in San Francisco, the new loyalty scheme "places Nordstrom in the Neiman Marcus category."

Retailers are also focusing on customer engagement. Customer acquisition is becoming more expensive as the cost of search engine promotion and postage rises. Mr. Greenberg also stated that the cost of starting and managing a customer loyalty program has decreased. The new offerings are anticipated to benefit the Nordstrom loyalty program. The retailer has not entirely abandoned traditional rewards. Earned points can still be redeemed for any Nordstrom goods or service. The combination of hard and soft benefits is anticipated to increase participation rates.[12]

Types of loyalty program

We are discussing the loyalty programs which are relevant to fashion businesses here. One of the most prevalent types of loyalty schemes on the market is point-based loyalty programs. Customers earn points every time they spend money in the most common arrangement, and the more they spend, the more reward points they receive. Customers may earn points for a variety of transaction-related activities, such as purchasing a specific item or a certain number of points per dollar spent. Non-transactional actions such as joining the program, referring a friend, celebrating their birthday, or sharing something on social media can also earn them points. Points can then be redeemed for rewards such as free goods, special offers, or discounts.

Another common type of loyalty scheme is the tiered loyalty program. Companies in this sort of retail loyalty program focus on providing better rewards to more valuable customers. Tiers are a sort of segment in which program participants are promoted based on the actions you want to inspire customers to take. Tiers can be determined by expenses, points, miles, or other factors that characterize customer engagement. Tiers grant access to improved offers, discounts, and other benefits. Tiers are recalculated on a frequent basis in more advanced configurations of tier loyalty program systems. As a consequence, customers must continue to spend in order to remain in the specific tier. For example, Neiman Marcus' famous InCircle program is twenty-five years old and considered the gold standard of customer loyalty programs.

Another possible type of loyalty program is to offer a retail loyalty program with a strategic partner, so-called

partner retail loyalty program. If the strategic partner shares the homophily company values, target market, and spending power, it can support the fashion business's promotional efforts. A collaboration in which partners trade discount coupons in co-promotional campaigns is an example of this type of loyalty campaign. Members of both loyalty programs benefit from this joint effort. The key to this type of collaboration is to find partners who are in the same industry as you but are not direct rivals.[13]

Self-Service Options

Self-service options such as kiosks are not new technology to most customers in the retail setting. Some are eager to use them, while others still prefer the human touch in their in-store shopping. Self-service price-check kiosks or checkouts are commonplace in supermarkets, home improvement, and some discount and specialty stores. The self-service kiosks could locate the products that customers are looking for and not in-stock in the physical store with additional exclusive assortments that are only available online.

In the case of Amazon, they launched their first Amazon Locker in 2011 in New York City, Seattle, and London. In June 2018, Lockers were available in more than 2,800 locations in over 70 cities around the world. As of September 2021, the number of Amazon Lockers grew to over 30,000 with the majority being operated in the United States. You can find them in grocery stores, convenience stores, transport hubs, shopping centers, residential properties, and universities. Lockers come in a variety of sizes and provide customers with a contact-free experience, which proved an excellent method during the pandemic (see Figure 8.4).

Amazon Hub Locker+ was first launched in 2017, which is a secure, self-service, completely automated kiosk that offers customers a convenient delivery option for picking up their Amazon packages plus returning the purchases without a box or packaging. In case of the trouble experienced by the customers, Amazon provides customer service twenty-four hours a day, seven days a week. Every Locker also has the direct Amazon Hub Locker customer support phone number printed on it. Here are their own words explaining their Amazon Hub and recruiting business partners to expand their service network.

Figure 8.4 One of the Amazon Lockers located in Kent, Ohio, displaying the self-service kiosk for checking on orders and deliveries in the center of the locker
(*Source*: Jihyun Vick)

> Amazon Hub is a worldwide network of pickup and return locations. Amazon Hub is looking for partners that have a physical location to offer secure package pickup and return services to Amazon customers; in turn, these partners can benefit from the potential increase in foot traffic and sales which new customers can bring to their location. Partners have the ability to choose an Amazon Hub program that meets their needs, as well as the needs of their customers.[14]

Personalization

Personalization as an optimal customer service can occur in a brick-and-mortar store or in an online website setting. As the customers seek one-of-a-kind, unique products to express their individuality, a personalization option given to the products has been a popular option for many fashion retailers to cater for their customers' needs and demands. In the omnichannel retail setting, AI-driven personalized product recommendations can add more power to the customer service goals. In addition, sending a personalized message to the customers also would enhance their perception of the retailer as a relationship building too.

Personalized recommendations

Personalized recommendation may be one of the most fantastic perks of email marketing to any business, especially for the omnichannel fashion retailer, due to the greater diversity in customers' styles, body types, size differences, and other preferences. It is a process to recommend products and services to a particular customer. It requires a good understanding of the target customer and browsing data through cookies and email click data. Customizing an email marketing message, campaign, or newsletter is similar to how mass customization creates made-to-order products and services specifically for individual customers.

Send anniversary promo codes (e.g., for birthdays)

Congratulating your customer on their birthday is a fantastic way to stay in touch more personally. Birthday emails are one of the most effective emails that retailers can send. "Birthday emails have a 481% higher transaction rate than promotional emails. Birthday emails generate 342% higher revenue per email than promotional emails. In addition, birthday emails have 179% higher unique click rates than promotional emails."[15] Birthday emails may contain discount coupons, "(digitally) scratch-it" mystery savings, a code for free gift, and/or free shipping. For instance, DSW (Designer Shoe Warehouse), a US omnichannel shoe retailer headquartered in the Columbus area of Ohio, knows how to get to the subscriber's wallet through attractive offers (and shoes, of course). Their birthday email promotion resonates with customers powerfully.

Return Products across Channels

Another optimal customer service can be a flexible return policy across retail channels. As the customer makes the purchase transactions online, they anticipate the order confirmation via email communication or text messages within a couple of hours, followed by the shipping confirmation and tracking information as part of the customer service for order and fulfillment. After the order has been delivered, not all customers may be pleased with their purchases and need to return the item to the retailer. Processing order returns is not only a critical factor when establishing an omnichannel logistics system, as discussed in Chapter 6, but also an essential component of customer service. Omnichannel customers expect and demand to be able to return the order to the retailer in-store or via mail. Omnichannel retailers must be ready to accept returns across channels, which may differ from those used for purchase transactions. In order to make this level of customer service available to the customers, the retailer must have seamless data integration in place across their channels.

In-Store Services

In this section, we will focus on how omnichannel businesses could deliver optimal customer service by fully understanding the need for excellent customer service at the physical store level. Some customers prefer the brick-and-mortar store setting over the e-commerce site because of the tactile nature of fashion goods and try-on opportunities to check on garment fit and sizes, among others. It will be very beneficial for omnichannel business owners to understand the expectations of the customers who choose the brick-and-mortar channel, so their customers can be delighted with the level of service in-store.

Front-End and Back-End Services

In the retail setting, we often encounter customer facing services which are called **front-end services**. It occurs on the retail selling floor or online to assist the customer's needs and inquiries. For instance, front-end services include cashiers, customer information, returns, and concierge services. On the other hand, other customer service functions are not readily viewable from the customer perspective, which are called **back-end services**. This is because such services take place behind the scenes or off a retailer's premises. Back-end services include alteration and installation services, deliveries, and repair work. In the omnichannel era, we still see both in-store personal shoppers (in the case of Saks Fifth Avenue) as well as e-client advisors (in the case of Dior). For example, Saks Fifth Avenue offers various enhanced services through their program, Fifth Avenue Club, where they offer private luxury dressing suites with pre-selected clothing in the customers' sizes and preference, personal shopping throughout the product categories from beauty to shoes to dresses, flexible scheduling with lunch service, and "precision alteration" of the purchased items.[16]

Experiential Value-Driven Features

When it comes to the brick-and-mortar store setting, the experiential factor and instant gratification are the most fantastic attractions for many shoppers.[17] Experiential value that can be perceived at the store level refers to the aspects of the store and events held in the store that create a positive and memorable shopping experience for the customers. Such shopping experiences stem from store design, layout, lighting, music, scent, displays, service quality, and ambiance.[18] These features can enhance the customer's emotional and cognitive responses to the store and its products and influence their purchase decisions and repeat visits.[19] Moreover, immersive in-store special events such as a mini fashion show or pop-up events in a temporary location can increase the memorable and engaging experience, which results in greater experiential value perceived by the customers. These experiential value-driven features rehappening in a brick-and-mortar retail setting can help omnichannel fashion retailers differentiate themselves from online-only retail competitors and foster brand loyalty and customer retention. All in all, fashion retailers should pay close attention to their stores' experiential features and design them to match their target market's preferences and expectations.

Online-Centered Services

Online customer services in omnichannel retailing are essential to provide a seamless and satisfying shopping experience for customers across different channels and platforms. Online customer services include responding to customer inquiries, complaints, feedback, and reviews through various digital means such as email, chat, social media, and video calls. Online customer services also involve providing personalized recommendations, offers, and loyalty programs based on the customer's preferences and purchase history. Online customer services can help omnichannel retailers to increase customer satisfaction, retention, and loyalty, as well as to gain insights into customer behavior and preferences. In this section, we will discuss communication-enhancing services such as product recommendation and email and chat services.

Communication-Enhancing Services

Online channels add much more than transactional channels. Through the internet and email communications, omnichannel businesses can communicate and promote their product offerings to their customers 24/7. Using advanced technologies such as artificial intelligence (AI) and machine learning (ML), the retailers can offer product recommendations via email or on their product webpage. In addition, email and chat services support customers around the clock and improve efficiencies on the end of the omnichannel retailers' operation. Let's discuss product recommendations first.

Product Recommendations

Product recommendations are possible based on AI and ML technologies applied in the fashion retail landscape. The "Algorithm fashion companion" function employed by ZALANDO[20] is a digital clothing combination tool based on machine learning and AI technology, providing customers with (almost) unlimited clothing suggestions (see Figure 8.5). For instance, when you look up a single product webpage of Nike performance T-shirts with the NBA New Orleans Pelicans logo, they also suggest how to put the outfit together by showing some related pieces. This also creates an up-selling opportunity for the business. If you scroll down to the bottom of that product page, customers may see other recommended NBA licensed products.

Personalized recommendation may be one of the most fantastic perks of email marketing to any business, especially for the omnichannel fashion retailer, due to the greater diversity in customers' styles, body types, size differences, and other preferences. It is a process of recommending products and services to a particular customer. It requires a good understanding of the target customer and browsing data through cookies and email click data. Customizing an email marketing message, campaign, or newsletter is similar to the way in which mass customization creates made-to-order products and services specifically for individual customers.

When personalizing recommendations via email, you may consider one or more combinations of the following critical matters: a) interactive by answering questions or coupon codes that one can use, b) animated GIF or graphics, c) audio or video contents, d) episodic contents based on prior engagement with the customers, and e) dynamic content blocks.

Figure 8.5 Algorithm fashion companion tools can generate AI- and ML-based recommendations to potential customers

Email and Chat Services

Engaging current customers is one of the core reasons for email marketing as a part of customer service. Engaging them in meaningful ways and reaching out to target customers can be the first step in serving the customers. In addition, email and chat services can be very effective when it comes to re-engaging past customers. As a part of global consumer trends, in general, consumers are interested in money-saving opportunities. Approximately 61 percent of customers use coupons, while about 97 percent of people are looking for a deal before purchasing online.[21] All this means deals, discounts, and even coupons are an excellent idea to re-engage these customers and get them to spend money on your business again.

When re-engaging former customers, omnichannel retailers should be much more thoughtful about the frequency and content of an email marketing campaign. Regardless, there is a reason why we call these customers "past," hinting that they used to be the ones who were relatively active with your business. On this occasion, retailers should offer a personalized email with well-crafted content including straightforward questions on the frequency and type of email communication the customer prefers. Of course, gently remind your past customers of the great benefits or transactions they may enjoy. For instance, H&M communicates with their former customers and how to re-engage with the customer base with a special discount offer.

Negative Impacts on Customer Services

Long before the rise of e-commerce, the retail industry had been experiencing various issues surrounding customer returns. Some returned goods can still be in good condition for sale on the floor or web; however, others are not suitable for sale and end up eroding the business's bottom line. In many cases, returned goods are donated to charity organizations like Goodwill or go to landfill, which negatively affects environmental sustainability. In this section, we will discuss customer returns, fraudulent returns, and consumer data security, and relevant issues as the factors causing adverse effects on the omnichannel retailer's customer service effort.

Customer Returns

There are many different reasons why the customers would return their purchases back to the retailers. Return rates for online retailing can be double those for stores. They suggest that omnichannel **returns management**—network configuration and returns management processes—has yet to fully mature.[22] As covered in detail in the Chapter 6 section on returns management systems, reducing the return rate is one of the great interests among the omnichannel retailers to improve their bottom line. **Reverse logistics** is very costly to business owners, especially when the returns are planned, and a generous return policy is abused by the customers.

Fraudulent Returns

As covered in Chapter 6, consider how consumers may feel when confronted with businesses using multichannel solutions. Products purchased online can only be shipped to a consumer's address. Items purchased in the store may have different prices than online sales. Meanwhile, promo codes from emails or online deals may not be accepted in brick-and-mortar stores. As a result, consumers become frustrated and face many different obstacles to completing orders when products are not available in their channel of choice. These issues may continue when it comes to the return process for customers and return management for the business. All in all, the return management process is part customer support, part (reverse) logistics, and part inventory management.

As mentioned in Chapter 6, critical issues in returns management can be bracketing and return fraud/wardrobing.[23] With e-commerce allowing for no direct or in-person contact for the return process, it has increased the tendency of this return fraud.[24] These unethical consumer return behaviors do hurt the fashion retailers' bottom line, especially when they offer free shipping and returns. The omnichannel retailers may consider implementing a more stringent return policy as appropriate. There are a couple of frequently used return management platforms/service providers such as Happy Returns,[25] which is a part of the PayPal Company, and Narvar, a post-purchase customer experience platform.[26] Both platforms offer greater confidence and efficiencies to fashion and other retailers by managing returns and exchanges on behalf of retailers. The latter is widely adopted by large corporations such as Gap, Inc., Lululemon, Crate and Barrel, Dyson, among others.

Consumer Data Security and Issues

There are several layers regarding e-commerce security which are critical for any omnichannel retailer to comply with. The convenience of storing customer data is crucial to retailers to provide customers with a seamless check-out convenience such as "One-Click Checkout" by PayPal or "Click to Pay" with Visa. Yet, when storing customer data, it is equally critical to establish utmost security safeguards to protect their privacy and information. For example, **integrity** in the context of e-commerce security refers to information shared by the consumer and will not be altered in any way by anyone, including the business owners or an unauthorized party. Integrity encompasses the consistency, accuracy, and trustworthiness of information over its entire business life cycle. The idea behind this critical dimension of e-commerce security is to ensure that businesses only use data that customers have given to a site. Any signs of data tampering will damage consumer confidence. The most common threat would be any unauthorized person intercepting and redirecting payment into a different account.

From a consumer's perspective, the best way to demonstrate integrity is to have a clear, written, and easily accessible data privacy and cookie policy that outlines how a business entity plans to process and store consumer data. A business can provide this policy document on their consumer consent form. For example, below is a clear message that Nike Inc. included in their 10-K report with their shareholders for its fiscal year of 2020. Nike Inc. communicates that they are subjective to data security and privacy risks that could adversely affect their business operations.

> *In addition to our own sensitive and proprietary business information, we handle transactional and personal information about our wholesale customers and consumers and users of our digital experiences, which include online distribution channels and product engagement, adaptive products and personal fitness applications. Hackers and data thieves are increasingly sophisticated and operate social engineering, such as phishing and large-scale, complex automated attacks that can evade detection for long periods of time. Any breach of our or our service providers' networks, or other vendor systems, may result in the loss of confidential business and financial data, misappropriation of our consumers', users' or employees' personal information or disruption of our business. Any of these outcomes could have a material adverse effect on our business, including unwanted media attention, impairment of our consumer and customer relationships, damage to our reputation, resulting in lost sales and consumers, fines, lawsuits, or significant legal and remediation expenses. We also may need to expend significant resources to protect against, respond to and/or redress problems caused by any breach.*[27]

Credit Card Fraud

There are two common frauds against the e-commerce industry: credit card fraud and fake returns. While shopping online, one may experience a threat called e-skimming, which refers to stealing credit card information and personal data from the payment card processing page on an e-commerce website. Attackers can visit your site through successful phishing attempts, brute force attacks, XSS, or third-party sabotage and then capture the payment information shoppers enter into the checkout page in real-time.[28]

It is crucial for e-commerce and omnichannel retailers to note substantial differences between online and in-store payments. When fraudulent transactions occur in the e-commerce setting, the e-commerce merchants are held liable for such incidences. Fraudulent transactions can significantly cost the e-commerce merchants lost merchandise and shipping charges, additional fees and penalties imposed by the card associations, and the cost of fulfillment—reviewing, processing, and preparing the orders to be shipped.

To prevent fraudulent transactions, e-commerce merchants can use a couple of different methods: an address verification system (AVS) can check the zip code of a cardholder, their shipping address, and/or card verification number (CVN). The merchants could also contact the customers manually to check on the purchases or opt-in to screen fraudulent activities and offer automated decision models. Last but not least, merchants could choose to implement an additional layer of protection via Card Association Payer Authentication services or negative lists. Negative lists refer to collecting and maintaining a list of black-listed customer profiles such as IP address, name shipping/billing address, and contact number. This method is used by approximately 40 percent of all e-commerce merchants. Merchants can run the list to check on existing problematic customers' profiles and the new order. If there is a match, then that could verify that the customer is a known problem.

Data Breach

One of the most well-known data breaches of a major retailer might be the one that occurred to Target in 2013. Cybercriminals had infected millions of consumers by installing malware on point-of-sale (POS) systems to steal data from cash registers. This kind of attack provides immediate benefits to the perpetrators, who can then sell credit card data on the dark web.[29] At the end of this chapter, we will examine a case study on data breach.

When your device or network is infected with malicious code or ransomware (a type of malicious code asking for a ransom), you may not be able to access all critical data and systems. System downtime is a potential loss of sales; regularly backing up site data can help avoid a catastrophic blow to your business. One of the most well-known malwares is Trojan Horse, which is a program usually designed to destroy your computer system. The source of this threat comes from a file that is downloaded by customers. These programs can collect data about credit or debit cards, transmit that information to hackers, crash the user's computer, or use PC resources for hackers' goals without the user's permission. These programs can quickly obtain any sensitive data and may also infect your website. Therefore, it is strongly advised to verify the sources before downloading any files.[30]

Mobile Platform and Cloud Computing Security Issues

Mobile applications are attractive targets for cybercriminals and constitute one of the most significant e-commerce security issues. Attackers discover that it is economically feasible to use bots and automated scripts to steal payment details, targeting many mobile websites. As the use of mobile applications increases, consumers face more significant risks from criminals targeting vulnerable applications, by redirecting customers to fake shopping carts and stealing payment information.

Cloud computing allows many benefits but can also present unique security issues and challenges. In the cloud, data is stored with a third-party provider and accessed over the internet. Cloud service providers view cloud security issues and risks as a shared responsibility between the service providers and the clients. The service providers are responsible for the security of the cloud itself. Cloud customers are responsible for protecting what they put in it, such as protecting their data from threats and controlling its access.

CASE STUDY 8.1

Data Breaches in Fashion Retailing

Target was founded in 1902 (as Dayton Dry Goods Company) and became a nationwide retailer by 1961. In 1979, Target reached $1 billion in annual sales across 74 stores in the United States. To become an even greater competitor, Target invested in technology and was the first mass merchandiser to implement UPC scanning throughout their stores. Throughout the following decades, Target continued to invest in technology innovation that would help improve customer experience. And in 2015, Target's annual revenue was reported at over $72.6 billion for the fiscal year, an increase of $1.34 billion (1.9 percent) from 2014.

Although Target saw major growth, Walmart and Amazon, Target's main competitors, began putting downward pressure on prices at Target to match competitors' discounted retail price points. As a result, Target struggled to keep up with technological advancements, and in 2013, Target faced a massive data breach of credit and debit card information of 40 million customers. The following year, they admitted that hackers stole email addresses, mailing addresses, and other personal information from 70 to 110 million customers. Following the data breach, Target planned to invest $5 million in data security and agreed to a $10 million settlement with victims of the security breach.[31]

After Target fell victim to one of the nation's most significant security breaches, several US organizations focused on preventing cybercrime. US organizations acknowledged their vulnerability regarding mobile payment security measures. Still, they faced many barriers because US organizations hesitated to invest in costly new security measures, such as machines accommodating Europay, Mastercard, and Visa (EMV) chip cards. Despite the resistance toward EMV chip card (also known as Smart Card) technology and the high costs involved in implementation, in 2015, the United States enforced new regulations that required merchants to use EMV chip card technology as a security measure. This EMV payment technology could significantly reduce future data breaches, as seen in other countries. Still, too many barriers exist to adopting advancing sophisticated data systems into the retail industry widely.[32]

More recently, Bonobos men's clothing store has suffered a massive data breach exposing millions of customers' personal information after a cloud backup of their database was downloaded by a threat actor. Bonobos stated that the corporate systems were not breached during the attack. Bonobos started as an online men's clothing store but later expanded to 60 locations to try on clothes before purchasing them. Walmart bought Bonobos in 2017 for $300 million to sell its clothing on their jet.com site.

This leaked database is a monstrous 70 GigabiteSQL file containing various internal tables used by the Bonobos website. The database also includes various data far more interesting to threat actors, such as customers' addresses, phone numbers, partial credit card numbers (last four digits), order information, and password histories. The number of records varies depending on the category of the data. For example, the address and phone numbers are for 7 million shipping addresses, account information for 1.8 million registered customers, and 3.5 million partial credit card records.[33]

BleepingComputer reported that the backup database was stolen from an external cloud environment and that an unauthorized third party was able to view a backup file hosted in an external cloud environment. After the incident, they notified the customers that an unauthorized third party might have viewed their contact information and encrypted passwords. Payment information was not affected by this issue. Though the database did not include complete payment information, threat actors can use the partial data in targeted phishing attacks.

Discussion Questions:

1. What are the negative consequences of such data breaches to the retailers beyond financial impacts?
2. From the customer's perspective, what are the security measures that one can take to avoid such data breaches?
3. What are the measures you, as a consumer, practice in the e-commerce environment to protect your privacy and personal data?

Career Opportunities

Job Titles	Key Responsibility
Concierge (International Cosmetic Brand)	The Concierge position will be part of the Digital Team and report directly to the Online Client Care and Fraud Prevention Associate, and will work closely with all departments (product development, retail, accounting, etc.) to ensure all client inquiries are fully answered, and direct-to-consumer after-sales business is supported. This role is based out of our corporate office in Brooklyn, NY. Responsibilities include but are not limited to: Order and Product Inquiry Resolution • Respond to client order and product inquiries via email and phone within the appropriate time frame, and according to identified business needs • Resolve product, order, and service issues in a high-touch empathic manner • Support to internal teams (outside of Ecommerce Operations) in providing client-facing relevant information pertaining to product, service, or online orders Online Order Liaison • Liaise with the order fulfillment team to ensure client requests are accommodated and fulfilled properly • Initiate communication with clients for online order fulfillment exceptions (delay, OOS, partial delivery) Client Purchase Support • Responsible for assisting clients with site navigation, order placement, or account registration, and troubleshooting Concierge Inbox Maintenance • Monitor and maintain concierge communication channels (email, phone) by categorizing requests according to inquiry type, and forwarding/assigning them to appropriate team members • Maintain the logs and forms, and actions on necessary items for general client care operations—e.g. returns log, OOS **Qualifications** • Strong empathic values, and active listening skills • Aptitude to provide excellent client service, and high-tough resolutions • Proficient in MAC OS, and MS Office applications • Self-motivated and adaptable—a team player, no task is too big or too small • Ability to multi-task, have a sense of urgency and can perform under pressure • Strong communication, interpersonal and analytical skills • Willingness and flexibility to work all shifts including weekends and overtime during busy periods. Required Education/Experience • Bachelor's degree • 1 year experience in retail, or call center environment • Cosmetics/skincare retail experience is a plus • French-speaking is a plus

Summary

In this chapter, we discuss the extensive planning requirements for customer service initiatives. Omnichannel customer service can be understood at two different levels: one is a macro view and the other is a micro view of customer service. A macro view of retail service approaches that retail service as their main intangible product offerings to the customers, while a micro view of retail service delineates customer service as a customer support endeavor to enhance the customer experience at a retail level. Many high-end retailers or specialty retailers frequently practice clienteling as one of their enhanced services. In addition, accepting various payment methods can be considered as customer service by enhancing their convenience and transactional experience. Due to the cross-channel nature of omnichannel retailing, customer service should be optimized throughout the various channels that the retailer operates. Flexible POS system, loyalty programs, self-service options, and accepting the returns across channels are some of the examples to enhance the omnichannel retailer's customer service effort. In the physical store environment, the omnichannel retailer may pay closer attention to coordination of the front-end and back-end services as well as experiential value-driven strategies, while online channels may enhance communication and promotional activities by utilizing product recommendations, automated email communication, or AI-powered chat services to engage and re-engage the customers. As a part of the dark side of consumer behavior, we discuss the issues caused by customer returns and their negative impacts on customer service. Lastly, consumer data security and issues are something that all omnichannel retailers must pay attention to to prevent such incidence which may erode the customer traffic to the retailer.

Key Terms

Back-end services
Biometric payment
Buy now pay later (BNPL)
Clienteling
Credit card fraud
E-skimming
E-micropayments
E-wallet
Front-end services
Integrity
Malicious code
Mobile payment
Mobile wallets
Partner retail loyalty program
Payment gateway
Personalized recommendation
Point-based loyalty programs
Point-of-sale (POS)
Prepaid cards
Proximity mobile wallets
Ransomware
Returns management
Reverse logistics
Shopify
Tiered loyalty program
Trojan horse
Vend

Reflection and Discussion Questions

1. What are the macro and micro views of retail service?
2. How has retail customer service expanded its scope through informational technological advancement?
3. What are the "must-have" basic/fundamental customer services? Think of an example of the failure of such customer service in the omnichannel retail setting.
4. What are enhanced customer services? Think of an example from your own prior experience in the omnichannel fashion retail setting.
5. What are the preferred payment options among college students? Explain pros and cons of those identified payment options.
6. Think of the best practice in a loyalty program from your own experience and explain what made you choose it for this question.
7. Propose three target markets who will find personalization as an optimal customer service in the omnichannel fashion retail context. Explain who they are in terms of demographics and why, based on their psychographics and lifestyles.
8. Think of one of the most experiential value-driven omnichannel fashion or other retailers that you encounter in person or through media. Explain why you found it an experientially driven retailer and the components of the customer service contributing to the level of experiential features.
9. Explain some of the critical security issues when it comes to consumer data. And give some examples of the available tools to better achieve omnichannel security.
10. Design an ideal enhanced customer services from a customer journey perspective. Then, share the ideas with a classmate and evaluate the customer services from a managerial perspective in terms of personnel expenses, staffing, and training, among others.

Business Considerations for Omnichannel Retailers

PART 3

Part 3 comprises Chapters 9 and 10. In these chapters, you will delve into the business considerations for omnichannel retailers. We will start by discussing the complex ethical and legal concerns for omnichannel retailing in Chapter 9. The chapter also examines issues concerning consumer privacy and information rights, intellectual property rights, evolving sales tax regulations in the US, and the regulation of social media marketing. Chapter 10 explores consumer-facing trends such as augmented reality (AR) and virtual reality (VR) integration, collaborative consumption, and visual search. Chapter 10 will also introduce retail tech trends, such as digital garment merchandising, personalized micro-production, and location-based technology. Additionally, it highlights emerging trends like artificial intelligence (AI) applications, the metaverse, and non-fungible tokens (NFTs). The vision for the future of retail emphasizes unique and authentic shopping experiences.

CHAPTER 9
Ethical and Legal Issues in Omnichannel Retailing

Learning Objectives

Upon completion of this chapter, you will be able to:

- Assess the contemporary ethical and legal issues involved in omnichannel retailing
- Examine fundamental concepts related to consumer privacy, consumer data rights, and relevant regulations
- Compare the various forms of intellectual property and justify how to protect intellectual property in fashion business
- Apply current sales tax regulations for omnichannel retailers
- Evaluate how social influencers comply with the FTC's influencer marketing regulation

With the advancement of technology, we as a society are confronted with various gray areas that lack clear legal boundaries. In this chapter, we will discuss the ethical and legal issues involved in omnichannel retailing, especially pertaining to consumer privacy and information rights, intellectual property rights, the changing landscape of sales tax regulations in the United States, and the US regulation of social media marketing.

Ethical and Legal Issues in Omnichannel Retailing

Like all businesses, omnichannel retailers try to offer new products and services and need to follow the laws in the spaces—both physical and virtual—in which the business operates. Different than traditional brick-and-mortar stores, omnichannel retailers rely on the internet and new technologies to make their business thrive in a competitive marketplace. Invented in the 1960s, the internet was established as an interconnected networks among government researchers to share information, where trust is built as an assumption. However, in the past six decades, the internet has evolved to be an any-to-any network (meaning a net where every node [i.e., computers] is connected [reachable] to any other node of the internet), while not everyone can be trusted. The inherent trust framework built into the internet has caused many problems that we see today, such as computer virus attacks, credit card fraud, and black markets pilfering personal data. Thus, information privacy and security have been important and controversial topics in the past decade.

In addition to information privacy and security, the internet, social media, and other technologies also provide opportunities and threats to omnichannel retailers. Therefore, protecting intellectual property rights under the law is crucial to gain competitive advantages. Moreover, while information technologies enable new platforms for businesses to reach customers they could not reach before, they also shift away revenue streams from local governments. The disruptive effect of e-commerce on local retailers and state governments can be observed through the sales tax battle between omnichannel retailers and state governments. In the following sections, we will discuss the important ethical and legal issues of information privacy, intellectual properties, and sales tax regulations.

Information Privacy and Security

Information privacy refers to consumers' ability to control how and to what extent their personal information is to be transmitted to others. As e-commerce continues to grow, consumers and brands become more connected via numerous communication channels and transactions on the internet; there is more and more data in the retailers' hands.

Research suggests that there is a discrepancy between online shoppers and their trusted online retailers regarding the kinds information collected.[1] A solid privacy strategy can fuel user adoption and revenue growth, and help companies increase or retain market share. Likewise, breaches of trust and unmet consumer expectations around privacy open up opportunities for competitors.[2]

For the last decade, consumer and privacy advocates have been discussing the tradeoffs posed by an economy fueled by data. For years, the "privacy paradox" has hung over this discussion—the idea that users' stated preferences do not always match their actual behaviors and choices. But concurrent forces have now reached an inflection point, making privacy a competitive differentiator. Shifts in the market demand for privacy, consumer norms, regulations, and product design suggest that the time has come for technology companies to make progress in building consumer trust and differentiating their privacy practices.

Cisco's June 2020 worldwide survey of consumers found that seven out of ten consumers were willing to spend time and money to protect their data, while nearly three out of ten have actually acted on those preferences and switched providers over their data policies or data-sharing practices.[3] Moreover, according to PwC's Global Trust Insights 2021 report, half of the executives said cybersecurity and privacy are now embedded into every business decision or plan.[4] Therefore, brands need to find effective ways to communicate with their consumers. In a speech to the Computers, Privacy, and Data Protection conference, Apple CEO Tim Cook suggested that businesses built on data exploitation without consumer choice deserves reform. In 2021, Apple rolled out Privacy Nutrition Labels (Figure 9.1), aiming to put policies in plain terms for users, requiring app publishers to describe what types of data are being collected and for what purpose. Nearly three-quarters (72 percent) of US iPhone and iPad owners indicated that they were aware of the privacy labels' introduction.[5]

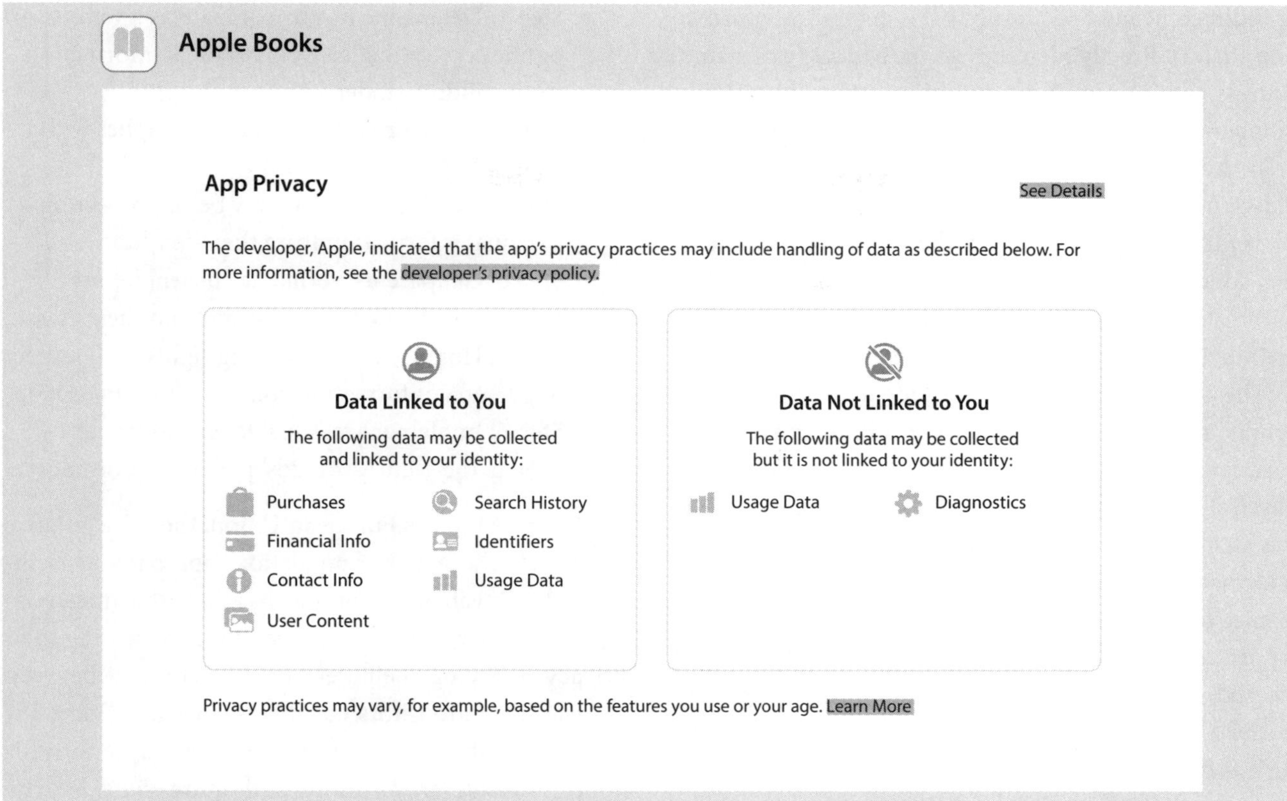

Figure 9.1 An example of "Privacy Nutrition Labels" from Apple's app store
(*Source*: Author)

Consumer Data and Omnichannel Retail Business

To provide omnichannel experiences, retailers must provide their customers with a seamlessly integrated user experience and relevant information across various channels. Their goal is to cater a unique experience to each customer's preferences and situations. Imagine the following scenarios and consider the consumer data needed in the example. First, a customer purchased a product online (through social media like Instagram or a brand website) and chose to pick it up at the retailer's brick-and-mortar store. Second, a customer is sent notifications through a retailer's app when they are near the retailer's store. Third, when a customer enters a store, the retailer may use near field communication (NFC) technology to send detailed product information or promotions to a customer's mobile device when they are interacting with that product. This highly personalized real-time experience will not be possible without consumer data such as location data, payment card data, mobile phone number, Instagram account, IP address, and browsing/shopping history, etc.

Although some may argue that privacy is not the top societal issue that worldwide consumers expect brands to address, it is still relatively high on the priority list. The Edelman's 2020 Trust Barometer report found that data privacy and cybersecurity ranked just after climate change, pandemic-related economic issues, poverty, and job loss due to automation. In the United States, consumers think companies (42 per cent) should be most responsible for protecting consumers' online privacy, compared with the federal government (32 percent) or individuals (17 percent).[6] Research has shown that transparency in company data practices, such as telling customers what data they collect, store, and use, and the disclosure steps should a data breach happen, can help protect a company from financial loss by its data breach and save hundreds of companies millions of dollars.[7]

Personal Identifiable Information

Personal identifiable information (PII) can be generally defined as any representation of information that permits the identity of an individual to whom the information applies to be reasonably inferred by either direct or indirect means. Specifically, PII is defined as information that: i) directly identifies an individual (e.g., name, address, social security number or other identifying number or code, telephone number, email address, etc.) or ii) by which an agency intends to identify specific individuals in conjunction with other data elements, i.e., indirect identification. In the online environment, the concept of personal identifiable information has diminished relevance as it becomes easier to associate an individual with a digital device.

These data elements may include a combination of gender, race, birth date, geographic indicator, and other descriptors. Additionally, information permitting the physical or online contacting of a specific individual is the same as personally identifiable information. This information can be maintained in either paper, electronic, or other media. A Federal Trade Commission report acknowledges "consumers' objections to being tracked, regardless of whether the tracker explicitly learns a consumer name, and the potential for harm, such as discriminatory pricing based on online browsing history, even without the use of PII."[8]

Who Owns Consumer Data? Privacy Policy and US Privacy Laws

Since the 1990s, consumer privacy issues have progressively moved to the forefront of consumer affairs and public policy research. At the federal level, the United States currently does not have a comprehensive data privacy law. Instead, there are only so-called sectoral privacy laws. Examples are the Telephone Consumer Protection Act (regarding telemarketing), the Fair Credit Reporting Act (regarding credit reports and employment background checks), the FACT Act (regarding financial privacy), and Health Insurance Portability and Accountability Act (HIPAA, regarding medical records privacy). This sectoral approach leaves many uses of personal information unprotected. For example, one's online shopping history and website preferences are not covered by any specific law in the United States.

For children under 13 years old, the Children's Online Privacy Protection Act (COPPA) puts parents in control. If your business collects personal information (such as full name, physical address, email or video chat ID, IP address, photo, etc.) from children under 13, you need to have certain information in your privacy policy and get parental consent. The FTC recommends following the six steps below to comply with the law.[9]

- Step 1: Determine if your company is a website or online service that collects personal information from children under 13.
- Step 2: Post a privacy policy that complies with COPPA.
- Step 3: Notify parents directly before collecting personal information from their children.
- Step 4: Get parents' verifiable consent before collecting personal information from their kids.
- Step 5: Honor parents' ongoing rights with respect to personal information collected from their kids.
- Step 6: Implement reasonable procedures to protect the security of kids' personal information.

Compared to the European Union, the US legislative institution chose a "self-regulation" approach to facilitate online businesses. This means asking the industry to regulate their consumer data practices by posting their privacy policy on their websites as a contract between the website and visitors/customers. In reality, very few people read those long and full-of-legal-jargon privacy policies. However, as more and more cybersecurity incidents have happened in the past decade, consumers are more concerned that their data may fall into the wrong hands. The recent development of the California Consumer Privacy Act (CCPA) made California the first state in the US to offer more comprehensive protections on consumer data rights. After California enacted its Privacy Act in 2020, Virginia and Colorado also passed similar laws that took effect in January and July 2023, respectively.

General Data Protection Regulation (GDPR) and California Consumer Privacy Act (CCPA)

General Data Protection Regulation (**GDPR**) and **California Consumer Privacy Act** (**CCPA**) are the two recent privacy regulations introduced in the EU and California, respectively. The newly established regulations have significantly impacted retailers' information privacy practices. Omnichannel retailers who serve or wish to serve customers in these two markets should make sure to be compliant with the regulations.

The General Data Protection Regulation (GDPR) was established by the European Commission in April 2016 and enforced as of May 25, 2018. This law was put in place to protect consumers in the European Union by giving them more control over their personal data in the form of subject data rights. These rights include the right to:

1. Access their data and obtain information about the processing of that data.
2. Restrict the processing of their data.
3. Withdraw consent at any time.
4. Correct any incorrect, inaccurate, or incomplete personal data.
5. Erase their personal data, cease further dissemination of their data, and halt processing of their data by third parties.
6. Receive their personal data in a commonly used and machine-readable format to transmit it to another controller.
7. Request that natural persons, not just computers, make decisions concerning their data.
8. Object to the processing of their data for direct marketing, research, or company interest purposes.[10]

The most distinct effect that makes GDPR different from the previous privacy laws is that GDPR can impose administrative fines for noncompliance up to €20 million ($24.1 million) or 4 percent of annual global revenue, whichever is the higher. Since GDPR's enactment, several international companies have been fined under the laws. For instance, H&M was fined €35.2 million ($41.3 million) for breaching the GDPR in relation to the monitoring of several hundred staff members by a German subsidiary.[1] Facebook's WhatsApp messaging service was fined nearly $270 million by Irish authorities for not being transparent about how it uses data collected from people and how the data was shared with other Facebook properties like its main social network and Instagram.[12]

The California Consumer Privacy Act of 2018 (CCPA) gives California residents more control over the personal information that businesses collect about them. This landmark law secures new privacy rights for California consumers, including: 1) the right to know about the personal information a business collects about them and how it is used and shared; 2) the right to delete personal information collected from them (with some exceptions); 3) the right to opt-out of the sale of their personal information; and 4) the right to nondiscrimination for exercising their CCPA rights. It also requires businesses to provide California consumers with clear notices on their privacy practices once a year and an obvious place for consumers to indicate their choice of "Do not sell my data" to data brokers on the websites. California Privacy Rights and Enforcement Act (CPRA) passed by California voters in November 2020 (California Proposition 24).

Implications of Omnichannel Retail Business

In the past ten years, a series of high-profile data breach scandals have heightened consumers' concerns. For instance, Target had a data breach in 2013 that affected 40 million customers' payment information before the Thanksgiving Holiday. The incident cost Target $202 million in settlements with the affected consumers and financial agencies such as Visa, Mastercard, and the banks that have to reissue new credits cards to those Target customers.[13] Under Armour's MyFitnessPal, a diet and exercise app, was breached in 2018. The incident impacted 150 million users' information, including usernames, passwords, and email addresses. A year later, this data from the MyFitnessPal hack was found on the dark web being sold for around $20,000 in Bitcoin. In 2021, 533 million Facebook users' data was leaked from more than 100 countries, including phone numbers, Facebook IDs, full names, email addresses, and more. With the data, hackers could impersonate people and commit fraud.

When companies' information systems are attacked, and customers' profiles are compromised after data breaches, customers may feel more vulnerable about their information privacy. Therefore, not only are consumers concerned about their data, but they are ready to put security and data practices into their purchase decisions. According to a McKinsey survey, 87 percent of consumers say they would not do business with a company if they had concerns about its security practices. Moreover, 71 percent said they would stop doing business with a company if it gave away sensitive data without permission. The 2020 Trustwave Global Security Report found that the retail sector as a whole (i.e., both e-commerce and brick-and-mortar stores) was the most compromised sector for cyberattacks, followed by the financial sector. Of course, any industry that secures a large amount of personal information or valuable intellectual property has the risk of becoming a target. Therefore, omnichannel retailers should be proactive on data collection, security, and compliance.

To provide more customized product suggestions and B2C communication, consumers' personal information on customers is one of the most important things for omnichannel retailers. However, maintaining and storing data cost money, and if the database is breached, the incident could cost more. Thus, omnichannel retailers should make sure they have legitimate reasons to collect every piece of information they store. In other words, if you do not need a piece of data, do not collect it.

Intellectual Property in E-Commerce and Fashion Retailing

Intellectual property (IP) refers to creations of the mind—everything from works of art to inventions, computer programs to trademarks and other commercial signs.[14] Intellectual property has been recognized by various legal systems for a long time. For instance, in 1416, Italy granted the first patent to provide exclusive rights to Ser Franciscus Petri of Rhodes for his technological invention of a wool-felting device.[15] Nowadays, IP rights are not only protected by most developed countries but also safeguarded by Article 27 of the Universal Declaration of Human Rights—"Everyone has the right to the protection of the moral and material interests resulting from any scientific, literary or artistic production of which he is the author."[16] Governments aim to foster an environment where creativity and innovation can flourish by providing exclusive rights to IP owners. If executed properly, more inventors would be willing to disclose their inventions or creations in exchange for the legal monopoly right for a given period of time. After the intellectual property right expires, the intellectual property will go into the public domain, and anyone can use it. The goal of intellectual property law is to strike the right balance between the interests of innovators and the public interest. In the United States, the US Patent and Trademark Office (USPTO) is the agency responsible for granting US patents and registering trademarks. USPTO is housed under the Department of Commerce. On the other hand, the Copyright Office, under the Library of Congress, administers the national copyright system in the US.

In the following section, we will discuss the major intellectual property rights (i.e., trademark, trade dress, patent, and copyright), which enable a business to protect the financial benefit from what they invent or create;[17] we will discuss relevant examples pertaining to omnichannel retailing for fashion brands.

Trademark

A **trademark** is any word, name, symbol, design, or color capable of distinguishing the goods or services of a business from others. For example, the trademark "Nike," along with the Nike "swoosh," identifies the shoes made by Nike and distinguishes them from shoes made by other companies (such as those made by Puma or Adidas). In Chapter 3, we briefly talked about how a new business can utilize the United States Patent and Trademark Office's TESS (Trademark Electronic Search System) database to search for any potential trademark conflict to avoid trademark infringement. In the US, trademark rights are governed by a first-to-use system, meaning that a party gains rights in a trademark by using it in commerce. Therefore, a company must be able to show the USPTO that they are actually using the trademark. This is different from countries that use the first-to-file system, which means whoever registers a trademark first has rights regardless of whether they were first to use the mark. The countries that use the first-to-file system include countries like China, Japan, Germany, and European Union.[18] For omnichannel retailers who want to strengthen their power against anyone who attempts to use a similar domain name to market similar services or products, they should register their domain name as a trademark. Trademark registration can also prevent anyone else from registering the same name as their own trademark. Products should be marked "™" as a trademark or "℠" as a service mark. These symbols indicate a registered mark and should be used only when a trademark registration has been issued by USPTO. To maintain legal trademark status and company data, retailers need to continue to pay the registration fee.

When registering a trademark, brands need to specify in which categories the trademark will be used. Therefore, even if a company creates a highly successful mark for apparel, you may not be able to stop someone using an identical mark for a luggage brand. In principle, a trademark will last forever as long as it is in use. Since trademark rights are required as soon as a mark is put into use, it is not strictly necessary to register. In the interest of saving cost, brands may not need to register some marks if they only intend to use them for one or two seasons.

When it comes to selecting a trademark for your brand, the best practice is to choose one that is unusual or a made-up word, for example, Nike or Etsy. Choosing a mark that is too simple or descriptive will make it very hard to protect. For instance, Virgil Abloh's fashion company, Off White, had a rocky road requesting a trademark for their new phrase "For Walking" on their new shoes (note: quotations are included). The USPTO refused to register its phrase because it fails to meet the requirements of what a trademark represents. By definition, a trademark should never "describe an ingredient, quality, characteristic, function, feature, purpose, or use of an applicant's goods and/or services." While USPTO's attorney has used this as their primary argument against the phrase "For Walking," Abloh argues that his use of quotation marks changes the phrase from what USPTO thinks is a "descriptive meaning" to a "double entendre." Off White's office stated that the quotation marks give the phrase a nondescriptive mark because "it changes the commercial impression." Though Off White has pushed for registration numerous times, the USPTO office will not change their mind and register this phrase (Figure 9.2).

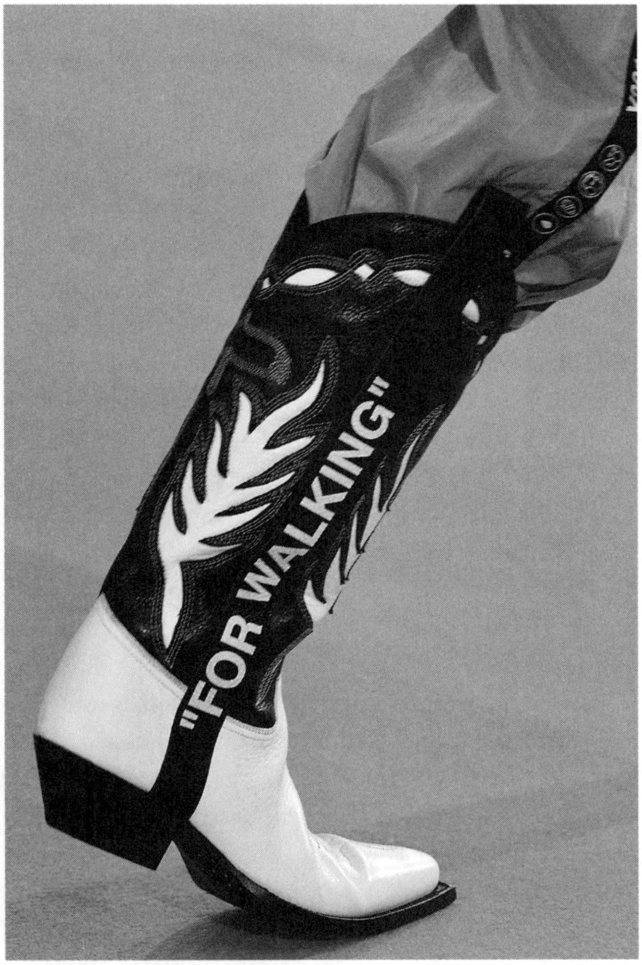

Figure 9.2 Off White's "For Walking" boots

Different Types of Trademarks

Different types of trademarks are listed in order of the strength of the mark in Table 9.1—from those that receive the strongest protection to those that do not receive protection at all.

Table 9.1 Types of Trademarks in Order of Strength of Mark

TYPES OF TRADEMARKS	DESCRIPTION
(a) Fanciful Marks Examples: Exxon® for petroleum or Pepsi® for soft drinks.	Those that have been invented for the sole purpose of functioning as a trademark and have no meaning other than acting as a mark. These are considered to be the strongest type of mark.
(b) Arbitrary Marks: Examples: APPLE for computers; TIDE for detergent; LOTUS for software.	Those that have been created from existing words but have no meaning in relation to the goods or services.
(c) Suggestive Marks: Examples: COPPERTONE for suntan lotion; BURGER KING for burger restaurants; MICROSOFT for software for microcomputers.	Those that suggest a quality or characteristic of the goods and services, rather than describing.
Unacceptable Marks	Description
(d) Descriptive Marks: Examples: American Airlines; Sharp televisions.	Those that merely describe the services or goods on which the mark is used. These are often difficult to enforce unless the trademark owner can show that the mark has become distinctive, such as if it is advertised so heavily that secondary meaning can be proven in the mind of consumers.
(e) Generic Terms: Examples: "Bicycle" for bicycles, or "E-ticket" for computerized reservation and ticketing of transportation services.	These refer to the common names of the goods or services to which they are applied. They are not capable of acquiring secondary meaning when used in their generic sense and, thus, are not protectable as trademarks.

(*Source*: USPTO, https://www.uspto.gov/trademarks/basics/strong-trademarks)

Trademark Infringement

Trademark infringement is the unauthorized use of a trademark or service mark (or a mark that is substantially similar to the underlying mark) on competing or related goods and services.[19] The key inquiry in a trademark infringement lawsuit is whether the defendant's use of the trademark causes a likelihood of confusion in the average consumer. For example, Michael Kors launched their new line of shoes, "Pippin" and "Olympia"—displaying a design with what looks like an N on the side of the shoe. New Balance claims that the shoes are identical to their own trademark: the letter N on all their athletic footwear (see Figure 9.3). New Balance has stated that Michael Kors' new launch should be seen as unfair competition because the company solely makes a profit by selling shoes with the letter N as a design. They have reported to the Federal Court issuing a complaint of "infringing products; copying, reproducing, or colorable imitation of the N Marks and N Mark; and advertising materials related to the infringing products in Defendant's possession." New Balance won the trademark case against Michael Kors. In 2021, New Balance also won another similar trademark infringement lawsuit in China and was awarded $3.85 million by the Shanghai Huangpu District Court. The lawsuit was one of the largest judgments awarded to a trademark holder in the sportswear market in China.

Trade dress protection is a form of IP that specifically protects the look or form of a product if the public can recognize the brand from its look. For example, the Chanel N° 5 perfume bottle is instantly recognizable as the Chanel N° 5 bottle, even without the "Chanel" name on it. The same holds true for the appearance/design of the Hermès Birkin bag. Note that trade dress does not protect the functional elements, and there is no expiration for trade dress protection. In other words, as long as it can continue to indicate the source of a product or service, it can last forever. Trade dress can be protected if the following factors are met:

1. The trade dress does not serve a "functional" purpose.
2. It is "distinctive" (either inherently or because it has acquired secondary meaning).
3. In the context of infringement, there is a likelihood of confusion between the parties' trade dress.

As discussed, functional features will not be protected by trade dress. Therefore, if the form of the product offers a certain function, it will not be qualified for trade dress protection. For example, a brand cannot monopolize the use of a particular unique handbag shape if that shape confers some sort of functional advantage (e.g., easier to grip).

Because trade dress requires resources to establish the wide recognition of the product and its source, it is advised that fashion brands should obtain copyright protection first because it is quick, relatively inexpensive, and very powerful in court. Brands should only use trade dress protection if no other form of protection is available. One recent example is Nike's Air Jordan 1. Although Nike started to sell Michael Jordan's first sneaker in 1985, the only protection Nike had for the Air Jordan 1 was a trade dress until the year 2021. However, Nike has not been successful in persuading the court that the alleged copycats create confusion in the market. Proving trademark or patent infringement, however, is much easier. Therefore, in 2020, Nike filed the Air Jordan 1 trademark application with the USPTO and was awarded the trademark (see Figure 9.4).

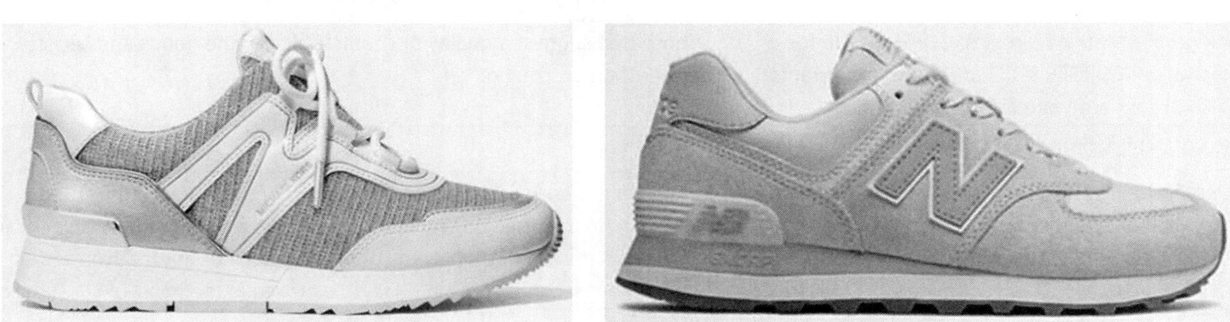

Figure 9.3 Michael Kors' Pippin shoe (left) and New Balance's 574 sneakers (right)
(*Source*: New Balance Athletics, Inc. v. Michael Kors U.S.A., Inc., 1:21-cv-11305 [D. Mass])

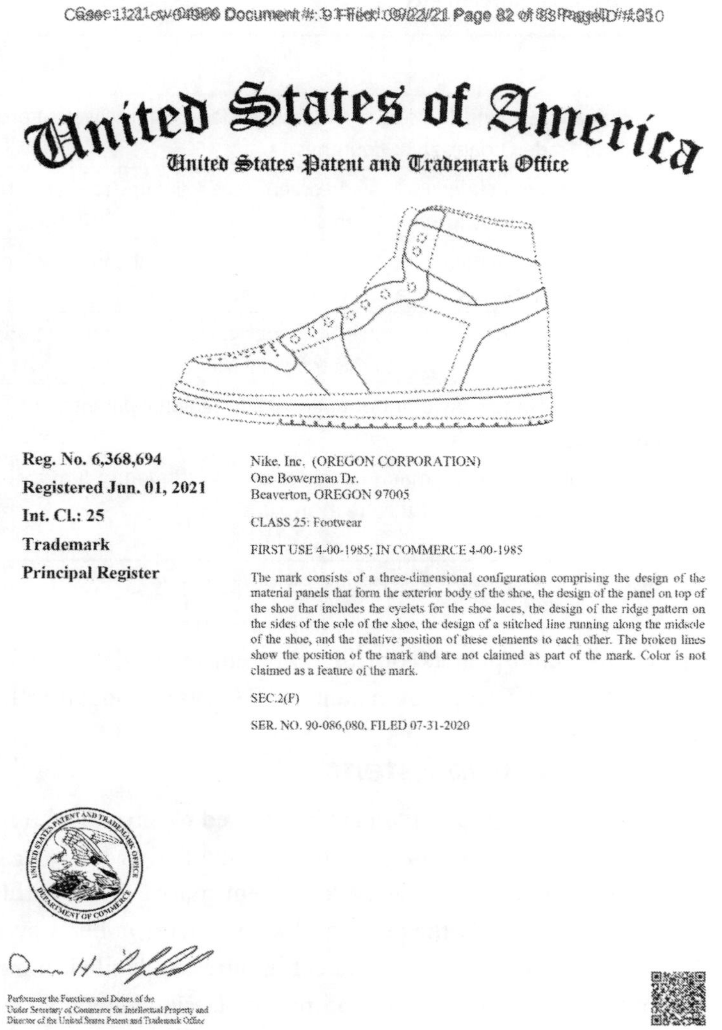

Case: 1:21-cv-04986 Document #: 9-1 Filed: 09/22/21 Page 82 of 83 PageID #:910

United States of America
United States Patent and Trademark Office

Reg. No. 6,368,694
Registered Jun. 01, 2021
Int. Cl.: 25
Trademark
Principal Register

Nike, Inc. (OREGON CORPORATION)
One Bowerman Dr.
Beaverton, OREGON 97005

CLASS 25: Footwear

FIRST USE 4-00-1985; IN COMMERCE 4-00-1985

The mark consists of a three-dimensional configuration comprising the design of the material panels that form the exterior body of the shoe, the design of the panel on top of the shoe that includes the eyelets for the shoe laces, the design of the ridge pattern on the sides of the sole of the shoe, the design of a stitched line running along the midsole of the shoe, and the relative position of these elements to each other. The broken lines show the position of the mark and are not claimed as part of the mark. Color is not claimed as a feature of the mark.

SEC.2(F)

SER. NO. 90-086,080, FILED 07-31-2020

Performing the Functions and Duties of the
Under Secretary of Commerce for Intellectual Property and
Director of the United States Patent and Trademark Office

Figure 9.4 Nike's Air Jordan 1 received trademark protection
(*Source*: USPTO, https://tsdr.uspto.gov/documentviewer?caseId=sn90086080&docId=ORC20210516025246#docIndex=1&page=1)

Patent

The United States has had patent protection since 1790, and the USPTO administers the patent and trademark laws and related activities. The role of the USPTO is to grant patents for the protection of inventions and to register trademarks. To help small businesses, USPTO provides a pro bono program for independent inventors and small businesses in securing patent protection (https://www.uspto.gov/patents/basics/using-legal-services/pro-bono/patent-pro-bono-program). A **patent** for an invention is the grant of a property right to the inventor. The term of a new patent can vary from one country to another. In the United States, the term is twenty years from the date on which the application for the patent was filed with the USPTO. Under certain circumstances, patent term extensions or adjustments may be available. The US patent grants are effective only within the United States, US territories, and US possessions. To gain protection in other countries, the US signed a treaty with 176 countries to recognize each other's intellectual property rights (see Table 9.2). Once a patent is granted, the patent right owner (assignee) has "the right to exclude others from making, using, offering for sale, or selling" the invention in the United States or "importing" the invention into the United States. Note that what is granted is the right to "exclude" others from making, using, offering for sale, selling, or importing the invention. The **assignee** is the entity that has the property right to the patent. If the inventor was employed by a business to create the invention, then the inventors may be under an obligation (e.g., employment contract) to assign the invention to the employer (the hiring company). The assignment of a patent is independent of inventorship.

Table 9.2 Intellectual Property Protection Treaties and International Agreements

AGREEMENTS AND TREATIES	DESCRIPTION
Agreement on Trade-Related Aspects of Intellectual Property Rights (TRIPS)	TRIPS is an international agreement that sets minimum standards for intellectual property protection for all World Trade Organization countries.
Anti-Counterfeiting Trade Agreement (ACTA)	Adopted in 2011, ACTA is a multilateral trade agreement that regulates counterfeiting, generic medicines, and online copyright infringement.
Berne Convention for the Protection of Literary and Artistic Works	Written in 1886, the Berne Convention was the first major multilateral convention on Copyright law. The United States became a party to this treaty in 1989.
Paris Convention for the Protection of Industrial Property	Established in 1883, the Paris Convention applies to trademarks, unfair competition, and patents. The United States became a party to this treaty in 1887.
Patent Cooperation Treaty (PCT)	A multilateral treaty that facilitates the grant of national and regional patents. The United States signed the PCT in 1970.
Protocol Relating to the Madrid Agreement Concerning the International Registration of Marks (Madrid Protocol)	The Madrid Protocol establishes an international trademark registration system for member states. The United States joined this treaty in 2003.

(Adapted from: University of Texas, Treaties of intellectual property law, https://tarlton.law.utexas.edu/treatises/intellectual-property-law)

In the United States, there are two types of patents that are relevant to omnichannel retailing: utility and design. In the following sections, we will discuss each and give you some examples.

Utility Patent

Utility patents may be granted to anyone who invents or discovers any new and useful process, machine, article of manufacture, or composition of matter, or any new and useful improvement thereof. The term of a new patent is twenty years from the application date. The four primary requirements for patentability are: new (novelty), useful, non-obvious, and accompanied by a written description of how to make and use the invention. In general, it takes about eighteen to twenty-two months from the date of filing a patent application for the USPTO to complete the examination process. The cost of applying for a patent, including attorney fees, can range from $5,000 to $15,000 or more, depending on how many claims are included in the invention.[20]

Some examples of utility patents that omnichannel retailers can obtain include 1) software program (e.g., Stylyze, Automated color processing, and selection platform, US10,387,938B2); 2) fulfillment center design (e.g., Amazon, multi-level fulfillment center for unmanned aerial vehicles, US9,777,502B2; Figure 9.5); 3) innovative product materials (Nike, Airbag for article of footwear, e.g., US10,524,540B1). For more information, you may search the patent numbers or the company names on Google Patent (https://www.google.com/patents) or USPTO patent search database (https://patft.uspto.gov/netahtml/PTO/search-bool.html).

Design Patent

Design patents may be granted to anyone who invents a new, original, and ornamental design for an article of manufacture. A design patent must be filed within one year after the product/design is made publicly available. Once the design patent application is filed, remember to mark "Patent Pending" or "Design Patent No. ###" to notify potential competitors of your IP.

Different brands may have different strategies for utilizing design patents for IP protection. For instance, Nike has applied more than 6,000 design patents to protect its shoes (e.g., D929,119), shoe insole (e.g., D919,273), garments (e.g., Jacket, D918,537; Pants, D918,534; Shorts, D918,535), display screen (e.g., D918,956), etc., while Adidas secured 244 design patents with USPTO.

Copyright

Copyright protects written or artistic expressions fixed in a tangible medium, such as graphic design, sculptures, novels, songs, videos, computer software, etc. In the United States, copyrights were built into the constitution "to promote the progress of science and useful arts, by securing for limited times to authors and inventors the exclusive right to their respective writings and discoveries" (Article 1, Section 8, Clause 8 of the US Constitution).[21] The owner of a copyrighted work has the

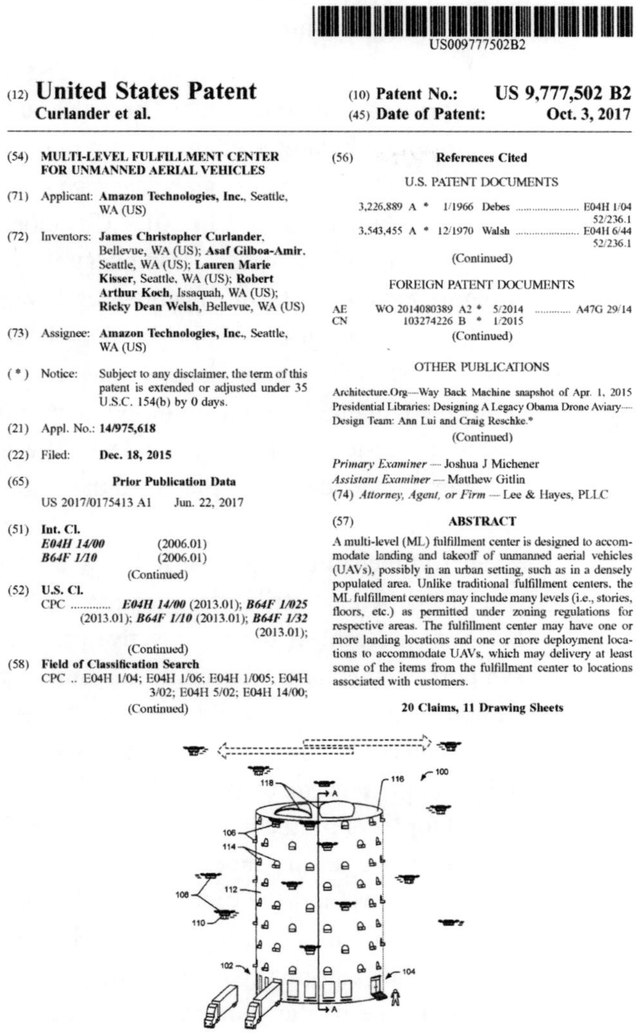

US009777502B2

(12) **United States Patent**
Curlander et al.

(10) **Patent No.: US 9,777,502 B2**
(45) **Date of Patent: Oct. 3, 2017**

(54) **MULTI-LEVEL FULFILLMENT CENTER FOR UNMANNED AERIAL VEHICLES**

(71) Applicant: **Amazon Technologies, Inc.**, Seattle, WA (US)

(72) Inventors: **James Christopher Curlander**, Bellevue, WA (US); **Asaf Gilboa-Amir**, Seattle, WA (US); **Lauren Marie Kisser**, Seattle, WA (US); **Robert Arthur Koch**, Issaquah, WA (US); **Ricky Dean Welsh**, Bellevue, WA (US)

(73) Assignee: **Amazon Technologies, Inc.**, Seattle, WA (US)

(*) Notice: Subject to any disclaimer, the term of this patent is extended or adjusted under 35 U.S.C. 154(b) by 0 days.

(21) Appl. No.: **14/975,618**

(22) Filed: **Dec. 18, 2015**

(65) **Prior Publication Data**

US 2017/0175413 A1 Jun. 22, 2017

(51) **Int. Cl.**
E04H 14/00 (2006.01)
B64F 1/10 (2006.01)
(Continued)

(52) **U.S. Cl.**
CPC ***E04H 14/00*** (2013.01); ***B64F 1/025*** (2013.01); ***B64F 1/10*** (2013.01); ***B64F 1/32*** (2013.01);
(Continued)

(58) **Field of Classification Search**
CPC .. E04H 1/04; E04H 1/06; E04H 1/005; E04H 3/02; E04H 5/02; E04H 14/00;
(Continued)

(56) **References Cited**

U.S. PATENT DOCUMENTS

3,226,889 A * 1/1966 Debes E04H 1/04 52/236.1
3,543,455 A * 12/1970 Walsh E04H 6/44 52/236.1
(Continued)

FOREIGN PATENT DOCUMENTS

AE WO 2014080389 A2 * 5/2014 .... A47G 29/14
CN 103274226 B * 1/2015
(Continued)

OTHER PUBLICATIONS

Architecture.Org—Way Back Machine snapshot of Apr. 1, 2015 Presidential Libraries: Designing A Legacy Obama Drone Aviary—Design Team: Ann Lui and Craig Reschke.*
(Continued)

Primary Examiner — Joshua J Michener
Assistant Examiner — Matthew Gitlin
(74) *Attorney, Agent, or Firm* — Lee & Hayes, PLLC

(57) **ABSTRACT**

A multi-level (ML) fulfillment center is designed to accommodate landing and takeoff of unmanned aerial vehicles (UAVs), possibly in an urban setting, such as in a densely populated area. Unlike traditional fulfillment centers, the ML fulfillment centers may include many levels (i.e., stories, floors, etc.) as permitted under zoning regulations for respective areas. The fulfillment center may have one or more landing locations and one or more deployment locations to accommodate UAVs, which may delivery at least some of the items from the fulfillment center to locations associated with customers.

20 Claims, 11 Drawing Sheets

Figure 9.5 Amazon's patent application of bee-hive-look fulfillment center design for drone delivery
(*Source*: USPTO.gov)

right to 1) reproduce it, 2) make derivative works from it (such as a fabric print based on a painting), 3) sell it or license it, 4) perform the work publicly, 5) display the work publicly, and 6) perform the work publicly via digital audio recordings (like audiobook or podcast). Copyright exists from the moment the work is created. Therefore, formal registration is not required to hold a copyright. However, if you decide to sue for copyright infringement, you will have to register.[22] Time is also crucial for filing copyright registration. It should be done within three months after the work is first becoming publicly available. Copyright owners should use a copyright notice to inform the public about the copyrighted work. A copyright notice should include the following three elements:

- The copyright symbol ©;
- The year of first publication of the work; and
- The name of the copyright owner.

For the length of copyright protection, currently, copyright law protects works of individuals for their lifetime plus 70 years beyond their life. Copyright protection has been extended several times in the last century.[23] The Sonny Bono Copyright Term Extension Act (CTEA) of 1998 (popularly known as the "Mickey Mouse Protection Act") extended the copyright for works created for hire and owned by corporations, such as Mickey Mouse of the Disney Corporation, to 95 years from the year of its first publication or for 120 years after initial creation.[24] On January 1, 2024, the world's favorite mouse in the version of its first presence in a Disney movie, *Steamboat Willie* (made in 1928), has entered the public domain. This means that the public (including brands and designers) can now copy, share, and build on the Mickey Mouse 1.0 version, as long as they don't mislead consumers into thinking the new design is produced or sponsored by Disney.[25]

Fair Use

Like any right, copyright is not absolute. To balance the interests of the public and copyright holders, fair use limits the exclusive right of the copyright owners. **Fair use** is a statutory doctrine that promotes freedom of expression by permitting the unlicensed use of copyright-protected works in certain circumstances, such as criticism, comment, news reporting, teaching, scholarship, and research. Section 107 of the Copyright Act provides the framework for determining whether something is of fair use. The following four factors are considered when it comes to evaluating a fair use case:

1. Purpose and character of the use, including whether the use is of a commercial nature or is for nonprofit educational purposes;
2. Nature of the copyrighted work—to what degree the work that was used relates to the copyright's purpose;
3. Amount and substantiality of the portion used in relation to the copyrighted work as a whole;
4. Effect of the use upon the potential market for or value of the copyrighted work.

(US Copyright Office, 2021)[26]

Since fair use claim is evaluated on a case-by-case basis, note that there is no formula to ensure that a small percentage or amount (e.g., 5 percent or 7 percent rule) of work—or a specific number of words, lines, pages, copies—may be used without permission.

Difference between Copyright and Other Forms of IP Protections

The difference between a copyright and a patent is that copyright protects original works of *expression*, while a patent protects the innovation of *utilitarian objects*. On the other hand, a trademark protects words, phrases, symbols, or designs by identifying the *source* of the goods or services and distinguishing them from others. Therefore, copyright can be a powerful protection for artistic works in the fashion business. For instance, a fabric print (as a graphic design) or a belt buckle (like a sculpture) can be protected under copyright law as long as these creative elements can be *conceptually* separated from the whole product.[27] In 2017, Unicolor, a pattern design company, brought a fashion apparel company to court for copyright infringement and was awarded $164,400 in damages and another $366,910 in fees and costs.[28] Copyright can also protect the creative content of an e-commerce site, including photographs, written material, music, graphics, and videos. The text-based programming code can be protected through patents or copyrights.

For omnichannel retailers, it is essential to recognize the different intellectual property involved in the business and protect their innovative product designs, symbols, trademarks, business methods, and even computer codes used in the business. When it comes to IP protection, a key concept to know is that a single object (e.g., a garment or shoe) may be covered by several forms of protection at the same time. For example, a pair of running shoes may have the brand logo, the sole design, and the innovative airbag for the foot protection that needs to be protected by IP. The logo and branding can be protected as trademarks, but the graphic image of the shoe can be protected by trade dress. The utility patent could protect the innovative airbag that the company developed for the running shoe. Thus, a running shoe can have three different kinds of IP protection. In the United States, fashion design for garments does not receive legal protection unless there are technical aspects of the design involved. However, the European Union provides a specific kind of copyright protection for fashion designs. Table 9.3 provides a summary of the major intellectual property rights, their scope of protection, and the pros and cons of using the rights.

Table 9.3 Intellectual Property Rights Protection in the United States

	SUBJECT MATTER	SCOPE OF PROTECTION (STANDARD FOR INFRINGEMENT)	ADVANTAGES/ DISADVANTAGES
Trademark/ Trade Dress	**Trademark:** Distinctive logos, names, images, designs that indicate the source of the product. **Trade dress:** The characteristic and distinctive visual presentation of a product; may include packaging and design elements.	**Trademark:** Registered trademarks provide nationwide protection against confusingly similar marks. **Trade dress:** Unregistered trade dress is protectable for distinctive packaging and for designs that have established secondary meaning by being recognized by the public. **Duration:** Indefinite, but the mark must continue to be used in commerce.	**Trademark:** **Pros:** Long duration, covers entire product line, rewards branding investments. **Cons:** International registrations or on multiple styles or product lines can become expensive. **Trade dress:** **Pros:** Can protect the "look" of a brand. **Cons:** May require the establishment of secondary meaning.
Patent	**Utility patent:** New, useful and non-obvious devices, processes, formula, or compositions, e.g., new fabrics, fasteners, production methods. **Design patent:** New ornamental designs for nonfunctional features or aspects of manufactured products.	**Utility patent:** Protects against products that make use of the patented process or composition or copy the patented product. **Design patent:** Protects against copies that appear to an ordinary observer to be the same as the patented design. **Duration:** Utility patent: 20 years. Design patent: 14 years.	**Utility patent:** **Pros:** Broad protection against infringing products. **Cons:** Application process is onerous, can be expensive, and difficult to obtain. **Design patent:** **Pros:** Strong protection for design elements of fashion products like shoes, eyewear, bags. **Cons:** Can take from 8 to 24 months to obtain, slow for fashion cycle.
Copyright	Original, creative works that have been fixed in a tangible medium. In fashion, can apply to fabric prints, jewelry, images on fashion items, photography, sculptural elements of fashion items or accessories, fashion photography.	Protects against copies that are substantially similar to the original. **Duration:** For works created by individuals: 70 years after the life of the creator. For works for hire (owned by corporations): 95 years after publication or 120 years after creation, whichever comes first.	**Pros:** Easy and inexpensive to obtain, long-lasting protection, good international protection. **Cons:** Does not apply to fashion designs or to elements of products that are dictated by functional rather than purely aesthetic considerations.

(Adapted from *Fashion Law: A Guide for Designers, Fashion Executives, and Attorneys,* 2nd edition, p. 25)[29]

Changing Landscape of Sales Tax Regulations

In the United States, a sales tax is exclusively collected by a retailer during the final sale of a good or service. It is paid by the end consumer and is considered one of the major revenue sources for state governments. If you lived in the United States, have you noticed that sometimes when you shop online, you did not pay the sales tax when you checked out? Have you wondered why? Below we will discuss some history of the legal battles between the US online retailers and state governments. We will also introduce the two tax principles: physical nexus and economic nexus in the following section.

Tax Battle on Internet Sales in the United States

Since the 1990s, as the internet made it possible for consumers to easily and frequently purchase goods from other jurisdictions, it has caused a number of challenges for states and retailers to collect sales tax. This was because, in 1992, the Supreme Court case Quill Corp. versus North Dakota determined that states could not collect sales tax on goods sold over the internet unless the seller had a *physical presence* in the state. For years, many states argued that they were losing a lot of money by not being able to collect sales tax on internet sales to customers located in their states. As e-commerce grew over the years, the law caused confusion as to which tax rate was applicable to which goods for many omnichannel retailers. Amazon used this ruling to justify not charging sales tax on its online sales, which gave it a competitive advantage over traditional brick-and-mortar retailers from 1995 until 2012 when pressure from states such as California and Texas brought Amazon to court and made Amazon collect sales tax for the states.[30,31]

The Current Practices of Collecting Tax in Omnichannel Retailing

In June 2018, the United States Supreme Court fundamentally changed the rules for the collection of sales tax by internet-based retailers, citing the fact that it is now much easier for internet-based retailers to determine where buyers are located and therefore collect the correct sales tax. In its decision in South Dakota versus Wayfair Inc., the Court stated that individual states could require online sellers to collect state sales tax on their sales if the retailer has a physical or economic nexus in the state. **Physical nexus** means a retailer has a physical presence in the state, whether it is an office, store, or warehouse. **Economic nexus** exists when a retailer earns above a sales or revenue threshold in that specific state. Currently, each state may impose different thresholds on the economic nexus. For instance, California has an annual sales threshold of $500K for out-of-state retailers. This means that an omnichannel retailer that does not have any physical presence in California needs to start collecting sales tax on the day they exceed the $500K threshold. As of January 2024, there are forty-six states (plus Washington DC) with economic nexus rules. Four states do not have any economic nexus laws (Oregon, New Hampshire, Montana, and Delaware) because they do not have state sales tax. Table 9.4 lists

Table 9.4 The Economic Nexus of the Top Ten Most Populated States

NO.	STATE	EFFECTIVE DATE OF LATEST LAW	THRESHOLD	MEASUREMENT DATE	INCLUDABLE SALES (GROSS, RETAIL, OR TAXABLE)	WHEN YOU NEED TO REGISTER ONCE YOU EXCEED THE THRESHOLD
1	**California**	1-Apr-19	$500,000	Preceding or current calendar year	Gross sales of tangible personal property. Marketplace sales included towards the threshold for individual sellers	The day you exceed the threshold
2	**Texas**	1-Oct-19	$500,000	Preceding 12 calendar months	Gross revenue: including taxable, nontaxable, and tax-exempt sales; Marketplace sales included towards the threshold for individual sellers	The first day of the fourth month after the month in which the seller exceeded the safe harbor threshold

Table 9.4 The Economic Nexus of the Top Ten Most Populated States, *continued*

NO.	STATE	EFFECTIVE DATE OF LATEST LAW	THRESHOLD	MEASUREMENT DATE	INCLUDABLE SALES (GROSS, RETAIL, OR TAXABLE)	WHEN YOU NEED TO REGISTER ONCE YOU EXCEED THE THRESHOLD
3	**Florida**	1-Jul-21	$100,000	Previous calendar year	Taxable sales. Marketplace sales are excluded from the threshold for individual sellers.	Next transaction (state doesn't specify)
4	**New York**	21-Jun-18 the date of the Wayfair decision	$500,000 in sales of tangible personal property and more than 100 sales	Immediately preceding four sales tax quarters	Gross receipts from sales of tangible personal property. Marketplace sales included towards the threshold for individual sellers	Register within 30 days after meeting the threshold and begin to collect tax 20 days thereafter
5	**Pennsylvania**	1-Jul-19	$100,000	Prior calendar year and then starting in the 2nd quarter. E.g., collection period 4/1/20–3/31/21 using the calendar year 2019	Gross sales on all channels, including taxable, exempt, and marketplace sales	April 1 following the calendar year when the threshold was exceeded
6	**Illinois**	1-Oct-18	$100,000 or more or 200 or more separate transactions	Preceding 12-month period	Retail sales. Marketplace sales are excluded from the threshold for individual sellers	The retailer shall determine on a quarterly basis whether they meet the criteria for the preceding 12-month period
7	**Ohio**	1-Aug-19	$100,000 or 200 or more separate transactions	Previous or current calendar year	Marketplace sales included towards the threshold for individual sellers	Marketplace facilitators: 1st of month following at least 30 days after meeting threshold; marketplace sellers next transaction (not specified)
8	**Georgia**	1-Jan-20	$100,000 or 200 or more sales*	Previous or current calendar year	Retail sales of tangible personal property delivered electronically or physically, whether taxable or exempt. Marketplace sales excluded from the threshold for individual sellers	Next transaction (state doesn't specify)
9	**North Carolina**	1-Nov-18	$100,000 or 200 or more separate transactions	Previous or current calendar year	Gross sales. Marketplace sales included towards the threshold for individual sellers	60 days after a remote seller meets the threshold
10	**Michigan**	1-Oct-18	$100,000 or 200 or more separate transactions	Previous calendar year	Gross sales. Marketplace sales are included towards the threshold for individual sellers	January 1 following the year the threshold is exceeded

(*Source*: US Census, https://www.census.gov/popclock/; Sales Tax Institute, Economic Nexus State Guide, https://www.salestaxinstitute.com/resources/economic-nexus-state-guide)

the top ten most populated states in the US and their economic nexus. For more details about the economic nexus for the forty-six states, visit the Economic Nexus State Guide at https://www.salestaxinstitute.com/resources/economic-nexus-state-guide.

Social Media Marketing Regulation

Social media platforms are essential channels for omnichannel retailers to engage and maintain customer relationships. Recently, many fashion brands have collaborated with influencers to deliver content that could engage their customers. Therefore, it is essential for retailers to make sure that the social influencers they work with comply with the disclosure requirement by the local regulation.

US Regulation on Influencer Marketing

In the US, influencer marketing is considered a type of endorsement advertisement. Since 2015, to prevent deceptive advertising, the FTC has been updating its guidelines (www.ftc.gov/influencer) on how social influencers should *disclose* the "material connection" and make it *obvious* to their followers. The "material connection" refers to the influencer's relationship with a brand that they endorsed on social media platforms—whether it is a personal/family/employee relationship, financial relationship (such as payment, discount, or free products or services). The disclosure should also be made obvious to the followers so that the endorsement information is transparent and allows followers to weight the value of the endorsement. In this section, we will discuss when to disclose, how to disclose, and the forms of disclosures following the FTC guideline.[32]

When to Disclose

According to the FTC, as long as an influencer has any financial, employment, personal, or family relationship with a brand, they should disclose the material connection. Any tags, likes, pins, or positive ways to show a preference for a brand, product, or services are considered endorsements—even if the brand did not ask the influencer to mention them or make any posts. For influencers, even if they consider their evaluations to be unbiased, as long as they have any relationship with a brand, they need to make a disclosure. However, if influencers just share what they like on social media, they do not need to declare that they do not have a relationship with the brand.

How to Disclose

In terms of how to disclose, the general rule is to make it obvious (hard to miss). The disclosure statement should be posted with the endorsement message itself (in the same language as the endorsement message) and not hidden in other places like the profile page, hashtags, or links. If the post is a photo posted on Instagram or Snapchat, the disclosure should be superimposed onto the photo, and viewers should have enough time to read the disclosure. If the post is a video, the disclosure should be included in the video itself in both audio and video format. This way, even if someone turned off the audio, they would still be able to see the disclosure text; or, if someone did not notice the disclosure words on the screen, they might hear the disclosure message. If an endorsement is live-streamed, the disclosure should be made periodically throughout the whole program so that someone who only views part of the live streaming can be notified too.

Forms of Disclosure

Simple explanations like "Thanks to MyFavoriteFashion brand for the free product" are often enough if placed in a way that is hard to miss. Hashtags like #MyFavoriteFashionPartner, #Ad, #Sponsored, or #Advertisement are good to include in the message/caption, but they are not necessary. Influencers should avoid using vague terms like "thank you" or "ambassador" or confusing acronyms (e.g., sp, spon, collab, etc.) as a form of disclosure. The FTC also advises that even if a social media platform has a disclosure tool, it is better for influencers to add their own (and good) disclosures. As more and more consumers are familiar with the concept of influencer marketing, market research has found that disclosure does not influence consumers' trust in the message as long as it fits well with the influencer's expertise and viewers' interests.

CASE STUDY 9.1

Privacy and Consumer Loyalty: Omnichannel Retailers' Strategies to Handle the Default Website Privacy Practices under Privacy Law

In the past two decades, e-commerce has witnessed unprecedented success, but this achievement has been accompanied by an increasing prominence of consumer privacy concerns. In 2013, Jai, Burns, and King employed the Stimulus–Organism–Response (SOR) model and Social Contract Theory to explore the impact of behavioral practices on consumers' evaluations of their online shopping experiences and repurchase intention toward online retailers.[34] Their findings revealed a disconnect between online shoppers and their trusted online retailers regarding the collection of information from customers. They found that most retailers involved in sharing information collected from customers with their affiliates or even with third-party companies for secondary uses like targeted advertising. The finding shows there is a disconnection between consumer expectations and actually business practices, which will harm the social contract between retailers and their customers and reduce consumers' repurchase intention toward their trusted retailers.[35]

Over the past ten years, the growing awareness of data breaches, unauthorized data sharing, and misuse of personal information has significantly influenced consumer attitudes toward data privacy, thereby impacting their loyalty to brands and retailers.[36] As a result, customers now demand greater transparency and control over their personal information, prompting businesses to reevaluate their data collection and usage practices. This shift in consumer expectations has compelled organizations across various sectors to navigate the challenge of balancing data-driven strategies with the imperative of protecting customer privacy. To address these concerns, the General Data Protection Regulation (GDPR) and the California Consumer Privacy Act (CCPA) have been enacted, driven by high-profile data breaches and scandals that have eroded consumer trust. These regulations place increased accountability and transparency requirements on businesses, necessitating explicit consent, clear data policies, and data breach notifications.

To handle default website privacy settings under the GDPR law, omnichannel retailers have implemented several strategies. They utilize Consent Management Platforms (CMPs) to effectively obtain and manage user consent. CMPs provide customizable consent banners or pop-ups, enabling users to make informed decisions about their data and privacy preferences in line with GDPR guidelines. An example of a Consent Management Platform is OneTrust. OneTrust offers a suite of privacy management tools, including a CMP, which enable organizations to comply with data privacy regulations and manage user consent effectively. Other examples of CMPs include TrustArc, Cookiebot, and Quantcast Choice.

Many omnichannel retailers also adopt an opt-in approach, setting privacy settings to a more privacy-friendly option by default and requiring users to actively opt-in to share additional data (e.g., receiving marketing newsletters, etc.). Additionally, granular privacy controls are offered to users, allowing them to specify the types of data they are comfortable sharing, the purposes for which their data can be used, and the duration of data retention. Clear and easily accessible privacy policies that outline data collection and usage practices are provided, along with regular auditing and compliance monitoring to ensure adherence to GDPR guidelines and prompt implementation of any regulatory updates or changes.

In a study conducted by Willis, Jai, and Lauderdale (2021), the researchers examined how a US retailer's decision to voluntarily apply GDPR data subject rights to US consumers affects the retailer–customer relationship.[37] The research found that when a retailer voluntarily applied GDPR consumer data rights to US consumers, it led to higher trust, lower privacy concerns, increased brand commitment, and positive consumer emotions. The study results suggest a promising approach for omnichannel retailers to earn consumers' trust and loyalty, particularly when customers engage with a retailer across multiple channels, leading to the sharing of more personal data. By effectively communicating their commitment to privacy, fostering transparent data practices, empowering users with control over their information, and making investments in secure technologies, omnichannel retailers can build trust and cultivate long-term customer loyalty in an era where privacy concerns are of paramount importance.

Discussion Questions:

1. How has the growing awareness of data breaches and unauthorized data sharing impacted consumer attitudes toward data privacy and their loyalty to brands and retailers?
2. How does the opt-in approach help businesses comply with the GDPR's requirement for explicit user consent? What are the potential benefits and challenges associated with implementing this approach?
3. Can you provide examples of how omnichannel retailers have implemented CMPs to effectively obtain and manage user consent? Do they all have the same default privacy preference? If not, which strategy will you adopt if you are a business owner? Please provide your rationale.
4. Examine your favorite omnichannel retailer's privacy policy—what element(s) in the privacy policy that you find informative? Is there anything surprising to you?
5. How do clear and accessible privacy policies contribute to building trust and enabling users to make informed decisions about their data?
6. What strategies can omnichannel retailers employ to balance data-driven strategies with the need to protect customer privacy? How can they effectively communicate their commitment to privacy to build trust and foster long-term customer loyalty?

CASE STUDY 9.2

Nike and MSCHF Reach a Settlement in the "Satan Shoes" Trademark Lawsuit

In March 2021, Lil Nas X, a Grammy-winning rapper, released "Satan Shoes" in collaboration with MSCHF, an art collective based in New York, to promote his latest music video, where he simulated hell and visited the devil. These shoes started a world of controversy due to the fact that they were created using Nike's Air Max 97s. Just 666 pairs of shoes were produced, with the 666 referring to the devil's number. The shoes have a pentagram pendant on the front, a reference to the Bible verse Luke 10:18 on the upper, and a drop of human blood mixed with red ink in the sole. The "Satan Shoes" were priced at $1,018 each, around six times the price of a pair of Air Max 97s sold by Nike.

After the products were dropped, Nike immediately came out stating that they had nothing to do with this shoe and they were not endorsing the sales of these shoes.[35] Boycotting and canceling of the brand was already underway until Nike had then filed a lawsuit against MSCHF for using their Nike swoosh logo and causing "confusion and dilution" to their brand. Many consumers believed that "Satan Shoes" were genuine Nike products and posted comments like:

> "This is terrible! Won't buy Nike again You are banned!"
> "no more Nike for anyone in my family"
> "I WILL NEVER WEAR ANOTHER PAIR OF NIKE AND I'M THROWING AWAY ALL THE ONES I HAVE NOW … WHAT A DISGRACE THIS IS PURE EVIL."

Their lawsuit places a special focus on the inclusion of Nike's Swoosh logo on the offending shoe, asserting that it is up to Nike, not third parties like MSCHF, to decide what products feature its logo. Although this shoe caused endless controversy, this is not the first time that MSCHF has debuted a religious-themed shoe. In 2019, MSCHF released what was called "the Jesus Shoe" (Figure 9.6). Like the "Satan shoe," it made several adjustments, attaching a crucifix to the front laces, injecting "holy water" in the sole and inserting a

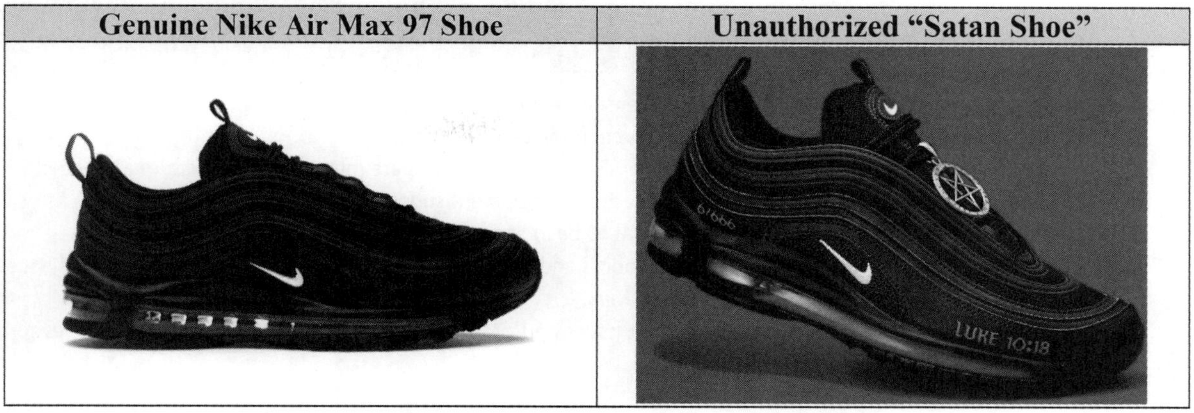

Figure 9.6 The genuine Nike Air Max97 shoe and Satan Shoe (*Source*: Nike, Inc. v. MSCHF Product Studio Inc., 1:21-cv-01679 [E.D.N.Y.])

religious-themed sockliner. They also kept the Nike logo unchanged. MSCHF first claimed that their shoes were protected under "the First Sale Doctrine." The doctrine is a statutory regulation that allows these third-party companies to sell trademarked goods.[38] However, Nike's argument against this is that "The doctrine is based on the premise that consumers are not being deceived because they are receiving what they have bargained for, the trademarked good."

In response to this, MSCHF then claimed that the shoes were protected under the First Amendment because they were "individually numbered works of art." Their attorney argued MSCHF was passionate about their artistic creations and believed that their work should not be punished because it is all about creativity. Moreover, all but one of the pairs of shoes had already been sold and shipped. Therefore, it would be pointless to continue with the lawsuit. Lil Nas X also expressed his frustration with the outcome, tweeting that he's "legally not allowed to give the 666th pair away anymore because of the crying nerds on the Internet," after teasing the giveaway earlier in the week.

After a week of filing the lawsuit, Nike and MSCHF came to a settlement between the selling of the shoes and the brands.[39] The settlement states that MSCHF would issue a "voluntary recall" of the shoes and offer a buy-back program as well. Even after the settlement was reached, though, MSCHF still stands by their belief that the shoes are a representation of art and individuality. The shoes are an arguable topic and will definitely be talked about in the future.

Geographic area of the case: United States.

Discussion Questions:

1. In your opinion, was MSCHF at fault for "wrongly" using/keeping the Nike swoosh on the shoes?
2. What can Nike do in the future to prevent something like this from happening?
3. Do you believe that these shoes are covered by the First Amendment as freedom of speech?
4. Would you buy the shoes if you were a fan of Nike? Why? Or why not?
5. How much creativity is too much creativity, in your opinion? Will this type of new product benefit any party involved?
6. Conduct an online search or visit The Fashion Law website (www.thefashionlaw.com/) to explore recent trademark/patent/copyright infringement cases. Select a case that captures your interest and provide a detailed explanation as to why you find it intriguing.

Career Opportunities

Job Titles	Key Responsibility
Production Assistant	• Support the printables and licensing team • Manage the costing and production for assigned categories • Monitor time & action calendar (TAC) to ensure dates are met and escalate issues as needed • Cost product and work with design/development/supply base to meet IMU% goals • Recommend product placement to be in line with sourcing strategy goals • Communicate directly with vendors and internal partners regarding all production related issues to ensure quality and on time delivery • Monitor product development issues and proactively communicate with applicable parties to find solutions **Qualifications** • A college degree preferably with course work in textiles and sourcing/production • High attention to detail • Ability to work in a global multicultural environment • Exceptional written/verbal communication skills • Good time management skills • Demonstrated organizational skills • Ability and willingness to work hard in a fast-paced, multi-tasking, team-oriented environment

Summary

Internet, social media, and other technologies provide opportunities and challenges to omnichannel retailers and the societies in which they operate their businesses. Ethical and legal issues in this sphere include information privacy and security, intellectual property, and tax regulations. In the past ten years, a series of high-profile data breach scandals have heightened consumers' concerns, and more consumers think companies should be responsible for protecting consumers' online privacy. General Data Protection Regulation (GDPR) and the California Consumer Privacy Act (CCPA) are the two recent privacy regulations introduced in the EU and California, respectively. The newly established regulations have greatly affected retailers' information privacy practices. In addition, omnichannel retailers may utilize different forms of IP protection (i.e., trademark, trade dress, patent, and copyright) to protect their domain names, logo, innovative materials, product designs, and relevant artistic expression of creations. Omnichannel retailers should also recognize the changing landscape of sales tax regulation. In 2018, the US Supreme Court changed the rules for the collection of sales tax by internet-based retailers. In addition to the physical nexus, the court added an economic nexus, which exists when a retailer earns above a sales or revenue threshold in that specific state. In other words, an omnichannel retailer who does not have any physical presence in a certain state will need to start collecting sales tax on the day they exceed the state-specified economic threshold. Last but not least, when omnichannel retailers work with social influencers on promotions, it is essential that retailers make sure that the social influencers comply with the FTC's guideline for influencer marketing.

Key Terms

Assignee
California Consumer Privacy Act (CCPA)
Copyright
Design patent
Economic nexus
Fair use
First-to-use system
First-to-file system
General Data Protection Regulation (GDPR)
Information privacy
Intellectual property
Material connection
Patent
Personal identifiable information (PII)
Physical nexus
Privacy Nutrition Labels
Privacy paradox
Sales tax
Trademark
Trademark infringement
Trade dress
USPTO
Utility patent

Reflection and Discussion Questions

1. As a consumer, do you have any of the following privacy invasion experiences? Please briefly describe one of your most recent experiences.
   - Spam/junk emails
   - ID theft
   - Credit card fraud
   - Computer virus attack
   - Behavioral ads that you found offensive
   - Behavioral ads that you found embarrassing
   - Others learning your personal info (e.g., account, password) from online activities
   - Others learning your shopping info (e.g., product purchased, search terms) that you don't expect other people to know
   - email read by someone other than the recipient
2. Do you think Apple's Privacy Nutrition Labels are helpful for consumers in making an app decision?
3. When you shop online, have you seen a pop-up screen asking you if you would like to allow all the cookies on this website or customize your cookie preference? Do you always select "allow all"? If not, please describe your experience of how you decide if you would give a retailer permission(s) to use different types of cookies to track you (e.g., performance cookies, targeting cookies, personal ads and content, use precise geolocation data, actively scan device characteristics for identification, etc.).
4. What kind of strategies do you think omnichannel retailers should do to reduce consumers' privacy concerns?
5. Go on the internet (e.g., https://www.thefashionlaw.com/) and search for a recent filing of trademark infringement (or other intellectual property infringement case) and share it with the class.
6. Assuming you and your business partner decided to open an Anime T-Shirts store online, what kind of intellectual properties should you consider filing for protection?
7. Search two or three social influencers on a social media of your choice. Please describe how they disclose their relationships with sponsors.
8. What types of copyrights do you have as an author?
9. What four factors are considered when it comes to evaluating a fair use case?
10. What is an economic nexus in the US tax law? In your home state, what's the rule of collecting online sales tax?

CHAPTER 10

Emerging Trends in Omnichannel Retailing

Learning Objectives

Upon completion of this chapter, you will be able to:

- Describe the retail technology trends in the fashion industry
- Identify the emerging technology and their applications in the omnichannel retail industry
- Apply the emerging retail trends to omnichannel retail business ideas

In this chapter, we discuss the technological trends of the retail business. Some of the trends may become standards in the next decade or so. Retail technological trends are discussed including augmented reality (AR) and digital garment and e-commerce visual merchandising, micro production for personalization, location-based technology, social shopping, Internet of Things application, digital transformation in supply chain and logistics, and customer relationship management (CRM) and email marketing. Secondly, emerging trends in other industries that are applicable to the fashion industry include artificial intelligence (AI) applications, Metaverse, non-fungible token, gamification, live commerce and social shopping, immortality of physical retail formats, cashier free, clerk-less retail formats, and the future retail's characteristics.

Retail Technology in the Fashion Industry

Omnichannel fashion businesses are facing one massive challenge—keeping up with fast-changing retail technologies. This challenge presents a frequent review of the emerging technology along with the investment costs in building the infrastructure within the business organization, training employees, and, most importantly, educating consumers about the new technologies that the business is implementing. However, the flip side of this challenge can be looking forward to the business opportunities to engage and expand their horizon into more technologically savvy consumer markets and proactively address these consumers' demands more effectively and efficiently through those emerging retail technologies. When e-commerce was introduced in the late 1990s, only the catalog-based fashion businesses hopped on to the bandwagon of embracing the e-commerce of another channel. Since then, we have clearly experienced the demise of the traditional brick and mortar retailers due to their sluggish transformation to morph into one of omnichannel retail business. In this section, we will discuss the imperative emerging trends in the retail world to keep your fashion business at the forefront of the field, including augmented reality and three-dimensional (3D) product development and presentation, product personalization through micro-production, visual search technology, emerging technologies supporting CRM and email marketing efforts, and AI implications in the consumer journey.

Design and Manufacturing Technology as Applied to the Retail Space

The advanced technology originally developed for design development and manufacturing yet now supporting the retail function as well, including augmented reality and digital garment development technology and microproduction for personalization is discussed. In this section, we will learn how they can be applied to the retail setting to improve the customer experience and their shopping journey in the context of omnichannel retail setting.

Augmented Reality and Digital Garments Development

Augmented reality (AR) is a technology where part of a user's physical world is enhanced with computer-generated perceptual information such as visual, auditory, haptic, and olfactory.[1] AR applications provide a practical and effective solution that enables customers and business employees to use smart devices to interact with the product, no matter where they are. Approximately 824,000 people are currently exposed to these technologies in the workplace. By 2030, 23 million jobs worldwide will be directly affected by AR and VR.[2] This technology enables product designers to see mockups of their designs overlaid into the real-world using applications such as Vusar's AR app.[3] AR has been widely used in fashion 3D product development and product presentation via the internet. The simplest example of AR technology is a QR code that makes goods and places "talk" to us. This technology has been used in fashion businesses, as providing consumers with virtual shopping options has become an important trend for fashion omnichannel retailers, such as Macy's, Adidas, and ModCloth, formerly owned by Walmart, between March 2017 and September 2019. They have turned the virtual fitting room into a reality for their customers, allowing customers to have a try-and-buy experience at home.[4] For instance, Converse Shoes offers their customers an AR try-on app, the so-called "Sample." Moreover, global fashion houses are catching on to this trend as well. For example, Burberry provides an Embedded Experience AR tool using Google search. In addition, Prada launched The Augmented Sunset Resort Show to highlight its new resort collection in 2019, while Chanel organized an event called Augmented Reality Snow Globe to celebrate winter holidays and engage with customers.[5]

A 3D garment development tool such as CLO Virtual Fashion allows omnichannel retailers to offer many benefits to customers. Often, online fashion customers point out the downside of online shopping is not being able to try on garments before purchasing them. Yet, 3D garment development tools can extend virtual fitting rooms technology where online customers can create an avatar by entering their body measurements and try on and style the garments online.[6] In addition, many omnichannel retailers such as Adidas and Dicks Sporting Goods are adopting virtual presentations of their products to be displayed on their e-commerce website and catalogs.

Micro Production for Personalization

Micro production refers to a strategy using small-batch manufacturing, which is highly automated, has small scale, needs fewer resources to set up and operate, and offers a broader range of process capabilities and startup businesses.[7,8] Due to its size, micro-production strategy offers fashion businesses more flexibility to shift between different product types.[9] Because of its agility and flexibility, this manufacturing strategy can be used to customize each new order while avoiding overstock situations. The make-to-order trend allows micro manufacturers to reduce supply chain costs by not over-ordering certain supplies and materials.[10] According to McKinsey and Company's industry trend report in 2019, personalization will become the main incentive for the retail industry's success in the next five years, affecting their sales revenues significantly.[11] The possibility of further purchases increases by 110 percent, and the chance of buyers spending beyond the plan rises by 40 percent.[12] For instance, the Berlin-based clothing company, Lesara, produces 90 percent of its products domestically through their micro-manufacturing facility and claims that it takes ten days to turn around from identifying fashion trends to launching the products on the market.[13]

Visual Search

Visual search refers to a technology that allows the users/customers/businesses to use real-world images such as screenshots, images downloaded from the internet, and/or personal photographs as the stimuli for online searches. Once pictures are submitted to search engines such as Google, AI deciphers the content and context of these images and generates a list of related results.[14]

This technology has been prevalent in the fashion industry. We often want to find a new look, clothing, or theme rather than a single object. Visual search makes online shopping easier. Many retailers, including ASOS, Neiman Marcus, and Wayfair, have built proprietary visual search tools.[15] For instance, Pinterest Lens has learned to identify more than 2.5 billion home furnishings and fashion items, processed nearly 600 million searches in the Pinterest app and browser extension, and has seen a 140 percent increase in search volume since its launch.[16] This technology is expected to increase the conversion by 85 percent.[17] Moreover, Shnap is a mobile app and browser extensions app using smart visual search technology which enable consumers to buy clothing by taking photos and automatically finding the source of purchase and comparing prices (Figure 10.1). For example, if a shopper sees a brand name, such as a Givenchy hoodie on Instagram, they can use an Android or iOS app to take a photo and upload it, and then Shnap will order it on a website like Farfetch.

Location-Based Technology

In addition to the location-based technology covered in Chapter 5, omnichannel retailers could consider a few more wonderful strategies to entice their customers when they are browsing in stores. Consumers' responses to text messaging as one of the mobile marketing efforts are quite positive.[18] Due to the influx of Covid-19 communications sent by companies to

Figure 10.1 Consumers can use their selfies to conduct a visual search online

customers, text messages were more important than ever in 2020. Geofencing or beacon technology allows the businesses to get permission from customers and send the relevant promotional contents through text messages while the customers are in the store. In addition, the company provides consumers with an opportunity to comment, rate, and share their business experiences. When 38 percent of smartphone owners turn on their GPS location, they can receive promotional messages via SMS. This statistic reveals opportunities for local marketing via text messages. Moreover, omnichannel retailers can implement AR and location-based technology to promote their current offerings (see Figure 10.2).

Another use of location-based technology can be tied to mobile app uses. When customers are downloading a mobile app, mobile app companies/marketers gain permission from customers regarding receiving push notifications (also known as drop messages) through the mobile app. In order to promote customers' participation to opt into this notification via the mobile app, businesses incentivize the customers with various loyalty programs and apps that allow them to earn points. For example, Shopkick will provide users with points ("kick") when they enter certain stores. People who subscribe to this kind of mobile app are more likely to buy goods because they are already in the store. For another example, if customers visit a shopping mall, they may receive a notification with an exciting offer from a nearby coffee shop. Customers are likely to consider such an offer because it is both relevant and timely. By offering these two qualities in advertising, location-based marketing can increase customer engagement and bring better results for your business.[19] For the most part, omnichannel fashion retailers have their own mobile app, which enables the customers not only shop for fashion goods but also tracks the consumer's purchase behavior and location-based features.

Figure 10.2 A combination of AR and location-based technology in the physical retail space

Social Shopping

Social shopping is defined as "the act of using social media to find reviews and recommendations about products (either product you're actively searching for or those you happen to stumble upon), then using those reviews to guide your purchase decision."[20] Social shopping brings social media and e-commerce together.[21] Social shopping occurs "when brands tag products to their social content and allow users to shop the products directly from the content."[22] "For instance, over 70 percent of shoppers worldwide use mobile apps to make purchases, driven by a desire for speed and simplicity, and this number is expected to increase over the next five years."[23] Over 90 percent of consumers said online reviews would influence their buying decision and 50 percent said they would pay more for a product with positive online reviews.[24] Instagram is the most popular social media shopping platform, with 70 percent of consumers expecting products to be discovered on Instagram, and Instagram has activated the new feature of Instagram Checkout, where purchases can be made in the app.[25] Brands can build entire stores on Facebook, and the most commonly used tools are Facebook Page Shops and Messenger. Brands can add and update products, sell directly from the brand's page, manage orders and shipping, and manage Facebook ads to promote the store.[26] Snapchat's shoppable show allows viewers to shop directly from the screen while watching.[27] Pinterest's Shop the Look feature allows consumers to take photos that interest them. Pinterest will search for similar products in its app and then link them to products on the retailer's website.[28,29] TikTok already operates an e-commerce shopping platform in China. It is working hard to provide support for users in the United States and Western Europe and is currently launching an in-app "Buy Now" button.[30] Lastly but not least, former Google and Starbucks executives have teamed up to launch a social shopping platform called Tuli, explicitly designed for the catering industry, where customers can order takeaway or takeaway food directly from photos and posts in the app.[31]

Internet of Things Application

The application of **Internet of Things (IoT)** is ubiquitous in our daily lives. The IoT refers to a network of electronic devices in the physical environment that are connected with the internet. Through the wired or wireless internet connection, the devices can communicate and exchange data with one another.[32] These devices range from ordinary household objects to sophisticated industrial tools to airplanes.[33] By 2025, there will be a total of 41.6 billion connected IoT devices and industrial and automotive equipment represents the most growth opportunity for the IoT applications.[34] Smart home systems are just one prominent example of the widespread adoption of IoT applications, which allows users to manage the data between devices seamlessly and—for example—control the thermostat from a remote location (see Figure 10.3).

Consumer-facing IoT applications are focused on individual users or families through the use of wearables and personal monitoring devices, such as Amazon's Echo, Google's Home, and Apple's HomePod.[35] The Apple Watch dominates the market as an example of wearable technology that can communicate with other Apple devices. The current Apple Watch can perform EKGs and is equipped with fall detection, notifying medical emergency services in the event of a fall,[36] which expands its function into a personal and wellness monitoring device. Finally, IoT application has been applied to monitoring companion animals staying home while their human friends are at work or at school (Figure 10.4). For instance, Furbo 360-degree Dog Camera allows the pet owners to monitor the activities of dog remotely on their mobile or tablet devices.

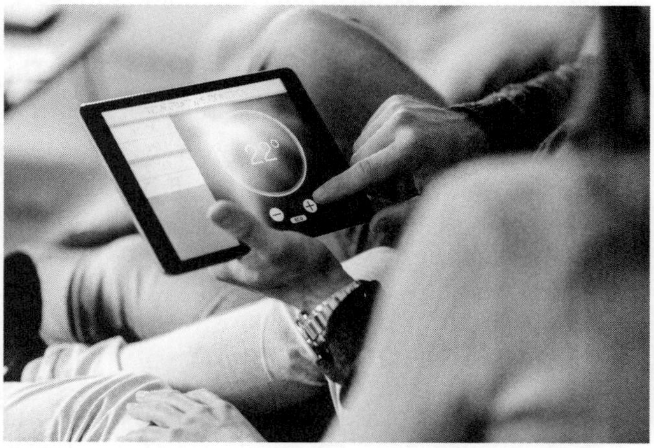

Figure 10.3 Consumers easily adjust indoor temperature using a smart home thermostat on their tablets and other mobile devices

Digital Transformation in Supply Chain and Logistics

One of the major issues experienced by retailers during the Covid-19 pandemic was in relation to the supply chain and logistics such as operational bottle neck in key hubs and transit points. According to a Business of Fashion (2022) article, these supply chain and logistic issues were amplified due to increase in consumer spending[37] boosted by the influx of governmental stimulus funds during that period.[38] Digital transformation in supply chain and logistics is the process of using digital technologies and data to optimize the flow of goods and services from production to consumption. Digital transformation can help supply chain and logistics organizations improve efficiency, agility, visibility, customer satisfaction, and sustainability. Coming out of the Covid-19 pandemic, many industry leaders called for putting more emphasis in building resilience in supply chain and logistics by adopting and implementing digital solutions in planning and sourcing, which are upstream of the supply chain, rather than downstream components of the supply chain management such as transportation and distribution.[39]

CRM and Email Marketing

A company's customer base is one of its most significant assets. And this is true for fashion businesses due to the industry's maturity, the proliferation of brands, and declining brand loyalty among consumers. This asset deserves strict management and supervision. CRM refers to tracking and managing interactions between existing

Figure 10.4 Your furry companion can be monitored using IoT while being away from home

and potential customers. Any business can hugely benefit from CRM using advanced software and retail technology to build and operate the customer base. Such CRM software enables fashion businesses to manage all of their interactions with their existing and potential customers. This technology may synchronize browsing and purchasing data with marketing automation and email marketing systems. As of 2020, there were more than 3.9 billion active users worldwide. Businesses can use email marketing and CRM platforms such as Salesforce together to organize contacts, automate activities, and store customer data.[40] CRM software offers a more personalized customer experience through the data collected with various touchpoints with customers. Such technology also monitors which marketing pieces each contact has received and opened. This technology tremendously helps the marketing campaign effort of omnichannel fashion businesses with recruitment and retention of their customer base.[41] According to Split Base (2021), 40 percent of all luxury purchases are affected by the customer's digital experience.[42] For example, Canada Goose's email opt-in form is an excellent example of a form that offers a benefit ("get exclusive access to products, experiences and more") without providing a discount.

Emerging Trends Applicable for Omnichannel Fashion Business

AI Implications in Consumer Journey

Artificial intelligence (AI) refers to the simulation of human intelligence in machines programmed to think like humans and mimic their actions through deep machine learning and problem-solving. According to IBM Institute for Business Value report published in 2020,[43] AI is successfully employed to provide an intelligent, convenient, and informed customer experience at any point along the customer journey. With this technology frequently applied in the retail industry, an omnichannel fashion business may achieve re-imagined customer experiences and end-to-end customer journeys that are integrated and more personal so that they feel more natural to customers.[44] With further developments in AI, retailers will gain the ability to provide more effortless and more satisfying outcomes at every phase in a customer journey, from product discovery to post-purchase customer service. Advanced machine learning and data analytics is the key to powering such experiences at scale.[45]

An industry article reported that the "hyper-personalized" future of the retail industry has emerged, especially in areas such as fashion and cosmetics.[46] For example, Stitch Fix, an online retailer, operates a **subscription business model** for shopping for curated outfits and accessories. The subscription business model refers to a business model in which a customer agrees to pay a recurring fee at regular intervals for access to a product/service. In the case of Stitch Fix customers take the survey to reveal their style preference, budget, and lifestyle first. Then they can either choose to work with a stylist who will curate a "Fix" for the customers' needs and wants within the budget or pick items from the recommendation made by Stitch Fix to have the garments and accessories shipped to their homes for trying on before buying them. If the customers do not like them, then they can simply send them back. It has been extremely popular among working professionals who may feel like they have no time and energy for shopping for clothes.

Stitch Fix uses machine learning algorithms and data analysis to learn about shoppers' tastes in clothing through personal style information filled out by shoppers online. Stitch Fix's system offers AI-based suggestions to the stylist to make personalized choices for the client while using the stylist's feedback to improve their offers. Similarly, Shiseido also uses machine learning of the data collected via a Treasure Data enterprise customer data platform to build a preference model and personalize its loyalty program, for example, by recommending different beauty products to customers to help them experience different stages of life. Moreover, The North Face has developed an in-store application that asks customers about their plans to wear the jacket they need and their activities while wearing the jacket. Then, IBM's Watson Analytics uses this customer information and makes personalized recommendations.[47]

Metaverse and Fashion

The **metaverse** is a concept that refers to the fusion of physical and digital worlds in which individuals can interact, create, and explore in an immersive environment. The fashion industry is one of the sectors that is embracing the metaverse as a new opportunity to reach and engage customers, showcase products, and express creativity. Some of the ways that fashion brands are using the metaverse include first creating virtual collections and skins that can be worn by avatars in games and social platforms, such as Balenciaga's collaboration with Fortnite[48] or Ralph Lauren's partnership with Zepeto.[49] Zepeto is a well-known South Korean metaverse mobile app with over 300 million users worldwide, which enable users to create 3D avatars to interact with other users. Second, fashion brands could launch digital showrooms and runways that allow customers to view and try on products in 3D, using technologies like AI and AR, such as Gucci's virtual garden in Roblox.[50] Third, fashion brands can sell **non-fungible tokens** (NFTs) that represent unique digital assets, such as artworks, designs, or experiences, that can be owned and traded by customers, such as Burberry's NFT collection with Mythical Games[51] or Dolce & Gabbana's Alta Moda NFT auction.[52] All in all, the metaverse offers fashion brands and omnichannel retailers a chance to innovate, differentiate, and connect with their customers in new and exciting ways.

Non-Fungible Tokens and Fashion

Non-fungible tokens (NFTs) are a novel way to create and own blockchain-based digital assets. They are one-of-a-kind, indivisible, and verifiable, which makes them perfect for representing rare and valuable physical and digital assets. NFTs have many applications in the fashion industry where authenticity and uniqueness are admired by the consumers. First, NFTs can be used to prove ownership and authenticity of physical and digital fashion items. For example, the fashion brand RTFKT Studios released limited edition sneakers as NFTs that are linked to physical shoes. This allows buyers to verify the authenticity of their physical shoes using the corresponding NFT. Later in 2021, this company was acquired by Nike.[53] Nike and RTFKT announced the release of Cryptokicks iRL in four colorways.[54] Second, NFTs can be used to create and sell digital fashion items that can be worn by avatars in virtual worlds or games. For example, The Fabricant, a digital fashion house, sold "Iridescence," a shimmering dress, on the blockchain for $9,500 in 2019.[55] Virtual fashion can also be used to express one's identity and creativity in the metaverse. Due to the innovativeness of the NFTs, it created a lot of buzz around fashion brands that were early adopters.

Gamification and Fashion

Gamification refers to the application of game elements and mechanics to non-game contexts, such as education, health, or business. How can gamification and fashion be combined to create engaging and meaningful experiences for consumers? As of 2023, there are thousands of fashion game apps available for Android and iOS including Covet Fashion, Fashion Fantasy, Love Nikki, and Super Stylist, to name a few.[56] For the consumer standpoint, these fashion game apps are adopted for their entertainment. For the business perspective, these fashion game apps can serve as wonderful advertising media to promote the lines or license the brand's fashion to the game company. Another possible way is to use gamification to enhance and personalize fashion design and production. For example, a fashion platform could allow users to create their own clothing items, accessories, or patterns using game-like tools and features. The platform could also enable users to share their creations with other users, receive feedback, and participate in competitions or collaborations. When the omnichannel retailer participates in such a platform, the platform users and the retailer can co-create a fashion item or even a line with a marketing or business potential. Moreover, in the metaverse game setting, users dress the avatar in certain outfits to express their virtual identity, which may be the same or different from their physical identity. In such a setting, the virtual fashion has shown great potential for future businesses.

Digital Retail Formats on Steroids: Live Commerce on Social Media Shopping

Live commerce is a new form of online shopping that combines live video streaming with e-commerce. Live commerce allows customers to watch and shop at the same time, and interact with the presenter and other viewers through a chatroom. Live commerce brings an element of "now or never" and "fear of missing out" which promotes experiential shopping and impulsive shopping. Many of the live commerce shoppers reported that they tend to enjoy a more engaging and entertaining shopping experience. According to Statista (2022), live commerce on platforms such as Taobao and TikTok is very popular in China, where it accounted for approximately $200 billion in sales, which was a 10.6 percent share of e-commerce sales in 2020. The sales revenue of Chinese live commerce was estimated to grow to a 24.3 percent share of all e-commerce sales in 2023.[57] This format is rapidly growing in popularity in the United States as well on social media platforms such as YouTube, Facebook, Instagram, TikTok, and Amazon Live.[58] In 2020, there was $11 billion of sales revenues from this format in the United States.[59] According to McKinsey & Company (2021), live commerce can help fashion brands and omnichannel retailers increase conversion rates, improve brand appeal and differentiation, and reach new and younger audiences.[60]

Immortality of Brick-and-Mortar Retail Formats

The decade-old "retail apocalypse" in the United States reflected the changes in consumer and retail trends in the twenty-first century. Since the inception of e-commerce in the late 1990s, consumers have been adopting it as a part of their shopping and purchasing channel and this trend became fully blown in the 2010s with the greater popularity of omnichannel retailers. For instance, Amazon's sales revenues grew from $6.92 billion in 2004 to $513.98 billion in 2022.[61] Over 9,000 stores closed in 2019 in United States. With the continued growth of e-commerce sales contributed by pure e-tailers and omnichannel retailers, the physical footprint for general retail may continue to shrink in the United States.[62] However, this may not affect the fashion retailers that concentrate on the experiential shopping experience or the luxury fashion segments.

During the 2010s, the millennial and Gen Z consumers' attention was captivated by the **pop-up shop** and event marketing efforts in the omnichannel retail environment. Pop-up shops are temporary retail spaces that allow businesses to sell their products in an environment completely designed and controlled by them.[63] This type of retail offering is "typically used to introduce a new product line, test a new market or generate awareness for a product or cause."[64] Pop-up shops operate a short opening time and commitment toward the retail venues; therefore, it offers the companies/businesses agility and flexibility[65] based on a relatively low operating and investment cost. These retail venues bring the businesses buzz as well as experiential marketing outcomes.[66] Due to the connectedness of our young adult consumers and teenage consumers via their smartphones and the ubiquity of the internet, these events have been prevalent (Figure 10.5). Consumers are eager to have a first-hand experience of tangible or intangible products or services. Also, the popularity of sharing experiences via social media boosted the popularity of these events. Pop-up shops have been widely adopted in the fashion industry. For instance, Bottega Veneta launched the Invisible Pop-up Store in Shanghai, China, in 2020, entirely made of mirrors.[67] This pop-up store covered an area of more than 1,080 square feet and displayed a series of 2020 autumn and winter collections for men and women, including ready-to-wear, handbags, small leather goods, shoes, jewelry, and glasses.[68] During the pandemic, the brand's revenue in China's high-value markets increased.[69] More recently, during the pandemic, global cosmetics brands including NARS, Charlotte Tilbury, Dior, and Lancôme have launched their virtual pop-up stores to create an experience and educate their customers beyond the product pages and description. These virtual pop-up stores were the ideal remedy for customers and businesses due to limited face-to-face interaction available during the pandemic.

In addition to the experiential aspects of the pop-up shops, consumers can use them to collect consumer preferences and data on payment systems. For example, due to the Covid-19 pandemic, consumers are more eager to use contactless payment systems. Therefore,

Figure 10.5 BTS Pop-Up: space of BTS in Hudson Yards area in Manhattan, NYC
(*Source*: Jihyun Vick)

marketers of the fashion industry could explore questions to address the checkout process and payment systems through pop-up shops before they invest the infrastructure in establishing business operational strategies.[70]

Cashier Free, Clerk-Less Retail Formats

As the labor costs increase and the convenience of access to merchandise 24/7 grows, convenience stores are going cashier free, clerk-less.[71] This phenomenon is quite common in the Far East. In the case of China, the spread of cashier-free shops comes in the context of an online retailing boom, while in Korea and Japan, the industry is seeking ways to respond to the labor shortage.[72,73] This phenomenon was realized through an Amazon Go store in Seattle, first opened in 2019.[74]

The fashion industry adopted a vending machine as a humanless automated self-serving retail format. For instance, Kylie Cosmetics launched vending machines in regional and international airports throughout the United States (Figure 10.6). In addition, YSL Beauty launched a vending machine called Lipstick Engraving ATM 2.0, which offers a customization option for customers to buy lipsticks with their names engraved on

Figure 10.6 Kylie Cosmetics vending machine located in the Cleveland Hopkins International Airport
(*Source*: Jihyun Vick)

the product in real-time.[75] In addition, Uniqlo's unique installation mainly focused on one item: warm vests for travelers who may not have packed properly for Northern California's difficult microclimate. Adidas wanted to promote their Splash Pack line, so they installed vending machines in sports bars based in LA and Boston during the baseball World Series. Consumers were allowed to win limited edition products based on the World Series such as cleats, autographs, and gears. The vending machine had digital printing features that unlocked new products. Lululemon focused on a certain target market—runners. They set up a machine at a Run Stop that included running gear and products like Lululemon socks and hats. Customers had to answer a questionnaire on their workout habits.[76]

Another fashion brand that adopted a vending machine as their way to reach out to the Gen Z target market is Jacquemus, a French fashion brand founded by Simon Porte Jacquemus in 2009. The brand is known for its minimalist and playful designs. The brand launched a vending machine for the fashion goods in Paris. Across one weekend, a two-day temporary pop-up period in December 2021, fans of Jacquemus could purchase the brand's highly sought accessories such as Bambino Long bag via the vending machine as soon as they drop. This temporary pop-up idea of using a vending machine was a hit. Of course, it went viral on Instagram via numerous posts of purchases made by its lucky fans.[77]

Future of Retail Is About an Authentic, Coherent, and New Shopping Experience

The future of retail is right around the corner with a coherent experience that focuses on the authentic brand personality of the business. Consumers are more willing to share their information and sales data among others to get pampered by the CRM technology adopted by the omnichannel retailers. Maybe more than everyday consumers would recognize, we are allowing businesses to gather data about us on a daily basis. For instance, the ads that appear while we are browsing and watching YouTube videos are supported by the cookie data collected by our device while we browse.

As more advanced retail technologies emerge, omnichannel fashion retailers need to stay relevant and promptly align their organization with the proper technologies to stay current with consumer demands and expectations. Keeping authenticity, coherence, consistency, and transparency as the core value to business operations, fashion businesses may flourish by catering to their customer journey to last for their lifetime. These experiences will be the key to maintaining customer satisfaction in the vast sea of brands and retailers competing for their business.

Box 10.1 Amazon Style: A Short-Lived Apparel Retail Store of Amazon Inc

On May 25, 2022, the online retail giant Amazon launched their first physical apparel store called Amazon Style in Glendale, California.[78] Within five months they launched their second Amazon Style store in Easton Town Center, located in Columbus, Ohio in October 2022.[79] Both stores were nearly 30,000 square feet in size and featured women's and men's clothing as well as shoes and accessories. They carried national brands such as Calvin Klein, Champion, Levi's, Lacoste, Theory, Equipment, and among others.[80] Amazon's own brands The Drop, Amazon Essentials, and Amazon Aware were also available. When we consider the fact that Amazon sells 10 percent of all clothes in the US,[81] it may be a reasonable step for the company to have physical store fronts.

Amazon Style was not your typical brick and mortar store. This is the experience of one of this book's authors at their Easton Town Center location in March 2023. Amazon Style had an inviting store front (Figure 10.7) and nice flow of the merchandise. It certainly merged online and offline operations by employing a variety of technologies at the forefront. I was instructed to use the Amazon Shopping app to enjoy a personalized shopping experience. I scanned a product's QR code using the Amazon Shopping app to obtain information such as sizes, colors, and ratings. The chosen items were then routed to a "contact-free" fitting room or to the pickup counter. Once I completed picking outfits to try on, I received a text message and notification via the Amazon Shopping app to come to one of their 36 specific fitting rooms to try on the items. The fitting room was stocked with the items I had chosen and additional recommended pieces from the backend staff. It also had a colorful, wall-mounted kiosk with touch screen to communicate with the backend staff about I liked the item, how it fitted or even if I wanted to try on other styles. The checkout was possible through Amazon One; yet I did it using the man-powered, physical check out. The purchase was bagged in their Amazon Styled reusable cotton duck fabric tote bag with their logo.

Some customers were getting excited about whether Amazon Style would come to their cities. The vision of Simoina Vasen, managing director of Amazon Style, existed for a very short time period. Amazon Inc. shuttered its two Amazon Style stores by November 9, 2023, which is just 17 months after opening the first store, as they sharpened their focus on grocery stores.[82] Amazon Style was a worthy attempt made during the closing of most of its Amazon-branded physical stores such as bookstores, Amazon 4-Star, and mall pop-up kiosks in 2022. In the meantime, Amazon hired Tony Hoggett, a former executive of British supermarket chain Tesco plc for over thirty years, to lead Amazon's physical retail stores in the US as Senior Vice President of Physical Stores.[83] Amazon Style is now in the history of omnichannel retailing, yet you can peek at the video regarding the store experience on About Amazon.[84]

Figure 10.7 The Amazon Style store front at Easton Town Center, located in Columbus, Ohio

CASE STUDY 10.1

Your Personal 3D Avatar for Shopping

During 2015, global sales of apparel and footwear reached $1.2 trillion; yet the retail industry experienced a high volume of merchandise return worth $62.4 billion due to improper fit.[85] This statistic presents the greater importance of accurate assessment of garment and footwear fit to the wearers. There is commercially available technology that can support the retail industry to reduce fit-related merchandise returns. For example, the latest retail technology of true-to-size 3D avatars is being adopted by fashion retailers, including Marks & Spencer, Calvin Klein, Wrangler, Diesel, and Desigual (Shopometry.com, 2021). With numeric information (height and weight) and visual data (a photograph of the user), a 3D avatar can be created via Virtual Outfits.com, allowing consumers to try on garments virtually in a digital fitting room. Farfetch, Yoox, Intermix, Boohoo, TopShop, BCBG, and Amazon are some retailers that use this technology on VirtualOutfits.com.

3DLook is another company that offers 3D visualization technology by processing and measuring the human body from only two photos taken by any mobile device.[86] This high-tech firm utilizes the computer vision algorithm and deep learning to analyze photographs and body measurements submitted by consumers. In order to accurately estimate the 3D model based on the visual and numeric data points, 3DLook operates its 3D body scanning lab collecting the 100+ data points on the human body and build ten body types, including trapezoid, oval, hourglass, athletic, pear, triangle, inverted-triangle, narrow rectangle, rectangle, and wide rectangle. Then, using neural networks and proprietary statistical modeling based on the visual landmarks, body measurements generate synthetic data for the consumer, which can be used later to build a 3D model of the customer. This company works with several partners in the fashion industry, including BROWZWEAR, Gerber technology, CLO, Professional Clothing Industry Association Worldwide, and LVMH.

Over the turn of the century, Lands' End and Levi's adopted this 3D virtual model to boost their sales and customer experience. Since then, many fashion retailers have stepped back from 3D virtual technology. However, with the pandemic in 2020 and 2021, the use of a 3D avatar was helpful with customer engagement, entertainment (gamification of the virtual try-on), subsequent sales, and reduction in returns. Overall, fashion retailers can apply 3D visualization technology to virtual dressing solutions, 3D mirrors, social shopping, fitness and healthcare, visual search applications, gaming/immersive content generation, and augmented/mixed reality.

The geographic area of the case: US, Europe.[85,86]

Discussion Questions:

1. Do you think 3D virtual try-on will continue to thrive in the market? Why or why not?
2. Check out the Virtual Outfits' website (https://style.me) and find out the efficiency and usability of the interface.
3. Apply the three principles of evaluating a website—appearance, functionality, and speed—to analyze Virtual Outfits' website. Summarize key points in each dimension and discuss why you would or would not adopt such technology for your next apparel shopping trip.
4. What other omnichannel fashion companies may adopt this technology? What target segments may find this technology more appealing for them to use? Why?

Career Opportunities

<table>
<tr><th>Job Titles</th><th>Key Responsibility</th></tr>
<tr><td>Analyst, Global Product Management</td><td>Daily Responsibility:
• Collaborating with cross-functional areas (UX, IT, Store Operations, Data Science, Analytics, Merchandising, Finance, Marketing) to identify and deliver value through a customer-first, digitally-enabled ecosystem.
• Developing compelling digital product visions and strategies grounded in customer needs, business goals, data, and insights.
• Translating product vision into outcome-focused roadmaps that communicate clear direction and digital product priorities across the organization based on the value that will be delivered.
• Managing multiple stakeholder expectations while delivering on the product vision, ensuring decisions that impact the product are grounded in material business and customer benefits.
• Establishing product goals, metrics, and analytics to measure product value outcomes; managing and grooming a product backlog based on performance while maintaining a balance between innovative capabilities and foundational refinements and enablers.
• Analyzing consumer needs, current market trends, and potential partnerships from a build/buy perspective, assessing current competitor offerings, identifying opportunities for differentiation.
• Partnering with finance and other teams to develop business cases and benefits to support investment in product features and functionality.
• Delivering the product's value through a highly collaborative, cross-functional team comprised of business, technology, and design disciplines working in an agile framework.
• Engaging relevant stakeholders to create deployment plans and internal communications, ensuring product capabilities are positioned for successful adoption across functions and brands.
• Providing end-to-end subject matter expertise for the digital product internally and as the primary point for any needs related to the product area.
• Participate and lead digital product activities (story mapping, scrums, stand-ups, design reviews, sprint demos, sprint planning, retrospectives, etc.).
• Translate and document requirements in the format of product epics, features, user stories, and acceptance criteria.
• Provide product level guidance across the UX and Digital Product Team.

Qualifications

• 4-year college degree or equivalent experience.
• 2 or more years of digital product management experience in consumer-facing mobile and web products with a track record of delivering new and innovative customer experiences to the market.
• 2 or more years of retail industry experience or equivalent domain experience.
• Proficiency at appropriately applying Design Thinking, Agile, and Lean methods to identify and deliver high-value business and customer outcomes through digital products.
• Well-versed in modern digital technologies and ability to facilitate communication and activities between business, technology, and design teams.
• Strong communication skills and proven ability to influence both at a strategic leadership level and cross-functionally.
• A proven track record of delivering innovative and engaging customer experiences informed by data and insights.
• Ability to perform well in high-pressure situations, balance competing priorities, and demonstrate the ability to work without direct supervision.</td></tr>
</table>

Summary

The future of retail may already be here. As a consumer, you may have experienced the major consumer trends mentioned in this chapter. Consumers today are getting much more tech-savvy as they flip through their social media feeds and shop through social shopping. They are highly interested in sustainable products/services, the sharing economy, and subscription of monthly fashion and accessories rentals. At home, consumers are connecting their electronic devices through the internet to manage their lives. Spontaneous pop-up events and subscription fashion business are on the rise to meet these customers' demands. Moreover, the retail trends are already commercially applied in the retail industry, and we anticipate seeing more applications of augmented reality and visual search among omnichannel fashion retailers in the near future. Ubiquitous mobile phone ownership and usages fuels the consumer adoptions of such retail technologies. Among many, artificial intelligence and machine learning seem like the keys to support the consumer journeys while gathering and transferring the invaluable data of the consumers back to the business. The future of retail is right around the corner with a coherent experience focused on an authentic brand personality of the business. Its authenticity will resonate with the consumers not only by their words/slogans but also through their omnichannel business strategies and consistent services based on well curated relationship management. These experiences will be the key to maintaining customer satisfaction in the vast sea of brands and retailers competing for their business.

Key Terms

Artificial intelligence (AI)
Augmented reality (AR)
Cashier free, clerk-less retail formats
Event marketing
Gamification
Internet of Things (IoT)
Live commerce
Metaverse
Micro production
Non-fungible token (NFT)
Pop-up shop
Social shopping
Subscription business model
Visual search

Reflection and Discussion Questions

1. What are the important consumer trends that omnichannel fashion businesses should consider?
2. Discuss an example of IoT applications that you, your family, or friends are using daily and the effectiveness of such applications.
3. Based on a synthesis of some of the retail trends covered in this chapter, ideate a possible mobile app which could enhance wardrobe management.
4. Describe social shopping and how it is applied to the omnichannel fashion business.
5. Discuss the application of visual search among fashion retailers.
6. List critical elements that retailers should pay attention to when developing a CRM strategy.
7. Describe how AI technology has been adopted in email marketing.
8. Discuss the importance of augmented reality and 3D visualization to the omnichannel fashion business.
9. Describe how AI technology has been adopted in the e-commerce sites of omnichannel retailers.
10. Discuss how micro production technology will improve the productivity of omnichannel fashion retailers.
11. From your email inbox, identify a couple of excellent examples of CRM via email communication and discuss why.

Glossary

Alternative Text (Alt Text). The descriptive text which conveys the meaning and context of a visual item in a digital setting, such as on an app or web page.

Artificial Intelligence (AI). It is the simulation of human intelligence in machines programmed to think like humans and mimic their actions through deep machine learning and problem-solving.

Assignee. The assignee is the entity that has the property right to a patent.

Augmented Reality (AR). A technology where part of a user's physical world is enhanced with computer-generated perceptual information such as visual, auditory, haptic, and olfactory.

Awareness Stage. Retailers focus on educating potential customers about their new product offerings or present the existing products as a new solution. The traditional media content to evoke customers' interests and awareness includes television ads, billboards, newspaper/magazine ads, radio, or word of mouth. In the online environment, omnichannel retailers can do things like shareable photographs, blog posts, social media posts, videos, e-catalogs, podcasts, etc.

Back-End Services. Customer service functions that are not readily viewable from the customer's perspective.

Biometric Payment. A method of payment using various parts of the body. Eye tracking, fingerprint scanning, and facial recognition are widely used biometric payment methods.

Boomerang Effect. Where customers keep coming back to a company multiple times in an effort to resolve a problem.

BOPIS. Buy online, pick up in-store. One of the most common omnichannel retailing services. Many major omnichannel retailers also offer curbside pick-up so that customers do not need to go into the store for pick-up.

Bounce Rate. The percentage of visitors to a particular website who only viewed one page divided by all the visitors.

Bracketing. The practice of buying a number of different sizes or colors of an article of clothing with the intention to return most, if not all, of the items.

Brand Ambassador. People who are hired by a business to work under contract to help them achieve specific business goals, such as increasing brand awareness and boosting conversions and sales.

Broadcasting Email/Text Messages. A one-time email campaign that the marketer sends to a specific group of customers or subscribers. Such emails include newsletters, promo campaigns, special offers, and featured blog posts, among others.

Business-to-Consumer (B2C) Marketplaces. The marketplaces that mainly focus on bringing shoppers and brands together.

California Consumer Privacy Act (CCPA). Enacted in 2020, California is the first state in the US to offer more comprehensive protections for consumer data rights.

Catalog Marketing. Using catalogs to sell to individual customers. Catalogs provide the tangibility and power of direct mail and have become an integral part of an omnichannel campaign by driving customers to digital experiences.

Clienteling. The practice of personal shopping in brick-and-mortar stores, which includes providing extensive merchandise help and fashion or technical assistance.

Content Marketing. A strategy that emphasizes creating and distributing valuable, relevant, and consistent content to attract and engage target customers, which will ultimately lead to sales and customer loyalty.

Content Marketing Funnel. A process from attracting a new customer to after the customer completes a transaction, including the awareness stage, evaluation stage, and conversion stage.

Conversion Rate. The number of visitors to a website that completed a desired goal (a conversion) out of the total number of visitors.

Conversion Stage. The stage in which consumers make a desirable action (e.g., complete a transaction, enroll in the email list, book an appointment, etc.).

Copyright. A property right that protects one's written or artistic expressions fixed in a tangible medium, such as graphic design, sculptures, novels, songs, videos, computer software, etc. The owner of a copyrighted work has the right to 1) reproduce it, 2) make derivative works from it (such as a fabric print based on a painting), 3) sell it or license it, 4) perform the work publicly, 5) display the work publicly, and 6) perform the work publicly via digital audio recordings (like audiobook or podcast). In the U.S. United States, copyright law protects the works of individuals for their lifetime plus seventy years beyond their life.

Crawling. A term describing the process of search engines like Google sending a bot to the internet to "read" the webpages and index the content for future search.

Cross-Selling. A marketing technique that makes a recommendation adjacent to the original product or sells an additional product or service to a customer.

Customer Lifetime Value (CLV). The total revenue a business can reasonably expect from a single customer account throughout the business relationship. It is a function of average annual revenue per customer divided by the average lifespan of a customer (average years that a customer continues to purchase from a brand).

Customer Relationship Management (CRM). It refers to a strategic management of acquiring new customers, retaining current customers, and nurturing preferably life-long interactions with customers.

Customer's Purchase Journey. The process a customer goes through to achieve their consumption goals with your company. A customer's purchase journey consists of five stages, namely, 1) awareness stage, 2) evaluation stage, 3) purchase (conversion) stage, 4) postpurchase stage, and 5) retention stage.

Deep Discount Stores. Stores that offer for sale primarily discounted items that are typically surplus, liquidated, out of season, discontinued, salvaged, part of an odd or partially damaged lot of goods, etc. Dollar Trees, Big Lot, Aldi, and Jacks Dollar Stores are some examples of deep discount stores.

Design Patents. A design patent may be granted to anyone who invents a new, original, and ornamental design for an article of manufacture. A design patent must be filed within one year after the product/design is made publicly available.

Direct Marketing. A form of communicating an offer (usually presented in ways like advertising), where organizations communicate directly to a pre-selected customer and supply a method for a direct response through various media such as mail (or email), catalog (or e-catalog), TV, mobile phones, or website.

Direct Selling. A business model that offers entrepreneurial opportunities to individuals as independent contractors to market and sell products and services, typically through one-to-one selling, in-home product demonstrations, parties, or online. Many direct-selling companies sell personal care and cosmetics products.

Direct-to-Consumer (D2C) Retailers. Retailers that utilize internet platforms to directly sell products/services to individual consumers.

Display Ads. Display ads are image or video ads on websites partnered with a display network. They can offer a visually engaging tool to drive sales, traffic, and brand awareness.

Distribution Order Management (DOM). This refers to fulfillment optimization management, so orders arrive to customers on time while incurring the lowest cost. DOM system encompasses order routing, order splitting, shipping, inventory forecasting, reordering, and inventory management.

Dual-Channel Retailers. Retailers that operate both in brick-and-mortar stores and online through e-commerce platforms or catalogs along with a website or mobile apps. The concept of dual-channel retailing emerged in the early days of e-commerce when online shopping became popular in the late 1990s and early 2000s.

Economic Nexus. In U.S. tax law, economic nexus exists when a retailer earns above a sales or revenue threshold in that specific state. Currently, each state may impose different thresholds on the economic nexus.

Email Marketing. Sending out emails to a list of accounts to reach a wider audience and engage with customers in a more interactive way than traditional mail marketing. It offers omnichannel retailers a cost-effective, personalized, and highly measurable way of marketing.

E-Micropayments. Small transactions occurring in the e-commerce environment.

Endless Aisle. A marketing and sales technique by which retailers can provide in-store customers with the opportunity to order products that are either not normally sold in the store or that are currently out of stock. It's also known as "buy in-store, ship to customer."

Engagement Rate. An important indicator to measure the effectiveness of social media marketing. It is calculated as total engagements (i.e., the sum of shares, comments, likes, etc.) divided by total followers, multiplied by 100 percent.

Enterprise Resource Planning (ERP). A process that integrates all back-office functions to create a master data environment including locations of each component and inventory.

E-Skimming. Stealing credit card information and personal data from the payment card processing page on an e-commerce website.

Ethical and Value-Based Shoppers. Shoppers who purchase goods/services from brands that align with their values whenever practical.

Evaluation Stage. When potential customers will determine whether they want to purchase the product. Many factors influence customers' evaluation of a product. The goal at this stage is to help eliminate consumers' doubt about making the purchase. Identifying the pain points that prevent a customer from making a purchase could be useful for identifying effective content at this stage.

Evergreen Content. The content that is continuously relevant to customers without seasonal effect.

E-Wallet. An advanced digital payment method integrated with mobile wallets which refers to the e-wallet system operated via mobile device and app.

Factory Outlet Store. Also known as designer outlet stores, these are typically located in outlet malls and have become popular destinations for value-seeking shoppers in the United States and many other countries. Shoppers are drawn to these malls for the opportunity to purchase designer goods at discounted prices.

Fair Use. A statutory doctrine that promotes freedom of expression by permitting the unlicensed use of copyright-protected works in certain circumstances, such as criticism, comment, news reporting, teaching, scholarship, and research. Section 107 of the Copyright Act provides the framework for determining whether something is of fair use.

Front-End Services. The customer-facing services that occur on the retail selling floor or online to assist the customer's needs and inquiries. For instance, front-end services include cashiers, customer information, returns, and concierge services.

Fulfillment System. The organized management of receiving, processing, and delivering orders to the customer.

Full-Line Department Store. A department store that offers many different lines of products, including both soft lines (e.g., apparel and household textile goods), hard lines (e.g., sporting goods, furniture, electrical goods, etc.), and many different services, including wrapping, delivery, and credit.

Full-Line Discount Stores. Retailers that sell various brand products at much lower costs.

Gamification. The application of game elements and mechanics to non-game contexts, such as education, health, or business.

General Data Protection Regulation (GDPR). Established by the European Commission in April 2016 and enforced on May 25, 2018, GDPR was implemented to protect consumers in the European Union by giving them more control over their personal data in the form of subject data rights. There are eight different types of rights included in the GDPR. The most distinct effect that makes GDPR different from the previous privacy laws is that GDPR can impose administrative fines for noncompliance up to €20 million ($24.1 million) or 4 percent of annual global revenue, whichever is the highest.

Horizontal Marketplace. A platform that serves as a one-stop-shop experience. The focus of the horizontal marketplace is to offer various product types to all different types of customers. They want to be the one-stop shop for many consumers and offer the platform to all different types of sellers. Examples of horizontal marketplaces are eBay, Amazon, and AliExpress.

In-App Notification. The notification sent when a customer opens the app.

In-Bound Logistics. Warehouse processes to ensure proper supervision of goods from entering the warehouse or receiving of the goods.

Independent Structures. Those in which all operating channels operate independently and information is not shared between them. This format is commonly used by smaller retail businesses.

Influencer Marketing. A marketing practice that employs leading, niche content creators (influencers) to improve brands' desired business outcomes.

Information Privacy. Consumers' ability to control how, and to what extent, their personal information is to be transmitted to others.

In-House Order Fulfillment. An order processed and fulfilled by the business itself, without seeking assistance from outside the business.

Integrity. Integrity in the context of e-commerce security refers to information shared by the consumer that will not be altered in any way by anyone, including the business owners or an unauthorized party.

Internet of Things (IoT). A term used to describe the network of physical objects—"things"—that are embedded with sensors, software, and other technologies to connect and exchange data with other devices and systems over the internet.

Key Opinion Leaders (KOLs). People who have high-level expertise on a specialized topic within a particular field.

Key Performance Indicator (KPI). A series of measurements that help a business determine if they are achieving their goals.

Keyword Planner. A tool that helps marketers identify the best keywords to use based on customers' interests and purchase intent. Google price keywords based on the search volume. The lower the Google keyword search volume, the cheaper it should be to win an auction and show your ad at the top of the SERP. The exact prices are determined by how many other businesses are bidding on the same keywords.

Limited-Line Department Store. A department store that carries a narrower range of merchandise than a full-line department store; typically, a limited-line department store usually has high-quality merchandise at high prices for the upscale market. For instance, Saks Fifth Avenue and Neiman Marcus.

Live Commerce. A new form of online shopping that combines live video streaming with e-commerce. Live commerce allows customers to watch and shop at the same time, and interact with the presenter and other viewers through chatroom.

Live Stream Shopping. This is modernized TV shopping programs which enable viewers to buy products directly from creator-hosted streamed events on the internet.

Local Campaigns. These promote store locations across channels such as Search, Display, Google Maps, and YouTube. To use local campaigns, omnichannel retailers need to have an account on platforms such as Google My Business (https://www.google.com/business/).

Logistics. The entire process of planning, implementing, and controlling the efficient flow of materials and products, services, information, energy, people, and other resources that move into, through, and out of a firm (in both the public and private sectors) to the customers.

Metaverse. A concept that refers to the fusion of physical and digital worlds in which individuals can interact, create, and explore in an immersive environment. The fashion industry is one of the sectors that is embracing the metaverse as a new opportunity to reach and engage customers, showcase products, and express creativity.

Micro Production. A strategy using small-batch manufacturing, which is highly automated, has a small scale, needs fewer resources to set up and operate, and offers a broader range of process capabilities and startup businesses.

Mobile Commerce. Business transactional activities occurring via a mobile device.

Mobile Marketing. It refers to two different marketing methods—one method is marketing on or with a mobile device (such as a mobile phone) and the other, more traditional method is marketing "on-the-go," or location-based or proximity marketing.

Mobile-First Design. The strategy of building your website for mobile devices before developing the desktop version. Mobile-first design is based on a strategy called progressive enhancement, which suggests that it is easier to begin with a simple prototype, in this case, a mobile page, and continue to add and adjust content to conform to the larger and more complex device formats such as desktops or tablets.

Multichannel Retailers. Retailers that operate in brick-and-mortar stores, direct marketing, direct selling, online, and other electronic methods to transact business with customers.

Multichannel Supply Chain Management (SCM). Offering additional transactional channels to consumers that allow them to access product information and purchase goods without geographical and temporal limitations.

Multi-Level Marketing. A compensation plan in which individuals may earn compensation based on personal sales and/or the sales of others in their sales organizations. Direct selling companies primarily use multi-level marketing compensation plans.

Non-Fungible Token (NFT). A novel way of creating and owning one-of-a-kind, indivisible, and verifiable blockchain-based digital assets.

Off-Price Retailers. Retailers that sell high-quality goods at low prices. These stores sell designer clothes, branded apparel, etc. An off-price retailer targets end-of-season stock, closeouts, overruns, returns, and inventory excess, so that they can offer significant discounts over the retail price.

Offsite SEO. Having third-party review sites or mentions may increase a retailer's website credibility, hence increasing the ranking results.

Omnichannel Retailers. Retailers that provide customers with an integrated shopping experience across various channels, including brick-and-mortar stores, online stores, mobile apps, social media platforms, and other channels.

Omnichannel Supply Chain Management (SCM). A set of processes to effectively and efficiently integrate suppliers, manufacturers, distribution centers, distributors, and retailers so that products are produced and distributed through collaborative planning of demand, production, logistics, and inventory deployment.

Onboarding Email/Text Messages. When customers sign up for an account or service, brands can show an immediate appreciation by sending onboarding emails or text messages. These emails usually welcome new customers, offer instructions on using their product or service, and encourage further engagement and interaction with the company.

Online Calls-to-Action. This can include buttons like "add to cart," "checkout now," "share with," "like on social," etc.

Online Marketplaces. Online marketplaces are defined by two criteria: 1) there are many sellers and buyers on the platforms, and 2) buyers can complete transactions without leaving the site. Omnichannel retailers utilize online marketplaces as one of the channels to sell.

Onsite SEO. The practice of optimizing your own website elements in order to rank higher in the SERP.

Order Automation. Orders that are automatically managed by software using the new order details that are sent from an e-commerce site to a warehouse.

Order Management System (OMS). A software platform that can track your sales, orders, fulfillment, inventory, and the process of linking them together.

Out-Bound Logistics. Warehouse processes to ensure proper supervision of goods from leaving the warehouse.

Partner Retail Loyalty Program. A type of loyalty program offering a retail loyalty program with a strategic partner.

Patent. A property right that is granted to the inventor(s) for an invention. The term of a new patent can vary from one country to another. In the United States, the term is twenty years from the date on which the application for the patent was filed with the United States Patent and Trademark Office (USPTO).

Pay-Per-Click (PPC). The pre-negotiated cost that a brand agrees to pay for each click ad received.

Personal Identifiable Information (PII). Any representation of information that permits the identity of an individual to whom the information applies to be reasonably inferred by either direct or indirect means. In the online environment, the concept of personal identifiable information (PII) has diminished relevance as it becomes easier to associate an individual with a digital device.

Physical Nexus. In U.S. tax law, physical nexus means a retailer has a physical presence in the state, whether it is an office, store, or warehouse.

Point of Sale (POS). The point of sale is the stage where customers are to be effectively served through smooth and pleasant transactional experience as a part of customer journey.

Pop-Up Shop. A temporary retail space which is typically used to introduce a new product line, test a new market, or generate awareness for a product or cause. Pop-up shops are evolving and taking on greater importance as brands lean into direct-to-consumer efforts and retail real estate firms see it as a robust driver of traffic.

Post-Purchase Stage. In the post-purchase stage, consumers will perform a post-purchase evaluation and see if they are satisfied with the purchase. If they are satisfied with the product, they may not have any reactions. However, if they are not satisfied with the product, they may complain to the retailers or return the product. For omnichannel retailers, they should send a follow-up email to ask their customers if they are satisfied once the products or services are delivered. They may also invite customers to write a review for them to provide positive word of mouth for them.

Product Inventory System. A method used to manage and locate inventory. The inventory control software can help fashion retailers manage product (re)ordering by monitoring all aspects of the inventory quantity on the shelves, storage rooms, and warehouses.

Proximity Marketing. This involves targeting potential consumers with personalized advertisements based on their interests and enticing them to make a purchasing decision in the immediate future. This marketing is possible due to the beacon technology.

Purchase (Conversion) Stage. This is when consumers take the desired action, such as completing a transaction, signing up for an email list, or booking an appointment. This stage is crucial for omnichannel retailers because it's when consumers feel confident in a product or service and are ready to take action. To ensure a successful transaction, it's essential to provide information related to shipping/delivery options, payments, and return policies.

Purchase Dissonance. Also known as buyer's remorse, purchase dissonance is a psychological state that occurs when a person feels regret or uncertainty after making a purchase.

Pure Play Retailers. Refers to online retailers that have never operated brick-and-mortar stores nor engaged in other types of nonstore distribution.

Push Notification. The notification is sent whether a customer opens the app or not.

Pyramid Schemes. Different from multi-level marketing, pyramid schemes describe an illegal investment pitch that relies on promising unrealistic returns from imaginary investments.

Re-Commerce. A system in which the used/pre-owned goods and services are shared, bartered, traded, and transacted between individuals free of charge or for a fee.

Responsive Design. Also known as adaptive design. Responsive design is a technique that suggests automatically adjusting a website design based on the size of the user's screens.

Retention Stage. Omnichannel retailers can fully integrate their ecosystem to offer free services, send out promotional incentives (e.g., discount codes, free samples, etc.), offer cross-sell recommendations, send out re-order reminders, or re-engagement to encourage customers who have not visited the website/store recently to do so.

Return on Investment (ROI). The monetary return a retailer gets back from an investment. ROI is an important indicator for retail upper management when deciding where to allocate operation and marketing budget.

Returns Management. The reverse logistics and order management process that can help the omnichannel retailers improve their customer's shopping experience.

Reverse Logistics. A way to handle the return, reuse, recycling, or disposal of products that make the reverse journey from the customer to the supplier.

Search Ads. (Also called paid-search ads). Search ads are ads served based on someone's search query. It is a great tool to reach people when they are searching for the products or services you offer. If done right, search ads can drive sales and traffic for omnichannel retailers.

Search Engine Marketing (SEM). A type of marketing strategy using a search engine algorithm which drives more new website visitors than any other online advertising method. It enables more precise targeting of ready-to-purchase customers.

Search Engine Optimization (SEO). A practice of optimizing the web content so search engines such as Google or Bing can recognize online channels and match them with search queries better.

Search Engine Results Pages (SERPs). A search engine's response to a keyword(s) query.

Seasonal Content. The content that is created for certain holidays, seasons, or events.

Semi-Integrated Structures. These share some but not all operational and informational tools across channels. For example, merchandising and pricing in a core brick-and-mortar business may differ from the company's online store, or some divisions may be run separately or partially integrated.

Shoppable Content. Any form of content that allows customers to buy the products directly from the content they are viewing in real-time, whether it's a social media post, image, video, or even a virtual reality game

Shopping Ads. These appear on search results and the Google Shopping tab. Shopping ads are ideal for omnichannel retailers who are looking to increase their sales.

Single-Channel Retailers. Retailers that reach customers through only one distribution option, regardless of whether it is online, catalog, mail-order, face-to-face selling, or traditional brick-and-mortar retail.

SMART Principle. A principle of choosing KPIs to evaluate business goals refers to selecting a Specific business goal; the goal should be Measurable, Achievable, Relevant to overall business objectives, and Time-bound.

Social Commerce. Selling products or services with social media websites, such as Facebook, Instagram, X (formerly Twitter), TikTok, Pinterest, or YouTube, which support user-generated content and social interaction.

Social Media (Social Networks). A group of internet-based applications that build on the ideological and technological foundations of Web 2.0 and allow the creation and exchange of user-generated content.

Social Media Advertising. The advertising and marketing promotional practices that use social networks to increase brand or company awareness or promote particular products, which eventually lead to sales.

Social Shopping. The act of using social media to find reviews and recommendations about products, and then using those reviews to guide your purchase decision. Social shopping brings social media and e-commerce together.

Social-Local-Mobile (Slo-Lo-Mo) Marketing. A marketing strategy that micro-targets prospects and consumers whenever, wherever, with contextually relevant content, information, or promotion that is designed to be shared on social media platforms.

Specialty Store. A store that focuses on selling a specific type of product or a narrow range of related products within a particular niche or category. These stores often have a more targeted and specialized selection of products than larger, general merchandise retailers.

Subscription Business Model. A business model in which a customer agrees to pay a recurring fee at regular intervals for access to a product/service.

Television Retailing. Also known as TV shopping or home shopping, this is a form of direct response marketing that involves selling products or services through a television program or channel.

Text Marketing. Text marketing can include short message service (SMS) and back-and-forth messaging, which allows recipients to respond to brief customer service questions and provide the company with information about their preferences.

Third-Party Logistics (3PL). Outsourcing of one or more functions of logistics services. Most common 3PL services are warehousing and fulfillment of the order.

Trademark. A trademark is any word, name, symbol, design, or color capable of distinguishing the goods or services of a business from others.

Trademark Infringement. Unauthorized use of a trademark or service mark (or a mark that is substantially similar to the underlying mark) on competing or related goods and services.

Transactional Email/Text Messages. Typically defined as automated email or text notifications regarding the purchases made via the e-commerce site and in-store retail environments. These emails/texts are activated when customers perform specific actions such as confirming the shipment of the orders or returns of the ordered products, activating/deactivating an account, starting a subscription, or requesting a password recovery, among others.

Transportation Management System (TMS). A platform/software providing the retailer with visibility into day-to-day transportation operations and streamlining the shipping process to make it easier for businesses to manage and optimize their transportation operations, whether they are by land, air, or sea.

Triggered Emails/Text Messages. Email or text messages that are triggered by an action taken (or not) by a website visitor or a change in a customer's behavior or profile via trigger marketing automation.

User Experience (UX). A good user experience provides customers with the ability to find information quickly, easily search for the products they want, and be able to pay as smoothly as possible.

User-Generated Content (UGC). UGC can be likes, ratings, reviews, questions and answers, and user-submitted images and videos.

Utility Patents. A utility patent may be granted to anyone who invents or discovers any new and useful process, machine, article of manufacture, or composition of matter, or any new and useful improvement thereof. Some examples of utility patents that omnichannel retailers can obtain include software programs, fulfillment center design, innovative product materials, etc.

Vend. This is one of the most adopted POS systems for online retailers, and is straightforward to use for in-store or online retailing and/or for a business operating multiple locations

Vertical Marketplaces. Vertical marketplaces focus on selling products within a specific segment or to an identified niche market. For instance, a vertical marketplace may focus on (re)selling luxury products, handmade crafts, or a single product category like sneakers.

Visual Search. A technology that allows users/customers/businesses to use real-world images such as screenshots, images downloaded from the internet, and/or your photographs as the stimuli for online searches. Once pictures are submitted to search engines such as Google, artificial intelligence (AI) deciphers the content and context of these images and generates a list of related results.

Wardrobing. Fraudulent activities that occur in both a traditional retail context and omnichannel retail context, where customers have purchased items with a clear intention to wear/use the items for a special occasion only to return the worn product for a refund later.

Warehouse Clubs. Retailers offer a more limited range of products than a traditional supermarket and aim to attract shoppers who wish to save money by buying in bulk. Costco, Sam's Club, and BJ's Wholesale Club are examples of warehouse clubs in the U.S.

Web 2.0. The second generation of World Wide Web technology enables individual users to interact and collaborate with each other on the web.

Website Usability. The level of ease and accessibility presented to visitors upon browsing and interacting with a website.

Notes

Chapter 1

1. Encyclopaedia Britannica. (2024). *Industrial revolution.* https://www.britannica.com/money/Industrial-Revolution
2. Tortora, P. G., & Marcketti, S. B. (2021). *Survey of historic costume.* New York: Fairchild Books .
3. Macy's. (2024). *Macy's brand heritage.* https://www.macys.com/s/brand-heritage/history/
4. Graff, C. (2022). *Making automobiles last during World War II.* The National WWII Museum. https://www.nationalww2museum.org/war/articles/automobile-rationing-world-war-ii
5. Companies History. (2023). *Carrefour SA history, profile and history video.* https://www.companieshistory.com/carrefour/
6. Mall of America. (2023). *Best in retail, entertainment + attractions.* https://mallofamerica.com/about
7. Sopadjieva, E., Dholakia, U. M., & Benjamin, B. (2017, January 3). *A study of 46,000 shoppers shows that omnichannel retailing works.* Harvard Business Review. https://hbr.org/2017/01/a-study-of-46000-shoppers-shows-that-omnichannel-retailing-works
8. Digital Commerce 360 Staff. (2022, August 23). *Share of Top 500 using omnichannel options soars compared to pre-pandemic.* https://www.digitalcommerce360.com/2022/08/23/the-share-of-top-500-retailers-using-omnichannel-options-soars-compared-to-the-pre-pandemic-era/
9. Rodríguez-Torrico, P., Cabezudo, R. S. J., & San-Martin, S. (2017). Tell me what they are like and I will tell you where they buy. An analysis of omnichannel consumer behavior. *Computers in Human Behavior, 68*, 465–471.
10. Beck, N., & Rygl, D. (2015). Categorization of multiple channel retailing in multi-, cross-, and omni-channel retailing for retailers and retailing. *Journal of Retailing and Consumer Services, 27,* 170–178.
11. Kats, R. (2021, March 8). *Retailers plan to increase investments across digital channels as many solidify their omnichannel plans.* Insider Intelligence. https://www.insiderintelligence.com/content/retailers-plan-increase-investments-across-digital-channels-many-solidify-their-omnichannel-plans
12. Aviso, A. (2024). *BOPIS statistics: Overview. Fit Small Business.* https://fitsmallbusiness.com/bopis-statistics/#bopis-statistics-overview
13. Total Retail. (2023). *2023 Top 100 omnichannel retailers report.* https://www.mytotalretail.com/article/total-retail-releases-its-2023-top-100-omnichannel-retailers-report/
14. Nordstrom, Inc. (2022, May 24). *Nordstrom reports first quarter 2022 earnings. Nordstrom.* https://press.nordstrom.com/news-releases/news-release-details/nordstrom-reports-first-quarter-2022-earnings
15. Vembar, K. (2023, January 17). *Macy's CEO: "We are in the final stretch" of closing stores.* Retail Dive. https://www.retaildive.com/news/macys-ceo-final-stretch-closing-stores/640465/
16. Howland, D. (2020, February 3). *Macy's launches new store concept in Texas.* Retail Dive. https://www.retaildive.com/news/macys-launches-new-store-concept-in-texas/571580/
17. Business Wire. (2022, July 20). *Macy's accelerates the growth of its off-mall, small-format strategy.* https://www.businesswire.com/news/home/20220720005342/en/
18. AEO Inc. (2022). *Quiet Platforms announces launch of new nationwide delivery network.* https://investors.ae.com/press-releases/news-details/2022/Quiet-Platforms-Announces-Launch-of-New-Nationwide-Delivery-Network/
19. Gray, C. (2022). Google Cloud announces partnership with H&M to advance AI. *AI Magazine.* https://aimagazine.com/machine-learning/google-cloud-announces-partnership-with-h-m-to-advance-ai
20. Keenan, J. (2019). *Stores at the center of Hibbett Sports' digital strategy.* TotalRetail.https://www.mytotalretail.com/article/stores-at-the-center-of-hibbett-sports-digital-strategy/
21. FCC, Federal Communications Commission. (2021) *Broadband speed guide.* https://www.fcc.gov/consumers/guides/broadband-speed-guide
22. Cooper, T. (2022, May 6). *The decade in broadband: 2020 statistics & predictions.* Broadbandnow Research. https://broadbandnow.com/research/broadband-2020
23. Laricchia, F. (2022, December 6). *Percentage of U.S. adults who own a smartphone from 2011 to 2021.* Statista. https://www.statista.com/statistics/219865/percentage-of-us-adults-who-own-a-smartphone/
24. StatCounter. (2023). *Desktop vs mobile vs tablet market share worldwide—January 2023.* https://gs.statcounter.com/platform-market-share/desktop-mobile-tablet/worldwide

25. Wurmser, Y. (2021, June 2). *US time spent with mobile 2021: Pandemic gains stick even as growth cools.* Insider Intelligence. https://content-na1.emarketer.com/us-time-spent-with-mobile-2021
26. McKinsey & Company. (2023). *McKinsey Quarterly: Five Fifty.* https://www.mckinsey.com/capabilities/strategy-and-corporate-finance/our-insights/five-fifty-the-quickening
27. *Social media fact sheet.* (2021, April 7). Pew Research Center. https://www.pewresearch.org/internet/fact-sheet/social-media/
28. Georgiev, D. (2023, January 31). *How much time do people spend on social media in 2023.* Techjury. https://techjury.net/blog/time-spent-on-social-media/
29. Statista Research Department. (2022, July 27). *Apparel, footwear and accessories retail e-commerce revenue in the United States from 2017 to 2025.* Statista. https://www.statista.com/statistics/278890/us-apparel-and-accessories-retail-e-commerce-revenue/
30. Insider Intelligence. (2020). *Which product categories have US Amazon Prime Members purchased digitally in the past month?* https://chart-na1.emarketer.com/235740/which-product-categories-have-us-amazon-prime-members-purchased-digitally-past-month-of-respondents-feb-april-2020
31. Smith, P. (2023, February 15). *Global apparel market—statistics & facts.* Statista. https://www.statista.com/topics/5091/apparel-market-worldwide/
32. Smith, P. (2023, February 13). *Revenue of the apparel market worldwide by country in 2022.* Statista. https://www.statista.com/forecasts/758683/revenue-of-the-apparel-market-worldwide-by-country
33. Statista.. (n.d.). *Apparel – Worldwide.* Retrieved February 27, 2023, from https://www.statista.com/outlook/cmo/apparel/womens-apparel/worldwide
34. Lebow, S. (2021, Aug. 19). *Worldwide ecommerce continues double-digit growth following pandemic push to online.* Insider Intelligence. https://content-na1.emarketer.com/worldwide-ecommerce-continues-double-digit-growth-following-pandemic-push-online?ecid=nl1014
35. Unglesbee, B. (2021, July 6). *Despite online growth, stores will still account for three-fourths of retail sales in 2024, Forrester says.* Retail Dive. https://www.retaildive.com/news/despite-online-growth-stores-will-still-account-for-three-fourths-of-retai/602862/
36. Zhang, K. Z., & Benyoucef, M. (2016). Consumer behavior in social commerce: A literature review. *Decision Support Systems, 86*, 95–108.
37. Chevalier, S. (2021, July 27). *Share of online consumers in the United States who use social media for online shopping in 2019.* Statista. https://www.statista.com/statistics/1130265/share-online-consumers-us-social-media-online-shopping/
38. Koetsier, J. (2022, January 22). *Livestream shopping: A $500 billion market in 2022 as Amazon, Google, Facebook, TikTok jump in?* Forbes. https://www.forbes.com/sites/johnkoetsier/2022/01/22/livestream-shopping-a-500-billion-market-in-2022-as-amazon-google-facebook-tiktok-jump-in/?sh=57fcc4493bc5
39. Amazon.com. (2023). *How to shop Amazon Go.* https://www.amazon.com/b?ie=UTF8&node=16008589011
40. World Economic Forum. (2021). *Net-zero challenge: The supply chain opportunity.* https://www3.weforum.org/docs/WEF_Net_Zero_Challenge_The_Supply_Chain_Opportunity_2021.pdf
41. Lowitt, E. (2011, October 3). *Patagonia's "Buy Less" campaign may lead to more revenue.* Harvard Business Review. https://hbr.org/2011/10/patagonias-buy-less-campai
42. DoneGood Collaborator. (2020, August 26). *What is ethical shopping – and why is it the world's most powerful force for change?* https://donegood.co/blogs/news/does-shopping-ethically-really-make-a-difference
43. The Centre for Retail Research. (2021). *Ethical consumer, the green shopper.* https://www.retailresearch.org/ethical-shoppers.html
44. Curtin, M. (2018). *73 percent of Millennials are willling to spend more money on this 1 type of product.* https://www.inc.com/melanie-curtin/73-percent-of-millennials-are-willing-to-spend-more-money-on-this-1-type-of-product.html
45. Edelson, S. (2018, December 18). Conscious consumers lead to retail shift. *WWD.* https://wwd.com/feature/conscious-consumers-lead-to-retail-shift-1202935386/
46. Ibid.
47. Petrov, C. (2021, March 26). *22 amazing sharing economy statistics to share in 2020.* SpendMeNot. https://spendmenot.com/blog/sharing-economy-statistics/.
48. Ibid.
49. Financial News Media. (2020, December 7). *Global sharing economy could reach $335 billion by 2025.* https://www.prnewswire.com/news-releases/global-sharing-economy-could-reach-335-billion-by-2025-301187042.html
50. PYMNTS. (2020, September 8). *Wardrobe: Recommerce meets the sharing economy.* https://www.pymnts.com/news/retail/2020/wardrobe-recommerce-meets-the-sharing-economy-in-bid-to-become-the-airbnb-of-fashion
51. Joinwardrob.com, 2023.
52. Tax Tips. (2020, January 16). *11 side business ideas for 2020.* https://sharedeconomycpa.com/blog/side-business-ideas-2020
53. Palmer, A. (2021). *Online clothing reseller Poshmark closes up more than 140% on the first day of trading.* CNBC. https://www.cnbc.com/2021/01/14/poshmark-ipo-posh-starts-trading-on-nasdaq.html
54. Retail Technology. (2022, July 4). *H&M fashions new data platform.* https://www.retailtechnology.co.uk/news/7752/hm-fashions-new-data-platform/

Chapter 2

1. Nelson, A. (2022). *I shopped at Macy's and JCPenney. Only one store won my money even though the other was way trendier.* Business Insider. https://www.businessinsider.com/macys-jcpenney-christmas-shopping-comparison-review-

2022-12#the-hickory-farms-display-at-jcpenney-left-something-to-be-desired-but-the-price-was-a-steal-the-original-price-for-a-seasonal-collection-was-60-but-on-sale-it-cost-24-31

2. Dawkins, J. (2024). JCPenney has become TikTokers' unlikely beauty obsession. Business Insider. https://www.businessinsider.com/tiktok-loves-jcpenney-beauty-2024-1&post-bottom-piano-recommendations
3. Smith, P. (2023). *Department store sales in the United States from 1992 to 2021.* Statista. https://www.statista.com/statistics/197712/annual-department-store-sales-in-the-us-since-1992/
4. Lal, R., & Alvarez, J. B. (2011). *Death knell for the category killers?* Harvard Business Review. https://hbr.org/2011/12/death-knell-for-the-category-k
5. Zhang, Z. J. (2023). *Why category killers can't survive.* Wharton Business Daily. https://knowledge.wharton.upenn.edu/podcast/wharton-business-daily-podcast/why-category-killers-cant-survive/
6. Dukes, A. J., Geylani, T. and Srinivasan, K. , *Consumption trends and the warehouse club retail format* (May 14, 2019). Available at SSRN: https://ssrn.com/abstract=3194302 or http://dx.doi.org/10.2139/ssrn.3194302
7. Meisenzahl, M. (2022, December 24). *I compared Costco, Sam's Club, and BJ's. Costco is the best, even though its membership is most expensive.* Business Insider. https://www.businessinsider.com/which-is-the-best-warehouse-club-costco-sams-club-bjs-compared-2022-6
8. Tighe, D. (2022). *U.S. dollar stores—statistics & facts.* Statista. https://www.statista.com/topics/1343/dollar-stores-in-the-us/#topicOverview
9. Wells, J. (2017, February 8). *Dollar disruptors: How discount stores are shaking up the grocery world.* Retail Dive. https://www.retaildive.com/news/dollar-disruptors-how-discount-stores-are-shaking-up-the-grocery-world/435559/
10. Target Dollar Spot Finds. @target.dollarspot.finds (2023, March 18). *Target Bullseye's Playground – Sharing my target finds.* Instagram. https://www.instagram.com/target.dollarspot.finds/related_profiles/?hl=en
11. Warner, A. (2022, March 27). *PSA: Everything from Target's dollar section is online — and it's overflowing with so many cute spring finds.* People. https://people.com/lifestyle/target-bullseye-shop-dollar-finds-march-2022/
12. der Weduwen, A., Pettegree, A., & Kemp, G. (Eds.). (2021). *Book trade catalogues in early modern Europe* (Vol. 93). Leiden: Brill.
13. National Day Calendar. (2022, November 8). *National mail order catalog day.* https://nationaldaycalendar.com/national-mail-order-catalog-day-august-18/
14. Ibid.
15. Direct Selling Association. (2023). *What is direct selling?* https://www.dsa.org/
16. Direct Selling News. (2023, March 18). *2022 global 100 list of top direct selling companies in the world based on 2021 revenue.* https://www.directsellingnews.com/global-100-lists/
17. Mary Kay. (2023, March 18). *About Mary Kay.* https://www.marykay.com/en-us/about-mary-kay
18. Lieber, C. (2018, November 1). *Why so many hip start-ups advertise with snail mail.* Vox. https://www.vox.com/the-goods/2018/11/1/18048418/mail-marketing-coupons-away-casper-harrys-glossier
19. Zhang, J. (2020, February 11). *Why catalogs are making a comeback.* Harvard Business Review. https://hbr.org/2020/02/why-catalogs-are-making-a-comeback
20. Zhang, J. (2022, July 19). *How paper catalogs remain relevant in a digital age.* Harvard Business Review. https://hbr.org/2022/07/how-paper-catalogs-remain-relevant-in-a-digital-age
21. Ibid.
22. Uniqode Phygital. (2024). *QR Codes on brochures: Colorful QR Codes to improve your ROI.* https://www.uniqode.com/qr-code-generator/for-brochures
23. Jai, T. M., & Tung, T. (2015). Fashion innovativeness, information technology innovativeness, and prior experience as factors influencing adoption of apparel mobile E-catalogs. *Journal of Global Fashion Marketing, 6*(3), 163–179.
24. Ibid.
25. IBIS World. (2023, January 10). *Telemarketing & call centers in the US – market size 2004 – 2029.* https://www.ibisworld.com/industry-statistics/market-size/telemarketing-call-centers-united-states/
26. Boada, N. (2021, June 21). *Lead generation: What is it & how forms can help.* Cyberclick. https://www.cyberclick.net/numericalblogen/lead-generation-what-is-it-how-forms-can-help
27. Dixon, M., McKenna, T., & Shepherd, T. (2021, February 16). *4 behaviors that boost inbound sales.* Harvard Business Review. https://hbr.org/2021/02/4-behaviors-that-boost-inbound-sales
28. Boada, N. (2021, June 21). *Lead generation: What is it & how forms can help.* Cyberclick. https://www.cyberclick.net/numericalblogen/lead-generation-what-is-it-how-forms-can-help
29. Boada, N. (2022, April 19). *What is telemarketing? Definition, advantages, and examples.* Cyberclick. https://www.cyberclick.net/numericalblogen/what-is-telemarketing-definition-advantages-and-examples
30. Ibid.
31. Big Commerce. (2023). *What is telemarketing?* https://www.bigcommerce.com/ecommerce-answers/what-is-telemarketing/
32. Textedly.com (2023). Pricing for SMS marketing built to scale. https://www.textedly.com/pricing/
33. Hott, A. (2021, March 25). *SMS marketing: The good, the bad, and the don't you dare.* Optinmonster. https://optinmonster.com/sms-marketing/
34. Direct Selling Association. (2022). *Releases data showing record high sales and customers in the U.S. in 2021.* https://www.dsa.org/events/news/individual-press-release/direct-selling-association-releases-data-showing-record-high-sales-and-customers-in-the-u.s.-in-2021

35. Direct Selling Association. (2023). *Direct selling in the United States: 2022 industry overview*. www.dsa.org/benefits/research
36. JPMorgan Chase & Co. (2023). *Enriching women's lives: The Mary Kay legacy*. https://www.jpmorganchase.com/news-stories/stories-mary-kay
37. Linge, M. (2021, October 2). How the founder of Mary Kay went from single mom to billion-dollar beauty queen. *NY Post*. https://nypost.com/2021/10/02/how-mary-kays-founder-went-from-single-mom-to-billion-dollar-beauty-queen/
38. Kidder, S. (2023). *5 luxury brands that bet big on pop-up stores*. Storefront. https://www.thestorefront.com/mag/5-luxury-brands-that-bet-big-on-pop-up-stores/
39. Louis Vuitton. (2021). *Opening of ephemeral pop-up store Louis Vuitton x Virgil Abloh at Quai de la Megisserie in Paris*. https://us.louisvuitton.com/eng-us/stories/louis-vuitton-and-nike-air-force-1#gallery
40. IBIS World. (2022, June 24). *Cable shopping networks in the US – market size 2007–2028*. https://www.ibisworld.com/industry-statistics/market-size/cable-shopping-networks-united-states/
41. Agee, T., & Martin, B. A. (2001). Planned or impulse purchases: How to create effective infomercials. *Journal of Advertising Research*, *41*(6), 35–42.
42. Script to Screen. (2021, September 9). *Next generation of infomercials*. https://www.scripttoscreen.com/next-generation-of-infomercials/
43. Martin, B. A., Bhimy, A. C., & Agee, T. (2002). Infomercials and advertising effectiveness: An empirical study. *Journal of Consumer Marketing*, *19*(6), 468–480.
44. Build. (2023). *Popular infomercial examples and how to write a successful infomercial script*. https://buildd.co/marketing/infomercial-examples
45. Walk-Morris, T. (2020, July 9). *How COVID-19 boosted QVC, HSN, and livestreaming*. Retail Dive. https://www.retaildive.com/news/how-covid-19-boosted-qvc-hsn-and-livestreaming/581016/
46. Keveney, B. (2020, September 7). *How QVC, HSN thrive during COVID-19 pandemic with the help of cookware, Skype and stay-at-home viewers*. USA Today. https://www.usatoday.com/story/entertainment/tv/2020/09/03/how-home-shopping-giants-qvc-hsn-weathered-pandemic/5608060002/
47. Conley, P. (2023, February 17). *US e-commerce in 2022 tops $1 trillion for first time*. Digital Commerce. https://www.digitalcommerce360.com/article/us-ecommerce-sales/
48. Lebow, S. (2021, August 19). *Worldwide e-commerce continues double-digit growth following pandemic push to online*. Insider Intelligence. https://content-na1.emarketer.com/worldwide-ecommerce-continues-double-digit-growth-following-pandemic-push-online?ecid=nl1014
49. Smith, P. (2023, February 15). *Global apparel market – statistics & facts*. Statista. https://www.statista.com/topics/5091/apparel-market-worldwide/
50. McKinsey & Company (2020). *How COVID-19 has pushed the technology tipping point and transformed business forever*. https://www.mckinsey.com/capabilities/strategy-and-corporate-finance/our-insights/how-covid-19-has-pushed-companies-over-the-technology-tipping-point-and-transformed-business-forever
51. Unglesbee, B. (2021, July 6). *Despite online growth, stores will still account for three-fourths of retail sales in 2024, Forrester says*. Retail Dive. https://www.retaildive.com/news/despite-online-growth-stores-will-still-account-for-three-fourths-of-retai/602862/
52. Anastasia, D., & G., Dmitriy. (2019, May 10). *Types of online marketplaces: Complete categorization with examples*. Ruby Garage. https://rubygarage.org/blog/types-of-online-marketplaces
53. Tarry, S. (2020). *Online resale marketplace StockX reports record-breaking cyber weekend*. Retail Insider. https://retail-insider.com/retail-insider/2020/12/online-resale-market-place-stockx-reports-record-breaking-cyber-weekend/
54. Laricchia, F. (2023, March 6). *Daily time spent on mobile phones in the U.S. from 2019 to 2024*. Statista. https://www.statista.com/statistics/1045353/mobile-device-daily-usage-time-in-the-us/
55. Ceci, L. (2023, March 6). *Share of global daily time spend online via mobile devices 2013–2022*. Statista. https://www.statista.com/statistics/1289723/share-time-spent-mobile-internet-daily/
56. Koch, L. (2019, September 12). *Deals and product search features drive retail app downloads for in-store shoppers*. Insider Intelligence. https://www.emarketer.com/content/in-store-shoppers-are-downloading-retailers-mobile-apps-driven-by-deals-search-features
57. Caboni, F, & Hagberg, J. (2019), Augmented reality in retailing: A review of features, applications and value. *International Journal of Retail and Distribution Management*, *47* 11, 1125–1140.
58. Koetsier, J. (2021, Feburary 15). *91% of us hate being forced to install apps to do business, costing brands billions*. Forbes. https://www.forbes.com/sites/johnkoetsier/2021/02/15/91-of-us-hate-being-forced-to-install-apps-to-do-business-costing-brands-billions/?sh=14afe7385da8
59. Kaplan, A. M., & Haenlein, M. (2010). Users of the world, unite! The challenges and opportunities of social media. *Business Horizons*, *53*(1), 59–68.
60. Dixon, S. (2023, February 14). *Global social networks ranked by number of users 2023*. Statista. https://www.statista.com/statistics/272014/global-social-networks-ranked-by-number-of-users/
61. Kelly, C. (2022, January 11). *Social commerce to grow 3 times as fast as e-commerce, Accenture predicts*. Retail Dive. https://www.retaildive.com/news/social-commerce-to-grow-3-times-as-fast-as-e-commerce-accenture-predicts/616972/
62. Ibid.
63. Dixon, S. (2023, January 20). *U.S. market share of leading social media websites 2022*. Statista. https://www.statista.com/statistics/265773/market-share-of-the-most-popular-social-media-websites-in-the-us/

64. CNBC. (2023, February 11). *Will live shopping on TikTok, Amazon and YouTube take off in the U.S.?* [Video]. YouTube. https://youtube.com/watch?v=ycAU__6C9pM&si=EnSIkaIECMiOmarE
65. Dixon, S. (2022, August 22). *Average daily time spend on social media worldwide 2012–2022*. Statista. https://www.statista.com/statistics/433871/daily-social-media-usage-worldwide/
66. Kumar, V., Aksoy, L., Donkers, B., Venkatesan, R., Wiesel, T., & Tillmans, S. (2010). Undervalued or overvalued customers: Capturing total customer engagement value. *Journal of Service Research, 13*(3), 297–310.
67. Strugatz, R. (2014, October 13). Fashion brands push social media ads. *WWD*. https://wwd.com/feature/fashion-brands-push-social-media-ads-7977246-1007285/
68. Mazouri, H. (2021, July 14). *User-generated content: 5 steps to turn customers into advocates*. Sprout Social. https://sproutsocial.com/insights/user-generated-content-guide/
69. Mathew, J. (2018, July 30). *Understanding influencer marketing and why it is so effective*. Forbes. https://www.forbes.com/sites/theyec/2018/07/30/understanding-influencer-marketing-and-why-it-is-so-effective/?sh=719b470e71a9
70. James, D. (2022, July 19). *Instagram launches payment-in-chat feature for businesses*. Retail Dive. https://www.retaildive.com/news/instagram-launches-payment-chat-business-feature/627529/
71. Trivette, H. (2022, October 14). *A guide to social media algorithms and SEO*. Forbes. https://www.forbes.com/sites/forbesagencycouncil/2022/10/14/a-guide-to-social-media-algorithms-and-seo/?sh=11c1f92b52a0
72. Peters, J. (2023, February 14). *Instagram is getting rid of live shopping*. The Verge. https://www.theverge.com/2023/2/14/23599924/instagram-live-shopping-removal
73. Cox, L. (2021, November 8). *5 social media algorithms marketers need to know about in 2022*. HubSpot. https://blog.hubspot.com/marketing/how-algorithm-works-facebook-twitter-instagram
74. Globe Newswire. (2021, June 15). *New research shows social media has created a more competitive landscape for brands, but is simultaneously key for staying ahead in their industry*. Martech Series. https://martechseries.com/social/social-media-marketing/new-research-shows-social-media-has-created-a-more-competitive-landscape-for-brands-but-is-simultaneously-key-for-staying-ahead-in-their-industry/
75. Kelly, C. (2022, January 11). *Social commerce to grow 3 times as fast as e-commerce, Accenture predicts*. Retail Dive. https://www.retaildive.com/news/social-commerce-to-grow-3-times-as-fast-as-e-commerce-accenture-predicts/616972/
76. Olivier, C., & Silve, T. (2023, January 11). The outside view: Fashion and luxury's social media responsibilities. *WWD*. https://wwd.com/business-news/business-features/camille-olivier-thomas-silve-influence-social-media-ctzar-1235462105/
77. Peiser, J., Paul, M., & Chong, L. (2023, February 24). The new TikTok trend is convincing people not to buy things. *The Washington Post*. https://www.washingtonpost.com/business/2023/02/24/tiktok-definfluencing-marketing-trend/
78. Keenan, J. (2022, November 9). *Nordstrom earns top ranking in top 100 omnichannel retailers report*. Total Retail. https://www.mytotalretail.com/article/nordstrom-earns-top-ranking-in-top-100-omnichannel-retailers-report/
79. Nordstrom, Inc. (2022). *10K*. https://press.nordstrom.com/static-files/879478f9-0ee8-4b1e-a66a-3bc0eddc83b0
80. Nordstrom.com. (2023). *Nordstrom local locations*. https://www.nordstrom.com/browse/services/nordstrom-local
81. Nordstrom.com. (2023). *Pop-In@Nordstrom eats more*. https://press.nordstrom.com/news-releases/news-release-details/pop-innordstrom-eats-more
82. Nordstrom.com (2021, March 17). *Nordstrom introduces livestream shopping*. https://press.nordstrom.com/node/45776/pdf
83. Nordstrom, Inc (2023). *Nordy Club: Terms–conditions*. https://www.nordstrom.com/browse/nordy-club/terms-conditions
84. *Fashion eCommerce: analyzing global top brands*. Statista. https://www.statista.com/study/112205/fashion-ecommerce-analyzing-global-top-brands/

Chapter 3

1. Jai, T. M. C., Fang, D., Bao, F. S., James III, R. N., Chen, T., & Cai, W. Seeing it is like touching it: Unraveling the effective product presentations on online apparel purchase decisions and brain activity (an fMRI study). *Journal of Interactive Marketing, 53*, 66–79.
2. Laubheimer, P. (2018, November 5). *Shopping cart or wishlist? Saving products for later in ecommerce*. Nielsen Norman Group. https://www.nngroup.com/articles/wishlist- or-cart/
3. Sweeney, J. C., Hausknecht, D., & Soutar, G. N. (2000). Cognitive dissonance after purchase: A multidimensional scale. *Psychology & Marketing, 17*(5), 369–385.
4. Sopadjieva, E., Dholakia, U., & Benjamin, B. (2017, January 3). *A study of 46,000 shoppers shows that omnichannel retailing works*. Harvard Business Review. https://hbr.org/2017/01/a-study-of-46000-shoppers-shows-that-omnichannel-retailing-works
5. Goic, M., Rojas, A., & Saavedra, I. (2021). The effectiveness of triggered email marketing in addressing browse abandonments. *Journal of Interactive Marketing, 55*(1), 118–145.
6. Amazon. (2023). *Prime Membership Benefits*. https://www.amazon.com/b/node=23945845011
7. Sephora. (2023). *Beauty Insider Benefits*. https://www.sephora.com/profile/BeautyInsider
8. Starbucks. (2023). *Starbucks Reviews*. https://www.starbucks.com/rewards
9. Nordstrom. (2023). *The Nordy Club*. https://www.nordstrom.com/browse/nordy-club
10. Target. (2023). *Circle*. https://www.target.com/circle
11. Gao, W., Fan, H., Li, W., & Wang, H. (2021). Crafting the customer experience in omnichannel contexts: The role

of channel integration. *Journal of Business Research, 126*, 12–22.

12. Ismail, K. (2020, July 1). *How silos are killing your omnichannel strategy*. CMS Wire. https://www.cmswire.com/digital-marketing/how-silos-are-killing-your-omnichannel- strategy/
13. Amazon. (2023). *Prime try before you buy*. https://www.amazon.com/tbyb/huc/ref=s9_acss_bw_cg_PTBYB_1a1_w?_encoding=UTF8&ref_=PTBYB_EVERGREEN_REFRESH_FALL_FAQ_DT_HDR&pf_rd_m=ATVPD-KIKX0DER&pf_rd_s=merchandised-search-2&pf_rd_r=V04N0X2EQRH6QGSQWV3W&pf_rd_t=101&pf_rd_p=41804423-29df-4a40-90e6-b28c7b0
14. H&M. (2023). *Online shopping*. https://www2.hm.com/en_us/customer-service/shopping-at-hm/scan-and-find.html
15. Macy's. (2023). *Macy's style crew*. https://www.macys.com/style-crew/
16. Anderssen S. R. (2021). *In search of speed: A new way for retailers to organize*. McKinsey & Company. https://www.mckinsey.com/industries/retail/our-insights/in-search-of-speed-a-new-way-for-retailers-to-organize
17. *The leap* (2021). McKinsey Quarterly. https://www.mckinsey.com/capabilities/strategy-and-corporate-finance/our-insights/five-fifty-the-quickening
18. Mullan, L. (2020, May 17). *Nike unveils new augmented reality technology to improve shoe sizing*. Technology. https://technologymagazine.com/data-and-data-analytics/nike-unveils-new-augmented-reality-technology-im-prove-shoe-sizing
19. Kohan, S. (2020, December 19). *Pandemic-proof Nike delivers another strong quarter with 9% sales increase*. Forbes. https://www.forbes.com/sites/shelleykohan/2020/12/19/pandemic-proof-nike-delivers-another-strong-quarter-with-9-sales-increase/
20. Think With Google. (2023). https://www.thinkwithgoogle.com/consumer-insights/consumer-trends/personalized-shopping-spending-statistics/
21. Marr, B. (2023, March 21). *Revolutionizing retail: How ChatGPT is changing the shopping experience*. Forbes. https://www.forbes.com/sites/bernardmarr/2023/03/21/revolutionizing-retail-how-chatgpt-is-changing-the-shopping-experience/?sh=6204417f2540
22. Time Staff. (2019). *The 25 most influential people on the internet*. https://time.com/5626827/the-25-most-influential-people-on-the-internet/
23. PacSun Snapchat account. (2024). https://www.snapchat.com/add/pacsun
24. Piper Sandler. (2023). *Taking stock with Teens®*. https://www.pipersandler.com/sites/default/files/document/TSWTSpring2023.pdf
25. Pacsun. (2021, May 11). *Pacsun brand continues rise in the ranks of favorite teen fashion brands*. PRNewswire. https://www.prnewswire.com/news-releases/pacsun-brand-continues-rise-in-the-ranks-of-favorite-teen-fashion-brands-301288174.html
26. Loudin, A. (2019, October 29). *How Nordstrom got a handle on omnichannel fulfillment*. Supply Chain Dive. https://www.supplychaindive.com/news/nordstrom-opex-omnichannel-fulfillment-technology/566077/
27. Rajeck, J. (2019, May 14). *Omnichannel in Indonesia: Trends, ambitions and frustrations*. Econsultancy. https://econsultancy.com/omnichannel-in-indonesia-trends-ambitions-and-frustrations/
28. Wei, T., & Sachet, G. (2021, June 2). *Omni-channel retail is key to survival, but retailers may not be ready*. KPMG. https://kpmg.com/sg/en/home/media/press-contributions/2021/06/omni-channel-retail-is-key-to-survival-but-retailers-may-not-be-ready.html
29. Flourish Consulting Services. (2023). *6 ineffective marketing strategies*. https://www.flourishconsultingservices.com/uncategorized/6-ineffective-marketing-strategies-infographic
30. Marketing Charts. (2022, December 6). *These are the top 10 spending industries on ads in the US*. https://www.marketingcharts.com/advertising-trends/spending-and-spenders-227936
31. Corselli, A. (2014, November 6). *Marketers fail to coordinate across channels*. DMNews. https://www.dmnews.com/marketers-fail-to-coordinate-across-channels/
32. Marinaki, A. (2024). *20+ cart abandonment stats to reduce your lost sales in 2024*. https://moosend.com/blog/cart-abandonment-stats/
33. Schooley, S. (2020, December 1). *How to use email marketing to reduce cart abandonment*. https://www.business.com/articles/recover-abandoned- carts/
34. Sukhraj, R. (2020, September 11). *15 effective re-engagement email examples you'll want to steal in 2021*. Impact. https://www.impactplus.com/blog/re-engagement-email-examples
35. Fontanella, C. (2023, February 8). *How to calculate Customer Lifetime Value (CVL) & why it matters*. HubSpot. https://blog.hubspot.com/service/how-to-calculate-customer-lifetime-value
36. Edelman, D. C., & Singer, M. (2015). *Competing on customer journeys*. Harvard Business Review. https://hbr.org/2015/11/competing-on-customer-journeys
37. TikTok. (2022). *The infinite loop: TikTok's unique retail path to purchase*. https://www.tiktok.com/business/en-US/blog/infinite-loop-tiktok-retail-path-to-purchase
38. Palmieri, J. E. (2020). Ralph Lauren going virtual for the holidays. *WWD*. https://wwd.com/business-news/marketing-promotion/ralph-lauren-going-virtual-for-the-holidays-1234654198/#!
39. National Retail Federation. (2023). *NRF Retail Leadership Series – Candid conversations with retail CEOs*. https://nrf.com/events/nrf-retail-leadership-series
40. Clark, E. (2020, December 16). Patrice Louvet on feeling Ralph Lauren online. *WWD*. https://wwd.com/business-news/business-features/patrice-louvet-ralph-lauren-online-digital-stores-1234674305/

41. Adidas. (2021, March 10). *Annual Report 2020 – income statement.* https://report.adidas-group.com/2020/en/group-management-report-financial-review/business-performance/income-statement.html
42. Adidas. (2021, March 10). *Annual Report 2020 – Strategy.* https://report.adidas-group.com/2020/en/group-management-report-our-company/strategy.html

Chapter 4

1. *TikTok E-Commerce Platform Integration FAQs.* TikTok.com. https://ads.tiktok.com/help/article/tiktok-e-commerce-platform-integration-faq?lang=en
2. Pernice, K., & Budiu, R. (2016, June 26). *Hamburger menus and hidden navigation hurt UX metrics.* Nielsen Normal Group. https://www.nngroup.com/articles/hamburger-menus/
3. Dixon, S. (2023, February 24). *Facebook access penetration 2022, by device.* Statista. https://www.statista.com/statistics/377808/distribution-of-facebook-users-by-device/
4. Mueller, J. (2020, March 5). *Announcing mobile first indexing for the whole web.* Google Search Central Blog. https://webmasters.googleblog.com/2020/03/announcing-mobile-first-indexing-for.html
5. Gonzalo, F. (2017, March 1). *Understanding the difference between mobile-first, adaptive and responsive design.* https://fredericgonzalo.com/en/2017/03/01/understanding-the-difference-between-mobile-first-adaptive-and-responsive-design/
6. Kaempf, D. (2022, July 20). *Mobile-first vs. responsive web design: Choose your strategy.* Darwin Digital. https://darwindigital.com/mobile-first-versus-responsive-web-design/
7. Sweor. (2023, March 6). *27 eye-opening website statistics: Is your website costing you clients?* https://www.sweor.com/firstimpressions
8. Kristensen, E. (2022, May 24). *15 cart abandonment statistics you must know in 2023.* Drip. https://sleeknote.com/blog/cart-abandonment-statistics
9. Baymard Institute. (2022, August 16). *48 cart abandonment rate statistics 2023.* https://baymard.com/lists/cart-abandonment-rate
10. Baymard Institute. (2024, February 16). *49 cart abandonment rate statistics 2024.* https://baymard.com/lists/cart-abandonment-rate#why-users-abandon-their-cart
11. Statista. (2023). *Primary reason for digital shoppers worldwide to abandon their carts as of January 2019.* https://www.statista.com/statistics/692771/online-shopping-primary-reasons-to-abandon-carts
12. CloudFare. (2023). *How website performance affects conversion rates.* https://www.cloudflare.com/learning/performance/more/website-performance-conversion-rates
13. Wilson, A. (2022, October 19). *Why site speed is so important: Conversions, loyalty, and Google search ranking.* Shopify. https://www.shopify.com/blog/site-speed-importance
14. Eaton, K. (2012, March 15). *How one second could cost Amazon $1.6 billion in sales.* Fast Company. https://www.fastcompany.com/1825005/how-one-second-could-cost-amazon-16-billion-sales
15. Airship. (2023). *Accengage push notification & in-app message benchmark for mobile apps.* https://www.accengage.com/benchmark-opt-in-and-reaction-rates-of-push-notifications-and-in-app-messages-for-mobile-apps-2018-edition/
16. Wightman-Stone, D. (2019, June 14). *ASOS launches its first augmented reality feature.* Fashion United. https://fashionunited.uk/news/retail/asos-launches-its-first-augmented-reality-feature/2019061443676?_ga=2.61643948.1632091562.1588097635-1278169893.1588097634
17. Lauchlan, S. (2019, July 4). *Nike goes the distance with omni-channel retail transformation.* Diginomica. https://diginomica.com/nike-goes-distance-omni-channel-retail-transformation
18. Wong, B. (2023). *Top social media statistics and trends of 2024.* Forbes. https://www.forbes.com/advisor/business/social-media-statistics/#source
19. Meta. (2024). *Stay connected to your customers with a Facebook Page.* https://www.facebook.com/business/m/facebook-business-page
20. Meta. (2023). *About lookalike audiences.* https://www.facebook.com/business/help/164749007013531?id=401668390442328
21. Gottfried, J. (2024). *Americans' social media use.* Pew Research. https://www.pewresearch.org/internet/2024/01/31/americans-social-media-use/
22. Statista Research Department. (2016, April 11). *Instagram: Global brand adoption rate 2016, by category.* https://www.statista.com/statistics/305292/worldwide-instagram-brand-adoption-rate-category/
23. *Chanel's official Instagram Page* (2024). https://www.instagram.com/chanelofficial/?hl=en
24. *Gucci's official Instagram Page* (2024). https://www.instagram.com/gucci/?hl=en
25. Dixon, S. (2023, January 24). *Instagram accounts with the most followers worldwide 2023.* Statista. https://www.statista.com/statistics/421169/most-followers-instagram/
26. Dixon, S. (2023, February 15). *Instagram: Number of users in the United States 2020–2023.* Statista. https://www.statista.com/statistics/293771/number-of-us-instagram-users/
27. Schiffer, J. (2019). *Do fashion brands need TikTok?* Vogue Business. https://www.voguebusiness.com/companies/tiktok-social-networking-video-app-gen-z-mac-ralph-lauren
28. Monteros, M. (2021, August 25). *TikTok partners with Shopify to pilot in-app shopping.* Retail Dive. https://www.retaildive.com/news/tiktok-partners-with-shopify-to-pilot-in-app-shopping/605565/
29. Pinterest. (2023). *Your audience is here.* https://business.pinterest.com/audience
30. Pinterest. (2023). *Super shoppers. Standout results.* https://business.pinterest.com/insights/shopping-on-pinterest/

31. eMarketer. (2019). *Pinterest is the talk of shoptalk as it eyes IPO*. https://content-na1.emarketer.com/pinterest-is-the-talk-of-shoptalk-as-it-eyes-ipo
32. Lipsman, A. (2020, March 26). *Direct-to-consumer brands 2020: Growing pains hit disruptor brands on their path to maturity*. eMarketer. https://content-na1.emarketer.com/direct-to-consumer-brands-2020
33. Clement, D. P. (2020 February 20). *DTC disruptors on IAB brands to watch list include Stitch Fix, Casper*. https://multichannelmerchant.com/ecommerce/dtc-disruptors-iab-brands-to-watch-list-include-stitch-fix-casper/
34. Schlesinger, L., Higgins, M., & Roseman, S. (2020, March 31). *Reinventing the direct-to-consumer business model*. Harvard Business Review. https://hbr.org/2020/03/reinventing-the-direct-to-consumer-business-model
35. Lindsey, K. (2015). *Amazon opens first physical store*. Retail Dive. https://www.retaildive.com/news/amazon-opens-first-physical-store/408515/
36. Amazon (2023). *Amazon physical stores locations*. https://www.amazon.com/find-your-store/
37. Tyler, J. (2018). *Glossier, the wildly popular startup that's raised $86 million in its mission to revolutionize makeup and skin-care, just opened its first flagship store. Here's what it's like to shop there*. Business Insider. https://www.businessinsider.com/where-to-buy-glossier-in-person-2018-11#at-the-top-of-the-stairs-are-employees-greeting-everyone-by-a-big-floral-display-3
38. Turra, A. (2017). Italian fashion companies bank on pop-up stores. *WWD*. https://wwd.com/feature/italian-companies-bank-pop-up-shops-furla-genny-paula-cademartori-milan-10843936/
39. Shoaib, M. (2022). *Coach brings circular programme to London with new pop-up store*. Vogue Business. https://www.voguebusiness.com/sustainability/coach-brings-circular-programme-to-london-with-new-pop-up-store
40. Chikhoune, R. (2023). Banana Republic pop-up home store opens in L.A. *WWD*. https://wwd.com/home-design/shop-home/banana-republic-pop-up-home-store-los-angeles-1235830464/
41. Ilchi, L. (2023). Start-ups like knitwear brand, PH5, host pop-up store in New York City. *WWD*. https://wwd.com/fashion-news/fashion-scoops/ph5-new-york-city-store-1235685621/
42. Goldstone, V. (2023). House of Sunny arrives in Soho. *WWD*. https://wwd.com/business-news/retail/house-of-sunny-store-soho-london-1235791311/
43. Nordstrom. (2023). *Nordstrom Local*. https://www.nordstrom.com/browse/services/nordstrom-local
44. Zaczkiewicz, A. (2020). Fulfillment doesn't have to be a painful, costly endeavor for brands. *WWD*. https://wwd.com/business-news/business-features/fulfillment-trends-1203511765/
45. TikTok.com (2024). TikTok creator marketplace. https://creatormarketplace.tiktok.com/
46. Marine, B. (2020, September 11). *Gucci embraces its parody on Tiktok with the #guccimodelchallenge*. Wmagazine. https://www.wmagazine.com/story/gucci-model-tik-tok-challenge
47. Long, D. (2022, November 30). *Amazon India target first time online shoppers with live streaming content*. The Drum. https://www.thedrum.com/news/2022/11/30/amazon-india-targets-first-time-online-shoppers-with-live-streaming-content
48. James, D. (2023, January 10). *Instagram to remove shopping tab*. Retail Dive. https://www.retaildive.com/news/instagram-meta-remove-shopping-tab/640040/

Chapter 5

1. Asmare, A., & Zewdie, S. (2022). Omnichannel retailing strategy: A systematic review. *International Review of Retail, Distribution and Consumer Research*, *32*(1), 59–79. https://www.tandfonline.com/doi/abs/10.1080/09593969.2021.2024447
2. Gruzbarg, T. (2019, November 15). Three ways to unlock the potential value of cross channel shopping. *WWD*. https://wwd.com/business-news/business-features/cross-channel-shopping-1203371453/
3. Ibid.
4. Kluge, P., Schmid, M., Silliman, E., & Villepelet, C., (2021, December). *Omnichannel: It's time for the online tail to wag the retail dog*. McKinsey & Company. https://www.mckinsey.com/industries/retail/our-insights/omnichannel-its-time-for-the-online-tail-to-wag-the-retail-dog
5. Picot-Coupey, K., Huré, E. and Piveteau, L. (2016). Channel design to enrich customers' shopping experiences: synchronizing clicks with bricks in an omni-channel perspective—the Direct Optic case. *International Journal of Retail & Distribution Management*, *44*(3), 336–368. https://doi.org/10.1108/IJRDM-04-2015-0056
6. Ibid.
7. Boohoo Group PLC. (2022). *Annual Report 2022*. https://www.boohoo-com-plc-annual-report-2022.pdf
8. ShopifyPlus. (2020, August 12), *Omnichannel commerce guide: Sell everywhere your customers buy*. https://enterprise.plus.shopify.com/rs/932-KRM-548/images/Omnichannel_Commerce_Guide.pdf?_gl=1*1ea427s*_ga*MTM4MDg3NzQ3Ni4xNjczNDYxMDk2*_ga_B7X5MKCR35*MTY3NzI2ODYzMy4yLjEuMTY3NzI-2ODgyOS4zMy4wLjA.*_fplc*c2xQTzdvRWpFYjZRSjh0RV-VTM1VVa2RpcnBlZ3NLaFVyUEJCOWhZUnlGNHFNS2g-0bG9qZFBpd2xhMDNKNXNMMnFuVW8ybEY4VWx-uNVFpRVVXbDlORkNSREMzVmhuYXBGTWdWR-G9aTFh4bmpJZDdmaiUyQkNaeXV2dTYxT2VJNGclM-0QlM0Q.&_ga=2.139300211.1100393073.1677268634-1380877476.1673461096
9. Schwans, M. (2022, September 22). *Where clothing retailers can adapt to today's omnichannel challenges*. Zebra. https://www.zebra.com/us/en/blog/posts/2022/where-clothing-retailers-can-adapt-to-maximize-omnichannel-profit.html

10. Louis Vuitton website. https://www.louisvuitton.com/dispatch?noDRP=true
11. Ann Taylor. (2023). Ann Taylor website. https://www.anntaylor.com
12. *GDPR compliance checklist for U.S. companies.* (2023). https://gdpr.eu/compliance-checklist-us-companies/
13. Graf, C., Lange, T., Seyfert, A., & van der Wijden, N., (2021, July 19). *Into the fast lane: How to master the omnichannel supply chain.* McKinsey and Company. https://www.mckinsey.com/industries/retail/our-insights/into-the-fast-lane-how-to-master-the-omnichannel-supply-chain
14. Polian, L. G. (2009). *Multi-channel retailing.* New York, NY: Fairchild Books.
15. Matei, A. (2019). Shock! Horror! Do you know how much time you spend on your phone? *The Guardian.* https://www.theguardian.com/lifeandstyle/2019/aug/21/cellphone-screen-time-average-habits
16. Digital Marketing Community. (2019). *Average time spent in the USA on using mobile devices versus watching TV, 2019.* https://www.digitalmarketingcommunity.com/indicators/mobile-devices-tv-usa-2019/
17. Rampton, J. (2020, October 16). *Five examples of brands using cross-channel tactics to drive real results.* Oracle. https://blogs.oracle.com/marketingcloud/post/5-examples-of-brands-using-cross-channel-tactics-to-drive-real-results
18. Edelman, G. (2021, November 29). *The father of Web 3.0 wants us to trust less.* Wired. https://www.wired.com/story/web3-gavin-wood-interview/
19. Aichner, T., Grünfelder, M., Maurer, O., & Jegeni, D. (2021). Twenty-five years of social media: A review of social media applications and definitions from 1994 to 2019. *Cyberpsychology, Behavior, and Social Networking, 24*(4), 215–222.
20. Dixon, S. J. (2022). *Percentage of U.S. population who currently use any social media from 2008 to 2021.* Statista. https://www.statista.com/statistics/273476/percentage-of-us-population-with-a-social-network-profile/
21. Dixon, S. J. (2022). *Average number of social media accounts per internet user from 2013 to 2018.* Statista. https://www.statista.com/statistics/788084/number-of-social-media-accounts/
22. Dixon, S. J. (2024). *Daily time spent on social networking by internet users worldwide from 2012 to 2024 (in minutes).* Statista. https://www.statista.com/statistics/433871/daily-social-media-usage-worldwide/
23. Dixon, S. J. (2024). *Number of monthly active Facebook users worldwide as of 4th quarter 2023 (in millions).* Statista. https://www.statista.com/statistics/264810/number-of-monthly-active-facebook-users-worldwide/
24. Perrin, A., & Anderson, M. (2019). *Social media usage in the U.S. in 2019.* Pew Research Center. https://www.pewresearch.org/fact-tank/2019/04/10/share-of-u-s-adults-using-social-media-including-facebook-is-mostly-unchanged-since-2018/
25. World Bank. 2021. *World development indicators—population.* https://databank.worldbank.org/data/download/POP.pdf
26. Thomala, L. L. (2024). *Number of monthly active WeChat users from 4th quarter 2013 to 4th quarter 2023 (in millions).* Statista. https://www.statista.com/statistics/255778/number-of-active-wechat-messenger-accounts/
27. Thomala, L. L. (2024). *Number of Sina Weibo users in China from 2017 to 2021 (in millions).* Statista. https://www.statista.com/statistics/941456/china-number-of-sina-weibo-users/
28. Cotton Incorporated. (2021). *2021 Sustainability & Health and Wellness Survey.* https://sourcingjournal.com/topics/lifestyle-monitor/kate-hudson-fabletics-hippo-knitting-instagram-accountability-social-media-crisis-284651/
29. D'Amato, J. (2021, January 9). *Why email marketing is still IMPORTANT* [Updated For 2021]. https://www.lonefircreative.com/blog/why-email-marketing-is-still-important-for-2021
30. Ibid.
31. Bustillos, M. (2021, February 16). *33+ email marketing Stats [2020 & 2021 edition] for businesses.* https://www.hostpapa.com/blog/email/email-marketing-stats-2020/#:~:text=Email%20Marketing%20Stats%20for%202020%20%26%202021,-Share&text=Email%20marketing%20is%20the%20most,by%20their%20owner%20every%20day
32. Sameh, F. (2021, May 05). *Best fashion email marketing campaigns to inspire you in 2021.* https://www.perzonalization.com/blog/best-fashion-email-marketing-campaigns-2021/
33. Kakovkina, V. (2021, April 06). *Hot or NOT: Email marketing trends for 2021.* https://nethunt.com/blog/email-marketing-trends/
34. Girard, A. (2021, April 22). *The top 15 best email marketing services in 2021.* https://blog.hubspot.com/marketing/best-email-marketing-services
35. *Google launches self-service advertising program.* http://googlepress.blogspot.com/2000/10/google-launches-self-service.html
36. *Google: Annual advertising revenue 2001–2020.* Statista. https://www.statista.com/statistics/266249/advertising-revenue-of-google/
37. Bianchi, T. (2024). *Market share of leading desktop search engines worldwide from January 2015 to January 2024.* Statista. https://www.statista.com/statistics/216573/worldwide-market-share-of-search-engines/
38. Bianchi, T. (2024). *Annual revenue of Alphabet from 2017 to 2023, by segment (in million U.S. dollars).* Statista. https://www.statista.com/statistics/633651/alphabet-annual-global-revenue-by-segment/
39. Polian, L. M. (2009). *Multi-channel retailing.* New York, NY: Fairchild.
40. Mali, N. (2021). *Your m-commerce deep dive: Data, trends and what's next in the mobile retail revenue world.* https://www.bigcommerce.com/blog/mobile-commerce/#what-is-mobile-commerce
41. Sands, K. (2021, February 1). *Top m-commerce trends to look for in 2021.* https://thepaypers.com/expert-opinion/top-m-commerce-trends-to-look-for-in-2021–1246978

42. Taylor, P. (2024). *Number of smartphone mobile network subscriptions worldwide from 2016 to 2023, with forecasts from 2023 to 2028 (in millions)*. Statista. https://www.statista.com/statistics/330695/number-of-smartphone-users-worldwide/
43. Lin, Y. (2021, April 22). *10 mobile usage statistics you should know in 2021*. https://www.oberlo.com/blog/mobile-usage-statistics
44. Milijic, M. (2021, February 07). *29+ smartphone usage statistics: Around the world in 2020*. https://leftronic.com/smartphone-usage-statistics/
45. Statista Research Department. (2024, April 30). *Global m-commerce revenue and share of total e-commerce 2017–2028*. https://www.statista.com/statistics/1449284/retail-mobile-commerce-revenue-worldwide/#:~:text=In%202023%2C%20approximately%2030%20percent,and%2066%20percent%20of%20orders
46. Padua, A. (2020, November 20). *What is location-based marketing & its advantages*. Techfunnel. https://www.techfunnel.com/martech/location-based-marketing/
47. Kruse, K. (2016). *The 80/20 rule and how it can change your life*. Forbes. https://www.forbes.com/sites/kevinkruse/2016/03/07/80-20-rule/?sh=57bbc5523814
48. Kuligowski, K. (2021, January 15). *How to use CRM and email marketing together*. Business News Daily. https://www.businessnewsdaily.com/15962-how-crm-streamlines-email-marketing-.html
49. FrogDog Marketing. (2021, February 22). *The difference between CRM and e-mail marketing*. https://www.frog-dog.com/magazine/the-difference-between-crm-and-e-mail-marketing#:~:text=CRM%20stands%20for%20customer%20relationship%20management.&text=A%20CRM%20system%E2%80%94which%20may,keep%20tabs%20on%20their%20contacts
50. SplitBase. (2021). *5 essentials to a high-converting e-mail opt-in for fashion ecommerce* https://splitbase.com/blog/luxury-ecommerce-crm
51. Girish, D. (2021, February 21). *Location-based marketing examples: 4 brands that are winning*. https://blog.beaconstac.com/2016/04/4-brands-that-are-winning-at-location-based-marketing-and-how/
52. CleverTap. (2018). *Proximity marketing with Beacons: CleverTap retail insights*. https://clevertap.com/blog/beacon-marketing/

Chapter 6

1. Bowersox, D. J., Closs, D. J., Cooper, M. B., & Bowersox, J. C. (2020). *Supply chain logistics management* (5th ed.). New York: NY: McGraw Hill Education.
2. RiverLogic. (2021). *10 things about omni channel supply chain you may not have known*. https://www.riverlogic.com/blog/10-things-about-omnichannel-supply-chain-you-may-not-have-known
3. Lumen. (2021). *Single channel, multichannel, and omnichannel retailing*. https://courses.lumenlearning.com/wmopen-retailmanagement/chapter/introduction-to-single-channel-multichannel-and-omnichannel-retailing/
4. Lee, H.-H., & Kim, J. (2010). Investigating dimensionality of multichannel retailer's crosschannel integration practices and effectiveness: Shopping orientation and loyalty intention. *Journal of Marketing Channels, 17*(4), 281–312.
5. Ibid.
6. SteadieSeifi, M. (2011). Logistics strategic decisions. In R. Z. Farahani, S. Rezapour, & L. Kardar (Eds.), *Logistics operations and management: Concepts and models* (pp. 43–53). London: Elsevier. https://www.sciencedirect.com/science/article/pii/B9780123852021000037
7. Resnick, N., & Ho, H. (2020, September 9). *Top omnichannel logistics and supply chain challenges in ecommerce*. Shopify. https://www.shopify.com/enterprise/top-omnichannel-logistics-supply-chain-challenges-ecommerce-founders-must-face
8. Amar, J., Raabe, J., & Roggenhofer, S. (2019). *How to capture what the customer wants*. McKinsey. https://www.mckinsey.com/business-functions/operations/our-insights/how-to-capture-what-the-customer-wants
9. Ibid.
10. Aleksic, M. (2020, June 30). *What is the impact of omni channel commerce on supply chains*. https://ccbill.com/blog/omnichannel-impact-on-supply-chains
11. Salesforce. (2024). *Customer journeys: How to keep customers connected and coming back*. https://www.salesforce.com/products/marketing-cloud/best-practices/customer-journeys/
12. FBAhelp. (2020). *Locations of Amazon fulfillment centers*. https://fba.help/list-of-amazon-fulfillment-centers
13. Bowersox, D. J., Closs, D. J., Cooper, M. B., & Bowersox, J. C. (2020). *Supply chain logistics management* (5th ed.). New York: NY: McGraw Hill Education.
14. Reid, H. (2020, July 24). *Tips for optimized omnichannel fulfillment*. https://dclcorp.com/blog/fulfillment/tips-for-optimized-omnichannel-fulfillment/
15. Thomas, L. (2019, December 5). *How Nordstrom uses robots and shelves inspired by ants to deliver lipstick faster*. CNBC. https://www.cnbc.com/2019/12/05/nordstrom-partners-with-attabotics-and-tompkins-robotics-for-faster-delivery.html
16. Bowersox, D. J., Closs, D. J., Cooper, M. B., & Bowersox, J. C. (2020). *Supply chain logistics management* (5th ed.). New York: NY: McGraw Hill Education.
17. Apparel Search Company. (2024). *Inventory management for the fashion industry*. https://www.apparelsearch.com/terms/i/inventory_management.html
18. Bowles, R. (2021, March 8). *The retailer's guide to clothing inventory management*. https://www.logiwa.com/blog/clothing-inventory-management
19. Jules. (2020, June 9). *In-house order fulfillment: Is it right for you?* https://www.easyship.com/blog/in-house-fulfillment-challenges
20. Bowersox, D. J., Closs, D. J., Cooper, M. B., & Bowersox, J. C. (2020). *Supply chain logistics management* (5th ed.) (p. 90). New York: NY: McGraw Hill Education.

21. United Parcel Service of America, Inc. (2024). *Warehousing & distribution.* https://www.ups.com/us/en/supplychain/logistics/distribution.page
22. Fulfillment Bridge, Inc. (2021). *Questions to ask when choosing a courier service for your business.* https://fulfillmentbridge.com/ecommerce-blog/choosing-a-courier-service/
23. Shopify. (2020, April 3). *3PL guide 2021: What is third party logistics and how to choose?* https://www.shopify.com/enterprise/third-party-logistics-3pl
24. OptimoRoute. (2020, November 10). *Order fulfillment: How to speed up your process.* https://optimoroute.com/order-fulfillment/#how-to
25. Arora, S. (2021, February 09). *What is ecommerce fulfillment & its scope in 2021.* https://www.shiprocket.in/blog/ecommerce-fulfillment/
26. Tanese, B. (2020, March 12). *In-house vs. outsourcing fulfillment.* https://www.shipmonk.com/blog/in-house-vs-outsourcing-fulfillment
27. OptimoRoute. (2020, November 10). *Order fulfillment: How to speed up your process.* https://optimoroute.com/order-fulfillment/#how-to
28. ConnectPOS. (2020, November 26). *Retail POS trends and statistics for 2021.* https://www.connectpos.com/retail-pos-trends-and-statistics-for-2021/
29. Brightpearl. (2024). *Multi-channel order management.* https://www.brightpearl.com/order-management-software
30. Oracle. (2024). *What is a transportation management system?* https://www.oracle.com/scm/what-is-transportation-management-system/
31. Bernon, M., Cullen, J., & Gorst, J. (2016). Online retail returns management: Integration within an omnichannel distribution context. *International Journal of Physical Distribution & Logistics Management, 46*(6/7), 584–605. https://www.emerald.com/insight/content/doi/10.1108/IJPDLM-01-2015-0010/full/html
32. Ibid.
33. Merchant Fraud Journal. (2024). *Return fraud: How merchants lost $25.3B in fraudulent returns.* https://www.merchantfraudjournal.com/return-fraud-how-merchants-lost-25-3b-in-fraudulent-returns/
34. Brannigan, M. (2022, December 8). How fashion can minimise the billion-dollar return problem. *Vogue Business.* https://www.voguebusiness.com/consumers/how-fashion-can-minimise-the-billion-dollar-return-problem
35. PYMNTS. (2021, January 11). *Trying to reason with returns season.* https://www.pymnts.com/news/retail/2021/trying-to-reason-with-returns-season-51-percent-of-consumers-would-keep-goods-for-discounts/
36. Sabarwal, M. (2022). *Top 10 reasons for refund and exchange that every online retailer must know.* https://wpswings.com/blog/reasons-for-refund-and-exchange/#:~:text=Top%2010%20Reasons%20For%20Returning%20An%20Item%201,The%20Time%20of%20Highest%20Return%20...%20More%20items /
37. McKinsey & Company (2021). *Returning to order: Improving returns management for apparel companies.* https://www.mckinsey.com/industries/retail/our-insights/returning-to-order-improving-returns-management-for-apparel-companies
38. Gorlin, J. (2020, August 3). *The top 7 reasons your customer returned your garment.* https://blog.newmine.com/blog/top-7-reasons-your-customer-returned-your-garment
39. Ibid.
40. Merchant Fraud Journal. (2024). *Return fraud: How merchants lost $25.3B in fraudulent returns.* https://www.merchantfraudjournal.com/return-fraud-how-merchants-lost-25-3b-in-fraudulent-returns/
41. Charlton, G. (2020, September 25). *Ecommerce returns: 2020 stats and trends.* https://www.salecycle.com/blog/featured/ecommerce-returns-2018-stats-trends/
42. Parker, T. (2020, July 11). *An expensive problem for the online fashion industry: Too many returns.* Medium. https://medium.com/@parker_content/an-expensive-problem-for-the-online-fashion-industry-too-many-returns-abc441ed1b51
43. McEachern, A. (2020, March 5). *The return metrics you need to know beyond return rate.* https://www.loopreturns.com/blog/the-return-metrics-you-need-to-know-beyond-return-rate/
44. Ibid.
45. Williams, J. (2021, March 18). *Creative directors are embracing data.* FashionUnited. https://fashionunited.uk/news/fashion/creative-directors-are-embracing-data/2021031854530
46. Countants. (2020, February 1). *AI and machine learning for fashion industry: Global trends & benefits.* https://www.countants.com/blogs/ai-and-machine-learning-for-fashion-industry-global-trends-benefits/
47. Bi, F. (2021, March 10). How AI could help fashion e-tailers reduce retail returns. *Rolling Stone.* https://www.rollingstone.com/culture-council/articles/ai-fashion-e-tailers-returns-1137813/
48. Digitalcommerce360. (2019, September 16). *Sizing issue is a top reason shoppers return online orders: Why online shoppers make returns.* https://www.digitalcommerce360.com/2019/09/12/sizing-issue-is-a-top-reason-shoppers-return-online-orders/
49. FitAnalytics. (2021). *3 ways to reduce returns in the apparel e-tail industry.* https://www.fitanalytics.com/3-ways-to-reduce-returns
50. Antoniades, K. (2022). *4 clothing stores that share user-submitted photos.* https://corporette.com/fashion-stores-that-use-real-women-as-models/
51. Davis, S., & Toney, L. (2021, March 31). *How coronavirus (COVID-19) is impacting ecommerce [MARCH 2021].* https://www.roirevolution.com/blog/2021/03/coronavirus-and-ecommerce/
52. Perez, S. (2021). *Fueled by pandemic, contactless mobile payments to surpass half of all smartphone users in*

US by 2025. https://techcrunch.com/2021/04/05/fueled-by-pandemic-contactless-mobile-payments-to-surpass-half-of-all-smartphone-users-in-u-s-by-2025/

53. Digitalcommerce360. (2019, September 16). *Sizing issue is a top reason that shoppers return online orders: Why online shoppers make returns.* https://www.digitalcommerce360.com/2019/09/12/sizing-issue-is-a-top-reason-shoppers-return-online-orders/
54. Rheude, J. (2020, July 8). *E-commerce returns and refunds: Best practices.* Red Stag Fulfillment. https://redstagfulfillment.com/best-practices-e-commerce-returns/
55. Adegeest, D.-A. (2021). *Fast fashion retailers are clothing their stores, shrinking global retail.* FashionUnited. https://fashionunited.com/news/retail/fast-fashion-retailers-are-closing-their-stores-shrinking-global-retail/2021031638923
56. Harapko, S. (2021, February 18). *How COVID-19 impacted supply chains and what comes next.* https://www.ey.com/en_gl/supply-chain/how-covid-19-impacted-supply-chains-and-what-comes-next
57. Shih, W. C. (2020, September/October). *Global supply chains in a post-pandemic world.* Harvard Business Review. https://hbr.org/2020/09/global-supply-chains-in-a-post-pandemic-world
58. Silver, S. (2021, February 18). *From the filings: Supply chain lessons from the pandemic.* Journal of Accountancy. https://www.journalofaccountancy.com/news/2021/feb/supply-chain-lessons-from-coronavirus-pandemic.html
59. Stekier, M., & Lark, R. (2020, September 09). *Supply chain issues will get worse in 2020. Here's what to do now.* Explore our Thinking: Plante Moran. https://www.plantemoran.com/explore-our-thinking/insight/2020/09/supply-chain-issues-will-get-worse-in-2020-heres-what-to-do
60. Hippold, S. (2021, February 10). *Gartner survey finds 87% of supply chain professionals plan to invest in resilience within the next 2 years.* https://www.gartner.com/en/newsroom/2021-02-10-gartner-survey-finds-87-of-supply-chain-professionals-plan-to-invest-in-resilience-within-the-next-2-years

Chapter 7

1. Louis Vuitton. (n.d.). *Louis Vuitton pass application is launched.* https://eu.louisvuitton.com/eng-e1/articles/louis-vuitton-pass-application-is-launched
2. Backlinko. (2022). *Google CTR stats: How many people click on search results?* https://backlinko.com/google-ctr-stats
3. Google.com. (2024). *Overview of crawling and indexing topics.* Google for Developers. https://developers.google.com/search/docs/crawling-indexing
4. Bianchi, T. (2023, April 27). *Share of website traffic coming from mobile devices worldwide from 2015 to 2023.* Statista. https://www.statista.com/statistics/277125/share-of-website-traffic-coming-from-mobile-devices/
5. Bianchi, T. (2023, September 20). *Worldwide market share of search engines from September 2010 to July 2023.* Statista. https://www.statista.com/statistics/216573/worldwide-market-share-of-search-engines/
6. Google Ads. (2023, March 20). *What is paid search advertising?* https://ads.google.com/intl/en_id/home/resources/what-is-paid-search/
7. Google Ads. (2023). *Types of display campaigns.* https://support.google.com/google-ads/answer/2567043#zippy=%2Ctypes-of-display-campaigns%2Ctypes-of-video-campaigns
8. Instagram. (2021). [Instagram TV video]. https://www.instagram.com/tv/CP9DDRyhJvj/?utm_source=ig_embed&ig_rid=429a3f02-de5c-422b-bc50-b3e22f275709
9. Macready, H. & Cohen, B. (2023, April 11). *How often to post to social media in 2023.* Hootsuite. https://blog.hootsuite.com/how-often-to-post-on-social-media10
10. Robertson, T. S., Gatignon, H., & Cesareo, L. (2018). Pop-ups, ephemerality, and consumer experience: the centrality of buzz. *Journal of the Association for Consumer Research, 3*(3), 425–439.
11. Sanak-Kosmowska, K. (2021). Chapter 5: Social proof as a key factor in social commerce. *Evaluating social media marketing: Social proof and online buyer behaviour.* London: Routledge. https://doi.org/10.4324/9781003128052
12. MarTech Series. (2021, June 15). *New research shows social media has created a more competitive landscape for brands but is simultaneously key for staying ahead in their industry.* https://martechseries.com/social/social-media-marketing/new-research-shows-social-media-has-created-a-more-competitive-landscape-for-brands-but-is-simultaneously-key-for-staying-ahead-in-their-industry/
13. Influencer Marketing Hub. (2024, June 24). *Instagram money & engagement calculator.* Influencer Marketing Hub. https://influencermarketinghub.com/instagram-money-calculator/
14. Santora, J. (2024, February 6). *17 key influencer marketing statistics to fuel your strategy.* Influencer Marketing Hub. https://influencermarketinghub.com/influencer-marketing-statistics/
15. Ibid.
16. Kavali, V. (2023, May 19). *Influencer marketing vs. social media ads: Cost, conversions, and ROI comparison.* https://www.affable.ai/blog/influencer-marketing-vs-social-media-ads
17. Geyser, W. (2023 March 24). *What is an influencer?—social media influencers defined [updated 2023].* https://influencermarketinghub.com/what-is-an-influencer/#toc-2
18. Salesforce. (2023). *What are customer expectations, and how have they changed? Customer expectations hit all-time high.* https://www.salesforce.com/resources/articles/customer-expectations
19. Khlystova, A. (2020, July 13). *Broadcast emailing 101: Tips, tools, examples.* https://helpcrunch.com/blog/broadcast-emailing/#Email_broadcast_vs_Email_autoresponder
20. Pieces. (n.d.). *About us.* https://www.pieces.com/en-gb/about-us/
21. Tatango.Inc. (2020). *33 of the best automated text message examples.* https://www.tatango.com/blog/examples-of-brands-using-text-message-marketing/

22. Alvarado-Karste, D., & Guzmán, F. (2020). The effect of brand identity-cognitive style fit and social influence on consumer-based brand equity. *Journal of Product & Brand Management, 29*(7), 971–984
23. Yotpo. (n.d.). *Content & community: 11 strategies to grow your brand's community and drive sales.* https://www.yotpo.com/direct-to-consumer-ecommerce-marketing/chapter-4/content-community/
24. Jai, T. M. C., Fang, D., Bao, F. S., James III, R. N., Chen, T., & Cai, W. (2021). Seeing it is like touching it: Unraveling the effective product presentations on online apparel purchase decisions and brain activity (an fMRI study). *Journal of Interactive Marketing, 53*, 66–79.
25. Laubheimer, P. (2018). *Shopping cart or wishlist? Saving products for later in ecommerce.* Nielsen Norman Group. https://www.nngroup.com/articles/wishlist-or-cart/
26. HubSpot. (2022). *The ultimate list of marketing statistics for 2022.* https://www.hubspot.com/marketing-statistics
27. Jacob, I., Khanna, M., & Rai, K. A. (2020). Attribution analysis of luxury brands: An investigation into consumer-brand congruence through conspicuous consumption. *Journal of Business Research, 116*, 597–607.
28. Burnasheva, R., Suh, Y. G., & Villalobos-Moron, K. (2019). Sense of community and social identity effect on brand love: Based on the online communities of a luxury fashion brands. *Journal of Global Fashion Marketing, 10*(1), 50–65.
29. Wyzowl. (2023). *Video marketing statistics 2023.* https://www.wyzowl.com/video-marketing-statistics/
30. Miles, K. (2023). *Everything about shoppable content with 12 best examples.* Taggbox. https://taggbox.com/blog/shoppable-content/
31. Snapchat for Business. (n.d.). Dior Sneakers [Webpage]. https://forbusiness.snapchat.com/inspiration/diorsneakers
32. Fontanella, C. (2023, September 18). *How to calculate customer lifetime value (clv) & why it matters.* HubSpot. https://blog.hubspot.com/service/how-to-calculate-customer-lifetime-value
33. Retail Touchpoint. (2022). *The evolution of retail media: powered by data, RMNs offer full-funnel advertising.* https://www.retailtouchpoints.com/resources/the-evolution-of-retail-media-powered-by-data-rmns-offer-full-funnel-advertising
34. Ibid.
35. Scott-Dawkins, K. (2022, September 20). *This Year, Next Year: 2022 e-commerce & retail media forecast. GroupM.* https://www.groupm.com/longform/this-year-next-year-2022-e-commerce-retail-media-forecast/
36. Zalando Marketing Services. (2022). ZMS Creative Guidelines [PDF]. https://zms.zalando.com/wp-content/uploads/2022/02/ZMS_CreativeGuidelines_20220524.pdf
37. Franke, M. (2021, December 7). *5 insights on the future of retail media.* Epsilon. https://www.epsilon.com/us/insights/blog/5-insights-on-the-future-of-retail-media

Chapter 8

1. IBM Institute for Business Value. (2022). *Consumers want it all: Hybrid shopping, sustainability, and purpose-driven brands.* https://cdn.nrf.com/sites/default/files/2022-01/Consumers%20want%20it%20all.pdf
2. Lyra. (2020, May 26). *Different types of payment methods for eCommerce.* https://www.lyra.com/in/payment-methods/
3. Muchmore, M. (2020, December 28). *The best mobile payment apps for 2021.* https://www.pcmag.com/picks/the-best-mobile-payment-apps
4. Antosz, D. (2021, February 19). *The best mobile payment services of 2021.* https://digital.com/mobile-payment-services/
5. Crowe, M. D., Rysman, M., & Stavins, J. (2010). Mobile payments in the United States at retail point of sale: current market and future prospects. *FRB of Boston Public Policy Discussion Paper No. 10-2.* 1–39. http://dx.doi.org/10.2139/ssrn.1615500
6. Merz, S. (2021, February 02). *Payments in 2021: What's after the digital boom.* https://www.mytotalretail.com/article/payments-in-2021-what-lies-ahead-after-the-digital-boom/
7. Lyra. (2020, May 26). *Different types of payment methods for eCommerce.* https://www.lyra.com/in/payment-methods/
8. Brown, J. (2020, July 30). *Point-of-Sale (POS): A U.S. news guide.* https://www.usnews.com/360-reviews/point-of-sale
9. NCR. (2021, March 10). *Omnichannel payments.* https://www.ncr.com/blogs/payments/omnichannel-payments
10. Sherman, M. (2021, April 20). *5 great POS systems with eCommerce integrations for 2021.* https://www.merchantmaverick.com/pos-ecommerce-integrations/
11. Boerbaitz, B., & Julius, J. (2022). *Building leading retail loyalty programs: Key drivers of customer loyalty in retail.* Deloitte. https://www2.deloitte.com/us/en/pages/consulting/articles/how-to-build-leading-retail-loyalty-programs.html
12. Yellin, J. (2020, July 28). *Guide to Nordstrom's loyalty program—"The Nordy Club."* The Points Guy. https://thepointsguy.com/news/nordstrom-rewards-loyalty-program/
13. Bzik, K. (2024). *Loyalty program for retailer: 10 winning examples.* https://www.openloyalty.io/insider/best-retail-loyalty-programs
14. Amazon. (2024). *About Amazon Hub.* https://www.amazon.co.uk/b?ie=UTF8&node=16721554031
15. Campaign Monitor. (2020, March). *Retail marketing guide to email marketing.* https://www.campaignmonitor.com/resources/guides/the-retailers-guide-to-email-marketing/
16. Saks Fifth Avenue. (2024). *Saks Services: The Fifth Avenue Club.* https://www.saksfifthavenue.com/c/content/fifth-avenue-club
17. Maloney, G. (2018, May 23). *6 dimensions of experiential retail, and the 20 retailers doing it best.* Forbes. https://www.forbes.com/sites/gregmaloney/2018/05/23/six-dimensions-of-experiential-retail-and-the-top-20-retailers-at-delivering-it/

18. Fiore, A. M., & Kim, J. (2007). An integrative framework capturing experiential and utilitarian shopping experience. *International Journal of Retail and Distribution Management, 35*(6), 421–442. https://doi.org/10.1108/09590550710750313
19. Lee, H.-H., Kim, J., & Fiore, A. M. (2010). Affective and cognitive online shopping experience: Effects of image interactivity technology and experimenting with appearance. *Clothing and Textiles Research Journal, 28*(2), 140–154. https://doi.org/10.1177/0887302X09341586
20. Zalando. (2024, May 14). *Zalando adopts responsibilities within management board to execute ecosystem strategy around B2C and B2B.* https://corporate.zalando.com/en/company/zalando-adapts-responsibilities-within-management-board-execute-ecosystem-strategy-around#:~:text=Berlin%2C%20May%2014%2C%202024%20%2F%2F,to%2DBusiness%20(B2B).
21. Sukhraj, R. (2020, September 11). *15 effective re-engagement email examples you'll want to steal in 2021.* https://www.impactplus.com/blog/re-engagement-email-examples
22. Ibid.
23. Gorlin, J. (2020, August 3). *The top 7 reasons your customer returned your garment.* Newmine. https://blog.newmine.com/blog/top-7-reasons-your-customer-returned-your-garment
24. Charlton, G. (2020, September 25). *Ecommerce returns: 2020 stats and trends.* https://www.salecycle.com/blog/featured/ecommerce-returns-2018-stats-trends/
25. Happy Returns. (2024). *Bigger network = more convenience.* https://happyreturns.com/
26. Navar. (2024). *From post-purchase to next-purchase.* https://corp.narvar.com/
27. Nike, Inc. (2021). *2020 Annual report and notice of annual meeting,* p. 9. https://s1.q4cdn.com/806093406/files/doc_financials/2020/ar/363224(1)_16_Nike-Inc_Combo_WR_R2.pdf
28. Phillips, S. (2021, January 14). *Ecommerce security: Securing against cyber threats (2021).* https://www.bigcommerce.com/blog/ecommerce-website-security/#the-biggest-security-threats-to-your-ecommerce-site
29. Singh, H. (2021). *E-commerce security issues: Threats and attack prevention.* https://thecyphere.com/blog/ecommerce-security-best-practices/
30. Temok. (2020, March 27). *Top e-commerce security threats and solutions in 2020.* https://www.temok.com/blog/e-commerce-security-threats-and-solutions/
31. Hoffman, A., & Gold, N. (2018, January 2). *Target Corp's tarnished reputation: Failure in Canada and a Massive Data Breach.* SAGE Knowledge. http://dx.doi.org/10.4135/9781526429308.
32. Gray, D., & Ladig, J. (2015). The implementation of EMV chip card technology to improve cyber-security accelerates in the U.S. following Target corporation's data breach. *International Journal of Business Administration, 6*(2), 60–67.
33. Abrams, L. (2021, January 22). *Bonobos clothing suffers a data breach, hacker leaks 70GB database.* https://www.bleepingcomputer.com/news/security/bonobos-clothing-store-suffers-a-data-breach-hacker-leaks-70gb-database/

Chapter 9

1. Jai, T. M. C., Burns, L. D., & King, N. J. (2013). The effect of behavioral tracking practices on consumers' shopping evaluations and repurchase intention toward trusted online retailers. *Computers in Human Behavior, 29*(3), 901–909.
2. Chen, H. S., & Jai, T. M. C. (2019). Cyber alarm: Determining the impacts of hotel's data breach messages. *International Journal of Hospitality Management, 82*, 326–334.
3. *Cisco 2020 Consumer Privacy Survey. Protecting data privacy to maintain digital trust.* https://www.cisco.com/c/dam/en_us/about/doing_business/trust-center/docs/cybersecurity-series-2020-cps.pdf
4. PwC.com. (2021). *Global digital trust insights survey 2021* https://www.pwc.ch/en/publications/2020/ch-Digital-Trust-Insights-Survey-2021-report.pdf
5. Mahipal, A. (2021, May 13). *Apple 2021 new products survey.* Sellcell. https://www.sellcell.com/blog/apple-2021-new-products-survey/
6. Watson, S. M. (2021). *eMarketer report: Privacy as a competitive advantage.* https://content-na1.emarketer.com/privacy-competitive-advantage
7. Martin, K. D., Borah, A., Palmatier, R. W. (2018). *Research: A strong privacy policy can save your company millions.* Harvard Business Review. https://hbr.org/2018/02/research-a-strong-privacy-policy-can-save-your-company-millions
8. Federal Trade Commission. (2012). *Protecting consumer privacy in an era of rapid change.* https://www.ftc.gov/sites/default/files/documents/reports/federal-trade-commission-report-protecting-consumer-privacy-era-rapid-change-recommendations/120326privacyreport.pdf
9. Federal Trade Commission. (2017 June). *Children's online privacy protection rule: A six-step compliance plan for your business.* https://www.ftc.gov/tips-advice/business-center/guidance/childrens-online-privacy-protection-rule-six-step-compliance
10. European Union. (2018, May 25). *General data protection regulation.* Intersoft consulting. https://gdpr-info.eu/
11. GDPR News. (2020, October 4). *H&M fined €35m in Germany for GDPR breaches related to staff record keeping.* Compliance junction. https://www.compliancejunction.com/hm-fined-e35m-in-germany-for-gdpr-breaches-related-to-staff-record-keeping/
12. Satariano, A. (2021, September 2). Facebook's WhatsApp is fined for breaking the E.U.'s data privacy law. *The New York Times.* https://www.nytimes.com/2021/09/02/business/facebook-whatsapp-privacy-fine.html
13. Lynch, V. (2017). *Cost of 2013 target data breach nears $300 million.* The SSL Store™. https://www.thesslstore.com/blog/2013-target-data-breach-settled/
14. World Intellectual Property Organization. (n.d.). *What is intellectual property?* https://www.wipo.int/about-ip/en/
15. Chirambo, C. M. K. (2019). *Introduction to the patent system.* World Intellectual Property Office (WIPO). https://

www.wipo.int/edocs/mdocs/pct/en/wipo_pct_gbe_19/wipo_pct_gbe_19_topic_1b.pdf

16. United Nations. (1948). *Universal Declaration of Human Rights.* https://www.un.org/en/about-us/universal-declaration-of-human-rights
17. World Intellectual Property Organization. (2020). *What is intellectual property?* https://www.wipo.int/edocs/pubdocs/en/wipo_pub_450_2020.pdf
18. Mar, A. (2019, May 5). *Trademarks: First-to-use and first-to-file countries.* Trademark angel. https://trademarkangel.com/trademarks-first-to-use-and-first-to-file-countries/
19. United States Patent and Trademark Office. (n.d.). *About trademark infringement.* https://www.uspto.gov/page/about-trademark-infringement
20. United States Patent and Trademark Office. (2021, June 25). *USPTO fee schedule.* https://www.uspto.gov/learning-and-resources/fees-and-payment/uspto-fee-schedule
21. Cornell Law School. (n.d). *Article I.* Legal information institute. https://www.law.cornell.edu/constitution/articlei#section8
22. US Copyright Office. (2021, September). *Copyright basics.* https://www.copyright.gov/circs/circ01.pdf
23. Cornell University Library. (2021, March 17). *Copyright term and the public domain in the United States.* https://copyright.cornell.edu/publicdomain
24. US Copyright Office. (n.d.). *How long does copyright protection last?* https://www.copyright.gov/help/faq/faq-duration.html
25. Jenkins, J. (2024). *Mickey, Disney, and the public domain: A 95-year love triangle.* Duke Center for the Study of the Public Domain. https://web.law.duke.edu/cspd/mickey/#jan1
26. US Copyright Office. (2021, June). *US copyright office fair use index.* https://www.copyright.gov/fair-use/
27. Kieselstein-Cord v. Accessories By Pearl, Inc. 489 F. Supp 732 (S.D.N.Y. 1980). Rev'd 632 F2s090 (2d Cir. 1980). https://scholar.google.com/scholar_case?case=1778794882377500420&hl=en&as_sdt=6&as_vis=1&oi=scholarr
28. Hoosear, J. F. (2017). *Urban outfitters hit with willful copyright infringement.* https://www.knobbe.com/news/2017/05/urban-outfitters-hit-willful-copyright-infringement
29. Jimenez, G. C., & Kolsun, B. (2014). *Fashion law. A guide for designers, fashion executives, and attorneys* (2nd ed.). New York: Bloomsbury USA.
30. Greene, J. (2011, September 8). *Amazon and California lawmakers cut sales tax deal.* CNET. https://www.cnet.com/tech/services-and-software/amazon-and-california-lawmakers-cut-sales-tax-deal/
31. Moyer, E. (2012, April 27). *Amazon settles with Texas over sales tax.* CNET. https://www.cnet.com/tech/services-and-software/amazon-settles-with-texas-over-sales-tax/
32. Federal Trade Commission. (2019). *Disclosures 101 for social media influencers.* FTC. https://www.ftc.gov/tips-advice/business-center/guidance/disclosures-101-social-media-influencers
33. The United States Department of Justice Archives. (2020, January 17). *1854. Copyright infringement—first sale doctrine.* https://www.justice.gov/archives/jm/criminal-resource-manual-1854-copyright-infringement-first-sale-doctrine
34. Jai, T., Burns, L. D., & King, N. J. (2013). The effect of behavioral tracking practices on consumers' shopping evaluations and repurchase intention toward trusted online retailers. *Computers in Human Behavior, 29*(3), 901–909.
35. Jai, T., & King, N. J. (2016). Privacy versus reward: Do loyalty programs increase consumers' willingness to share personal information with third-party advertisers and data brokers? *Journal of Retailing and Consumer Services, 28*, 296–303.
36. Chen, H. S., & Jai, T. M. (2021). Trust fall: Data breach perceptions from loyalty and non-loyalty customers. *The Service Industries Journal, 41*(13–14), 947–963.
37. Willis, B., Jai, T., & Lauderdale, M. (2021). Trust and commitment: Effect of applying consumer data rights on US Consumers' attitudes toward online retailers in the big data era. *Journal of Consumer Behaviour, 20*(6), 1575–1590.
38. Pietsch, B. (2021, March 28th). Nike sues over unauthorized 'Satan Shoes'. *New York Times.* https://www.nytimes.com/2021/03/28/style/nike-satan-shoes-lil-Nas-x.html
39. Madani, D. (2021, April, 8th). Nike and MSCHF reach settlement in 'Satan Shoes' trademark lawsuit. *NBC News.* https://www.nbcnews.com/business/business-news/nike-mschf-reach-settlement-satan-shoes-trademark-lawsuit-n1263567)

Chapter 10

1. The Interaction Design Foundation. (2021). *What is augmented reality?* https://www.interaction-design.org/literature/topics/augmented-reality
2. Bossen, K. (2020, June 24). *The benefits of AR technology in product development.* https://dmexco.com/stories/how-ar-technology-can-optimize-product-development
3. Wiltz, C. (2020, February 27). *4 ways AR can enhance product design.* Design News. https://www.designnews.com/design-hardware-software/4-ways-ar-can-enhance-product-design
4. Biron, B. (2020, August 9). *Retailers like Macy's, Adidas, and Modcloth are turning to virtual fitting rooms to let consumers 'try on' clothing before buying it online.* Business Insider. https://www.businessinsider.com/retailers-like-macys-adidas-are-turning-to-virtual-fitting-rooms-2020-8
5. Belova, K. (2020, October 29). *Top AR & VR solutions in fashion and retail.* https://pixelplex.io/blog/how-ar-and-vr-transform-the-fashion-industry
6. Business of Fashion Team. (2020). *At CLO Virtual Fashion, digitising the design process to drive transformation.* https://www.businessoffashion.com/articles/technology/at-clo-virtual-fashion-digitising-the-design-process-to-drive-transformation/
7. Formlabs. (2021). *Versatile production: 4 steps for starting a microfactory.* https://formlabs.com/blog/4-steps-starting-a-microfactory

8. Kathiala, R. (2020, February 7). *Micro-factories—The future of fashion manufacturing?* Just Style. https://www.just-style.com/analysis/micro-factories-the-future-of-fashion-manufacturing_id137976.aspx
9. Ibid.
10. White, G. (2020, May 16). *TREND REPORT: The rise of the micro-manufacturer.*. Manufacturing Digital. https://www.manufacturingglobal.com/lean-manufacturing/trend-report-rise-micro-manufacturer
11. Boudet, J., Gregg, B., Rathje, K., Stein, E., & Vollhardt, K. (2019, June 18). *The future of personalization–and how to get ready for it.* McKinsey. https://www.mckinsey.com/business-functions/marketing-and-sales/our-insights/the-future-of-personalization-and-how-to-get-ready-for-it
12. Yukhnevich, A. (2020, February 7). *Personalization and customization trends in fashion retail.* Texel. https://texel.graphics/news/personalization-fashion-retail
13. Amed, I., Balchandani, A., Beltrami, M., Berg, A., Hedrich, S., & Rölkens, F. (2019, February 19). *Fashion on demand.* McKinsey. https://www.mckinsey.com/industries/retail/our-insights/fashion-on-demand
14. Boyd, C. (2021, February 24). *Visual search-The ultimate guide: Statistics, news, trends, and tips.* Medium. https://clarkboyd.medium.com/visual-search-trends-statistics-tips-and-uses-in-everyday-life-d20084dc4b0a
15. Ibid.
16. Popsop. (2021, January 2). *Visual search.* https://popsop.com/2021/01/visual-search
17. Nguyen, M. H. (2020, November 1). *Visual search—A must-have for fashion & apparel online sellers in 2021.* https://www.sharitek.com/post/visual-search-a-must-have-for-fashion-apparel-online-sellers-in-2021
18. Zipwhip. (2020). State of texting. https://www.zipwhip.com/state-of-texting/
19. Zozulya, S. (2020, August 7). 5 hot ideas for location-based apps and how to create a location-based application. Stfalcon. https://stfalcon.com/en/blog/post/5-hot-ideas-for-location-based-apps
20. Widmer, B. (2020, September 18). *What is social shopping and why you should get on board.* Photoslurp. https://hi.photoslurp.com/blog/social-shopping-ecommerce-brand-get-board/
21. Atul. (2021, February 10). *Social shopping in 2021: What is it & why your brand needs it now?* https://taggbox.com/blog/social-shopping/
22. Ibid.
23. Prados, M. (2020, April 30). *What social shopping looks like across 5 popular platforms.* Retail TouchPoints https://retailtouchpoints.com/topics/digital-commerce/social-commerce/what-social-shopping-looks-like-across-5-popular-platforms
24. Widmer, B. (2020, September 18). *What is social shopping and why you should get on board.* Photoslurp. https://hi.photoslurp.com/blog/social-shopping-ecommerce-brand-get-board/
25. Hurwitz, A. (2020, March 2). *Social media shopping in 2020.* Bigdrop. https://www.bigdropinc.com/blog/social-media-shopping-2020
26. Ibid.
27. Baggs, M. (2020, August 12). *How is social shopping changing in 2020?* The Social Element. https://thesocialelement.agency/how-is-social-shopping-changing-in-2020
28. Ibid.
29. Prados, M. (2020, April 30). *What social shopping looks like across 5 popular platforms.* Retail TouchPoints https://retailtouchpoints.com/topics/digital-commerce/social-commerce/what-social-shopping-looks-like-across-5-popular-platforms
30. Ibid.
31. Baggs, M. (2020, August 12). *How is social shopping changing in 2020?* The Social Element. https://thesocialelement.agency/how-is-social-shopping-changing-in-2020
32. Oracle. (2021). *What is the Internet of Things (IoT)?* https://www.oracle.com/internet-of-things/what-is-iot
33. Ranger, S. (2020, February 3). *What is the IoT? Everything you need to know about the Internet of Things right now.* ZD Net. https://www.zdnet.com/article/what-is-the-internet-of-things-everything-you-need-to-know-about-the-iot-right-now
34. Ibid.
35. Hernandez, M. (2019, July 17). *IoT: Consumer & commercial vs. industrial—Main overview.* Ubidots. https://ubidots.com/blog/iot-consumer-vs-commercial-vs-industrial-main-overview
36. Gonzalez, C. M. (2020). *IoT consumer market trends for 2020.* ASME. https://www.asme.org/topics-resources/content/iot-2020-trends-for-everyday-consumer-products
37. Lee, D., & Malik, R. (2022, March 2). *BoF Insights: Building resilience and value in fashion's supply chain.* Business of Fashion. https://www.businessoffashion.com/reports/retail/building-resilience-and-value-in-fashions-supply-chain-bof-insights/
38. Reuters & Mutikani, L. (2021, April 30). *Stimulus checks boost U.S. consumer spending; inflation warming up.* https://www.reuters.com/business/us-consumer-spending-income-rebound-march-2021-04-30/
39. Ibid.
40. Kuligowski, K. (2021, January 15). *How to use CRM and email marketing together.* Business News Daily. https://www.businessnewsdaily.com/15962-how-crm-streamlines-email-marketing-.html
41. FrogDog Magazine. (2021, February 22). *The difference between CRM and e-mail marketing.* https://www.frog-dog.com/magazine/the-difference-between-crm-and-e-mail-marketing#:~:text=CRM%20stands%20for%20customer%20relationship%20management.&text=A%20CRM%20system%E2%80%94which%20may,keep%20tabs%20on%20their%20contacts
42. SplitBase. (2021). *5 essentials to a high-converting e-mail opt-in for fashion ecommerce.* https://splitbase.com/blog/luxury-ecommerce-crm

43. IBM Institute for Business Value. (2020). *The coming AI revolution in retail and consumer products: Intelligent automation transforms both industries in unexpected ways.* https://www.ibm.com/thought-leadership/institute-business-value/report/ai-retail-consumer-products
44. Thiel, W. (2020, November 19). *Discover the role of AI in customer experience.* https://www.pointillist.com/blog/role-of-ai-in-customer-experience
45. Treanor, T. (2021, January 19). *AI and retail customer experience.* https://www.business.com/articles/ai-retail-customer-experience
46. Ibid.
47. McKinnon, T., & Rudolph, B. (2020, May 19). *20 Innovative examples of artificial intelligence in retail.* Indigo9 Digital. https://www.indigo9digital.com/blog
48. Yotka, S. (2021). Balenciaga and Fortnite team up for a digital-to-physical partnership. *Vogue.* https://www.vogue.com/article/balenciaga-fortnite-partnership
49. Ralph Lauren Corporation. (2021). *Ralph Lauren announces an exclusive partnership with Zepeto.* https://corporate.ralphlauren.com/pr_210825_ZepetoPartnership.html
50. Hahn, J. (2021). *Gucci hosts virtual exhibition in online game Roblox to mark centenary.* Dezeen. https://www.dezeen.com/2021/05/20/gucci-garden-roblox-virtual-exhibition/
51. Burberry. (2022). *Burberry announces new partnership with Mythical Games.* https://www.burberryplc.com/en/news/brand/2022/burberry-announces-new-partnership-with-mythical-games-
52. Thomas, D. (2021, October 4). Dolce & Gabbana just set a $6 million record for the fashion NTFs. *New York Times.* https://www.nytimes.com/2021/10/04/style/dolce-gabbana-nft.html
53. Lawler, R. (2021, December 14). *Nike just brought a virtual shoe company that makes NFTs and sneakers 'for the metaverse.'* The Verge. https://www.theverge.com/22833369/nike-rtfkt-nft-sneaker-shoe-metaverse-company
54. Le, M. (2022, December 7). *RTFKT and Nike announce the public draw of Cryptokicks iRL, the first native Web2 sneaker.* Sneaker News. https://sneakernews.com/2022/12/07/nike-cryptokicks-irl-release-date/
55. The Fabricant. (n.d.). *Digi-couture: Iridescence.* https://www.thefabricant.com/iridescence
56. Edelmayer, S. (2020, July 8) *The best fashion games to play dress-up on your phone.* Make Use Of. https://www.makeuseof.com/tag/best-fashion-games-play-dress-up/#:~:text=The%20Best%20Fashion%20Games%20to%20Play%20Dress-Up%20on,genre%20of%20gameplay%20to%20the%20next%20level.%20
57. Ou, X. (2024). *Proportion of livestreaming e-commerce's GMV in online shopping in China from 2017 to 2022.* Statista. https://www.statista.com/statistics/1192066/china-share-of-livestreaming-ecommerce-in-online-shopping/#:~:text=In%202020%2C%20the%20gross%20merchandise%20value%20of%20e-commerce,estimated%20to%20grow%20to%2024.3%20percent%20in%202023
58. Chevalier, S. (2022). *Most popular platforms for livestream e-commerce in the United States in 2021.* Statista. https://www.statista.com/statistics/1276274/most-popular-live-commerce-platforms-united-states/#:~:text=Social%20media%20networks%20are%20the%20most%20popular%20platforms,Instagram%2C%20and%20TikTok%20as%20well%20as%20Amazon%20Live.
59. Basiouny, A. (2022, August 31). *Why livestream commerce is on the rise.* Knowledge at Wharton. https://knowledge.wharton.upenn.edu/article/why-livestream-commerce-is-on-the-rise/#:~:text=Livestream%20commerce%2C%20in%20which%20brands%20sell%20their%20products,2020.%20Those%20numbers%20are%20only%20expected%20to%20climb
60. Arora, A., Glaser, D., Kim, A., Kluge, P., Kohli, S., & Sak, N. (2021). *It's showtime! How live commerce is transforming the shopping experience.* McKinsey. https://www.mckinsey.com/capabilities/mckinsey-digital/our-insights/its-showtime-how-live-commerce-is-transforming-the-shopping-experience
61. Statista Research Department. (2024). *Annual net sales revenue of Amazon from 2004 to 2023.* https://www.statista.com/statistics/266282/annual-net-revenue-of-amazoncom/
62. Rambourg, E. (2020). *Future luxe: What's ahead for business of luxury.* Vancouver, BC: Figure 1 Publishing, Inc.
63. Cook, K. (2021). *15 creative examples of branded pop-up shops.* HubSpot. https://blog.hubspot.com/marketing/creative-pop-up-events
64. Lutkevich, B. (2020, March 20). *What is a pop-up shop?* TechTarget. What Is? https://whatis.techtarget.com/definition/pop-up-shop
65. BigCommerce. (2021). *What is a pop-up shop?* https://www.bigcommerce.com/ecommerce-answers/what-pop-shop
66. Trotter, C. (2021, March 23). *Retail industry trends: The power of the pop-up shop.* Lightspeed. https://www.lightspeedhq.com/blog/retail-industry-trends-the-power-of-the-pop-up-shop
67. Zargani, L. (2020, July 2). *Bottega* Veneta introduces the invisible pop-up store. *WWD.* https://wwd.com/fashion-news/fashion-scoops/bottega-veneta-introduces-the-invisible-pop-up-store-1203664183
68. Ibid.
69. Parisi, D. (2020, July 8). *The new pop-up: Brands are rethinking the purpose of a temporary store.* Glossy. https://www.glossy.co/fashion/the-new-pop-up-brands-are-rethinking-the-purpose-of-a-temporary-store
70. Ibid.
71. Francis, C. (2018). *The (in)convenience of clerkless c-stores.* Convenience Store News. https://csnews.com/inconvenience-clerkless-c-stores
72. Harashima, D., & Matsuda, S. (2018). *China and Japan try cashier-free stores – for different reasons.* Nikkei Asia. https://asia.nikkei.com/Business/China-and-Japan-try-cashier-free-stores-for-different-reasons

73. Lung, T. (2021). *Japan's checkout-free grocery store is giving Amazon a run for its money*. Forbes. https://www.forbes.com/sites/tiffanylung/2021/01/28/japans-checkout-free-grocery-store-gives-amazon-a-run-for-their-money/?sh=310425c04b00

74. Ibid.

75. Pijak, J. (2015). *14 fashion vending machines: From cosmetic nail polish kiosks to vending machine window displays.* Trendhunter. https://www.trendhunter.com/slideshow/fashion-vending-machine

76. Hausse, A. (2021, July 12). *4 fashion brands that included smart vending machines in their marketing strategy*. Hackernoon. https://hackernoon.com/4-fashion-brands-that-included-smart-vending-machines-in-their-marketing-strategy-0obe37h9

77. Dazed. (2021). *There are Jacquemus vending machines now, and more fashion news you missed.* https://www.dazeddigital.com/fashion/article/54966/1/jacquemus-vending-machines-fashion-news-virgil-abloh-dior-house-of-gucci

78. Vembar, K. (2022, January 20). *Amazon opens first fashion retail store*. Retail Dive. https://www.retaildive.com/news/amazon-to-open-first-physical-clothing-store/617416/

79. Moorman, T. (2022, October 18). Second Amazon Style location in the country opens in Ohio. *Cincinnati Enquirer.* https://www.cincinnati.com/story/news/2022/10/18/amazons-style-store-opens-second-location-in-the-united-states/69571808007/

80. D'innocenzio, A. (2022, January 20). Amazon plans clothing store for Americana mall in Glendale. *Los Angeles Times.* https://www.latimes.com/business/story/2022-01-20/amazon-shopping-clothing-store-california-americana-glendale-retail

81. Ibid.

82. Day, M. (2023, November 2). *Amazon is clothing Style apparel stores as grocery push ramps up*. Bloomberg. https://www.bloomberg.com/news/articles/2023-11-02/amazon-is-closing-style-apparel-stores-as-grocery-push-ramps-up?utm_source=Triggermail&utm_medium=email&utm_campaign=Retail%20Daily%2011.3.23&utm_term=eMarketer%20Retail%20Active%20List

83. Reuters. (2021, July 9). *Amazon hires Tesco veteran Tony Hoggett to run stores.* Reuters.https://www.reuters.com/business/amazon-uk-poaches-tesco-veteran-tony-hoggett-run-stores-2021-07-09/

84. Vasen, S. (2022, January 20). *Amazon reimagines in-store shopping with Amazon Style.* About Amazon. https://www.aboutamazon.com/news/retail/amazon-reimagines-in-store-shopping-with-amazon-style

85. Frankel, J. (2017, February 20). *Shopping with an avatar.* Huffpost. https://www.huffpost.com/entry/shopping-with-an-avatar_b_58ab1b93e4b0b0e1e0e20dfe

86. 3DLook. (2023). *Body measuring apps: Providing customers with the perfect fit.* https://3dlook.me/blog/body-measuring-apps-providing-customers-with-the-perfect-fit/

Art Credits

All illustrations © Fairchild Books/Rendered by Daniel Kison

Chapter 1

1.1 Siegfried Layda/The Image Bank/Getty Images
1.2 SHAUN CURRY/AFP via Getty Images
1.5 Courtesy of Shatina Chen
1.6 Maskot/Getty Images
1.7 seksan Mongkhonkhamsao/Getty Images
1.8 SOPA Images/LightRocket/Getty Images

Chapter 2

2.2 Courtesy of Direct Selling Association
2.3 Edward Berthelot/Getty Images
2.4a&b Courtesy of Catherine Jai

Chapter 4

4.2 Fairchild Books/Rendered by Daniel Kison; photo: nicoletaionescu
4.3 Fairchild Books/Rendered by Daniel Kison; photos: top left: Klaus Vedfelt/DigitalVision/Getty Images; top center: Westend61/Getty Images; top right: Eva Carollo Photography/Moment/Getty Images; bottom left: Westend61/Getty Images; bottom center: AzmanJaka/iStock.com; bottom right: SEAN GLADWELL/Moment/Getty Images
4.5 JulPo/iStock.com

Chapter 5

5.1 Thomas Barwick/DivitalVision/Getty Images

Chapter 7

7.1–7.3 Courtesy of Catherine Jai
7.7 Fairchild Books/Rendered by Daniel Kison; Photos from left to right: Foremniakowski/Stock.com; Foremniakowski/Stock.com; Febriana Suwarningsih/iStock.com: NYS444/iStock.com; Jenson/iStock.com; bonetta/iStock.com; Finsterbush Photography/iStock.com

Chapter 8

8.1 Hispanolistic/iStock.com
8.2 Dowell/Moment/Getty Images
8.4 Courtesy of Jihyun Vick
8.5 lambada/iStock.com

Chapter 9

9.2 SAVIKO/Gamma-Rapho via Getty Images
9.3 New Balance Athletics, Inc. v. Michael Kors U.S.A., Inc., 1:21-cv-11305 (D. Mass.)
9.4–9.6 USPTO

Chapter 10

10.1 MStudioImages/iStock.com
10.2 Prasit Photo/Getty Images
10.3 AzmanJaka/iStock.com
10.4 Westend61/Getty Images
10.5–10.7 Courtesy of Jihyun Vick

Index

Bold page numbers indicate tables, *italic* numbers indicate figures.

D

E

T

U

V

W

Y

Z